Squid
The Definitive Guide

Other resources from O'Reilly

Related titles   Web Caching   Web Performance Tuning
                            Apache: The Definitive Guide   Perl for Web Site
                            Apache Cookbook   Management

oreilly.com   *oreilly.com* is more than a complete catalog of O'Reilly books. You'll also find links to news, events, articles, weblogs, sample chapters, and code examples.

oreillynet.com is the essential portal for developers interested in open and emerging technologies, including new platforms, programming languages, and operating systems.

Conferences   O'Reilly & Associates brings diverse innovators together to nurture the ideas that spark revolutionary industries. We specialize in documenting the latest tools and systems, translating the innovator's knowledge into useful skills for those in the trenches. Visit *conferences.oreilly.com* for our upcoming events.

Safari Bookshelf (*safari.oreilly.com*) is the premier online reference library for programmers and IT professionals. Conduct searches across more than 1,000 books. Subscribers can zero in on answers to time-critical questions in a matter of seconds. Read the books on your Bookshelf from cover to cover or simply flip to the page you need. Try it today with a free trial.

Squid
The Definitive Guide

Duane Wessels

O'REILLY®

Beijing · Cambridge · Farnham · Köln · Paris · Sebastopol · Taipei · Tokyo

Squid: The Definitive Guide
by Duane Wessels

Published by O'Reilly & Associates, Inc., 1005 Gravenstein Highway North, Sebastopol, CA 95472.

O'Reilly & Associates books may be purchased for educational, business, or sales promotional use. Online editions are also available for most titles (*safari.oreilly.com*). For more information, contact our corporate/institutional sales department: (800) 998-9938 or *corporate@oreilly.com*.

Editor:	Tatiana Apandi Diaz
Production Editor:	Mary Anne Weeks Mayo
Cover Designer:	Ellie Volckhausen
Interior Designer:	Melanie Wang

Printing History:

January 2004:	First Edition.

ISBN: 0-596-00162-2

[M]

To my darling Anne.
You have no idea.

Table of Contents

Preface

About This Book

I started the Squid project eight years ago while working at the National Laboratory for Applied Network Research and the University of California. Back then I certainly enjoyed writing code and fixing bugs but always felt bad about the lack of decent documentation. This book is my attempt to rectify that situation. It's been a long time coming and almost didn't happen. Like they say, "better late than never!"

This book is written for those who are tasked with setting up and maintaining one or more Squid caches. If you're new to Squid, I'll show you how to download, compile, and install the code. Those of you who have been using Squid for a while will be more interested in the later chapters, where I talk about disk cache performance, modifying requests, surrogate mode, caching hierarchies, monitoring Squid, and more.

In order to use this book, you should have a basic knowledge of Unix systems. Many of the book's examples are based on free operating systems, such as Linux, FreeBSD, NetBSD, and OpenBSD. I also have some tips for Solaris users. If you're more comfortable with Windows systems, you can use Squid under a Unix emulator or give the native NT port a try.

Here's an overview of the book's contents:

Chapter 1, Introduction
> This chapter introduces you to Squid and web caching. I give a brief history of the project, and a few notes on our future work. I explain how you can find additional support and information, including a FAQ, on the Squid web site.

Chapter 2, Getting Squid
> In this chapter, I explain how and why you should download Squid's source code. You may prefer to install a precompiled binary or use a preconfigured package. I also talk about staying up to date with Squid using the anonymous CVS server.

Chapter 3, Compiling and Installing

Assuming you've downloaded the source code, this chapter explains how to configure and compile Squid. In some cases you may need to tune your system before compiling Squid. For example, your kernel may have relatively low file-descriptor limits that affect Squid's performance.

Chapter 4, Configuration Guide for the Eager

Here, I give a brief introduction to Squid's configuration file. If you are the impatient type and can't wait to start using Squid, this chapter will leave you with a minimal configuration file you can start playing with.

Chapter 5, Running Squid

In this chapter, I explain how to run Squid for the first time and how to test Squid in a terminal window. Following that, I suggest a number of ways to configure your system so that Squid starts each time it boots. I also explain how to reconfigure Squid while it is running and how to safely shut it down.

Chapter 6, All About Access Controls

I talk extensively about access controls in this chapter. Squid has a powerful collection of access control features and a number of different rule sets that determine how requests and responses are treated. This is an important chapter because a mistake in your access controls may leave your cache, or even internal systems, vulnerable to abuse from outsiders.

Chapter 7, Disk Cache Basics

This chapter is about Squid's primary function: storing cached responses on disk. I explain how to configure the disk cache, including replacement policies and freshness controls. I also show you how to manually remove unwanted objects from the cache.

Chapter 8, Advanced Disk Cache Topics

In this chapter, I explain how to improve the performance of Squid's disk cache. I'll talk about Squid's different storage schemes and a number of filesystem tuning options that may help. If your Squid cache handles a relatively light load, you probably don't need to worry about disk performance.

Chapter 9, Interception Caching

Here, I explain how to configure Squid for HTTP interception, sometimes also called transparent caching. Actually, configuring Squid is the easy part. The difficulty comes from setting up a router or switch on your network and the host from which Squid is running. I explain how to configure networking equipment from Cisco, Alteon, Foundry, and Extreme. I'll also show you how to configure your operating system (Linux, FreeBSD, NetBSD, OpenBSD, and Solaris) for HTTP interception. Finally, I talk about WCCP.

Chapter 10, Talking to Other Squids

In this chapter, I cover the ins and outs of cache cooperation, including meshes, arrays, and hierarchies. You may also find it useful if you simply need to forward requests from Squid to another proxy or intermediary. I'll talk about the various intercache protocols supported by Squid (ICP, HTCP, Cache Digests, and CARP) and how Squid chooses the next-hop location for a given cache miss.

Chapter 11, Redirectors

Redirectors are the best way to make Squid rewrite HTTP requests before forwarding them. I describe the interface between Squid and a redirector program so that you can write your own. I also present a few of the more popular third-party redirectors available.

Chapter 12, Authentication Helpers

In this chapter, I explain how Squid interfaces with external authentication databases such as LDAP, NT domain controllers, and password files. Squid comes with a number of authentication helpers and understands Basic, Digest, and NTLM authentication credentials. I also document the API for each, in case you want to develop your own helper.

Chapter 13, Log Files

I cover Squid's various log files in this chapter, including *access.log, store.log, cache.log,* and others. I explain what each log file contains and how you should periodically maintain them.

Chapter 14, Monitoring Squid

This chapter provides a lot of information on monitoring Squid's operation. I cover both SNMP and Squid's own cache manager interface. You'll find it useful for both long-term monitoring and short-term problem diagnosis.

Chapter 15, Server Accelerator Mode

Squid's server accelerator mode is useful in a number of situations. You can use it to boost your origin server's poor performance, as a firewall to protect the server, or even to build your own content delivery network. I show how to set up Squid and make sure that outsiders can't abuse your service.

Chapter 16, Debugging and Troubleshooting

The book's final chapter explains how to debug and troubleshoot problems with Squid. You may find that some sites, or some user agents, don't work properly with Squid. I show how to isolate and reproduce the problem and how to present the information to Squid developers for assistance.

Appendix A, Config File Reference

This appendix is a reference guide for each of Squid's 200 configuration file directives. Each has a description, syntax, defaults, and examples.

Appendix B, The Memory Cache

This brief appendix explains a little about Squid's memory cache.

Appendix C, Delay Pools

You can use Squid's delay pools feature to limit bandwidth consumed by web surfers. I explain how the delay pools work and provide a number of example configurations.

Appendix D, Filesystem Performance Benchmarks

In this appendix, I present the results of numerous filesystem benchmarks. These may help you make informed decisions regarding particular operating systems, filesystem features, and Squid's storage techniques.

Appendix E, Squid on Windows

Have a look at this appendix if you'd like to run Squid on your Windows box. I talk about using Cygwin and about a native port of Squid, called SquidNT.

Appendix F, Configuring Squid Clients

This appendix contains information on how to configure various user agents to use Squid. I talk about manual configuration, environment variables, Proxy Auto-Configuration functions, and the Web Proxy Auto Discovery protocol.

As I'm finishing up this book, the latest stable version is Squid-2.5.STABLE4, and the development version is Squid-3.0. Perhaps the most important difference between the two is that Squid-3 is being rewritten in C++. You should find that most things are backward-compatible, although a few new configuration directives have been created. Please read the release notes carefully if you use Squid-3.0 or later.

I have created a web site for the book, located at *http://squidbook.org/*. There, you will find errata, supplemental information, and links to online resources.

Topics Not Covered

Due to a lack of time and space, there are some topics I was unable to cover in this book; they include:

Non-HTTP protocols

You'll find that I mostly talk about HTTP, even though Squid also supports FTP, Gopher, and some other relatively obscure protocols.

Customizing error messages

Squid's error messages can be customized and the source distribution includes versions of the error messages in a number of different languages. You can probably figure out how to customize the error messages by modifying the default pages or by reading Squid's source code.

Load balancing Squids

Load balancing is a popular way to increase the capacity of a caching service. Refer to one of the load balancing books mentioned in the following section if necessary.

What is cachable

HTTP has a number of somewhat complicated rules for determining what may, or may not be, cached, and for how long. Refer to *Web Caching*, or *HTTP: The Definitive Guide* (for more information, see the next section).

Copyright
> A number of nontechnical issues surround web caching. These include copyrights and privacy.

Modifying the source
> I don't go into detail about Squid's source code in this book. The Squid project hosts a programmers' guide, which is generally incomplete and out of date. If you have questions about the source code, please join the *squid-dev* mailing list.

SOCKS
> Squid doesn't support the SOCKS protocol at this time.

Recommended Reading

While reading this book, you may want to consult some of these other resources for more information (I'll refer to them throughout this book):

- *The Design and Implementation of the 4.4 BSD Operating System* by Marshall Kirk McKusick, Kieth Bostic, Michael J. Karels, and John S. Quarterman (Addison-Wesley Longman)
- *DNS and BIND* by Paul Albitz and Cricket Liu (O'Reilly & Associates)
- *HTTP: The Definitive Guide* by David Gourley and Brian Totty (O'Reilly)
- *Load Balancing Servers, Firewalls, and Caches* by Chandra Koopurapu (John Wiley & Sons)
- *Mastering Regular Expressions* by Jeffrey E. F. Friedl (O'Reilly)
- *Server Load Balancing* by Tony Bourke (O'Reilly)
- *Unix System Administration Handbook* and *Linux System Administration Handbook* by Evi Nemeth, Garth Snyder, Scott Seebass, and Trent R. Hein (Prentice Hall)
- My book, *Web Caching* (O'Reilly)
- RFC 1413: Identification Protocol
- RFC 1738: Uniform Resource Locators (URL)
- RFC 2186: Internet Cache Protocol (ICP), Version 2
- RFC 2187: Application of Internet Cache Protocol (ICP), Version 2
- RFC 2396: Uniform Resource Identifiers (URI): Generic Syntax
- RFC 2616: Hypertext Transfer Protocol—HTTP/1.1
- RFC 2617: HTTP Authentication: Basic and Digest Access Authentication
- RFC 2756: Hypertext Caching Protocol
- RFC 2817: Upgrading to TLS Within HTTP/1.1
- RFC 3040: Internet Web Replication and Caching Taxonomy

- RFC 3143: Known HTTP Proxy/Caching Problems
- Caching-related web sites, such as *http://www.caching.com/* and *http://www.web-cache.com/*

Conventions Used in This Book

I use the following typesetting conventions in this book:

Italic

> Used for new terms where they are defined, buttons, pages, configuration file directives, filenames, modules, ACLs, directories, and URI/URLs

Constant width

> Used for configuration file examples, program output, HTTP header names and directives, scripts, options, environment variables, functions, methods, rules, keywords, libraries, and command names

Constant width italic

> Used for replaceable text within examples and code pieces

Constant width bold

> Used to indicate commands to be typed verbatim

When displaying a Unix command, I'll include a shell prompt, like this:

```
% ls -l
```

If the command is specific to the Bourne shell (sh) or C shell (csh), the prompt will indicate which you should use:

```
sh$ ulimit -a
csh% limits
```

If the command requires super-user privileges, the shell prompt is a hash mark:

```
# make install
```

Occasionally, I provide configuration file examples with long lines. If the line is too wide to fit on the page, it's wrapped around and indented. Squid doesn't accept this sort of syntax, so you must make sure to place everything on one line.

 This icon signifies a tip, suggestion, or general note.

 This icon indicates a warning or caution.

Comments and Questions

Please address comments and questions concerning this book to the publisher:

O'Reilly & Associates, Inc.
1005 Gravenstein Highway North
Sebastopol, CA 95472
(800) 998-9938 (in the United States or Canada)
(707) 829-0515 (international or local)
(707) 829-0104 (fax)

There is a web page for this book, which lists errata, examples, and any additional information. You can access this page at:

http://www.oreilly.com/catalog/squid

To comment or ask technical questions about this book, send email to:

bookquestions@oreilly.com

For more information about books, conferences, Resource Centers, and the O'Reilly Network, check the O'Reilly web site at:

http://www.oreilly.com

You can contact the author at *wessels@packet-pushers.com*.

Acknowledgments

Looking back at the events and people that allowed me to write this book makes me feel extremely humble and grateful. I'm so happy to have been a part of the Harvest project with Mike Schwartz, Peter Danzig, and the others. That led directly to my work with kc claffy and Hans-Werner Braun at NLANR/UCSD. The Squid project would have never been at all without their support, and the grant from the National Science Foundation.

I'm also very thankful for all the hard work put in by the small crew of Squid developers: Henrik Nordström, Robert Collins, Adrian Chadd, and everyone else who has contributed time and code to the project. And I'm sorry that you ever had to read and/or fix any ugly code I wrote.

To all the reviewers who read the drafts—Joe Cooper, Scott Pepple, Robert Collins, and Adrian Chadd—thanks for finding my mistakes and suggesting ways to make the book better. I also owe so much to the people at O'Reilly for making the book possible, and for making it all come together. My editors Tatiana Diaz and Nat Torkington, the production editor Mary Anne Mayo, the graphic designer Melanie Wang, the illustrator, Rob Romano, the XML mungers Andrew Savikas and Joe Wizda, and the countless other folks working behind the scenes for me.

To my good friend, and business partner, Alex Rousskov: thanks for giving me the time and freedom to see this little project through. Finally, to the members of my new family, Annie and Blooey, thanks for putting up with the late nights. Can I make it up to you with extra back scratches?

## CHAPTER 1

Introduction

This long-overdue book is about Squid: a popular open source caching proxy for the Web. With Squid you can:

- Use less bandwidth on your Internet connection when surfing the Web
- Reduce the amount of time web pages take to load
- Protect the hosts on your internal network by proxying their web traffic
- Collect statistics about web traffic on your network
- Prevent users from visiting inappropriate web sites at work or school
- Ensure that only authorized users can surf the Internet
- Enhance your user's privacy by filtering sensitive information from web requests
- Reduce the load on your own web server(s)
- Convert encrypted (HTTPS) requests on one side, to unencrypted (HTTP) requests on the other

Squid's job is to be both a *proxy* and a *cache*. As a proxy, Squid is an intermediary in a web transaction. It accepts a request from a client, processes that request, and then forwards the request to the origin server. The request may be logged, rejected, and even modified before forwarding. As a cache, Squid stores recently retrieved web content for possible reuse later. Subsequent requests for the same content may be served from the cache, rather than contacting the origin server again. You can disable the caching part of Squid if you like, but the proxying part is essential.

As Figure 1-1 shows, Squid accepts HTTP (and HTTPS) requests from clients, and speaks a number of protocols to servers. In particular, Squid knows how to talk to HTTP, FTP, and Gopher servers.* Conceptually, Squid has two "sides." The *client-side* talks to web clients (e.g., browsers and user-agents); the *server-side* talks to

---

* Gopher servers are quite rare these days. Squid also knows about WAIS and whois, but these are even more obscure.

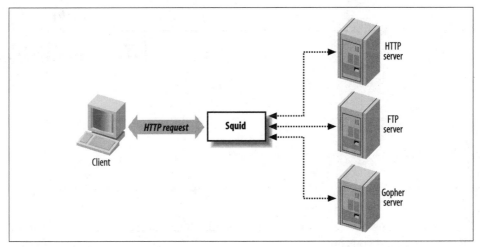

Figure 1-1. Squid sits between clients and servers

HTTP, FTP, and Gopher servers. These are called *origin servers*, because they are the origin location for the data they serve.

Note that Squid's client-side understands only HTTP (and HTTP encrypted with SSL/TLS). This means, for example, that you can't make an FTP client talk to Squid (unless the FTP client is also an HTTP client). Furthermore, Squid can't proxy protocols for email (SMTP), instant messaging, or Internet Relay Chat.

Web Caching

Web caching refers to the act of storing certain web resources (i.e., pages and other data files) for possible future reuse. For example, Matilda is the first person in the office each morning, and she likes to read the local newspaper online with her wakeup coffee. As she visits the various sections, the Squid cache on their office network stores the HTML pages and JPEG images. Harry comes in a short while later and also reads the newspaper online. For him, the site loads much faster because much of the content is served from Squid. Additionally, Harry's browsing doesn't waste the bandwidth of the company's DSL line by transferring the exact same data as when Matilda viewed the site.

A *cache hit* occurs each time Squid satisfies an HTTP request from its cache. The *cache hit ratio*, or *cache hit rate*, is the percentage of all requests satisfied as hits. Web caches typically achieve hit ratios between 30% and 60%. A similar metric, the *byte hit ratio*, represents the volume of data (i.e., number of bytes) served from the cache.

A *cache miss* occurs when Squid can't satisfy a request from the cache. A miss can happen for any number of reasons. Obviously, the first time Squid receives a request for a particular resource, it is a cache miss. Similarly, Squid may have purged the cached copy to make room for new objects.

Another possibility is that the resource is uncachable. Origin servers can instruct caches on how to treat the response. For example, they can say that the data must never be cached, can be reused only within a certain amount of time, and so on. Squid also uses a few internal heuristics to determine what should, or should not, be saved for future use.

Cache validation is a process that ensures Squid doesn't serve stale data to the user. Before reusing a cached response, Squid often validates it with the origin server. If the server indicates that Squid's copy is still valid, the data is sent from Squid. Otherwise, Squid updates its cached copy as it relays the response to the client. Squid generally performs validation using timestamps. The origin server's response usually contains a *last-modified* timestamp. Squid sends the timestamp back to the origin server to find if the original resource has changed.

For a detailed treatment of web caching, have a look at my book *Web Caching*, also by O'Reilly.

A Brief History of Squid

In the beginning was the CERN HTTP server. In addition to functioning as an HTTP server, it was also the first caching proxy. The caching module was written by Ari Luotonen in 1994.

That same year, the Internet Research Task Force Group on Resource Discovery (IRTF-RD) started the Harvest project. It was "an integrated set of tools to gather, extract, organize, search, cache, and replicate" Internet information. I joined the Harvest project near the end of 1994. While most people used Harvest as a local (or distributed) search engine, the Object Cache component was quite popular as well. The Harvest cache boasted three major improvements over the CERN cache: faster use of the filesystem, a single process design, and caching hierarchies via the Internet Cache Protocol.

Towards the end of 1995, many Harvest team members made the move to the exciting world of Internet-based startup companies. The original authors of the Harvest cache code, Peter Danzig and Anawat Chankhunthod, turned it into a commercial product. Their company was later acquired by Network Appliance. In early 1996, I joined the National Laboratory for Applied Network Research (NLANR) to work on the Information Resource Caching (IRCache) project, funded by the National Science Foundation. Under this project, we took the Harvest cache code, renamed it Squid, and released it under the GNU General Public License.

Since that time Squid has grown in size and features. It now supports a number of cool things such as URL redirection, traffic shaping, sophisticated access controls, numerous authentication modules, advanced disk storage options, HTTP interception, and surrogate mode (a.k.a. HTTP server acceleration).

Funding for the IRCache project ended in July 2000. Today, a number of volunteers continue to develop and support Squid. We occasionally receive financial or other types of support from companies that benefit from Squid.

Looking towards the future, we are rewriting Squid in C++ and, at the same time, fixing a number of design issues in the older code that are limiting to new features. We are adding support for protocols such as Edge Side Includes (ESI) and Internet Content Adaptation Protocol (ICAP). We also plan to make Squid support IPv6. A few developers are constantly making Squid run better on Microsoft Windows platforms. Finally, we will add more and more HTTP/1.1 features and work towards full compliance with the latest protocol specification.

Hardware and Operating System Requirements

Squid runs on all popular Unix systems, as well as Microsoft Windows. Although Squid's Windows support is improving all the time, you may have an easier time with Unix. If you have a favorite operating system, I'd suggest using that one. Otherwise, if you're looking for a recommendation, I really like FreeBSD.

Squid's hardware requirements are generally modest. Memory is often the most important resource. A memory shortage causes a drastic degradation in performance. Disk space is, naturally, another important factor. More disk space means more cached objects and higher hit ratios. Fast disks and interfaces are also beneficial. SCSI performs better than ATA, if you can justify the higher costs. While fast CPUs are nice, they aren't critical to good performance.

Because Squid uses a small amount of memory for every cached response, there is a relationship between disk space and memory requirements. As a rule of thumb, you need 32 MB of memory for each GB of disk space. Thus, a system with 512 MB of RAM can support a 16-GB disk cache. Your mileage may vary, of course. Memory requirements depend on factors such as the mean object size, CPU architecture (32- or 64-bit), the number of concurrent users, and particular features that you use.

People often ask such questions as, "I have a network with X users. What kind of hardware do I need for Squid?" These questions are difficult to answer for a number of reasons. In particular, it's hard to say how much traffic X users will generate. I usually find it easier to look at bandwidth usage, and go from there. I tell people to build a system with enough disk space to hold 3–7 days worth of web traffic. For example, if your users consume 1 Mbps (HTTP and FTP traffic only) for 8 hours per day, that's about 3.5 GB per day. So, I'd say you want between 10 and 25 GB of disk space for each Mbps of web traffic.

Squid Is Open Source

Squid is free software and a collaborative project. If you find Squid useful, please consider contributing back to the project in one or more of the following ways:

- Participate on the *squid-users* discussion list. Answer questions and help out new users.
- Try out new versions and report bugs or other problems.
- Contribute to the online documentation and Frequently Asked Questions (FAQ). If you notice an inconsistency, report it to the maintainers.
- Submit your local modifications back to the developers for inclusion into the code base.
- Provide financial support to one or more developers through small development contracts.
- Tell the developers about features you would like to have.
- Tell your friends and colleagues that Squid is cool.

Squid is released as free software under the GNU General Public License. This means, for example, that anyone who distributes Squid must make the source code available to you. See *http://www.gnu.org/licenses/gpl-faq.html* for more information about the GPL.

Squid's Home on the Web

The main source for up-to-date information about Squid is *http://www.squid-cache.org*. There you can:

- Download the source code.
- Read the FAQ and other documentation.
- Subscribe to the mailing list, or read the archives.
- Contact the developers.
- Find links to third-party applications.
- And more!

Getting Help

Given that Squid is free software, you may need to rely on the kindness of strangers for occasional assistance. The best place to do this is the *squid-users* mailing list. Before posting a message to the mailing list, however, you should check Squid's FAQ document to see if your question has already been asked and answered. If neither resource provides the help you need, you can contact one of the many services offering professional support for Squid.

Frequently Asked Questions

Squid's FAQ document, located at *http://www.squid-cache.org/Doc/FAQ/FAQ.html*, is a good source of information for new users. The FAQ evolves over time, so it will contain entries written after this book. The FAQ also contains some historical information that may be irrelevant today.

Even so, the FAQ is one of the first places you should look for answers to your questions. This is especially true if you are a new user. While it is certainly less effort for you to simply write to the mailing list for help, veteran mailing list members grow tired of reading and answering the same questions. If your question is frequently asked, it may simply be ignored.

The FAQ is quite large. The HTML version exists as approximately 25 different chapters, each in a separate file. These can be difficult to search for keywords and awkward to print. You can also download PostScript, PDF, and text versions by following links at the top of the HTML version.

Mailing Lists

Squid has three mailing lists you might find useful. I explain how to become a subscriber below, but you may want to check Squid's mailing list page, *http://www.squid-cache.org/mailing-lists.html*, for possibly more up-to-date information.

squid-users

The *squid-users* mailing list is an excellent place to find answers for such questions as:

- How do I ... ?
- Is this a bug ... ?
- Does this feature/program work on my platform?
- What does this error message mean?

Note that you must subscribe before you can post a message. To subscribe to the *squid-users* list, send a message to *squid-users-subscribe@squid-cache.org*.

If you prefer, you can receive the digest version of the list. In this case, you'll receive multiple postings in a single email message. To sign up this way, send a message to *squid-users-digest-subscribe@squid-cache.org*.

Once you subscribe, you can post a message to the list by writing to *squid-users@squid-cache.org*. If you have a question, consider checking the FAQ and/or mailing list archives first. You can browse the list archive by visiting *http://www.squid-cache.org/mail-archive/squid-users/*. However, if you are looking for something specific, you'll probably have more luck with the search interface at *http://www.squid-cache.org/search/*.

squid-announce

The moderated *squid-announce* list is used to announce new Squid versions and important security updates. The volume is quite low, usually less than one message per month. Write to *squid-announce-subscribe@squid-cache.org* if you'd like to subscribe.

squid-dev

The *squid-dev* list is a place where Squid hackers and developers can exchange ideas and information. Anyone can post a message to *squid-dev*, but subscriptions are moderated. If you'd like to join the discussion, please send a message about yourself and your interests in Squid. One of the list members should subscribe you within a few days.

The *squid-dev* messages are archived at *http://www.squid-cache.org/mail-archive/squid-dev/*, where anyone may browse them.

Professional Support

A number of companies now offer professional assistance for Squid. They may be able to help you get started with Squid for the first time, recommend a configuration for your network environment, and even fix some bugs.

Some of the consulting companies are associated with core Squid developers. By giving them your business, you ensure that fixes and features will be committed to future Squid software releases. If necessary, you can also arrange for development of private features.

Visit *http://www.squid-cache.org/Support/services.html* for the list of professional support services.

Getting Started with Squid

If you are new to Squid, the next few chapters will help you get started. First, I'll show you how to get the code, either the original source or precompiled binaries. In Chapter 3, I go through the steps necessary to compile and install Squid on your Unix system; this chapter is important because you'll probably need to tune your system before compiling the source code. Chapter 4 provides a very brief introduction to Squid's configuration file. Finally, Chapter 5 explains how to run Squid.

If you've already had a little experience installing and running Squid, you may want to skip ahead to Chapter 6.

Exercises

- Visit the Squid site and locate the *squid-users* mailing list archive. Browse the messages for the past few weeks.
- Search the Squid FAQ for information about file descriptors.
- Check one of the Squid mirror sites. Is it up to date with the primary site?

## CHAPTER 2

Getting Squid

Squid is normally distributed as source code. This means you'll probably need to compile it, as described in Chapter 3. The installation process should be relatively painless. The developers put a lot of effort into making sure Squid compiles easily on all the popular operating systems.

You can also find precompiled binaries for some operating systems. Linux users can get Squid in one of the various package formats (e.g., RPM, Debian, etc.). The FreeBSD, NetBSD, and OpenBSD projects offer Squid *ports*. The BSD ports aren't binary distributions but rather a small set of files that know how to download, compile, and install the Squid source. While these precompiled or preconfigured packages may be easier to install, I recommend that you download and compile the source yourself.

Anonymous CVS is a great way for developers and users to stay current with the official source tree. Instead of downloading entire new releases, you run a command to retrieve only the parts that have changed since your last update.

Versions and Releases

The Squid developers make periodic releases of the source code. Each release has a version number, such as 2.5.STABLE4. The third component starts either with STABLE or DEVEL (short for *development*).

As you can probably guess, the DEVEL releases tend to have newer, experimental features. They are also more likely to have bugs. Inexperienced users should not run DEVEL releases. If you choose to try a DEVEL release, and you encounter problems, please report them to the Squid maintainers.

After spending some time in the development state, the version number changes to STABLE. These releases are suitable for all users. Of course, even the stable releases may have some bugs. The higher-numbered stable versions (e.g., STABLE3,

STABLE4) are likely to have fewer bugs. If you are really concerned about stability, you may want to wait for one of these later releases.

Use the Source, Luke

So why can't you just copy a precompiled binary to your system and expect it to work perfectly? The primary reason is that the code needs to know about certain operating system parameters. In particular, the most important parameter is the maximum number of open file descriptors. Squid's ./configure script (see Chapter 3) probes for these values before compiling. If you take a Squid binary built for one value and run it on a system with a different value, you may encounter problems.

Another reason is that many of Squid's features must be enabled at compile time. If you take a binary that somebody else compiled, and it doesn't include the code for the features that you want, you'll need to compile your own version anyway.

Finally, note that shared libraries sometimes make it difficult to share executable files between systems. Shared libraries are loaded at runtime. This is also known as *dynamic linking*. Squid's ./configure script probes your system to find out certain things about your C library functions (if they are present, if they work, etc.). Although library functions don't usually change, it is possible that two different systems have slightly different shared C libraries. This may become a problem for Squid if the two systems are different enough.

Getting the Squid source code is really quite easy. To get it, visit the Squid home page, *http://www.squid-cache.org/*. The home page has links to the current stable and development releases. If you aren't located in the United States, you can select one of the many mirror sites. The mirror sites are usually named "wwwN.CC. squid-cache.org," where N is a number and CC is a two-letter country code. For example, *www1.au.squid-cache.org* is an Australian mirror site. The home page has links to the current mirror sites.

Each Squid release branch (e.g., Squid-2.5) has its own HTML page. This page has links to the source code releases and "diffs" between releases. If you are upgrading from one release to the next, you may want to download the diff file and apply the patch as described in Chapter 3. The release pages describe the new features and important changes in each version, and also have links to bugs that have been fixed.

When web access isn't an option, you can get the source release from the *ftp.squid-cache.org* FTP server or one of the FTP mirror sites. For the current versions, look in the *pub/squid-2/DEVEL* or *pub/squid-2/STABLE* directories. The Squid FTP site is mirrored at many locations as well. You can use the same country-code trick to guess some mirror sites, such as *ftp1.uk.squid-cache.org*.

The current Squid release distributions are about 1 MB in size. After downloading the compressed tar file, you can proceed to Chapter 3.

Precompiled Binaries

Some Unix distributions include, or make available, precompiled Squid packages. For Linux, you can easily find Squid RPMs. Often the Squid RPM is included on Linux CD-ROMs you can buy. The FreeBSD/NetBSD/OpenBSD distributions also contain Squid in their ports and/or packages collections.

While RPMs and precompiled packages may initially save you some time, they also have some drawbacks. As I already mentioned, certain features must be enabled or disabled *before* you start compiling Squid. The precompiled package that you install may not have the particular feature you want. Furthermore, Squid's ./configure script probes your operating system for certain parameters. These parameters may be configured differently on your machine on which Squid was compiled. Finally, if you want to apply a patch to Squid, you'll either have to wait for someone to build a new RPM/package or get the source and do it yourself.

I strongly encourage you to compile Squid from the source, but the decision is yours to make.

Anonymous CVS

The Concurrent Versioning System (CVS) is a nifty package that allows you to simultaneously edit and manage source code and other files. Almost every open source software project uses CVS.

You can anonymously access Squid's CVS files (read-only) to keep your source code up to date. The nice thing about CVS is that you can easily retrieve only the changes (diffs) of your current version. Thus, it is easy to see what has changed recently. Applying the changes to your current files efficiently synchronizes your source code with the official version.

CVS uses a tree-like indexing system. The trunk of the tree is called the *head branch*. For Squid's repository, this is where all new changes and features are placed. The head branch usually contains experimental and, possibly unstable, code. The stable code is typically found on other branches.

To effectively use Squid's anonymous CVS server, you first need to understand how different versions and branches are *tagged*. For example, the Version 2.5 branch is named *SQUID_2_5*. Particular releases, which represent a snapshot in time, have longer names, such as *SQUID_2_5_STABLE4*. To get exactly Squid Version 2.5. STABLE4, use the *SQUID_2_5_STABLE4* tag; to get the latest code on the 2.5 branch, use *SQUID_2_5*.

To use the Squid anonymous CVS server, you first need to set the CVSROOT environment variable:

```
csh% setenv CVSROOT :pserver:anoncvs@cvs.squid-cache.org:/squid
```

Or, for Bourne shell users:

```
sh$ CVSROOT=:pserver:anoncvs@cvs.squid-cache.org:/squid
sh$ export CVSROOT
```

You then log in to the server:

```
% cvs login
(Logging in to anoncvs@cvs.squid-cache.org)
CVS password:
```

At the prompt, enter **anoncvs** for the password. Now you can check out the source tree with this command:

```
% cvs checkout -r SQUID_2_5 -d squid-2.5 squid
```

The -r option specifies the revision tag to retrieve. Omitting the -r option gets you the head branch. The -d option changes the top-level directory name in which files are placed. If you omit the -d option, the top-level directory is the same as the module name. The final command-line argument (squid) is the name of the module to check out.

Once you have the Squid source tree checked out, you can run the cvs update command to update your files and synchronize with the master repository. Additional interesting commands are cvs diff, cvs log, and cvs annotate.

To learn more about CVS, visit *http://www.cvshome.org/*.

devel.squid-cache.org

The Squid developers maintain a separate site, currently hosted at SourceForge, for experimental Squid features. Check it out at *http://devel.squid-cache.org/*. There you'll find a number of cutting-edge development projects that haven't yet been integrated into the official Squid code base. You can access these projects through SourceForge's anonymous CVS server or download diff files based on the standard releases.

Exercises

- Visit the Squid web site or FTP server and look at the recent stable and development releases. How often are new releases made?
- Download the most recent stable code.
- Use Squid's anonymous CVS server to check out the recent stable branch. Change one of the source files by inserting a blank line, then run **cvs diff**.

Compiling and Installing

Squid is designed to be portable and should compile on all major Unix systems, including Linux, BSD/OS, FreeBSD, NetBSD, OpenBSD, Solaris, HP-UX, OSF/DUNIX/TRU-64, Mac OS/X, IRIX, and AIX. Squid also runs on Microsoft Windows. Please see Appendix E for instructions on compiling and running Squid on Windows.

Compiling Squid is relatively straightforward. If you've installed more than a few open source packages, you're probably already familiar with the procedure. You first use a program called ./configure to probe your system and then a program called make to do the actual compiling.

Before getting to that step, however, let's talk about tuning your system in preparation for Squid. Your operating system may have default resource limits that are too low for Squid to run correctly. Most importantly, you need to worry about the number of available file descriptors.

Before You Start

If you've been using Unix for a while, chances are that you've already compiled a number of other software packages. If so, you can probably quickly scan this chapter. The procedure for compiling and installing Squid is similar to many other software distributions.

To compile Squid, you need an ANSI C compiler. Don't be too alarmed by the "ANSI" part. Chances are that if you already have a C compiler, it is compliant with the ANSI specification. The GNU C compiler (gcc) is an excellent choice and widely available. Most operating systems come with a C compiler as a part of the standard installation. The common exceptions are Solaris and HP-UX. If you're using one of those operating systems, you might not have a compiler installed.

Ideally you should compile Squid on the same system on which it will run. Part of the installation process probes your system for certain parameters, such as the number of available file descriptors. However, if your system doesn't have a C compiler, you may be able to compile Squid elsewhere and then copy the binaries back. If the operating systems are different, Squid may encounter some problems. Also, Squid may become confused if the two systems have different kernel configurations.

In addition to a C compiler, you'll also need Perl and awk. awk is a standard program on all Unix systems, so you shouldn't need to worry about it. Perl is quite common, but it may not be installed on your system by default. You may need the gzip program to uncompress the source distribution file.

Solaris users, make sure that */usr/ccs/bin* is in your PATH, even if you're using gcc. To compile Squid, you may need the make and ar programs found in that directory.

Unpacking the Source

After downloading the source distribution, you need to unpack it somewhere. The particular location doesn't really matter. You can unpack Squid in your home directory or anywhere; you'll need about 20 MB of free disk space. Personally, I like to use */tmp*. Use the tar command to extract the source directory:

```
% cd /tmp
% tar xzvf /some/where/squid-2.5.STABLE4-src.tar.gz
squid-2.5.STABLE4/
squid-2.5.STABLE4/CONTRIBUTORS
squid-2.5.STABLE4/COPYING
squid-2.5.STABLE4/COPYRIGHT
squid-2.5.STABLE4/CREDITS
squid-2.5.STABLE4/ChangeLog
squid-2.5.STABLE4/INSTALL
squid-2.5.STABLE4/QUICKSTART
squid-2.5.STABLE4/README
...
```

Some tar programs don't have the z option, which automatically uncompresses gzip files. In that case, you'll need to use this command:

```
% gzip -dc /some/where/squid-2.5.STABLE4-src.tar.gz | tar xvf -
```

Once the source code has been unpacked, the next step is usually to configure the source tree. However, if this is the first time you're compiling Squid, you should make sure certain kernel resource limits are high enough; to find out how, read on.

Pretuning Your Kernel

Squid requires a fair amount of kernel resources under moderate and high loads. In particular, you may need to configure your system with a higher-than-normal number of file descriptors and mbuf clusters. The file-descriptor limit can be especially annoying. You'd be better off to increase the limit before compiling Squid.

At this point, you might be tempted to get the precompiled binaries to avoid the hassle of building a new kernel.* Unfortunately, you need to make a new kernel, regardless. Squid and the kernel exchange information through data structures that must not exceed the set file-descriptor limits. Squid checks these limits at runtime and uses the safest (smallest) value. Thus, even if a precompiled binary has higher file descriptors than the kernel, the kernel value takes precedence.

To change some settings, you must build and install a new kernel. This procedure varies among different operating systems. Consult *Unix System Administration Handbook* (Prentice Hall) or your operating-system documentation if necessary. If you're using Linux, you probably don't need to recompile your kernel.

File Descriptors

File descriptors are simply integers that identify each file and socket that a process has opened. The first opened file is 0, the second is 1, and so on. Unix operating systems usually impose a limit on the number of file descriptors that each process can open. Furthermore, Unix also normally has a systemwide limit.

Because of the way Squid works, the file-descriptor limits may adversely affect performance. When Squid uses up all the available file descriptors, it is unable to accept new connections from users. In other words, running out of file descriptors causes denial of service. Squid can't accept new requests until some of the current requests complete, and the corresponding files and sockets are closed. Squid issues a warning when it detects a file-descriptor shortage.

You can save yourself some trouble by making sure the file descriptor limits are appropriate before running ./configure. In most cases, 1024 file descriptors will be sufficient. Very busy caches may require 4096 or more. When configuring file descriptor limits, I recommend setting the systemwide limit to twice the per-process limit.

You can usually discover your system's file-descriptor limit from your Unix shell. All C shells and similar have the built-in limit command. Newer Bourne shells and similar have a command called ulimit. To find your file-descriptor limits, try running these commands:

```
csh% limit descriptors unlimited
csh% limit descriptors
descriptors    4096
```

or:

```
sh$ ulimit -n unlimited
sh$ ulimit -n
4096
```

---

* Not all operating systems require building a new kernel. Some may be tunable at runtime.

On FreeBSD, you can also use the sysctl command:

```
% sysctl -a | grep maxfiles
kern.maxfiles: 8192
kern.maxfilesperproc: 4096
```

If you can't figure out the file-descriptor limit, Squid's ./configure script can do it for you. When you run ./configure, as described in the section "The configure Script," watch for output like this near the end:

```
checking Maximum number of file descriptors we can open... 4096
```

If either limit, ulimit, or ./configure report a value less than 1024, you should invest the time to increase the limit before compiling Squid. Otherwise, Squid's performance will be poor under a moderate load.

Increasing the file descriptor limit varies from system to system. The following sections offer some tips to help get you started.

FreeBSD, NetBSD, OpenBSD

Edit your kernel configuration file, and add a line like this:

```
options        MAXFILES=8192
```

On OpenBSD, use option instead of options. Then, configure, compile, and install the new kernel. Reboot your system so the change takes effect.

Linux

Configuring file descriptors on Linux is a little complicated. You must edit one of the system include files, and execute some shell commands before compiling and running Squid. Start off by editing the file */usr/include/bits/types.h*. Change the value for __FD_SETSIZE as follows:

```
#define __FD_SETSIZE    8192
```

Next, increase the kernel file descriptor limit with this command:

```
# echo 8192 > /proc/sys/fs/file-max
```

Finally, increase the process file-descriptor limit in the same shell in which you will configure and compile Squid:

```
sh# ulimit -Hn 8192
```

This command must be executed as *root* and only works from the bash shell. There is no need to reboot on Linux.

 With this technique, you must execute the echo and ulimit commands each time your system boots, or at least before starting Squid. If you use an *rc.d* script to start Squid (see Chapter 5), that is a good place to stick these commands.

Solaris

Add this line to your */etc/system* file:

```
set rlim_fd_max = 4096
```

Then, reboot the system for the change to take effect.

Mbuf Clusters

The BSD-based networking code uses a data structure known as an *mbuf* (see W.R. Stevens' book, *TCP/IP Illustrated, Vol 2)*. Mbufs are typically small (e.g., 128 octets) chunks of memory. The data for larger network packets are stored in mbuf *clusters*. The kernel may enforce an upper limit on the total number of mbuf clusters available in the system. You can find this limit with the netstat command:

```
% netstat -m
196/6368/32768 mbufs in use (current/peak/max):
        146 mbufs allocated to data
        50 mbufs allocated to packet headers
103/6182/8192 mbuf clusters in use (current/peak/max)
13956 Kbytes allocated to network (56% of mb_map in use)
0 requests for memory denied
0 requests for memory delayed
0 calls to protocol drain routines
```

In this example, there are 8,192 mbuf clusters available, but there are never more than 6,182 used at once. When the system runs out of mbuf clusters, I/O routines such as read( ) and write( ) return the "No buffer space available" error message.

NetBSD and OpenBSD don't display mbuf usage in netstat -m output. Instead, they report "WARNING: mclpool limit reached" via syslog.

To increase the number of mbuf clusters, you need to add an option to your kernel configuration file:

```
options         NMBCLUSTERS=16384
```

Ephemeral Port Range

Ephemeral ports are the local port numbers the TCP/IP stack assigns to outgoing connections. In other words, when Squid makes a connection to an origin server, the kernel assigns a port number to the local socket. These local port numbers fall within a certain range. On FreeBSD, for example, the default ephemeral port range is 1024–5000.

A shortage of ephemeral ports may adversely affect performance for very busy proxies (i.e., hundreds of requests per second). This is because some TCP connections enter a TIME_WAIT state when they are closed. An ephemeral port number can't be reused while the connection is in the TIME_WAIT state.

You can see how many connections are in this state with the `netstat` command:

```
% netstat -n | grep TIME_WAIT
Proto Recv-Q Send-Q  Local Address         Foreign Address         (state)
tcp4      0      0   192.43.244.42.19583   212.67.202.80.80        TIME_WAIT
tcp4      0      0   192.43.244.42.19597   202.158.66.190.80       TIME_WAIT
tcp4      0      0   192.43.244.42.19600   207.99.19.230.80        TIME_WAIT
tcp4      0      0   192.43.244.42.19601   216.131.72.121.80       TIME_WAIT
tcp4      0      0   192.43.244.42.19602   209.61.183.115.80       TIME_WAIT
tcp4      0      0   192.43.244.42.3128    128.109.131.47.25666    TIME_WAIT
tcp4      0      0   192.43.244.42.3128    128.109.131.47.25795    TIME_WAIT
tcp4      0      0   192.43.244.42.3128    128.182.72.190.1488     TIME_WAIT
tcp4      0      0   192.43.244.42.3128    128.182.72.190.2194     TIME_WAIT
```

Note that this example has both client- and server-side connections. Client-side connections have 3128 as the local port number; server-side connections have 80 as the remote (foreign) port number. The ephemeral port numbers appear under the Local Address heading. In this example, they are in the 19,000s.

Unless you see thousands of ephemeral ports in the TIME_WAIT state, you probably don't need to increase the range. On FreeBSD, you can increase the range with this command:

```
# sysctl -w net.inet.ip.portrange.last=30000
```

On OpenBSD, the command is almost the same, but the sysctl variable has a different name:

```
# sysctl -w net.inet.ip.portlast=49151
```

On NetBSD, things work a little differently. The default range is 49,152–65,535. To increase the range, change the lower limit:

```
# sysctl -w net.inet.ip.anonportmin=10000
```

On Linux, simply write a pair of numbers to the following special file:

```
# echo "1024 40000" > /proc/sys/net/ipv4/ip_local_port_range
```

Don't forget to add these commands to your system startup scripts so that they take effect each time your machine reboots.

The configure Script

Like many other Unix software packages, Squid uses a `./configure` script to learn about an operating system before compiling. The `./configure` script is generated by the popular GNU autoconf program. When the script runs, it probes the system in various ways to find out about libraries, functions, types, parameters, and features that may or may not be present. One of the first things that `./configure` does is look for a working C compiler. If the compiler can't be found or fails to compile a simple test program, the `./configure` script can't proceed.

The `./configure` script has a number of different options. The most important is the installation prefix. Before running `./configure`, you need to decide where Squid should live. The installation prefix determines the default locations for the Squid logs, binaries, and configuration files. You can change the location for those files after installing, but it's easier if you decide now.

The default installation prefix is */usr/local/squid*. Squid puts files in seven different subdirectories under the prefix:

```
% ls -l /usr/local/squid
total 5
drwxr-x---  2 wessels  wheel  512 Apr 28 20:42 bin
drwxr-x---  2 wessels  wheel  512 Apr 28 20:42 etc
drwxr-x---  2 wessels  wheel  512 Apr 28 20:42 libexec
drwxr-x---  3 wessels  wheel  512 Apr 28 20:43 man
drwxr-x---  2 wessels  wheel  512 Apr 28 20:42 sbin
drwxr-x---  4 wessels  wheel  512 Apr 28 20:42 share
drwxr-x---  4 wessels  wheel  512 Apr 28 20:43 var
```

Squid uses the *bin*, *etc*, *libexec*, *man*, *sbin*, and *share* directories for a few, relatively small files (or other directories) that don't change very often. The files under the *var* directory, however, are a different story. This is where you'll find Squid's log files, which may grow quite large (tens or hundreds of megabytes). *var* is also the default location for the actual disk cache. You may want to put *var* on a different partition with plenty of space. One easy way to do this is with the `--localstatedir` option:

```
% ./configure --localstatedir=/bigdisk/var
```

You don't need to worry too much about pathnames when configuring Squid. You can always change the pathnames later, in the *squid.conf* file.

configure Options

The `./configure` script has a number of different options that all start with `--`. You can see the full list of options by typing **`./configure --help`**. Some of these options are common to all configure scripts, and some are unique to Squid. Here are the standard options that you might find useful:

`--prefix=PREFIX`
> This sets the installation prefix directory, as described earlier. The installation prefix is the default directory for all executables, logs, and configuration files. Throughout this book, *$prefix* refers to your choice for the installation prefix.

`--localstatedir=DIR`
> This option allows you to change the location for the *var* directory. The default is *$prefix/var*, but you might want to change it so that Squid's disk cache and log files are stored elsewhere.

`--sysconfdir=DIR`
> This option allows you to change the location for the *etc* directory. The default is *$prefix/etc*. If you like to use */usr* as the installation prefix, you might want to set `--sysconfdir` to */etc*.

Here are the Squid-specific `./configure` options:

`--enable-dlmalloc[=LIB]`
> On some systems, the built-in memory allocation (malloc) functions have poor performance characteristics when used with Squid. Using the `--enable-dlmalloc` option builds and links with the `dlmalloc` package included in the Squid source code. If you already have `dlmalloc` built on your system, you can specify the library's pathname as the `=LIB` argument. See *http://g.oswego.edu/dl/html/malloc. html* for more information on `dlmalloc`.

`--enable-gnuregex`
> Squid uses *regular expressions* for pattern matching in access control lists and other configuration directives. The GNU regular expression library comes with the Squid source code; it can be used on operating systems that don't have built-in regular expression functions. The `./configure` script probes your system for a regular expression library and enables the use of GNU regex if necessary. If, for some reason, you want to force the usage of GNU regex, you can add this option to the `./configure` command.

`--enable-carp`
> The Cache Array Routing Protocol (CARP) is useful for forwarding cache misses to an array, or cluster, of parent caches. There's more about CARP in Chapter 10.

`--enable-async-io[=N_THREADS]`
> Async I/O refers to one of Squid's techniques for improved storage performance. The *aufs* storage module uses a number of thread processes to perform disk I/O operations. This code works only on Linux and Solaris systems. The `=N_THREADS` argument changes the number of thread processes Squid uses. *aufs* and Async I/O are discussed in the section called Chapter 8.

> Note that the `--enable-async-io` option is a shortcut that turns on three other `./configure` options. It is equivalent to specifying:
> ```
> --with-aufs-threads=N_THREADS
> --with-pthreads
> --enable-storeio=ufs,aufs
> ```

`--with-pthreads`
> The `--with-pthreads` option causes the compilation procedure to link with your system's Pthreads library. The *aufs* storage module is the only part of Squid that uses threads. Normally, you don't specify this option on the `./configure` command line because it's enabled automatically when you use `--enable-async-io`.

`--enable-storeio=LIST`

Squid supports a number of different storage modules. With this option, you tell `./configure` which modules to compile. The *ufs*, *aufs*, *diskd*, *coss*, and *null* modules are supported in Squid-2.5. You can also get a list by looking at the directories under *src/fs*.

LIST is a comma-separated list of module names. For example:

```
% ./configure --enable-storeio=afus,diskd,ufs
```

The *ufs* module is the default and least likely to cause problems. Unfortunately, it also has limited performance characteristics. The other modules may not necessarily compile on your particular operating system. For a complete description of Squid's storage modules, see Chapter 8.

`--with-aufs-threads=N_THREADS`

Specifies the number of threads to use for the *aufs* storage scheme (see Chapter 8). By default, Squid automatically calculates how many threads to use, based on the number of cache directories.

`--enable-heap-replacement`

This option has been deprecated but remains for backward compatibility. You should always use the `--enable-removal-policies` option instead.

`--enable-removal-policies=LIST`

Removal policies are the algorithms Squid uses to eject cached objects when making room for new ones. Squid-2.5 supports three removal policies: least recently used (LRU), greed dual size (GDS), and least frequently used (LFU).

However, for some reason, the `./configure` options blur the distinction between a particular replacement policy and the underlying data structures required to implement them. LRU, which is the default, is implemented with a doubly linked list. The GDS and LFU implementations use a data structure known as a *heap*.

To use the GDS or LFU policies, you specify:

```
% ./configure --enable-removal-policies=heap
```

You then select between GDS and LFU in the Squid configuration file. If you want to retain the option of using LRU, specify:

```
% ./configure --enable-removal-policies=heap,lru
```

There's more about replacement policies in Chapter 7.

`--enable-icmp`

As you'll see in Chapter 10, Squid can make round-trip time measurements with ICMP messages, much like the `ping` program. You can use this option to enable these features.

`--enable-delay-pools`

Delay pools are Squid's technique for traffic shaping or bandwidth limiting. The pools consist of groups of client IP addresses. When requests from these clients are cache misses, their responses may be artificially delayed. See more about delay pools in Appendix C.

`--enable-useragent-log`

This option enables logging of the HTTP `User-Agent` header from client requests. See more about this in Chapter 13.

`--enable-referer-log`

This option enables logging of the HTTP `referer` header from client requests. See more about this in Chapter 13.

`--disable-wccp`

The Web Cache Coordination Protocol (WCCP) is Cisco's once-proprietary protocol for intercepting and distributing HTTP requests to one or more caches. WCCP is enabled by default, but you can use this option to prevent compilation of the WCCP code if you like.

`--enable-snmp`

The Simple Network Management Protocol (SNMP) is a popular way to monitor network devices and servers. This option causes the build procedure to compile all of the SNMP-related code, including a cut-down version of the CMU SNMP library.

`--enable-cachemgr-hostname`*[=hostname]*

cachemgr is a CGI program you can use to administratively query Squid. By default, *cachemgr*'s hostname field is blank, but you can create a default value with this option. For example:

```
% ./configure --enable-cachemgr-hostname=mycache.myorg.net
```

`--enable-arp-acl`

Squid supports ARP, or Ethernet address, access control lists on some operating systems. The code to implement ARP ACLs uses nonstandard function interfaces, so it is disabled by default. If you run Squid on Linux or Solaris, you may be able to use this feature.

`--enable-htcp`

HTCP is the Hypertext Caching Protocol—an intercache protocol similar to ICP. See Chapter 10 for more information.

`--enable-ssl`

Use this option to give Squid the ability to terminate SSL/TLS connections. Note this only works for accelerated requests in surrogate mode. See Chapter 15 for more information.

`--with-openssl`*[=DIR]*

This option exists so that you can tell the compiler where to find the OpenSSL libraries and header files, if necessary. If they aren't in the default location, enter the parent directory after this option. For example:

```
% ./configure --enable-ssl --with-ssl=/opt/foo/openssl
```

Given this example, your compiler looks for the OpenSSL header files in */opt/foo/openssl/include*, and for libraries in */opt/foo/openssl/lib*.

`--enable-cache-digests`

Cache Digests are another alternative to ICP, but with significantly different characteristics. See Chapter 10.

`--enable-err-languages="lang1 lang2 ..."`

Squid supports customizable error messages and comes with error messages in many different languages. This option determines the languages that are copied to the installation directory (*$prefix/share/errors*). If you don't use this option, all available languages are installed. To see which languages are available, look at a directory listing of the *errors* directory in the source distribution. Here's how to enable more than one language:

```
% ./configure --enable-err-languages="Dutch German French" ...
```

`--enable-default-err-language=lang`

This option sets the default value for the *error_directory* directive. For example, if you want to use Dutch error messages, you can use this `./configure` option:

```
% ./configure --enable-default-err-language=Dutch
```

You can also set the *error_directory* directive in *squid.conf*, as described in Appendix A. English is the default error language if you omit this option.

`--with-coss-membuf-size=N`

The Cyclic Object Storage System (*coss*) is an experimental storage scheme for Squid. This option sets the memory buffer size for *coss* cache directories. Note that in order to use *coss*, you must specify it as a storage type in the --enable-storeio option.

The argument is given in bytes. The default is 1,048,576 bytes or 1 MB. You can specify a 2-MB buffer like this:

```
% ./configure --with-coss-membuf-size=2097152
```

`--enable-poll`

Unix provides two similar functions that scan open file descriptors for I/O events: select( ) and poll( ). The `./configure` script usually does a very good job of figuring out when to use poll( ) over select( ). Use this option if you want to override the `./configure` script and force it to use poll( ).

`--disable-poll`

Similarly, Unix gurus may want to force `./configure` to not use poll( ).

`--disable-http-violations`

By default, Squid can be configured to violate the HTTP protocol specifications. You can use this option to remove the code completely that would violate HTTP.

--enable-ipf-transparent

In Chapter 9, I'll describe how to configure Squid for interception caching. Some operating systems use the IP Filter package to assist with the interception. In these cases you should use this `./configure` option. If you enable this option and get compiler errors on the *src/client_side.c* file, chances are that the IP Filter package isn't actually (or correctly) installed on your system.

--enable-pf-transparent

You may need this option to use HTTP interception on systems that use the PF packet filter. PF is the standard packet filter for OpenBSD and may have been ported to other systems as well. If you enable this option and get compiler errors on the *src/client_side.c* file, chances are that PF isn't actually installed on your system.

--enable-linux-netfilter

Netfilter is the name of the Linux packet filter for the 2.4 kernel series. Enable this option if you want to use HTTP interception with Linux 2.4 or later.

--disable-ident-lookups

ident is a simple protocol that allows a server to find the username associated with a client's particular TCP connection. If you use this option, the compiler excludes completely the code that performs such lookups. Even if you leave the code enabled at compile time, Squid doesn't make *ident* lookups unless you configure them in *squid.conf*.

--disable-internal-dns

The Squid source code includes two different DNS resolution implementations, called *internal* and *external*. Internal lookups are the default, but some people prefer the external technique. This option disables the internal functionality and reverts to the older method.

Internal lookups use Squid's own implementation of the DNS protocol. That is, Squid generates raw DNS queries and sends them to a resolver. It retransmits queries that time out, and you can specify any number of resolvers. One of the benefits to this implementation is that Squid gets accurate TTLs for DNS replies.

External lookups use the C library's gethostbyname( ) and gethostbyaddr( ) functions. Since these routines block the process until the answer comes back, they must be called from external, helper processes. Squid uses a pool of external processes to make queries in parallel. The primary drawback to external DNS resolution is that you need more helper processes as Squid's load increases. Another annoyance is that the C library functions don't convey TTLs with the answers, in which case Squid uses a constant value supplied by the *positive_dns_ttl* directive.

--enable-truncate

The truncate( ) system call is an alternative to using unlink( ). While unlink( ) removes a cache file altogether, truncate( ) sets the file size to zero. This frees the disk space associated with the file but leaves the directory entry in place.

This option exists because some people believed (or hoped) that truncate() would produce better performance than unlink(). However, benchmarks have shown little or no real difference.

`--disable-hostname-checks`

By default, Squid requires that URL hostnames conform to the somewhat archaic specifications in RFC 1034:

> The labels must follow the rules for ARPANET host names. They must start with a letter, end with a letter or digit, and have as interior characters only letters, digits, and hyphen.

Here, "letter" means the ASCII characters A through Z. Since internationalized domain names are becoming increasingly popular, you may want to use this option to remove the restriction.

`--enable-underscores`

This option controls Squid's behavior regarding underscore characters in hostnames. General consensus is that hostnames must not include underscore characters, although some people disagree. Squid, by default, generates an error message for requests that have an underscore in a URL hostname. You can use this option to make Squid treat them as valid. However, your DNS resolver may also enforce the no-underscore requirement and fail to resolve such hostnames.

`--enable-auth[=LIST]`

This option controls which HTTP authentication schemes to support in the Squid binary. You can select any combination of the following schemes: *basic*, *digest*, and *ntlm*. If you omit the option, Squid supports only basic authentication. If you give the `--enable-auth` option without any arguments, the build process adds support for all schemes. Otherwise, you can give a comma-separated list of schemes to support:

```
% ./configure --enable-auth=digest,ntlm
```

I talk more about authentication in Chapters 6 and 12.

`--enable-auth-helpers=LIST`

This old option is now deprecated, but still remains for backward compatibility. You should use `--enable-basic-auth-helpers=LIST` instead.

`--enable-basic-auth-helpers=LIST`

With this option, you can build one or more of the HTTP Basic authentication helper programs found in *helpers/basic_auth*. See Chapter 12 for their names and descriptions.

`--enable-ntlm-auth-helpers=LIST`

With this option, you can build one or more of the HTTP NTLM authentication helper programs found in *helpers/ntlm_auth*. See Chapter 12 for their names and descriptions.

--enable-ntlm-fail-open

When you enable this option, Squid's NTLM authentication module defaults to allow access in the event of an error or problem.

--enable-digest-auth-modules=*LIST*

With this option, you can build one or more of the HTTP Digest authentication helper programs found in *helpers/digest_auth*. See Chapter 12 for their names and descriptions.

--enable-external-acl-helpers=*LIST*

With this option, you can build one or more of the external ACL helper programs that I discuss in Chapter 12. For example:

```
% ./configure --enable-external-acl-helpers=ip_user,ldap_group
```

--disable-unlinkd

Unlinkd is another one of Squid's external helper processes. Its sole job is to execute the unlink( ) (or truncate( )) system call on cache files. Squid realizes a significant performance gain by implementing file deletion in an external process. Use this option to disable the external unlink daemon feature.

--enable-stacktrace

Some operating systems support automatic generation of stack trace data in the event of a program crash. When you enable this feature and Squid crashes, the stack trace information is written to the *cache.log* file. This information is often helpful to developers in tracking down programming bugs.

--enable-x-accelerator-vary

This advanced feature may be used when Squid is configured as a surrogate. It instructs Squid to look for X-Accelerator-Vary headers in responses from back-end origin servers. See Chapter 15.

Running configure

Now we're ready to run the ./configure script. Go to the top-level source directory and type ./configure, followed by any of the options mentioned previously. For example:

```
% cd squid-2.5.STABLE4
% ./configure --enable-icmp --enable-htcp
```

./configure's job is to probe your operating system and find out which things are available, and which are not. One of the first things it does is make sure your C compiler is working. If ./configure detects a problem with your C compiler, the script exits with this error message:

```
configure: error: installation or configuration problem: C compiler
cannot create executables.
```

Most likely, you'll never see that message. If you do, it means either your system doesn't have a C compiler at all or that the compiler isn't installed correctly. Look at the *config.log* file for hints as to the exact problem. If your system has more than one C compiler, you can tell ./configure which to use by setting the CC environment variable before running ./configure:

```
% setenv CC /usr/local/bin/gcc
% ./configure ...
```

After ./configure checks out the compiler, it looks for a long list of header files, libraries, and functions. Normally you won't have to worry about this part. In some cases, ./configure pauses to get your attention about something that may be a problem (such as not enough file descriptors). It may also stop if you specify incompatible or unreasonable command-line options. If something does go wrong, check the *config.log* output. ./configure's final task is to create *Makefile*s and other files based on the things it learned about your system. At this point, you're ready to begin compiling.

make

Once ./configure has done its job, you can simply type make to begin compiling the source code:

```
% make
```

Normally, this part goes smoothly. You'll see a lot of lines that look like this:*

```
source='cbdata.c' object='cbdata.o' libtool=no  depfile='.deps/cbdata.Po'
tmpdepfile='.deps/cbdata.TPo'  depmode=gcc /bin/sh ../cfgaux/depcomp  gcc -DHAVE_
CONFIG_H -DDEFAULT_CONFIG_FILE=\"/usr/local/squid/etc/squid.conf\" -I. -I. -I../
include -I. -I. -I../include -I../include     -g -O2 -Wall -c 'test -f cbdata.c ||
echo './''cbdata.c
source='client_db.c' object='client_db.o' libtool=no  depfile='.deps/client_db.Po'
tmpdepfile='.deps/client_db.TPo'  depmode=gcc /bin/sh ../cfgaux/depcomp  gcc -DHAVE_
CONFIG_H -DDEFAULT_CONFIG_FILE=\"/usr/local/squid/etc/squid.conf\" -I. -I. -I../
include -I. -I. -I../include -I../include     -g -O2 -Wall -c 'test -f client_db.c ||
echo './''client_db.c
source='client_side.c' object='client_side.o' libtool=no  depfile='.deps/client_side.
Po' tmpdepfile='.deps/client_side.TPo'  depmode=gcc /bin/sh ../cfgaux/depcomp  gcc -
DHAVE_CONFIG_H -DDEFAULT_CONFIG_FILE=\"/usr/local/squid/etc/squid.conf\" -I. -I. -I..
/include -I. -I. -I../include -I../include     -g -O2 -Wall -c 'test -f client_side.c
|| echo './''client_side.c
source='comm.c' object='comm.o' libtool=no  depfile='.deps/comm.Po' tmpdepfile='.
deps/comm.TPo'  depmode=gcc /bin/sh ../cfgaux/depcomp  gcc -DHAVE_CONFIG_H -DDEFAULT_
CONFIG_FILE=\"/usr/local/squid/etc/squid.conf\" -I. -I. -I../include -I. -I. -I../
include -I../include     -g -O2 -Wall -c 'test -f comm.c || echo './''comm.c
```

You may see some compiler warnings. In most cases, it is safe to ignore these. If you see a lot of them or something that looks really serious, report it to the developers as described in Chapter 16.

---

* The make output used to be much prettier, but such is the price we pay for advanced compiling tools such as automake.

If the compilation gets all the way to the end without any errors, you can move to the next section, which describes how to install the programs you just built.

To verify that compilation was successful, you can run make again. You should see this output:*

```
% make
Making all in lib...
Making all in scripts...
Making all in src...
Making all in fs...
Making all in repl...
'squid' is up to date.
'client' is up to date.
'unlinkd' is up to date.
'cachemgr.cgi' is up to date.
Making all in icons...
Making all in errors...
Making all in auth_modules...
```

The compilation step may fail for a number of reasons, including:

Source code bugs

Usually the Squid source code is thoroughly debugged. However, you may encounter some bugs or problems that prevent Squid from compiling. You're more likely to find these sorts of bugs in the newer development versions. Report these to the developers.

Compiler installation problems

An improperly installed C compiler probably won't be able to compile Squid or any other moderately sized software package. Usually, compilers come pre-installed with the operating system, so you don't have to worry about that. However, if you attempt to upgrade your compiler after installing the operating system, you might make a mistake. Never copy a compiler installation from one machine to another, unless you are absolutely sure about what you are doing. I feel it is always better to install the compiler on each machine separately.

Always make sure that your compiler's header files are synchronized with the library files. The header files normally reside in */usr/include*, while libraries are found in */usr/lib*. Linux's popular RPM system makes it possible to upgrade one, but not the other. If the libraries are based on different header files, Squid may not compile.

If you want to upgrade the compiler on one of the open-source BSD variants, be sure to run make world from the */usr/src* directory, rather than from the */usr/src/lib* or */usr/src/include* directories.

---

* If make recompiles the source every time you run it, and there are no errors, your system clock may be set wrong.

Here are some common compilation problems and error messages:

`Solaris: make[1]: *** [libmiscutil.a] Error 255`

This means that `./configure` didn't find the ar program. Make sure */usr/ccs/bin* is listed in your `PATH` environment variable. If you don't have the Sun compiler installed, you'll need the GNU binutils (*http://www.gnu.org/directory/binutils. html*).

`Linux: storage size of 'rl' isn't known`

This happens when the header and library files don't match, as described earlier. Be sure to upgrade both packages at the same time.

`Digital Unix: Don't know how to make EXTRA_libmiscutil_a_SOURCES. Stop.`

Digital Unix's make program isn't tolerant of the *Makefile* produced by the automake package. For example, *lib/Makefile.in* contains these lines:

```
noinst_LIBRARIES = \
        @LIBDLMALLOC@ \
        libmiscutil.a \
        libntlmauth.a \
        @LIBREGEX@
```

After substitution, when *lib/Makefile* is created, it looks like this:

```
noinst_LIBRARIES = \
        \
        libmiscutil.a \
        libntlmauth.a \
        <TAB>
```

As shown above, the last line contains an (invisible) TAB character, which confuses make. You can get past this problem by installing and using GNU make, or by manually editing *lib/Makefile* (and any others exhibiting this problem) to make it look like this:

```
noinst_LIBRARIES = \
        \
        libmiscutil.a \
        libntlmauth.a
```

If you have problems compiling Squid, check the FAQ first. You may also want to search the Squid web site (use the search box on the home page). Finally, if you're still stuck, send email to the *squid-users@squid-cache.org* list.

make Install

After compiling, you need to install the programs into their permanent directories. This might require superuser privileges, to put files in the installation directories. If so, become *root* first:

```
% su
Password:
# make install
```

If you enable Squid's ICMP measurement features with the `--enable-icmp` option, you must install the `pinger` program. The `pinger` program must be installed with superuser privileges because only *root* is allowed to send and receive ICMP messages. The following command installs `pinger` with the appropriate permissions:

```
# make install-pinger
```

After installing Squid, you should see the following directories and files listed under the installation prefix directory (*/usr/local/squid* by default):

sbin

The *sbin* directory contains programs normally started by *root*.

sbin/squid

This is the main Squid program.

bin

The *bin* directory contains programs for all users.

bin/RunCache

RunCache is a shell script you can use to start Squid. If Squid dies, this script automatically starts it again, unless it detects frequent restarts. The *RunCache* script is a relic from the time when Squid was not a daemon process. With the current versions, *RunCache* is less useful because Squid automatically restarts itself when you don't use the -N option.

bin/RunAccel

The *RunAccel* script is nearly identical to *RunCache*, except that it adds a command-line argument that tells Squid where to listen for HTTP requests.

bin/squidclient

squidclient is a simple HTTP client you can use to test Squid. It also has some special features for making management requests to a running Squid process.

libexec

The *libexec* directory traditionally contains helper programs. These are commands that you wouldn't normally run yourself. Rather, these programs are normally started by other programs.

libexec/unlinkd

unlinkd is a helper program that removes files from the cache directories. As you'll see later, file deletion can be a significant bottleneck. By implementing the delete operation in an external process, Squid achieves some performance gain.

libexec/cachemgr.cgi

cachemgr.cgi is a CGI interface to Squid's management functions. To use it, you'll probably need to copy this program to your HTTP server's *cgi-bin* directory. You'll see more about this in Chapter 14.

libexec/diskd (optional)

You get this only if you specify `--enable-storeio=diskd`.

libexec/pinger (optional)

You get this only if you specify --enable-icmp.

etc

The *etc* directory contains Squid's configuration files.

etc/squid.conf

This is the primary configuration file for Squid. Initially, this file contains a lot of comments to explain what each option does. After you understand the configuration directives, it's a good idea to remove the comments to make the configuration file smaller and easier to read. Note that the installation procedure doesn't overwrite this file if it already exists.

etc/squid.conf.default

This is a copy of the default configuration file from the source distribution. You may find it useful to have a copy of the current default configuration file after upgrading your Squid installation. New configuration directives may be added, and some of the existing directives may have changed.

etc/mime.conf

The *mime.conf* file tells Squid which MIME types to use for data retrieved from FTP and Gopher servers. The file is a table that correlates filename extensions to MIME types. Normally, you won't need to edit this file. However, you may need to add entries for special file types used within your organization.

etc/mime.conf.default

This is the default *mime.conf* file from the source distribution.

share

The *share* directory normally contains read-only data files used by Squid.

share/mib.txt

This is the SNMP Management Information Base (MIB) file for Squid. Squid doesn't use this file itself. Rather, your SNMP agent software (such as snmpget and Multi-Router Traffic Grapher (MRTG)) needs this file to understand the SNMP objects available from Squid.

share/icons

The *share/icons* directory contains a number of small icon files Squid uses in FTP and Gopher directory listings. Normally, you won't need to worry about these files, but you can change them if you want.

share/errors

The *share/errors* directory contains templates for the error messages Squid shows to users. These files are copied from the source directory when you install Squid. You can edit them if you like. However, the installation procedure always overwrites these files every time you run make install. So if you want to have customized error messages, it's a good idea to put them in a different directory.

var

> The *var* directory contains files that aren't critical and that change frequently. These are the sort of files you don't normally back up.

var/logs

> The *var/logs* directory is the default location for Squid's various log files. It is empty when you first install Squid. Once Squid gets running, you can expect to find files here named *access.log*, *cache.log*, and *store.log*.

var/cache

> This is the default cache directory (*cache_dir*) if you don't specify one in *squid. conf*. See Chapter 7 for all the details about cache directories.

Applying a Patch

After you've been running Squid for a while, you may find that you need to patch the source code to fix a bug or add an experimental feature. Patches are posted for important bug fixes on the *squid-cache.org* web site. If you don't want to wait for the next official release, you can download and apply the patch to your source code. You will then need to recompile Squid.

To apply a patch—also sometimes called a *diff*—you need a program called patch. Chances are that your operating system already has the patch program. If not, you can download it from the GNU collection (*http://www.gnu.org/directory/patch.html*). Note that if you're using anonymous CVS (see Chapter 2), you don't need to worry about patching files. The CVS system does it for you automatically when you update your tree.

To apply a patch, you need to save the patch file somewhere on your system. Then cd to the Squid source directory and run the command like this:

```
% cd squid-2.5.STABLE4
% patch < /tmp/patch_file
```

By default, the patch program tells you what it's doing as it runs. Usually this output scrolls by very quickly, unless there is a problem. You can safely ignore the warnings that say offset NNN lines. If you don't want to see all this output, use the -s option to make patch silent.

When patch updates the source files, it creates a backup copy of the original file. For example, if you're applying a patch to *src/http.c*, patch names the backup file *src/http. c.orig*. Thus, if you want to undo the patch after applying it, you can simply rename all the *.orig* files back to their former names. To use this technique successfully, it's a good idea to remove all *.orig* files before applying a patch.

If patch encounters a problem, it stops and prompts you for advice. Common problems are as follows:

- Running `patch` from the wrong directory. To fix this problem, you may need to `cd` to a different directory or use `patch`'s `-p` option.

- Patch is already applied. `patch` can usually tell if the patch file has already been applied. In this case, it asks if you want to unpatch the file.

- The `patch` program doesn't understand the file you are giving it. Patch files come in three flavors: normal, context, and unified. Old versions of `patch` may not understand context or unified diff output. Getting the latest version from the GNU FTP site will solve this problem.

- Corrupted patch file. If you aren't careful when downloading and saving the patch file, it may become corrupted. Sometimes people send patch files in email messages, and it is tempting to simply cut-and-paste them into a new window. On some systems, cut-and-paste can change Tab characters into spaces, or incorrectly wrap long lines. Both changes confuse `patch`. The `-l` option may be helpful, but it's best to make sure you copy and save the patch file correctly.

Sometimes `patch` can't apply part or all of the diff. In these cases, you'll see such messages as `Hunk 3 of 4 failed`. The failed sections are saved to files named *.rej*. For example, if a failure occurs while processing *src/http.c*, `patch` saves that piece of the diff to *src/http.c.rej*. In some cases, you may be able to fix these by hand, but it's usually not worth the trouble. If you have a lot of "failed hunks" or *.rej* files, it's a good idea to download a whole new copy of the latest source code.

After you apply a patch, you need to recompile Squid. One of the great things about `make` is that it only recompiles the files that have changed. But sometimes `make` doesn't comprehend all the intricate dependencies, and it doesn't rebuild enough of the files. To be safe, it's usually a good idea to recompile everything. The best way to do this is to clean the source tree before recompiling:

```
% make clean
% make
```

Running configure Later

Sometimes you may find it necessary to rerun `./configure`. For example, if you tune your kernel parameters, you must run `./configure` again so it picks up the new settings. As you read this book, you may also find that you want to use features that must be enabled with `./configure` options.

To rerun `./configure` with the same options, use this command:

```
% ./config.status --recheck
```

Another technique is to "touch" the *config.status* file, which updates its timestamp. This causes `make` to re-run the `./configure` script before compiling the source code:

```
% touch config.status
% make
```

To add or remove ./configure options, you need to type in the whole command again. If you can't remember the previous options, just look at the top of the *config. status* file. For example:

```
% head config.status
#! /bin/sh
# Generated automatically by configure.
# Run this file to recreate the current configuration.
# This directory was configured as follows,
# on host foo.life-gone-hazy.com:
#
# ./configure  --enable-storeio=ufs,diskd --enable-carp \
#   --enable-auth-modules=NCSA
# Compiler output produced by configure, useful for debugging
# configure, is in ./config.log if it exists.
```

After rerunning ./configure, you must compile and install Squid again. To be safe, it's a good idea to run make clean first:

```
% make clean
% make
```

Recall that ./configure caches the things it discovers about your system. In some situations, you'll want to clear this cache and start the compilation process from the very beginning. You can simply remove the *config.cache* file if you like. Then, the next time ./configure runs, it won't use the previous values. You can also restore the Squid source tree to its preconfigure state with the following command:

```
% make distclean
```

This removes all object files and other files created by the ./configure and make commands.

Exercises

- After compiling Squid, remove one or more of the *.o* files and run make again.
- Use the ulimit or limits command to change the file descriptor limit to some small value before compiling Squid. Does ./configure obey or ignore your new limit?
- Compile Squid with a high file-descriptor limit, then try to run it on a system with a lower limit. Does Squid use the lower or higher limit?
- What happens if you mistype one of the --enable options? What if you specify an invalid storage scheme with the --enable-store-io option?
- After compiling Squid, remove *src/Makefile* and try to compile it again. What's the easiest way to restore the file?

## CHAPTER 4

Configuration Guide for the Eager

After compiling and installing Squid, your next task is to delve into the configuration file. If you're new to Squid, you're likely to find it a bit overwhelming. The most recent version has approximately 200 configuration file directives and 2700 lines of comments. I certainly don't expect you to read about, and configure, every directive before starting Squid. This chapter can help you get Squid running quickly.

All the *squid.conf* directives have default values. You might be able to get Squid going without even touching the configuration file. However, I don't recommend trying that. You'll be much happier if you read the following sections first.

If you are really turned off by Squid's configuration file syntax, you might want to try the Webmin graphical user interface. It allows you to configure Squid (and numerous other programs) from your web browser. See *http://www.webmin.com* and *The Book of Webmin* by Joe Cooper (No Starch Press) for more information.

The squid.conf Syntax

Squid's configuration file is relatively straightforward. It is similar in style to many other Unix programs. Each line begins with a configuration directive, followed by some number of values and/or keywords. Squid ignores empty lines and comment lines (beginning with #) when reading the configuration file. Here are some sample configuration lines:

```
cache_log /squid/var/cache.log

# define the localhost ACL
acl Localhost src 127.0.0.1/32

connect_timeout 2 minutes

log_fqdn on
```

Some directives take a single value. For these, repeating the directive with a different value overwrites the previous value. For example, there is only one *connect_timeout* value. The first line in the following example has no effect because the second line overwrites it:

```
connect_timeout 2 minutes
connect_timeout 1 hour
```

On the other hand, some directives are actually lists of values. For these, each occurrence of the directive adds a new value to the list. The *extension_methods* directive works this way:

```
extension_methods UNGET
extension_methods UNPUT
extension_methods UNPOST
```

For these list-based directives, you can also usually put multiple values on the same line:

```
extension_methods UNGET UNPUT UNPOST
```

Many of the directives have common types. For example, *connect_timeout* is a time specification that has a number followed by a unit of time. For example:

```
connect_timeout 3 hours
client_lifetime 4 days
negative_ttl 27 minutes
```

Similarly, a number of directives refer to the size of a file or chunk of memory. For these, you can write a size specification as a decimal number, followed by bytes, KB, MB, or GB. For example:

```
minimum_object_size 12 bytes
request_header_max_size 10 KB
maximum_object_size 187 MB
```

Another type worth mentioning is the toggle, which can be either on or off. Many directives use this type. For example:

```
server_persistent_connections on
strip_query_terms off
prefer_direct on
```

In general, the configuration file directives may appear in any order. However, the order is important when one directive makes reference to something defined by another. Access controls are a good example. An *acl* must be defined before it can be used in an *http_access* rule:

```
acl Foo src 1.2.3.4
http_access deny Foo
```

Many things in *squid.conf* are case-sensitive, such as directive names. You can't write *HTTP_port* instead of *http_port*.

The default *squid.conf* file contains comments describing each directive, as well as the default values. For example:

```
#  TAG: persistent_request_timeout
#        How long to wait for the next HTTP request on a persistent
#        connection after the previous request completes.
#
#Default:
# persistent_request_timeout 1 minute
```

Each time you install Squid, the current default configuration file is saved as *squid.conf.default* in the *$prefix/etc* directory. Since directives change from time to time, you can refer to this file for the most up-to-date documentation on *squid.conf*.

The rest of this chapter is about the handful of directives you need to know before running Squid for the very first time.

User IDs

As you probably know, Unix processes and files have *user* and *group* ownership attributes. You need to select a user and group for Squid. This user and group combination must have read and write access to most of the Squid-related files and directories.

I highly recommend creating a dedicated *squid* user and group. This minimizes the chance that someone can exploit Squid to read other files on the system. If more than one person has administrative authority over Squid, you can add them to the *squid* group.

Unix processes inherit their parent process' ownership attributes. That is, if you start Squid as user *joe*, Squid also runs as user *joe*. If you don't want Squid to run as *joe*, you need to change your user ID beforehand. This is typically accomplished with the su command. For example:

```
joe% su - squid
squid% /usr/local/squid/sbin/squid
```

Unfortunately, running Squid isn't always so simple. In some cases, you may need to start Squid as *root*, depending on your configuration. For example, only *root* can bind a TCP socket to privileged ports like port 80. If you need to start Squid as *root*, you must set the *cache_effective_user* directive. It tells Squid which user to become after performing the tasks that require special privileges. For example:

```
cache_effective_user squid
```

The name that you provide must be a valid user (i.e., in the */etc/passwd* file). Furthermore, note that this directive is used only when you start Squid as *root*. Only *root* has the ability to become another user. If you start Squid as *joe*, it can't switch to user *squid*.

You might be tempted to just run Squid as *root* without setting *cache_effective_user*. If you try, you'll find that Squid refuses to run. This, again, is due to security concerns. If an outsider were somehow able to compromise or exploit Squid, he could gain full access to your system. Although we strive to make Squid secure and bug-free, this requirement provides some extra insurance, just in case.

If you start Squid as *root* without setting *cache_effective_user*, Squid uses nobody as the default value. Whatever user ID you choose for Squid, make sure it has read access to the files installed in *$prefix/etc*, *$prefix/libexec*, and *$prefix/share*. The user ID must also have write access to the log files and cache directory.

Squid also has a *cache_effective_group* directive, but you probably don't need to set it. By default, Squid uses the *cache_effective_user*'s default group (from the password file).

Port Numbers

The *http_port* directive tells Squid which port number to listen on for HTTP requests. The default is port 3128:

```
http_port 3128
```

If you are running Squid as a surrogate (see Chapter 15), you should probably set this to 80.

You can instruct Squid to listen on multiple ports with additional *http_port* lines. This is often useful if you must support groups of clients that have been configured differently. For example, the browsers from one department may be sending requests to port 3128, while another department uses port 8080. Simply list both port numbers as follows:

```
http_port 3128
http_port 8080
```

You can also use the *http_port* directive to make Squid listen on specific interface addresses. When Squid is used on a firewall, it should have two network interfaces: one internal and one external. You probably don't want to accept HTTP requests coming from the external side. To make Squid listen on only the internal interface, simply put the IP address in front of the port number:

```
http_port 192.168.1.1:3128
```

Log File Pathnames

I'll discuss all the details of Squid's log files in Chapter 13. For now the only thing you may need to worry about is where you want Squid to put its log files. The default location is a directory named *logs* under the installation prefix. For example, if you don't use the --prefix= option with ./configure, the default log file directory is */usr/local/squid/var/logs*.

You need to make sure that log files are stored on a disk partition with enough space. When Squid receives a write error for a log file, it exits and restarts. The primary reason for this behavior is to grab your attention. Squid wants to make sure you don't miss any important logging information, especially if your system is being abused or attacked.

Squid has three main log files: *cache.log*, *access.log*, and *store.log*. The first of these, *cache.log*, contains informational and debugging messages. When you start Squid the first few times, you should closely watch this file. If Squid refuses to run, the reason is probably at the end of *cache.log*. Under normal conditions, this log file doesn't become large enough to warrant any special attention. Also note that if you start Squid with the -s option, the important *cache.log* messages are also sent to your syslog daemon. You can change the location for this log file with the *cache_log* directive:

```
cache_log /squid/logs/cache.log
```

The *access.log* file contains a single line for each client request made to Squid. On average, each line is about 150 bytes. In other words, it takes about 150 MB to log one million client requests. Use the *cache_access_log* directive to change the location of this log file:

```
cache_access_log /squid/logs/access.log
```

If, for some reason, you don't want Squid to log client requests, you can specify the log file pathname as */dev/null*.

The *store.log* file is probably not very useful to most cache administrators. It contains a record for each object that enters and leaves the cache. The average record size is typically 175–200 bytes. However, Squid doesn't create an entry in *store.log* for cache hits, so it contains fewer records than *access.log*. Use the *cache_store_log* directive to change the location:

```
cache_store_log /squid/logs/store.log
```

You can easily disable *store.log* altogether by specifying the location as none:

```
cache_store_log none
```

If you're not careful, Squid's log files increase in size without limit. Some operating systems enforce a 2-GB file size limit, even if you have plenty of free disk space. Exceeding this limit results in a write error, which then causes Squid to exit. To keep log file sizes reasonable, you should create a *cron* job that regularly renames and archives the log files. Squid has a built-in feature to make this easy. See Chapter 13 for an explanation of log file rotation.

Access Controls

I'll have a lot to say about access controls in Chapter 6. For now, I'll cover a few controls so that more enthusiastic readers can quickly start using Squid.

Squid's default configuration file denies every client request. You must place additional access control rules in *squid.conf* before anyone can use the proxy. The simplest approach is to define an ACL that corresponds to your user's IP addresses and an access rule that tells Squid to allow HTTP requests from those addresses. Squid has many different ACL types. The *src* type matches client IP addresses, and the *http_access* rules are checked for client HTTP requests. Thus, you need to add only two lines:

```
acl MyNetwork src 192.168.0.0/16
http_access allow MyNetwork
```

The tricky part is putting these lines in the right place. The order of *http_access* lines is very important, but the order of *acl* lines doesn't matter. You should also be aware that the default configuration file contains some important access controls. You shouldn't change or disrupt these until you fully comprehend their significance. When you edit *squid.conf* for the first time, look for this comment:

```
#
# INSERT YOUR OWN RULE(S) HERE TO ALLOW ACCESS FROM YOUR CLIENTS
#
```

Insert your new rules below this comment, and before the *http_access deny All* line.

For the sake of completeness, here is a suitable initial access control configuration, including the recommended default controls and the example earlier:

```
acl All src 0/0
acl Manager proto cache_object
acl Localhost src 127.0.0.1/32
acl Safe_ports port 80 21 443 563 70 210 280 488 591 777 1025-65535
acl SSL_ports 443 563
acl CONNECT method CONNECT
acl MyNetwork src 192.168.0.0/16

http_access allow Manager Localhost
http_access deny Manager
http_access deny !Safe_ports
http_access deny CONNECT !SSL_ports
http_access allow MyNetwork
http_access deny All
```

Visible Hostname

Hopefully, you won't need to worry about the *visible_hostname* directive. However, you'll need to set it if Squid can't figure out the hostname of the machine on which it is running. When this happens, Squid complains and refuses to run:

```
% squid -Nd1
FATAL: Could not determine fully qualified hostname.  Please set 'visible_hostname'
```

Squid wants to be sure about its hostname for a number of reasons:

- The hostname appears in Squid's error messages. This helps users identify the source of potential problems.

- The hostname appears in the HTTP Via header of cache misses that Squid forwards. When the request arrives at the origin server, the Via header contains a list of all proxies involved in the transaction. Squid also uses the Via header to detect forwarding loops. I'll talk about forwarding loops in Chapter 10.

- Squid uses internal URLs for certain things, such as the icons for FTP directory listings. When Squid generates an HTML page for an FTP directory, it inserts embedded images for little icons that indicate the type of each file in the directory. The icon URLs contain the cache's hostname so that web browsers request them directly from Squid.

- Each HTTP reply from Squid includes an X-Cache header. This isn't an official HTTP header. Rather, it is an extension header that indicates if the response was a cache hit or a cache miss. Since requests and responses may flow through more than one cache, each X-Cache header includes the name of the cache reporting hit or miss. Here's a sample response that passed through two caches:

```
HTTP/1.0 200 OK
Date: Mon, 29 Sep 2003 22:57:23 GMT
Content-type: text/html
Content-length: 733
X-Cache: HIT from bo2.us.ircache.net
X-Cache: MISS from bo1.us.ircache.net
```

Squid tries to figure out the hostname automatically at startup. First it calls the gethostname( ) function, which usually returns the correct hostname. Next, Squid attempts a DNS lookup on the hostname with gethostbyname( ). This function typically returns both IP addresses and the *canonical* name for the system. If gethostbyname( ) succeeds, Squid uses the canonical name in error messages, Via headers, etc.

Squid may be unable to determine its fully qualified hostname for a number of reasons, including:

- The hostname may not be set.
- The hostname may be missing from the DNS zone or */etc/hosts* files.
- The Squid system's DNS client configuration may be incorrect or missing. On Unix, you should check the */etc/resolv.conf* and */etc/host.conf* files.

If you see the fatal message mentioned previously, you need either to fix the hostname and DNS information or explicitly configure the hostname for Squid. In most cases, it is sufficient to ensure the hostname command returns a fully qualified hostname and add an entry to */etc/hosts*. If that doesn't work, just set the visible hostname in *squid.conf*:

```
visible_hostname squid.packet-pushers.net
```

Administrative Contact Information

You should set the *cache_mgr* directive as a favor to your users. The value is an email address users can write to in case a problem surfaces. The *cache_mgr* address appears in Squid's error messages by default. For example:

```
cache_mgr squid@web-cache.net
```

Next Steps

After creating the minimal configuration file, you're more or less ready to run Squid for the first time. To do that, just follow the instructions in the next chapter.

When you've mastered starting and stopping Squid, you can spend some time beefing up the configuration file. You may want to add more sophisticated access controls, which you'll find documented in Chapter 6. Since I didn't say anything about the disk cache yet, you should also spend a fair amount of time in Chapters 7 and 8.

Exercises

- Parse Squid's configuration file with **squid -k parse** and check the process exit status.
- Intentionally introduce a some errors into the configuration file and run **squid -k parse** again. Notice how Squid reports different errors.
- Insert comments into the configuration file. Can you start a comment anywhere, even after a valid directive?
- Why do you think some configuration file errors are fatal, but others are not?

## CHAPTER 5

Running Squid

Now that you have Squid installed, and maybe even configured, you need to learn the ins and outs of running Squid. Although most of the configuration occurs in *squid.conf*, you may find some of Squid's command-line options useful. For example, one of the first things you must do is use the -z option to initialize the cache directories. You may also find the -d option useful for debugging.

Squid normally runs as a daemon process. If you are new to Squid, however, I recommend running Squid in the foreground from a terminal window until you are confident that it is working properly. Following that, you can run Squid as a daemon, in the background. Most likely, you'll want to start Squid each time your system boots. Different operating systems have different approaches to startup scripts. I'll show you how to make it happen in three different ways.

You can send signals to the running Squid process to execute various tasks, such as halting and reconfiguring Squid, and rotating the log files. Although you can use the kill command to send signals, it is easier to use the squid -k commands.

Squid Command-Line Options

Before getting too far into other things, let's look at Squid's command-line options. Many of these you will never use and some are useful only when debugging problems:

-a *port*
> Specifies a new *http_port* value. This option always overrides the value from *squid.conf*. Note, however, that you can specify multiple values in *squid.conf*. The -a option overrides only the first value from the config file. (This option uses the letter "a" because in the Harvest cache, the HTTP port was called the ASCII port.)

-d *level*

    Makes Squid write its debugging messages to *stderr* (as well as *cache.log* and syslog, if configured). The *level* argument specifies the maximum level for messages that should be shown on *stderr*. In most cases -d1 works well. See Chapter 16 for a description of debugging levels.

-f *file*

    Specifies an alternate configuration file.

-h   Displays the usage information.

-k *function*

    Signals Squid to perform various administrative functions. The *function* argument may be one of the following: reconfigure, rotate, shutdown, interrupt, kill, debug, check, or parse. reconfigure causes the running Squid process to reread its configuration file. rotate causes Squid to rotate its log files, which involves closing them, possibly renaming them, and opening them again. shutdown sends the signal to shut down the Squid process. interrupt also shuts down Squid but does so immediately, without waiting for active transactions to finish. kill sends the unstoppable KILL signal to Squid, which should only be used as a last resort. debug puts Squid into full debugging mode. It can quickly fill up your disk space if your cache is busy. check simply checks for a running Squid process. The process return value indicates whether Squid is running or not. Finally, parse simply parses the *squid.conf* file. The process return value is non-zero if the configuration file contains errors.

-s   Enables logging to the syslog daemon. Squid uses the LOCAL4 syslog facility. Level 0 debug messages are logged with priority LOG_WARNING, and level 1 messages are logged with LOG_NOTICE. Higher level debugging messages aren't sent to syslogd. You might use an entry like this in */etc/syslogd.conf*:

```
local4.warning                 /var/log/squid.log
```

-u *port*

    Specifies an alternate ICP port number, overriding *icp_port* in *squid.conf*.

-v   Prints the version string.

-z   Initializes cache, or swap, directories. You must use this option when running Squid for the first time or whenever you add a new cache directory.

-C   Prevents the installation of signal handlers that trap certain fatal signals such as SIGBUS and SIGSEGV. Normally, the signals are trapped by Squid so that it can attempt a clean shutdown. However, trapping the signal may make it harder to debug the problem afterwards. With this option, the fatal signals cause their default actions, which is usually to dump core.

-D   Disables initial DNS tests. Normally, Squid won't start until it verifies that its DNS server is working. This option prevents that check. You can also alter or remove the *dns_testnames* option in *squid.conf*.

-F Makes Squid refuse all requests until it rebuilds the storage metadata. If your cache is busy, this option may shorten the time required to rebuild the metadata. If your cache is large, however, the rebuild procedure may take a long time anyway.

-N Prevents Squid from becoming a background daemon process.

-R Prevents Squid from using the SO_REUSEADDR option before binding to the HTTP port.

-V Enables virtual host surrogate mode. Similar to entering *httpd_accel_host virtual* in *squid.conf*.

-X Forces full debugging, as though you had specified *debug_options ALL,9* in *squid.conf*.

-Y Returns ICP_MISS_NOFETCH instead of ICP_MISS when rebuilding store metadata. For busy parent caches, this option may result in less load while the cache is rebuilding. See Chapter 10.

Check Your Configuration File for Errors

Before trying to start Squid, you should verify that your *squid.conf* file makes sense. This is easy to do. Just run the following command:

```
% squid -k parse
```

If you see no output, the configuration file is valid, and you can proceed to the next step.

However, if your configuration file contains an error, Squid tells you about it:

```
squid.conf line 62: http_access allow okay2
aclParseAccessLine: ACL name 'okay2' not found.
```

Here you can see that the *http_access* directive on line 62 references an ACL that doesn't exist. Sometimes the error messages are less informative:

```
FATAL: Bungled squid.conf line 76: memory_pools
```

In this case, we forgot to put either on or off after the *memory_pools* directive on line 76.

It's a good idea to develop the habit of using squid -k parse every time you modify your configuration file. If you don't bother, and your file has some errors, Squid tells you about them and refuses to start anyway. If you end up managing a number of caches, it is likely that you'll develop some scripts to automate starting, stopping, and reconfiguring Squid. You can use this feature in your scripts to ensure that the configuration files are always valid.

Initializing Cache Directories

Before running Squid for the first time, and whenever you add a new *cache_dir*, you must initialize the cache directories. The command is simply:

```
% squid -z
```

For the UFS-related storage schemes (*ufs*, *aufs*, and *diskd*; see Chapter 8), this command creates the subdirectories needed under each *cache_dir*. You don't need to worry that Squid will wipe out your current cache directories (if any).

Ownership and permissions are a common problem at this stage. Squid runs under a certain user ID, specified with *cache_effective_user* in *squid.conf*. This user ID must have read and write permission under each *cache_dir* directory. If not, you'll see a message like this:

```
Creating Swap Directories
FATAL: Failed to make swap directory /usr/local/squid/var/cache/00:
    (13) Permission denied
```

In this case, you should make sure that all components of */usr/local/squid/var/cache* are accessible to the user ID given in *squid.conf*. The final component—the *cache* directory—must be writable by this user ID as well.

Cache directory initialization may take a couple of minutes, depending on the size and number of cache directories, and the speed of your disk drives. If you want to watch the progress, use the -X option:

```
% squid -zX
```

Testing Squid in a Terminal Window

Once you've initialized the cache directories, you should run Squid in a terminal window with logging to *stderr*. This way, you can easily spot any errors or problems and make sure that Squid successfully starts. Use the -N option to keep Squid in the foreground and the -d1 option to display level 1 debugging on *stderr*:

```
% squid -N -d1
```

You should see output like this:

```
2003/09/29 12:57:52| Starting Squid Cache version 2.5.STABLE4 for i386-unknown-
freebsd4.8...
2003/09/29 12:57:52| Process ID 294
2003/09/29 12:57:52| With 1064 file descriptors available
2003/09/29 12:57:52| DNS Socket created on FD 4
2003/09/29 12:57:52| Adding nameserver 206.107.176.2 from /etc/resolv.conf
2003/09/29 12:57:52| Adding nameserver 205.162.184.2 from /etc/resolv.conf
2003/09/29 12:57:52| Unlinkd pipe opened on FD 9
2003/09/29 12:57:52| Swap maxSize 102400 KB, estimated 7876 objects
2003/09/29 12:57:52| Target number of buckets: 393
2003/09/29 12:57:52| Using 8192 Store buckets
```

```
2003/09/29 12:57:52| Max Mem  size: 8192 KB
2003/09/29 12:57:52| Max Swap size: 102400 KB
2003/09/29 12:57:52| Rebuilding storage in /usr/local/squid/var/cache (DIRTY)
2003/09/29 12:57:52| Using Least Load store dir selection
2003/09/29 12:57:52| Set Current Directory to /usr/local/squid/var/cache
2003/09/29 12:57:52| Loaded Icons.
2003/09/29 12:57:52| Accepting HTTP connections at 0.0.0.0, port 3128, FD 11.
2003/09/29 12:57:52| Accepting ICP messages at 0.0.0.0, port 3130, FD 12.
2003/09/29 12:57:52| WCCP Disabled.
2003/09/29 12:57:52| Ready to serve requests.
```

If you see an error message, you need to fix it before proceeding. Be sure to check the first few lines of output for warning messages. The most common errors are file/directory permissions and configuration file syntax errors. If you see an error message that doesn't make sense, have a look at Chapter 16 for advice and information on troubleshooting Squid. If that doesn't help, check the Squid FAQ, or search the mailing list archives for an explanation.

Once you see the Ready to serve requests message, test Squid with a few HTTP requests. You can do this by configuring your browser to use Squid as a proxy and then open a web page. If Squid is working correctly, the page should load as quickly as it would without using Squid. Alternatively, you can use the *squidclient* program that comes with Squid:

```
% squidclient http://www.squid-cache.org/
```

If this works, Squid's home page HTML file will scroll across your terminal window. Once you're confident that Squid works okay, you can interrupt the Squid process (i.e., with Ctrl-C) and run Squid as a daemon.

Running Squid as a Daemon Process

Normally you'll want to run Squid as a daemon process (i.e., not attached to your terminal window). The easiest way to do this is simply execute Squid as follows:

```
% squid -s
```

The -s option causes Squid to write important status and warning messages to syslogd. Squid uses the LOCAL4 facility and the LOG_WARNING and LOG_NOTICE priorities. Your syslog daemon may or may not actually log Squid's messages, depending on how it is configured. These same messages are written to the *cache.log* file, so it is safe to omit the -s option if you prefer.

When you start Squid without the -N option (as shown earlier), Squid automatically backgrounds itself and creates a parent/child process pair. The child process is the one that does all the real work. The parent process makes sure that a child process is always running. Thus, if the child process dies unexpectedly, the parent starts another so that Squid remains in operation. You can see this parent/child process interaction by looking at your syslog messages:

```
Jul 31 14:58:35 zapp squid[294]: Squid Parent: child process 296 started
```

Here you can see that the parent is process ID 294, and the child is 296. When you look at ps output, you'll see that the child process is listed as (squid):

```
% ps ax | grep squid
  294 ??  Is     0:00.01 squid -sD
  296 ??  S      0:00.27 (squid) -sD (squid)
```

If the child Squid process dies unexpectedly, the parent starts another. For example:

```
Jul 31 15:02:53 zapp squid[294]:SquidParent:child process 296 exited due to signal 6
Jul 31 15:02:56 zapp squid[294]: Squid Parent: child process 359 started
```

In some situations, the child Squid process may die immediately. Rather than constantly spawning new Squid processes, the parent process gives up if the child processes won't stay running for at least 10 seconds five times in a row:

```
Jul 31 15:13:48 zapp squid[455]: Squid Parent: child process 474 exited with status 1
Jul 31 15:13:48 zapp squid[455]: Exiting due to repeated, frequent failures
```

If this happens to you, check syslog and Squid's *cache.log* for error messages.

The squid_start Script

When Squid runs as a daemon process, it looks for a file named *squid_start* in the same directory as the *squid* binary. If found, this program is executed before the parent process forks to run the child process. You can use this script for certain administrative tasks, such as notifying someone that Squid is starting, managing log files, etc. Squid doesn't start the child process until the *squid_start* program exits.

> The *squid_start* script only works when you start Squid by its absolute or relative pathname. In other words, Squid doesn't use the PATH environment variable to locate *squid_start*. Thus, you may want to develop the habit of starting Squid like this:
>
> ```
> % /usr/local/squid/sbin/squid -sD
> ```
>
> rather than starting Squid like this:
>
> ```
> % squid -sD
> ```

Boot Scripts

Most likely, you'll want Squid to start automatically every time your computer boots. Different operating systems vary widely in how their boot-up scripts work. I'll describe some common environments here, but you may need to refer to your particular operating system for specific information.

/etc/rc.local

One of the easiest schemes is the */etc/rc.local* script. This is simply a shell script that runs as *root* each time the system boots. Using this script to start Squid is as easy as adding the following line:

```
/usr/local/squid/sbin/squid -s
```

Of course your installation prefix may be different, and you may like to use some other command-line options. Don't use the -N option here.

If, for some reason, you're not using the *cache_effective_user* directive, you can try using su to start Squid as a non-*root* user:

```
/usr/bin/su nobody -c '/usr/local/squid/sbin/squid -s'
```

init.d and rc.d

The *init.d* and *rc.d* schemes use a separate shell script to start different services. These scripts are often located in one of the following directories: */sbin/init.d*, */etc/init.d*, and */usr/local/etc/rc.d*. The scripts usually take a single command-line argument, which is either *start* or *stop*. Some systems only use the start argument. Here's a basic script for starting Squid:

```
#!/bin/sh
#
# this script starts and stops Squid

case "$1" in
start)
        /usr/local/squid/sbin/squid -s
        echo -n ' Squid'
        ;;
stop)
        /usr/local/squid/sbin/squid -k shutdown
        ;;
esac
```

 Linux users may want to add commands that set the file-descriptor limits before running Squid. For example:

```
echo 8192 > /proc/sys/fs/file-max
limit -HSn 8192
```

To use this script, find the appropriate directory in which such scripts are stored. Give it a meaningful name, similar to the others. Perhaps *S98squid* or simply *squid. sh*. Be sure to test the script by rebooting your computer rather than assuming it will work.

/etc/inittab

Another scheme supported on some operating systems is the *letc/inittab* file. On these systems, the init process starts and stops services based on the *run level*. A typical *inittab* entry looks like this:

```
sq:2345:once:/usr/local/squid/sbin/squid -s
```

With this entry, the init process starts Squid just once and then forgets about it. Squid makes sure it stays running as described previously. Alternatively, you can do it like this:

```
sq:2345:respawn:/usr/local/squid/sbin/squid -Ns
```

Here, since we use the respawn option, init restarts Squid if the process exits. If you use respawn, be sure to use the -N option.

After editing the *inittab* file, use this command to make init reread its configuration file and start Squid:

```
# init q
```

A chroot Environment

Some people like to run Squid in a *chroot* environment. This is a Unix feature that gives a process a new root filesystem directory. It provides an extra level of security in the event that Squid is compromised. If an attacker somehow gains access to the operating system through Squid, she can only access files under the *chroot* filesystem. The other system files, outside of the *chroot* tree, remain inaccessible.

The easiest way to run Squid in a *chroot* environment is by specifying the new root directory in the *squid.conf* file with this directive:

```
chroot /new/root/directory
```

 The chroot( ) system call requires superuser privileges, so you must start Squid as *root* to use this feature.

The *chroot* environment isn't for first-time Unix users. It is a little tricky because you must replicate a number of files underneath the new root directory. For example, if the default configuration file is normally *lusr/local/squid/etc/squid.conf*, and you use the *chroot* directive, the file must be located at *lnew/root/directory/usr/local/squid/etc/squid.conf*. You must copy all of the files under *$prefix/etc*, *$prefix/share*, and *$prefix/libexec* to the *chroot* directory. Make sure that *$prefix/var* and the cache directories exist and are writable under the *chroot* directory as well.

Chances are that your operating system requires a number of files in the *chroot* directory, such as *letc/resolv.conf* and *ldev/null*. If you use an external helper program, such as a redirector (see Chapter 11) or an authenticator (see Chapter 12), you'll also need some shared libraries from */usr/lib*. You can use the ldd utility to find out which shared libraries are required for a given program:

```
% ldd /usr/local/squid/libexec/ncsa_auth
/usr/local/squid/libexec/ncsa_auth:
        libcrypt.so.2 => /usr/lib/libcrypt.so.2 (0x28067000)
        libm.so.2 => /usr/lib/libm.so.2 (0x28080000)
        libc.so.4 => /usr/lib/libc.so.4 (0x28098000)
```

You can also use the chroot command to test helpers:

```
# chroot /new/root/directory /usr/local/squid/libexec/ncsa_auth
/usr/libexec/ld-elf.so.1: Shared object "libcrypt.so.2" not found
```

For more information on *chroot*, see the chroot( ) manpage on your system.

Stopping Squid

The safest way to shut down Squid is with the squid -k shutdown command:

```
% squid -k shutdown
```

This command sends the TERM signal to the running Squid process. Upon receipt of the TERM signal, Squid closes its incoming sockets so that new requests aren't accepted. It then waits some amount of time for outstanding requests to complete. The default is 30 seconds, which you can change with the *shutdown_lifetime* directive.

If, for some reason, the *squid.pid* file is missing or unreadable, the squid -k commands don't work. In this case, you can manually kill Squid by finding the process ID with ps. For example:

```
% ps ax | grep squid
```

If you see more than one Squid process, be sure to kill the one that shows up as (squid). For example:

```
% ps ax | grep squid
  294 ??  Is      0:00.01 squid -sD
  296 ??  S       0:00.27 (squid) -sD (squid)
% kill -TERM 296
```

After sending the TERM signal, you may want to watch the log file to double-check that Squid is shutting down:

```
% tail -f logs/cache.log
2003/09/29 21:49:30| Preparing for shutdown after 9316 requests
2003/09/29 21:49:30| Waiting 10 seconds for active connections to finish
2003/09/29 21:49:30| FD 11 Closing HTTP connection
2003/09/29 21:49:31| Shutting down...
2003/09/29 21:49:31| FD 12 Closing ICP connection
2003/09/29 21:49:31| Closing unlinkd pipe on FD 9
2003/09/29 21:49:31| storeDirWriteCleanLogs: Starting...
2003/09/29 21:49:32| Finished.  Wrote 253 entries.
```

```
2003/09/29 21:49:32| Took 0.1 seconds (1957.6 entries/sec).
2003/09/29 21:49:32| Squid Cache (Version 2.5.STABLE4): Exiting normally.
```

If you use squid -k interrupt, Squid shuts down immediately, without waiting for active requests to complete. This is equivalent to sending the INT signal with kill.

Reconfiguring a Running Squid Process

As you learn more about Squid, you'll probably find yourself making many changes to the *squid.conf* file. To have the new settings take effect, you can either shut down and restart Squid, or you can reconfigure Squid while it is running.

The best way to reconfigure a running Squid process is with the squid -k reconfigure command:

```
% squid -k reconfigure
```

When you run this command, a HUP signal is sent to the running Squid process. Squid then reads and parses the *squid.conf* file. If the operation is successful, you'll see this in *cache.log*:

```
2003/09/29 22:02:25| Restarting Squid Cache (version 2.5.STABLE4)...
2003/09/29 22:02:25| FD 12 Closing HTTP connection
2003/09/29 22:02:25| FD 13 Closing ICP connection
2003/09/29 22:02:25| Cache dir '/usr/local/squid/var/cache' size remains unchanged
                     at 102400 KB
2003/09/29 22:02:25| DNS Socket created on FD 5
2003/09/29 22:02:25| Adding nameserver 10.0.0.1 from /etc/resolv.conf
2003/09/29 22:02:25| Accepting HTTP connections at 0.0.0.0, port 3128, FD 9.
2003/09/29 22:02:25| Accepting ICP messages at 0.0.0.0, port 3130, FD 11.
2003/09/29 22:02:25| WCCP Disabled.
2003/09/29 22:02:25| Loaded Icons.
2003/09/29 22:02:25| Ready to serve requests.
```

You need to be a little careful with the reconfigure option because it's possible to make changes that cause a fatal error. For example, note that Squid closes and reopens the incoming HTTP and ICP sockets. If you change the *http_port* to a port number that Squid can't open, it exits with a fatal error message.

Certain options and directives can't be changed while Squid is running. This includes:

* Removal of cache directories (*cache_dir* directive).
* Changes to the *store_log* directive.
* Changing the block-size value for *coss cache_dir*s. In fact, whenever you change this value, you must reinitialize the *coss cache_dir*.
* The *coredump_dir* directive isn't examined during the reconfigure procedure. Thus, you can't make Squid change its current directory after it has started.

Solaris users may experience a subtle problem when reconfiguring Squid. The fopen() call in the Solaris *stdio* implementation requires an unused file descriptor less than 256. The *FILE* structure stores the file descriptor as an 8-bit value. Normally this isn't a problem because Squid uses raw I/O (e.g., open()) to open cache files. However, certain tasks that occur during the reconfigure procedure use fopen(). These may fail if the first 256 file descriptors are already allocated.

Rotating the Log Files

Squid writes to a number of log files unless you disable them in *squid.conf*. You must periodically *rotate* the log files to prevent them from consuming too much disk space. Squid places a lot of importance on log files and exits with an error message when it can't write to them. To keep disk space consumption under control, use the following command in a *cron* job:

```
% squid -k rotate
```

For example, this *crontab* entry rotates the logs every 24 hours, at 4 A.M.:

```
0 4 * * * /usr/local/squid/sbin/squid -k rotate
```

This command does two things. First, it closes the currently open log files. Then, it renames the *cache.log*, *store.log*, and *access.log* files by appending a numeric extension. For example, *cache.log* becomes *cache.log.0*, *cache.log.0* becomes *cache.log.1*, and so on, up to the value of the *logfile_rotate* option.

Squid keeps only the last *logfile_rotate* versions of each log file. The older versions are simply removed during the renaming process. If you want to keep more copies, you need to increase the *logfile_rotate* limit or write some custom scripts that move the log files to a different location.

See Chapter 13 for additional information about rotating log files.

Exercises

- Use Squid's -s option and verify that its messages are saved by your syslog daemon.
- Run **squid -X -d9**, and examine some of the debugging messages.
- Write a shell script that stops Squid but doesn't exit until all Squid processes exit.
- Play with **squid -k rotate**. What happens if you have **tail -f cache.log** running when you rotate the log files?

## CHAPTER 6

All About Access Controls

Access controls are the most important part of your Squid configuration file. You'll use them to grant access to your authorized users and to keep out the bad guys. You can use them to restrict, or prevent access to, certain material; to control request rewriting; to route requests through a hierarchy; and to support different qualities of service.

Access controls are built from two different components. First, you define a number of access control list (ACL) elements. These elements refer to specific aspects of client requests, such as IP addresses, URL hostnames, request methods, and origin server port numbers. After defining the necessary elements, you combine them into a number of access list rules. The rules apply to particular services or operations within Squid. For example, the *http_access* rules are applied to incoming HTTP requests. I cover the access control elements first, and then the rules later in this chapter.

Access Control Elements

ACL elements are the building blocks of Squid's access control implementation. These are how you specify things such as IP addresses, port numbers, hostnames, and URL patterns. Each ACL element has a name, which you refer to when writing the access list rules. The basic syntax of an ACL element is as follows:

```
acl name type value1 value2 ...
```

For example:

```
acl Workstations src 10.0.0.0/16
```

In most cases, you can list multiple values for one ACL element. You can also have multiple acl lines with the same name. For example, the following two configurations are equivalent:

```
acl Http_ports port 80 8000 8080

acl Http_ports port 80
acl Http_ports port 8000
acl Http_ports port 8080
```

A Few Base ACL Types

Squid has approximately 25 different ACL types, some of which have a common base type. For example, both *src* and *dst* ACLs use IP addresses as their base type. To avoid being redundant, I'll cover the base types first and then describe each type of ACL in the following sections.

IP addresses

Used by: *src, dst, myip*

Squid has a powerful syntax for specifying IP addresses in ACLs. You can write addresses as subnets, address ranges, and domain names. Squid supports both "dotted quad" and CIDR prefix* subnet specifications. In addition, if you omit a netmask, Squid calculates the appropriate netmask for you. For example, each group in the next example are equivalent:

```
acl Foo src 172.16.44.21/255.255.255.255
acl Foo src 172.16.44.21/32
acl Foo src 172.16.44.21

acl Xyz src 172.16.55.32/255.255.255.248
acl Xyz src 172.16.55.32/28

acl Bar src 172.16.66.0/255.255.255.0
acl Bar src 172.16.66.0/24
acl Bar src 172.16.66.0
```

When you specify a netmask, Squid checks your work. If your netmask masks out non-zero bits of the IP address, Squid issues a warning. For example, the following lines results in the subsequent warning:

```
acl Foo src 127.0.0.1/8
```

```
aclParseIpData: WARNING: Netmask masks away part of the specified IP in 'Foo'
```

The problem here is that the /8 netmask (255.0.0.0) has all zeros in the last three octets, but the IP address 127.0.0.1 doesn't. Squid warns you about the problem so you can eliminate the ambiguity. To be correct, you should write:

```
acl Foo src 127.0.0.1/32
```

---

* CIDR stands for Classless Inter-Domain Routing. It is from an Internet-wide effort to support routing by any prefix length, instead of the old class A, B, and C subnet lengths.

or:

```
acl Foo src 127.0.0.0/8
```

Sometimes you may need to list multiple, contiguous subnets. In these cases, it may be easier to specify an address range. For example:

```
acl Bar src 172.16.10.0-172.16.19.0/24
```

This is equivalent to, and more efficient than, this approach:

```
acl Foo src 172.16.10.0/24
acl Foo src 172.16.11.0/24
acl Foo src 172.16.12.0/24
acl Foo src 172.16.13.0/24
acl Foo src 172.16.14.0/24
acl Foo src 172.16.15.0/24
acl Foo src 172.16.16.0/24
acl Foo src 172.16.18.0/24
acl Foo src 172.16.19.0/24
```

Note that with IP address ranges, the netmask goes only at the very end. You can't specify different netmasks for the beginning and ending range values.

You can also specify hostnames in IP ACLs. For example:

```
acl Squid dst www.squid-cache.org
```

 Squid converts hostnames to IP addresses at startup. Once started, Squid never makes another DNS lookup for the hostname's address. Thus, Squid never notices if the address changes while it's running.

If the hostname resolves to multiple addresses, Squid adds each to the ACL. Also note that you can't use netmasks with hostnames.

Using hostnames in address-based ACLs is usually a bad idea. Squid parses the configuration file before initializing other components, so these DNS lookups don't use Squid's nonblocking IP cache interface. Instead, they use the blocking gethostbyname( ) function. Thus, the need to convert ACL hostnames to addresses can delay Squid's startup procedure. Avoid using hostnames in *src*, *dst*, and *myip* ACLs unless absolutely necessary.

Squid stores IP address ACLs in memory with a data structure known as an *splay tree* (see *http://www.link.cs.cmu.edu/splay/*). The splay tree has some interesting self-organizing properties, one of which being that the list automatically adjusts itself as lookups occur. When a matching element is found in the list, that element becomes the new root of the tree. In this way frequently referenced items migrate to the top of the tree, which reduces the time for future lookups.

All subnets and ranges belonging to a single ACL element must not overlap. Squid warns you if you make a mistake. For example, this isn't allowed:

```
acl Foo src 1.2.3.0/24
acl Foo src 1.2.3.4/32
```

It causes Squid to print a warning in *cache.log*:

```
WARNING: '1.2.3.4' is a subnetwork of '1.2.3.0/255.255.255.0'
WARNING: because of this '1.2.3.4' is ignored to keep splay tree searching
         predictable
WARNING: You should probably remove '1.2.3.4' from the ACL named 'Foo'
```

In this case, you need to fix the problem, either by removing one of the ACL values or by placing them into different ACL lists.

Domain names

Used by: *srcdomain*, *dstdomain*, and the *cache_host_domain* directive

A domain name is simply a DNS name or zone. For example, the following are all valid domain names:

```
www.squid-cache.org
squid-cache.org
org
```

Domain name ACLs are tricky because of a subtle difference relating to matching domain names and subdomains. When the ACL domain name begins with a period, Squid treats it as a wildcard, and it matches any hostname in that domain, even the domain name itself. If, on the other hand, the ACL domain name doesn't begin with a period, Squid uses exact string comparison, and the hostname must be exactly the same for a match.

Table 6-1 shows Squid's rules for matching domain and hostnames. The first column shows hostnames taken from requested URLs (or client hostnames for *srcdomain* ACLs). The second column indicates whether or not the hostname matches *lrrr.org*. The third column shows whether the hostname matches an *.lrrr.org* ACL. As you can see, the only difference is in the second case.

Table 6-1. Domain name matching

URL hostname	Matches ACL lrrr.org?	Matches ACL .lrrr.org?
lrrr.org	Yes	Yes
i.am.lrrr.org	No	Yes
iamlrrr.org	No	No

Domain name matching can be confusing, so let's look at another example so that you really understand it. Here are two slightly different ACLs:

```
acl A dstdomain foo.com
acl B dstdomain .foo.com
```

A user's request to get *http://www.foo.com/* matches ACL B, but not A. ACL A requires an exact string match, but the leading dot in ACL B is like a wildcard.

On the other hand, a user's request to get *http://foo.com/* matches both ACLs A and B. Even though there is no word before *foo.com* in the URL hostname, the leading dot in ACL B still causes a match.

Squid uses splay trees to store domain name ACLs, just as it does for IP addresses. However, Squid's domain name matching algorithm presents an interesting problem for splay trees. The splay tree technique requires that only one key can match any particular search term. For example, let's say the search term (from a URL) is *i.am.lrrr.org*. This hostname would be a match for both *.lrrr.org* and *.am.lrrr.org*. The fact that two ACL values match one hostname confuses the splay algorithm. In other words, it is a mistake to put something like this in your configuration file:

```
acl Foo dstdomain .lrrr.org .am.lrrr.org
```

If you do, Squid generates the following warning message:

```
WARNING: '.am.lrrr.org' is a subdomain of '.lrrr.org'
WARNING: because of this '.am.lrrr.org' is ignored to keep splay tree searching
predictable
WARNING: You should probably remove '.am.lrrr.org' from the ACL named 'Foo'
```

You should follow Squid's advice in this case. Remove one of the related domains so that Squid does exactly what you intend. Note that you can use both domain names as long as you put them in different ACLs:

```
acl Foo dstdomain .lrrr.org
acl Bar dstdomain .am.lrrr.org
```

This is allowed because each named ACL uses its own splay tree.

Usernames

Used by: *ident, proxy_auth*

ACLs of this type are designed to match usernames. Squid may learn a username through the RFC 1413 ident protocol or via HTTP authentication headers. Usernames must be matched exactly. For example, bob doesn't match bobby. Squid also has related ACLs (*ident_regex* and *proxy_auth_regex*) that use regular-expression pattern matching on usernames.

You can use the word REQUIRED as a special value to match any username. If Squid can't determine the username, the ACL isn't matched. This is how Squid is usually configured when using username-based access controls.

Regular expressions

Used by: *srcdom_regex, dstdom_regex, url_regex, urlpath_regex, browser, referer_regex, ident_regex, proxy_auth_regex, req_mime_type, rep_mime_type*

A number of ACLs use *regular expressions* (regex) to match character strings. (For a complete regular-expression reference, see O'Reilly's *Mastering Regular Expressions*.) For Squid, the most commonly used regex features match the beginning and/or end of a string. For example, the ^ character is special because it matches the beginning of a line or string:

```
^http://
```

This regex matches any URL that begins with http://. The $ character is also special because it matches the end of a line or string:

```
.jpg$
```

Actually, the previous example is slightly wrong because the . character is special too. It is a wildcard that matches any character. What we really want is this:

```
\.jpg$
```

The backslash escapes the . so that its specialness is taken away. This regex matches any string that ends with .jpg. If you don't use the ^ or $ characters, regular expressions behave like standard substring searches. They match an occurrence of the word (or words) anywhere in the string.

With all of Squid's regex types, you have the option to use case-insensitive comparison. Matching is case-sensitive by default. To make it case-insensitive, use the -i option after the ACL type. For example:

```
acl Foo url_regex -i ^http://www
```

TCP port numbers

Used by: *port, myport*

This type is relatively straightforward. The values are individual port numbers or port number ranges. Recall that TCP port numbers are 16-bit values and, therefore, must be greater than 0 and less than 65,536. Here are some examples:

```
acl Foo port 123
acl Bar port 1-1024
```

Autonomous system numbers

Used by: *src_as, dst_as*

Internet routers use Autonomous System (AS) numbers to construct routing tables. Essentially, an AS number refers to a collection of IP networks managed by a single organization. For example, my ISP has been assigned the following network blocks: 134.116.0.0/16, 137.41.0.0/16, 206.168.0.0/16, and many more. In the Internet routing tables, these networks are advertised as belonging to AS 3404. When routers forward packets, they typically select the path that traverses the fewest autonomous systems. If none of this makes sense to you, don't worry. AS-based ACLs should only be used by networking gurus.

Here's how the AS-based types work: when Squid first starts up, it sends a special query to a *whois* server. The query essentially says, "Tell me which IP networks belong to this AS number." This information is collected and managed by the Routing Arbiter Database (RADB). Once Squid receives the list of IP networks, it treats them similarly to the IP address-based ACLs.

AS-based types only work well when ISPs keep their RADB information up to date. Some ISPs are better than others about updating their RADB entries; many don't bother with it at all. Also note that Squid converts AS numbers to networks only at startup or when you signal it to reconfigure. If the ISP updates its RADB entry, your cache won't know about the changes until you restart or reconfigure Squid.

Another problem is that the RADB server may be unreachable when your Squid process starts. If Squid can't contact the RADB server, it removes the AS entries from the access control configuration. The default server, *whois.ra.net*, may be too far away from many users to be reliable.

ACL Types

Now we can focus on the ACL types themselves. I present them here roughly in order of decreasing importance.

src

IP addresses are the most commonly used access control elements. Most sites use IP address controls to specify clients that are allowed to access Squid and those that aren't. The *src* type refers to client (source) IP addresses. That is, when an *src* ACL appears in an access list, Squid compares it to the IP address of the client issuing the request.

Normally you want to allow requests from hosts inside your network and block all others. For example, if your organization is using the 192.168.0.0 subnet, you can use an ACL like this:

```
acl MyNetwork src 192.168.0.0
```

If you have many subnets, you can list them all on the same *acl* line:

```
acl MyNetwork src 192.168.0.0 10.0.1.0/24 10.0.5.0/24 172.16.0.0/12
```

Squid has a number of other ACL types that check the client's address. The *srcdomain* type compares the client's fully qualified domain name. It requires a reverse DNS lookup, which may add some delay to processing the request. The *srcdom_regex* ACL is similar, but it allows you to use a regular expression to compare domain names. Finally, the *src_as* type compares the client's AS number.

dst

The *dst* type refers to origin server (destination) IP addresses. Among other things, you can use this to prevent some or all of your users from visiting certain web sites. However, you need to be a little careful with the *dst* ACL. Most of the requests received by Squid have origin server hostnames. For example:

```
GET http://www.web-cache.com/ HTTP/1.0
```

Here, *www.web-cache.com* is the hostname. When an access list rule includes a *dst* element, Squid must find the IP addresses for the hostname. If Squid's IP cache contains a valid entry for the hostname, the ACL is checked immediately. Otherwise, Squid postpones request processing while the DNS lookup is in progress. This can add significant delay to some requests. To avoid those delays, you should use the *dst-domain* ACL type (instead of *dst*) whenever possible.[*]

Here is a simple *dst* ACL example:

```
acl AdServers dst 1.2.3.0/24
```

Note that one problem with *dst* ACLs is that the origin server you are trying to allow or deny may change its IP address. If you don't notice the change, you won't bother to update *squid.conf*. You can put a hostname on the *acl* line, but that adds some delay at startup. If you need many hostnames in ACLs, you may want to preprocess the configuration file and turn the hostnames into IP addresses.

myip

The *myip* type refers to the IP address where clients connect to Squid. This is what you see under the *Local Address* column when you run netstat -n on the Squid box. Most Squid installations don't use this type. Usually, all clients connect to the same IP address, so this ACL element is useful only on systems that have more than one IP address.

To understand how *myip* may be useful, consider a simple company local area network with two subnets. All users on subnet-1 are programmers and engineers. Subnet-2 consists of accounting, marketing, and other administrative departments. The system on which Squid runs has three network interfaces: one on subnet-1, one on subnet-2, and the third connecting to the outbound Internet connection (see Figure 6-1).

When properly configured, all users on subnet-1 connect to Squid's IP address on that subnet, and similarly, all subnet-2 users connect to Squid's second IP address.

---

[*] Apart from access controls, Squid only needs an origin server's IP address when establishing a connection to that server. DNS lookups normally occur much later in request processing. If the HTTP request results in a cache hit, Squid doesn't need to know the server's address. Additionally, Squid doesn't need IP addresses for cache misses that are forwarded to a neighbor cache.

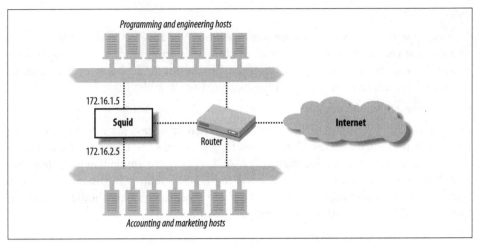

Figure 6-1. An application of the myip ACL

You can use this to give the technical staff on subnet-1 full access, while limiting the administrative staff to only work-related web sites.

The ACLs might look like this:

```
acl Eng myip 172.16.1.5
acl Admin myip 172.16.2.5
```

Note, however, that with this scheme you must take special measures to prevent users on one subnet from connecting to Squid's address on the other subnet. Otherwise, clever users on the accounting and marketing subnet can connect through the programming and engineering subnet and bypass your restrictions.

dstdomain

In some cases, you're likely to find that name-based access controls make a lot of sense. You can use them to block access to certain sites, to control how Squid forwards requests and to make some responses uncachable. The *dstdomain* type is very useful because it checks the hostname in requested URLs.

First, however, I want to clarify the difference between the following two lines:

```
acl A dst www.squid-cache.org
acl B dstdomain www.squid-cache.org
```

A is really an IP address ACL. When Squid parses the configuration file, it looks up the IP address for *www.squid-cache.org* and stores the address in memory. It doesn't store the name. If the IP address for *www.squid-cache.org* changes while Squid is running, Squid continues using the old address.

The *dstdomain* ACL, on the other hand, is stored as a domain name (i.e., a string), not as an IP address. When Squid checks ACL B, it uses string comparison functions on the hostname part of the URL. In this case, it doesn't really matter if the *www. squid-cache.org* IP changes while Squid is running.

The primary problem with *dstdomain* ACLs is that some URLs have IP addresses instead of hostnames. If your goal is to block access to certain sites with *dstdomain* ACLs, savvy users can simply look up the site's IP address manually and insert it into the URL. For example, these two URLs bring up the same page:

```
http://www.squid-cache.org/docs/FAQ/
http://206.168.0.9/docs/FAQ/
```

The first can be easily matched with *dstdomain* ACLs, but the second can't. Thus, if you elect to rely on *dstdomain* ACLs, you may want to also block all requests that use an IP address instead of a hostname. See the later section "Denying Requests with IP Addresses" for an example.

srcdomain

The *srcdomain* ACL is somewhat tricky as well. It requires a so-called reverse DNS lookup on each client's IP address. Technically, Squid requests a DNS PTR record for the address. The answer—a fully qualified domain name (FQDN)—is what Squid compares to the ACL value. (Refer to O'Reilly's *DNS and BIND* for more information about DNS PTR records.)

As with *dst* ACLs, FQDN lookups are a potential source of significant delay. The request is postponed until the FQDN answer comes back. FQDN answers are cached, so the *srcdomain* lookup delay usually occurs only for the client's first request.

Unfortunately, *srcdomain* lookups sometimes don't work. Many organizations fail to keep their reverse lookup databases current. If an address doesn't have a PTR record, the ACL check fails. In some cases, requests may be postponed for a very long time (e.g., two minutes) until the DNS lookup times out. If you choose to use the *srcdomain* ACL, make sure that your own DNS *in-addr.arpa* zones are properly configured and working. Assuming that they are, you can use an ACL like this:

```
acl LocalHosts srcdomain .users.example.com
```

port

Most likely, you'll want to use the *port* ACL to limit access to certain origin server port numbers. As I'll explain shortly, Squid really shouldn't connect to certain services, such as email and IRC servers. The *port* ACL allows you to define individual ports, and port ranges. Here is an example:

```
acl HTTPports port 80 8000-8010 8080
```

HTTP is similar in design to other protocols, such as SMTP. This means that clever users can trick Squid into relaying email messages to an SMTP server. Email relays are one of the primary reasons we must deal with a daily deluge of spam.

Historically, spam relays have been actual mail servers. Recently, however, more and more spammers are using open HTTP proxies to hide their tracks. You definitely don't want your Squid cache to be used as a spam relay. If it is, your IP address is likely to end up on one of the many mail-relay blacklists (MAPS, ORDB, spamhaus, etc.). In addition to email, there are a number of other TCP/IP services that Squid shouldn't normally communicate with. These include IRC, Telnet, DNS, POP, and NNTP. Your policy regarding port numbers should be either to deny the known-to-be-dangerous ports and allow the rest, or to allow the known-to-be-safe ports and deny the rest.

My preference is to be conservative and allow only the safe ports. The default *squid.conf* includes the following Safe_ports ACL:

```
acl Safe_ports port 80          # http
acl Safe_ports port 21          # ftp
acl Safe_ports port 443 563     # https, snews
acl Safe_ports port 70          # gopher
acl Safe_ports port 210         # wais
acl Safe_ports port 1025-65535  # unregistered ports
acl Safe_ports port 280         # http-mgmt
acl Safe_ports port 488         # gss-http
acl Safe_ports port 591         # filemaker
acl Safe_ports port 777         # multiling http

http_access deny !Safe_ports
```

This is a sensible approach. It allows users to connect to any nonprivileged port (1025–65535), but only specific ports in the privileged range. If one of your users tries to request a URL, such as *http://www.lrrr.org:123/*, Squid returns an access denied error message. In some cases, you may need to add additional port numbers to the Safe_ports ACL to keep your users happy.

A more liberal approach is to deny access to certain ports that are known to be particularly dangerous. The Squid FAQ includes an example of this:

```
acl Dangerous_ports 7 9 19 22 23 25 53 109 110 119

http_access deny Dangerous_ports
```

One drawback to the *Dangerous_ports* approach is that Squid ends up searching the entire list for almost every request. This places a little extra burden on your CPU. Most likely, 99% of the requests reaching Squid are for port 80, which doesn't appear in the *Dangerous_ports* list. The list is searched for all of these requests without resulting in a match. However, integer comparison is a fast operation and should not significantly impact performance.

myport

Squid also has a *myport* ACL. Whereas the *port* ACL refers to the origin server port number, *myport* refers to the port where Squid receives client requests. Squid listens on different port numbers if you specify more than one with the *http_port* directive.

The *myport* ACL is particularly useful if you use Squid as an HTTP accelerator for your web site and as a proxy for your users. You can accept the accelerator requests on port 80 and the proxy requests on port 3128. You probably want the world to access the accelerator, but only your users should access Squid as a proxy. Your ACLs may look something like this:

```
acl AccelPort myport 80
acl ProxyPort myport 3128
acl MyNet src 172.16.0.0/22

http_access allow AccelPort          # anyone
http_access allow ProxyPort MyNet    # only my users
http_access deny ProxyPort           # deny others
```

method

The *method* ACL refers to the HTTP request method. GET is typically the most common method, followed by POST, PUT, and others. This example demonstrates how to use the *method* ACL:

```
acl Uploads method PUT POST
```

Squid knows about the following standard HTTP methods: GET, POST, PUT, HEAD, CONNECT, TRACE, OPTIONS, and DELETE. In addition, Squid knows about the following methods from the WEBDAV specification, RFC 2518: PROPFIND, PROPPATCH, MKCOL, COPY, MOVE, LOCK, UNLOCK.* Certain Microsoft products use nonstandard WEBDAV methods, so Squid knows about them as well: BMOVE, BDELETE, BPROPFIND. Finally, you can configure Squid to understand additional request methods with the *extension_methods* directive. See Appendix A.

Note that the CONNECT method is special in a number of ways. It is the method used for tunneling certain requests through HTTP proxies (see also RFC 2817: Upgrading to TLS Within HTTP/1.1). Be especially careful with the CONNECT method and remote server port numbers. As I talked about in the previous section, you don't want Squid to connect to certain remote services. You should limit the CONNECT method to only the HTTPS/SSL and perhaps NNTPS ports (443 and 563, respectively). The default *squid.conf* does this:

```
acl CONNECT method CONNECT
acl SSL_ports 443 563
```

---

* For the RFC database, visit *http://www.rfc-editor.org/rfc.html*.

```
http_access allow CONNECT SSL_ports
http_access deny CONNECT
```

With this configuration, Squid only allows tunneled requests to ports 443 (HTTPS/ SSL) and 563 (NNTPS). CONNECT method requests to all other ports are denied.

PURGE is another special request method. It is specific to Squid and not defined in any of the RFCs. It provides a way for the administrator to forcibly remove cached objects. Since this method is somewhat dangerous, Squid denies PURGE requests by default, unless you define an ACL that references the method. Otherwise, anyone with access to the cache may be able to remove any cached object. I recommend allowing PURGE from *localhost* only:

```
acl Purge method PURGE
acl Localhost src 127.0.0.1
http_access allow Purge Localhost
http_access deny Purge
```

See Chapter 7 for more information on removing objects from Squid's cache.

proto

This type refers to a URI's access (or transfer) protocol. Valid values are the following: http, https (same as HTTP/TLS), ftp, gopher, urn, whois, and cache_object. In other words, these are the URL scheme names (RFC 1738 terminology) supported by Squid. For example, suppose that you want to deny all FTP requests. You can use the following directives:

```
acl FTP proto FTP
http_access deny FTP
```

The *cache_object* scheme is a feature specific to Squid. It is used to access Squid's cache management interface, which I'll talk about in Chapter 14. Unfortunately, it's not a very good name, and it should probably be changed.

The default *squid.conf* file has a couple of lines that restrict cache manager access:

```
acl Manager proto cache_object
acl Localhost src 127.0.0.1

http_access allow Manager Localhost
http_access deny Manager
```

These configuration lines allow cache-manager requests only when they come from the localhost address. All other cache-manager requests are denied. This means that any user with an account on the Squid machine can access the potentially sensitive cache-manager information. You may want to modify the cache-manager access controls or protect certain pages with passwords. I'll talk about that in Chapter 14.

time

The *time* ACL allows you to control access based on the time of day and the day of the week. The syntax is somewhat cryptic:

```
acl name [days] [h1:m1-h2:m2]
```

You can specify days of the week, starting and stopping times, or both. Days are specified by the single-letter codes shown in Table 6-2. Times are specified in 24-hour format. The starting time must be less than the ending time, which makes it awkward to write *time* ACLs that span "midnights."

Table 6-2. Day codes for the time ACL

Code	Day
S	Sunday
M	Monday
T	Tuesday
W	Wednesday
H	Thursday
F	Friday
A	Saturday
D	All weekdays (M-F)

 Days and times are interpreted with the localtime( ) function, which takes into account your local time zone and daylight savings time settings. Make sure that your computer knows what time zone it is in! You'll also want to make sure that your clock is synchronized to the correct time.

To specify a *time* ACL that matches your weekday working hours, you can write:

```
acl Working_hours MTWHF 08:00-17:00
```

or:

```
acl Working_hours D 08:00-17:00
```

Let's look at a trickier example. Perhaps you're an ISP that relaxes access during off-peak hours, say 8 P.M. to 4 A.M. Since this time spans midnight, you can't write "20:00-04:00." Instead you'll need either to split this into two ACLs or define the peak hours and use negation. For example:

```
acl Offpeak1 20:00-23:59
acl Offpeak2 00:00-04:00
http_access allow Offpeak1 ...
http_access allow Offpeak2 ...
```

Alternatively, you can do it like this:

```
acl Peak 04:00-20:00
http_access allow !Peak ...
```

Although Squid allows it, you probably shouldn't put more than one day list and time range on a single *time* ACL line. The parser isn't always smart enough to figure out what you want. For example, if you enter this:

```
acl Blah time M 08:00-10:00 W 09:00-11:00
```

what you really end up with is this:

```
acl Blah time MW 09:00-11:00
```

The parser ORs weekdays together and uses only the last time range. It does work, however, if you write it like this, on two separate lines:

```
acl Blah time M 08:00-10:00
acl Blah time W 09:00-11:00
```

ident

The *ident* ACL matches usernames returned by the ident protocol. This is a simple protocol, that's documented in RFC 1413. It works something like this:

1. A user-agent (client) establishes a TCP connection to Squid.
2. Squid connects to the ident port (113) on the client's system.
3. Squid writes a line containing the two TCP port numbers of the client's first connection. The Squid-side port number is probably 3128 (or whatever you configured in *squid.conf*). The client-side port is more or less random.
4. The client's ident server writes back the username belonging to the process that opened the first connection.
5. Squid records the username for access control purposes and for logging in *access. log*.

When Squid encounters an *ident* ACL for a particular request, that request is postponed until the ident lookup is complete. Thus, the *ident* ACL may add some significant delays to your users' requests.

We recommend using the *ident* ACL only on local area networks and only if all or most of the client workstations run the ident server. If Squid and the client workstations are connected to a LAN with low latency, the *ident* ACL can work well. Using *ident* for clients connecting over WAN links is likely to frustrate both you and your users.

The ident protocol isn't very secure. Savvy users will be able to replace their normal ident server with a fake server that returns any username they select. For example, if I know that connections from the user administrator are always allowed, I can write a simple program that answers every ident request with that username.

You can't use *ident* ACLs with interception caching (see Chapter 9). When Squid is configured for interception caching, the operating system pretends that it is the origin server. This means that the local socket address for intercepted TCP connections has the origin server's IP address. If you run netstat -n on Squid, you'll see a lot of foreign IP addresses in the *Local Address* column. When Squid makes an ident query, it creates a new TCP socket and binds the local endpoint to the same IP address as the local end of the client's TCP connection. Since the local address isn't really local (it's some far away origin server's IP address), the bind() system call fails. Squid handles this as a failed ident query.

Note that Squid also has a feature to perform "lazy" ident lookups on clients. In this case, requests aren't delayed while waiting for the ident query. Squid logs the ident information if it is available by the time the HTTP request is complete. You can enable this feature with the *ident_lookup_access* directive, which I'll discuss later in this chapter.

proxy_auth

Squid has a powerful, and somewhat confusing, set of features to support HTTP proxy authentication. With proxy authentication, the client's HTTP request includes a header containing authentication credentials. Usually, this is simply a username and password. Squid decodes the credential information and then queries an external authentication process to find out if the credentials are valid.

Squid currently supports three techniques for receiving user credentials: the HTTP Basic protocol, Digest authentication protocol, and NTLM. Basic authentication has been around for a long time. By today's standards, it is a very insecure technique. Usernames and passwords are sent together, essentially in cleartext. Digest authentication is more secure, but also more complicated. Both Basic and Digest authentication are documented in RFC 2617. NTLM also has better security than Basic authentication. However, it is a proprietary protocol developed by Microsoft. A handful of Squid developers have essentially reverse-engineered it.

In order to use proxy authentication, you must also configure Squid to spawn a number of external helper processes. The Squid source code includes some programs that authenticate against a number of standard databases, including LDAP, NTLM, NCSA-style password files, and the standard Unix password database. The *auth_param* directive controls the configuration of all helper programs. I'll go through it in detail in Chapter 12.

The *auth_param* directive and *proxy_auth* ACL is one of the few cases where their order in the configuration file is important. You must define at least one authentication helper (with *auth_param*) before any *proxy_auth* ACLs. If you don't, Squid prints an error message and ignores the *proxy_auth* ACLs. This isn't a fatal error, so Squid may start anyway, and all your users' requests may be denied.

The *proxy_auth* ACL takes usernames as values. However, most installations simply use the special value REQUIRED:

```
auth_param ...
acl Auth1 proxy_auth REQUIRED
```

In this case, any request with valid credentials matches the ACL. If you need fine-grained control, you can specify individual usernames:

```
auth_param ...
acl Auth1 proxy_auth allan bob charlie
acl Auth2 proxy_auth dave eric frank
```

 Proxy authentication doesn't work with HTTP interception because the user-agent doesn't realize it's talking to a proxy rather than the origin server. The user-agent doesn't know that it should send a Proxy-Authorization header in its requests. See Chapter 9 for additional details.

src_as

This type checks that the client (source) IP address belongs to a specific AS number. (See the earlier section "Autonomous system numbers" for information on how Squid maps AS numbers to IP addresses.) As an example, consider the fictitious ISP that uses AS 64222 and advertises the 10.0.0.0/8, 172.16.0.0/12, and 192.168.0.0/16 networks. You can write an ACL like this, which allows requests from any host in the ISP's address space:

```
acl TheISP src 10.0.0.0/8
acl TheISP src 172.16.0.0/12
acl TheISP src 192.168.0.0/16
http_access allow TheISP
```

Alternatively, you can write it like this:

```
acl TheISP src_as 64222
http_access allow TheISP
```

Not only is the second form shorter, it also means that if the ISP adds more networks, you won't have to update your ACL configuration.

dst_as

The *dst_as* ACL is often used with the *cache_peer_access* directive. In this way, Squid can forward cache misses in a manner consistent with IP routing. Consider an ISP that exchanges routes with a few other ISPs. Each ISP operates their own caching proxy, and these proxies can forward requests to each other. Ideally, ISP A forwards cache misses for servers on ISP B's network to ISP B's caching proxy. An easy way to do this is with AS ACLs and the *cache_peer_access* directive:

```
acl ISP-B-AS dst_as 64222
acl ISP-C-AS dst_as 64333
cache_peer proxy.isp-b.net parent 3128 3130
cache_peer proxy.isp-c.net parent 3128 3130
cache_peer_access proxy.isb-b.net allow ISP-B-AS
cache_peer_access proxy.isb-c.net allow ISP-C-AS
```

These access controls make sure that the only requests sent to the two ISPs are for their own origin servers. I'll talk further about cache cooperation in Chapter 10.

snmp_community

The *snmp_community* ACL is meaningful only for SNMP queries, which are controlled by the *snmp_access* directive. For example, you might write:

```
acl OurCommunityName snmp_community hIgHsEcUrItY
acl All src 0/0
snmp_access allow OurCommunityName
snmp_access deny All
```

In this case, an SNMP query is allowed only if the community name is set to hIgHsEcUrItY.

maxconn

The *maxconn* ACL refers to the number of simultaneous connections from a client's IP address. Some Squid administrators find this a useful way to prevent users from abusing the proxy or consuming too many resources.

The *maxconn* ACL matches a request when that request exceeds the number you specify. For this reason, you should use *maxconn* ACLs only in *deny* rules. Consider this example:

```
acl OverConnLimit maxconn 4
http_access deny OverConnLimit
```

In this case, Squid allows up to four connections at once from each IP address. When a client makes the fifth connection, the *OverConnLimit* ACL is matched, and the *http_access* rule denies the request.

The *maxconn* ACL feature relies on Squid's client database. This database keeps a small data structure in memory for each client IP address. If you have a lot of clients, this database may consume a significant amount of memory. You can disable the client database in the configuration file with the *client_db* directive. However, if you disable the client database, the *maxconn* ACL will no longer work.

arp

The *arp* ACL is used to check the Media Access Control (MAC) address (typically Ethernet) of cache clients. The Address Resolution Protocol (ARP) is the way that hosts find the MAC address corresponding to an IP address. This feature came about when some university students discovered that, under Microsoft Windows, they could set a system's IP address to any value. Thus, they were able to circumvent Squid's address-based controls. To escalate this arms race, a savvy system administrator gave Squid the ability to check the client's Ethernet addresses.

Unfortunately, this feature uses nonportable code. If you use Solaris or Linux, you should be able to use *arp* ACLs. If not, you're out of luck. The best way to find out is to add the --enable-arp-acl option when you run ./configure.

The *arp* ACL feature contains another important limitation. ARP is a datalink layer protocol. It works only for hosts on the same subnet as Squid. You can't easily discover the MAC address of a host on a different subnet. If you have routers between Squid and your users, you probably can't use *arp* ACLs.

Now that you know when not to use them, let's see how *arp* ACLs actually look. The values are Ethernet addresses, as you would see in ifconfig and arp output. For example:

```
acl WinBoxes arp 00:00:21:55:ed:22
acl WinBoxes arp 00:00:21:ff:55:38
```

srcdom_regex

The *srcdom_regex* ACL allows you to use regular expression matching on client domain names. This is similar to the *srcdomain* ACL, which uses modified substring matching. The same caveats apply here: some client addresses don't resolve back to domain names. As an example, the following ACL matches hostnames that begin with dhcp:

```
acl DHCPUser srcdom_regex -i ^dhcp
```

Because of the leading ^ symbol, this ACL matches the hostname *dhcp12.example. com*, but not *host12.dhcp.example.com*.

dstdom_regex

The *dstdom_regex* ACL is obviously similar, except that it applies to origin server names. The issues with *dstdomain* are relevant here, too. The following example matches hostnames that begin with *www*:

```
acl WebSite dstdom_regex -i ^www\.
```

Here is another useful regular expression that matches IP addresses given in URL hostnames:

```
acl IPaddr dstdom_regex [0-9]$
```

This works because Squid requires URL hostnames to be fully qualified. Since none of the global top-level domains end with a digit, this ACL matches only IP addresses, which do end with a number.

url_regex

You can use the *url_regex* ACL to match any part of a requested URL, including the transfer protocol and origin server hostname. For example, this ACL matches MP3 files requested from FTP servers:

```
acl FTPMP3 url_regex -i ^ftp://.*\.mp3$
```

urlpath_regex

The *urlpath_regex* ACL is very similar to *url_regex*, except that the transfer protocol and hostname aren't included in the comparison. This makes certain types of checks much easier. For example, let's say you need to deny requests with sex in the URL, but still possibly allow requests that have sex in their hostname:

```
acl Sex urlpath_regex sex
```

As another example, let's say you want to provide special treatment for cgi-bin requests. You can catch some of them with this ACL:

```
acl CGI1 urlpath_regex ^/cgi-bin
```

Of course, CGI programs aren't necessarily kept under */cgi-bin/*, so you'd probably want to write additional ACLs to catch the others.

browser

Most HTTP requests include a User-Agent header. The value of this header is typically something strange like:

```
Mozilla/4.51 [en] (X11; I; Linux 2.2.5-15 i686)
```

The *browser* ACL performs regular expression matching on the value of the User-Agent header. For example, to deny requests that don't come from a Mozilla browser, you can use:

```
acl Mozilla browser Mozilla
http_access deny !Mozilla
```

Before using the *browser* ACL, be sure that you fully understand the User-Agent strings your cache receives. Some user-agents lie about their identity. Even Squid has a feature to rewrite User-agent headers in requests that it forwards. With browsers such as Opera and KDE's Konqueror, users can send different user-agent strings to different origin servers or omit them altogether.

req_mime_type

The *req_mime_type* ACL refers to the Content-Type header of the client's HTTP request. Content-Type headers usually appear only in requests with message bodies. POST and PUT requests might include the header, but GET requests don't. You might be able to use the *req_mime_type* ACL to detect certain file uploads and some types of HTTP tunneling requests.

The *req_mime_type* ACL values are regular expressions. To catch audio file types, you can use an ACL like this:

```
acl AuidoFileUploads req_mime_type -i ^audio/
```

rep_mime_type

The *rep_mime_type* ACL refers to the Content-Type header of the origin server's HTTP response. It is really only meaningful when used in an *http_reply_access* rule. All other access control forms are based on aspects of the client's request. This one is based on the response.

If you want to try blocking Java code with Squid, you might use some access rules like this:

```
acl JavaDownload rep_mime_type application/x-java
http_reply_access deny JavaDownload
```

ident_regex

You saw the *ident* ACL earlier in this section. The *ident_regex* simply allows you to use regular expressions, instead of exact string matching on usernames returned by the ident protocol. For example, this ACL matches usernames that contain a digit:

```
acl NumberInName ident_regex [0-9]
```

proxy_auth_regex

As with *ident*, the *proxy_auth_regex* ACL allows you to use regular expressions on proxy authentication usernames. For example, this ACL matches admin, administrator, and administrators:

```
acl Admins proxy_auth_regex -i ^admin
```

External ACLs

Squid Version 2.5 introduces a new feature: *external ACLs*. You instruct Squid to send certain pieces of information to an external process. This helper process then tells Squid whether the given data is a match or not.

Squid comes with a number of external ACL helper programs; most determine whether or not the named user is a member of a particular group. See Chapter 12 for descriptions of those programs and for information on how to write your own. For now, I'll explain how to define and utilize an external ACL type.

The *external_acl_type* directive defines a new external ACL type. Here's the general syntax:

```
external_acl_type type-name [options] format helper-command
```

type-name is a user-defined string. You'll also use it in an *acl* line to reference this particular helper.

Squid currently supports the following options:

ttl=*n*
> The amount of time, in seconds, to cache the result for values that are a match. The default is 3600 seconds, or 1 hour.

negative_ttl=*n*
> The amount of time, in seconds, to cache the result for values that aren't a match. The default is 3600 seconds, or 1 hour.

concurrency=*n*
> The number of helper processes to spawn. The default is 5.

cache=*n*
> The maximum number of results to cache. The default is 0, which doesn't limit the cache size.

format is one or more keywords that begin with the % character. Squid currently supports the following format tokens:

%LOGIN
> The username, taken from proxy authentication credentials.

%IDENT
> The username, taken from an RFC 1413 ident query.

%SRC
> The IP address of the client.

%DST
> The IP address of the origin server.

%PROTO
> The transfer protocol (e.g., HTTP, FTP, etc.).

%PORT
> The origin server TCP port number.

%METHOD
> The HTTP request method.

%{Header}

The value of an HTTP request header; for example, %{User-Agent} causes Squid to send strings like this to the authenticator:

```
"Mozilla/4.0 (compatible; MSIE 6.0; Win32)"
```

%{Hdr:member}

Selects certain members of list-based HTTP headers, such as Cache-Control; for example, given this HTTP header:

```
X-Some-Header: foo=xyzzy, bar=plugh, foo=zoinks
```

and the token %{X-Some-Header:foo}, Squid sends this string to the external ACL process:

```
foo=xyzzy, foo=zoinks
```

%{Hdr:;member}

The same as %{Hdr:*member*}, except that the ; character is the list separator. You can use any nonalphanumeric character as the separator.

helper-command is the command that Squid spawns for the helper. You may include command arguments here as well. For example, the entire command may be something like:

```
/usr/local/squid/libexec/my-acl-prog.pl -X -5 /usr/local/squid/etc/datafile
```

Putting all these together results in a long line. Squid's configuration file doesn't support the backslash line-continuation technique shown here, so remember that all these must go on a single line:

```
external_acl_type MyAclType cache=100 %LOGIN %{User-Agent} \
    /usr/local/squid/libexec/my-acl-prog.pl -X -5 \
    /usr/local/squid/share/usernames \
    /usr/local/squid/share/useragents
```

Now that you know how to define an external ACL, the next step is to write an *acl* line that references it. This is relatively straightforward. The syntax is as follows:

```
acl acl-name external type-name [args ...]
```

Here is a simple example:

```
acl MyAcl external MyAclType
```

Squid accepts any number of optional arguments following the *type-name*. These are sent to the helper program for each request, after the expanded tokens. See my description of the *unix_group* helper in Chapter 12 for an example of this feature.

Dealing with Long ACL Lists

ACL lists can sometimes be very long. Such lists are awkward to maintain inside the *squid.conf* file. Also, you may need to generate Squid ACL lists automatically from other sources. In these cases, you'll be happy to know that you can include ACL lists from external files. The syntax is as follows:

```
acl name "filename"
```

The double quotes here instruct Squid to open *filename* and assign its contents to the ACL. For example, instead of this:

```
acl Foo BadClients 1.2.3.4 1.2.3.5 1.2.3.6 1.2.3.7 1.2.3.9 ...
```

you can do this:

```
acl Foo BadClients "/usr/local/squid/etc/BadClients"
```

and put the IP addresses into the *BadClients* file:

```
1.2.3.4
1.2.3.5
1.2.3.6
1.2.3.7
1.2.3.9
...
```

Your file may include comments that begin with a # character. Note that each entry in the file must be on a separate line. Whereas a space character delimits values on an *acl* line, newlines are the delimiter for files containing ACL values.

How Squid Matches Access Control Elements

It is important to understand how Squid searches ACL elements for a match. When an ACL element has more than one value, any single value can cause a match. In other words, Squid uses OR logic when checking ACL element values. Squid stops searching when it finds the first value that causes a match. This means that you can reduce delays by placing likely matches at the beginning of a list.

Let's look at a specific example. Consider this ACL definition:

```
acl Simpsons ident Maggie Lisa Bart Marge Homer
```

When Squid encounters the *Simpsons* ACL in an access list, it performs the ident lookup. Let's see what happens when the user's ident server returns Marge. Squid's ACL code compares this value to Maggie, Lisa, and Bart before finding a match with Marge. At this point, the search terminates, and we say that the *Simpsons* ACL matches the request.

Actually, that's a bit of a lie. The *ident* ACL values aren't stored as an unordered list. Rather, they are stored as an splay tree. This means that Squid doesn't end up searching all the names in the event of a nonmatch. Searching an splay tree with N items requires $log(N)$ comparisons. Many other ACL types use splay trees as well. The regular expression-based types, however, don't.

Since regular expressions can't be sorted, they are stored as linked lists. This makes them inefficient for large lists, especially for requests that don't match any of the regular expressions in the list. In an attempt to improve this situation, Squid moves a regular expression to the top of the list when a match occurs. In fact, due to the nature of the ACL matching code, Squid moves matched entries to the second position in the list. Thus, commonly matched values naturally migrate to the top of the ACL list, which should reduce the number of comparisons.

Let's look at another simple example:

```
acl Schmever port 80-90 101 103 107 1 2 3 9999
```

This ACL is a match for a request to an origin server port between 80 and 90, and all the other individual listed port numbers. For a request to port 80, Squid matches the ACL by looking at the first value. For port 9999, all the other values are checked first. For a port number not listed, Squid checks every value before declaring the ACL isn't a match. As I've said before, you can optimize the ACL matching by placing the more common values first.

Access Control Rules

As I mentioned earlier, ACL elements are the first step in building access controls. The second step is the access control rules, where you combine elements to allow or deny certain actions. You've already seen some *http_access* rules in the preceding examples. Squid has a number of other access control lists:

http_access
> This is your most important access list. It determines which client HTTP requests are allowed, and which are denied. If you get the *http_access* configuration wrong, your Squid cache may be vulnerable to attacks and abuse from people who shouldn't have access to it.

http_reply_access
> The *http_reply_access* list is similar to *http_access*. The difference is that the former list is checked when Squid receives a *reply* from an origin server or upstream proxy. Most access controls are based on aspects of the client's request, in which case the *http_access* list is sufficient. However, some people prefer also to allow or deny requests based on the reply content type. Because Squid doesn't know the content type value until it receives the server's reply, this additional access list is necessary. See the later section "An http_reply_access Example" for more information.

icp_access
> If your Squid cache is configured to serve ICP replies (see Chapter 10), you should use the *icp_access* list. In most cases, you'll want to allow ICP requests only from your neighbor caches.

no_cache
> You can use the *no_cache* access list to tell Squid it must never store certain responses (on disk or in memory). This list is typically used in conjunction with *dst*, *dstdomain*, and *url_regex* ACLs.

The "no" in *no_cache* causes some confusion because of double negatives. A request that is denied by the *no_cache* list isn't cached. In other words no_cache deny ... is the way to make something uncachable. See the later section "Preventing Cache Hits for Local Sites" for an example.

miss_access

The *miss_access* list is primarily useful for a Squid cache with sibling neighbors. It determines how Squid handles requests that are cache misses. This feature is necessary for Squid to enforce sibling relationships with its neighbors. See the later section "Preventing Abuse from Siblings" for an example.

redirector_access

This access list determines which requests are sent to one of the redirector processes (see Chapter 11). By default, all requests go through a redirector if you are using one. You can use the *redirector_access* list to prevent certain requests from being rewritten. This is particularly useful because a redirector receives less information about a particular request than does the access control system.

ident_lookup_access

The *ident_lookup_access* list is similar to *redirector_access*. It enables you to make "lazy" ident lookups for certain requests. Squid doesn't issue ident queries by default. It does so only for requests that are allowed by the *ident_lookup_ access* rules (or by an *ident* ACL).

always_direct

This access list affects how a Squid cache with neighbors forwards cache misses. Usually Squid tries to forward cache misses to a parent cache, and/or Squid uses ICP to locate cached responses in neighbors. However, when a request matches an *always_direct* rule, Squid forwards the request directly to the origin server.

With this list, matching an allow rule causes Squid to forward the request directly. See Chapter 10 for more information and an example.

never_direct

Not surprisingly, *never_direct* is the opposite of *always_direct*. Cache miss requests that match this list must be sent to a neighbor cache. This is particularly useful for proxies behind firewalls.

With this list, matching an allow rule causes Squid to forward the request to a neighbor. See Chapter 10 for more information and an example.

snmp_access

This access list applies to queries sent to Squid's SNMP port. The ACLs that you can use with this list are *snmp_community* and *src*. You can also use *srcdomain*, *srcdom_regex*, and *src_as* if you really want to. See Chapter 14 for an example.

broken_posts

This access list affects the way that Squid handles certain POST requests. Some older user-agents are known to send an extra CRLF (carriage return and linefeed) at the end of the request body. That is, the message body is two bytes longer than indicated by the Content-Length header. Even worse, some older HTTP servers actually rely on this incorrect behavior. When a request matches this access list, Squid emulates the buggy client and sends the extra CRLF characters.

Squid has a number of additional configuration directives that use ACL elements. Some of these used to be global settings that were modified to use ACLs to provide more flexibility.

cache_peer_access
> This access list controls the HTTP requests and ICP/HTCP queries that are sent to a neighbor cache. See Chapter 10 for more information and examples.

reply_body_max_size
> This access list restricts the maximum acceptable size of an HTTP reply body. See Appendix A for more information.

delay_access
> This access rule list controls whether or not the delay pools are applied to the (cache miss) response for this request. See Appendix C.

tcp_outgoing_address
> This access list binds server-side TCP connections to specific local IP addresses. See Appendix A.

tcp_outgoing_tos
> This access list can set different TOS/Diffserv values in TCP connections to origin servers and neighbors. See Appendix A.

header_access
> With this directive, you can configure Squid to remove certain HTTP headers from the requests that it forwards. For example, you might want to automatically filter out Cookie headers in requests sent to certain origin servers, such as *doubleclick.net*. See Appendix A.

header_replace
> This directive allows you to replace, rather than just remove, the contents of HTTP headers. For example, you can set the User-Agent header to a bogus value to keep certain origin servers happy while still protecting your privacy. See Appendix A.

Access Rule Syntax

The syntax for an access control rule is as follows:

    access_list allow|deny [!]ACLname ...

For example:

```
http_access allow MyClients
http_access deny !Safe_Ports
http_access allow GameSites AfterHours
```

When reading the configuration file, Squid makes only one pass through the access control lines. Thus, you must define the ACL elements (with an acl line) before referencing them in an access list. Furthermore, the order of the access list rules is very important. Incoming requests are checked in the same order that you write them. Placing the most common ACLs early in the list may reduce Squid's CPU usage.

 For most of the access lists, the meaning of deny and allow are obvious. Some of them, however, aren't so intuitive. In particular, pay close attention when writing *always_direct*, *never_direct*, and *no_cache* rules. In the case of *always_direct*, an allow rule means that matching requests are forwarded directly to origin servers. An *always_direct* deny rule means that matching requests aren't forced to go directly to origin servers, but may still do so if, for example, all neighbor caches are unreachable. The *no_cache* rules are tricky as well. Here, you must use deny for requests that must not be cached.

How Squid Matches Access Rules

Recall that Squid uses OR logic when searching ACL elements. Any single value in an *acl* can cause a match.

It's the opposite for access rules, however. For *http_access* and the other rule sets, Squid uses AND logic. Consider this generic example:

```
access_list allow ACL1 ACL2 ACL3
```

For this rule to be a match, the request must match each of *ACL1*, *ACL2*, and *ACL3*. If any of those ACLs don't match the request, Squid stops searching this rule and proceeds to the next. Within a single rule, you can optimize rule searching by putting least-likely-to-match ACLs first. Consider this simple example:

```
acl A method http
acl B port 8080
http_access deny A B
```

This *http_access* rule is somewhat inefficient because the A ACL is more likely to be matched than B. It is better to reverse the order so that, in most cases, Squid only makes one ACL check, instead of two:

```
http_access deny B A
```

One mistake people commonly make is to write a rule that can never be true. For example:

```
acl A src 1.2.3.4
acl B src 5.6.7.8
http_access allow A B
```

This rule is never going to be true because a source IP address can't be equal to both 1.2.3.4 and 5.6.7.8 at the same time. Most likely, someone who writes a rule like that really means this:

```
acl A src 1.2.3.4 5.6.7.8
http_access allow A
```

As with the algorithm for matching the values of an ACL, when Squid finds a matching rule in an access list, the search terminates. If none of the access rules result in a match, the default action is the *opposite* of the last rule in the list. For example, consider this simple access configuration:

```
acl Bob ident bob
http_access allow Bob
```

Now if the user Mary makes a request, she is denied. The last (and only) rule in the list is an allow rule, and it doesn't match the username Mary. Thus, the default action is the opposite of allow, so the request is denied. Similarly, if the last entry is a deny rule, the default action is to allow the request. It is good practice always to end your access lists with explicit rules that either allow or deny all requests. To be perfectly clear, the previous example should be written this way:

```
acl All src 0/0
acl Bob ident bob
http_access allow Bob
http_access deny All
```

The src 0/0 ACL is an easy way to match each and every type of request.

Access List Style

Squid's access control syntax is very powerful. In most cases, you can probably think of two or more ways to accomplish the same thing. In general, you should put the more specific and restrictive access controls first. For example, rather than:

```
acl All src 0/0
acl Net1 src 1.2.3.0/24
acl Net2 src 1.2.4.0/24
acl Net3 src 1.2.5.0/24
acl Net4 src 1.2.6.0/24
acl WorkingHours time 08:00-17:00

http_access allow Net1 WorkingHours
http_access allow Net2 WorkingHours
http_access allow Net3 WorkingHours
http_access allow Net4
http_access deny All
```

you might find it easier to maintain and understand the access control configuration if you write it like this:

```
http_access allow Net4
http_access deny !WorkingHours
```

```
http_access allow Net1
http_access allow Net2
http_access allow Net3
http_access deny All
```

Whenever you have a rule with two or more ACL elements, it's always a good idea to follow it up with an opposite, more general rule. For example, the default Squid configuration denies cache manager requests that don't come from the localhost IP address. You might be tempted to write it like this:

```
acl CacheManager proto cache_object
acl Localhost src 127.0.0.1
http_access deny CacheManager !Localhost
```

However, the problem here is that you haven't yet allowed the cache manager requests that do come from localhost. Subsequent rules may cause the request to be denied anyway. These rules have this undesirable behavior:

```
acl CacheManager proto cache_object
acl Localhost src 127.0.0.1
acl MyNet 10.0.0.0/24
acl All src 0/0
http_access deny CacheManager !Localhost
http_access allow MyNet
http_access deny All
```

Since a request from localhost doesn't match MyNet, it gets denied. A better way to write the rules is like this:

```
http_access allow CacheManager localhost
http_access deny CacheManager
http_access allow MyNet
http_access deny All
```

Delayed Checks

Some ACLs can't be checked in one pass because the necessary information is unavailable. The *ident*, *dst*, *srcdomain*, and *proxy_auth* types fall into this category. When Squid encounters an ACL that can't be checked, it postpones the decision and issues a query for the necessary information (IP address, domain name, username, etc.). When the information is available, Squid checks the rules all over again, starting at the beginning of the list. It doesn't continue where the previous check left off. If possible, you may want to move these likely-to-be-delayed ACLs near the top of your rules to avoid unnecessary, repeated checks.

Because these delays are costly (in terms of time), Squid caches the information whenever possible. Ident lookups occur for each *connection*, rather than each request. This means that persistent HTTP connections can really benefit you in situations where you use ident queries. Hostnames and IP addresses are cached as specified by the DNS replies, unless you're using the older external *dnsserver* processes.

Proxy Authentication information is cached as I described previously in the "proxy_auth" section.

Slow and Fast Rule Checks

Internally, Squid considers some access rule checks *fast*, and others *slow*. The difference is whether or not Squid postpones its decision to wait for additional information. In other words, a slow check may be deferred while Squid asks for additional data, such as:

- A reverse DNS lookup: the hostname for a client's IP address
- An RFC 1413 ident query: the username associated with a client's TCP connection
- An authenticator: validating the user's credentials
- A forward DNS lookup: the origin server's IP address
- An external, user-defined ACL

Some access rules use fast checks out of necessity. For example, the *icp_access* rule is a fast check. It must be fast, to serve ICP queries quickly. Furthermore, certain ACL types, such as *proxy_auth*, are meaningless for ICP queries. The following access rules are fast checks:

- *header_access*
- *reply_body_max_size*
- *reply_access*
- *ident_lookup*
- *delay_access*
- *miss_access*
- *broken_posts*
- *icp_access*
- *cache_peer_access*
- *redirector_access*
- *snmp_access*

The following ACL types may require information from external sources (DNS, authenticators, etc.) and are thus incompatible with fast access rules:

- *srcdomain, dstdomain, srcdom_regex, dstdom_regex*
- *dst, dst_as*
- *proxy_auth*
- *ident*
- *external_acl_type*

This means, for example, that you can't reliably use an *ident* ACL in a *header_access* rule.

Common Scenarios

Because access controls can be complicated, this section contains a few examples. They demonstrate some of the common uses for access controls. You should be able to adapt them to your particular needs.

Allowing Local Clients Only

Almost every Squid installation should restrict access based on client IP addresses. This is one of the best ways to protect your system from abuses. The easiest way to do this is write an ACL that contains your IP address space and then allow HTTP requests for that ACL and deny all others:

```
acl All src 0/0
acl MyNetwork src 172.16.5.0/24 172.16.6.0/24

http_access allow MyNetwork
http_access deny All
```

Most likely, this access control configuration will be too simple, so you'll need to add more lines. Remember that the order of the *http_access* lines is important. Don't add anything after deny All. Instead, add the new rules before or after allow MyNetwork as necessary.

Blocking a Few Misbehaving Clients

For one reason or another, you may find it necessary to deny access for a particular client IP address. This can happen, for example, if an employee or student launches an aggressive web crawling agent that consumes too much bandwidth or other resources. Until you can stop the problem at the source, you can block the requests coming to Squid with this configuration:

```
acl All src 0/0
acl MyNetwork src 172.16.5.0/24 172.16.6.0/24
acl ProblemHost src 172.16.5.9

http_access deny ProblemHost
http_access allow MyNetwork
http_access deny All
```

Denying Pornography

Blocking access to certain content is a touchy subject. Often, the hardest part about using Squid to deny pornography is coming up with the list of sites that should be blocked. You may want to maintain such a list yourself, or get one from somewhere else. The "Access Controls" section of the Squid FAQ has links to freely available lists.

The ACL syntax for using such a list depends on its contents. If the list contains regular expressions, you probably want something like this:

```
acl PornSites url_regex "/usr/local/squid/etc/pornlist"
http_access deny PornSites
```

On the other hand, if the list contains origin server hostnames, simply change *url_regex* to *dstdomain* in this example.

Restricting Usage During Working Hours

Some corporations like to restrict web usage during working hours, either to save bandwidth, or because policy forbids employees from doing certain things while working. The hardest part about this is differentiating between appropriate and inappropriate use of the Internet during these times. Unfortunately, I can't help you with that. For this example, I'm assuming that you've somehow collected or acquired a list of web site domain names that are known to be inappropriate. The easy part is configuring Squid:

```
acl NotWorkRelated dstdomain "/usr/local/squid/etc/not-work-related-sites"
acl WorkingHours time D 08:00-17:30

http_access deny !WorkingHours NotWorkRelated
```

Notice that I've placed the !WorkingHours ACL first in the rule. The *dstdomain* ACL is expensive (comparing strings and traversing lists), but the *time* ACL is a simple inequality check.

Let's take this a step further and understand how to combine something like this with the source address controls described previously. Here's one way to do it:

```
acl All src 0/0
acl MyNetwork src 172.16.5.0/24 172.16.6.0/24
acl NotWorkRelated dstdomain "/usr/local/squid/etc/not-work-related-sites"
acl WorkingHours time D 08:00-17:30

http_access deny !WorkingHours NotWorkRelated
http_access allow MyNetwork
http_access deny All
```

This scheme works because it accomplishes our goal of denying certain requests during working hours and allowing requests only from your own network. However, it might be somewhat inefficient. Note that the NotWorkRelated ACL is searched for all requests, regardless of the source IP address. If that list is long, you'll waste CPU resources by searching it for requests from outside your network. Thus, you may want to change the rules around somewhat:

```
http_access deny !MyNetwork
http_access deny !WorkingHours NotWorkRelated
http_access Allow All
```

Here we've delayed the most expensive check until the very end. Outsiders that may be trying to abuse Squid will not be wasting your CPU cycles.

Preventing Squid from Talking to Non-HTTP Servers

You need to minimize the chance that Squid can communicate with certain types of TCP/IP servers. For example, people should never be able to use your Squid cache to relay SMTP (email) traffic. I covered this previously when introducing the *port* ACL. However, it is such an important part of your access controls that I'm presenting it here as well.

First of all, you have to worry about the CONNECT request method. User agents use this method to tunnel TCP connections through an HTTP proxy. It was invented for HTTP/TLS (a.k.a SSL) requests, and this remains the primary use for the CONNECT method. Some user-agents may also tunnel NNTP/TLS traffic through firewall proxies. All other uses should be rejected. Thus, you'll need an access list that allows CONNECT requests to HTTP/TLS and NNTP/TLS ports only.

Secondly, you should prevent Squid from connecting to certain services such as SMTP. You can either allow safe ports or deny dangerous ports. I'll give examples for both techniques.

Let's start with the rules present in the default *squid.conf* file:

```
acl Safe_ports port 80          # http
acl Safe_ports port 21          # ftp
acl Safe_ports port 443 563     # https, snews
acl Safe_ports port 70          # gopher
acl Safe_ports port 210         # wais
acl Safe_ports port 280         # http-mgmt
acl Safe_ports port 488         # gss-http
acl Safe_ports port 591         # filemaker
acl Safe_ports port 777         # multiling http
acl Safe_ports port 1025-65535  # unregistered ports

acl SSL_ports port 443 563
acl CONNECT method CONNECT

http_access deny !Safe_ports
http_access deny CONNECT !SSL_ports
<additional http_access lines as necessary...>
```

Our Safe_ports ACL lists all privileged ports (less than 1024) to which Squid may have valid reasons for connecting. It also lists the entire nonprivileged port range. Notice that the Safe_ports ACL includes the secure HTTP and NNTP ports (443 and 563) even though they also appear in the SSL_ports ACL. This is because the Safe_ ports ACL is checked first in the rules. If you swap the order of the first two http_ access lines, you could probably remove 443 and 563 from the Safe_ports list, but it's hardly worth the trouble.

The other way to approach this is to list the privileged ports that are known to be unsafe:

```
acl Dangerous_ports 7 9 19 22 23 25 53 109 110 119
acl SSL_ports port 443 563
acl CONNECT method CONNECT

http_access deny Dangerous_ports
http_access deny CONNECT !SSL_ports
<additional http_access lines as necessary...>
```

Don't worry if you're not familiar with all these strange port numbers. You can find out what each one is for by reading the */etc/services* file on a Unix system or by reading IANA's list of registered TCP/UDP port numbers at *http://www.iana.org/ assignments/port-numbers*.

Giving Certain Users Special Access

Organizations that employ username-based access controls often need to give certain users special privileges. In this simple example, there are three elements: all authenticated users, the usernames of the administrators, and a list of pornographic web sites. Normal users aren't allowed to view pornography, but the admins have the dubious job of maintaining the list. They need to connect to all servers to verify whether or not a particular site should be placed in the pornography list. Here's how to accomplish the task:

```
auth_param basic program /usr/local/squid/libexec/ncsa_auth
    /usr/local/squid/etc/passwd

acl Authenticated proxy_auth REQUIRED
acl Admins proxy_auth Pat Jean Chris
acl Porn dstdomain "/usr/local/squid/etc/porn.domains"
acl All src 0/0

http_access allow Admins
http_access deny Porn
http_access allow Authenticated
http_access deny All
```

Let's examine how this all works. First, there are three ACL definitions. The *Authenticated* ACL matches any valid proxy authentication credentials. The *Admins* ACL matches valid credentials from users Pat, Jean, and Chris. The *Porn* ACL matches certain origin server hostnames found in the *porn.domains* file.

This example has four access control rules. The first checks only the *Admins* ACL and allows all requests from Pat, Jean, and Chris. For other users, Squid moves on to the next rule. According to the second rule, a request is denied if its origin server hostname is in the *porn.domains* file. For requests that don't match the *Porn* ACL, Squid moves on to the third rule. Here, the request is allowed if it contains valid authentication credentials. The external authenticator (ncsa_auth in this case) is responsible for deciding whether or not the credentials are valid. If they aren't, the final rule applies, and the request is denied.

Note that the ncsa_auth authenticator isn't a requirement. You can use any of the numerous authentication helpers described in Chapter 12.

Preventing Abuse from Siblings

If you open up your cache to peer with other caches, you need to take additional precautions. Caches often use ICP to discover which objects are stored in their neighbors. You should accept ICP queries only from known and approved neighbors.

Furthermore, you can configure Squid to enforce a sibling relationship by using the miss_access rule list. Squid checks these rules only when forwarding cache misses, never cache hits. Thus, all requests must first pass the http_access rules before the miss_access list comes into play.

In this example, there are three separate ACLs. One is for the local users that connect directly to this cache. Another is for a child cache, which is allowed to forward requests that are cache misses. The third is a sibling cache, which must never forward a request that results in a cache miss. Here's how it all works:

```
alc All src 0/0
acl OurUsers src 172.16.5.0/24
acl ChildCache src 192.168.1.1
acl SiblingCache src 192.168.3.3

http_access allow OurUsers
http_access allow ChildCache
http_access allow SiblingCache
http_access deny All

miss_access deny SiblingCache

icp_access allow ChildCache
icp_access allow SiblingCache
icp_access deny All
```

Denying Requests with IP Addresses

As I mentioned in the "dstdomain" section, the *dstdomain* type is good for blocking access to specific origin servers. However, clever users might be able to get around the rule by replacing URL hostnames with their IP addresses. If you are desperate to stop such requests, you may want to block all requests that contain an IP address.

You can do so with a redirector (see Chapter 11) or with a semicomplicated *dstdom_regex* ACL like this:

```
acl IPForHostname dstdom_regex ^[0-9]+\.[0-9]+\.[0-9]+\.[0-9]+$
http_access deny IPForHostname
```

An http_reply_access Example

Recall that the response's content type is the only new information available when Squid checks the *http_reply_access* rules. Thus, you can keep the *http_reply_access* rules very simple. You need only check the *rep_mime_type* ACLs. For example, here's how you can deny responses with certain content types:

```
acl All src 0/0
acl Movies rep_mime_type video/mpeg
acl MP3s rep_mime_type audio/mpeg
http_reply_access deny Movies
http_reply_access deny MP3s
http_reply_access allow All
```

You don't need to repeat your *http_access* rules in the *http_reply_access* list. The *allow All* rule shown here doesn't mean that all requests to Squid are allowed. Any request that is denied by *http_access* never makes it to the stage where Squid checks the *http_reply_access* rules.

Preventing Cache Hits for Local Sites

If you have a number of origin servers on your network, you may want to configure Squid so that their responses are never cached. Because the servers are nearby, they don't benefit too much from cache hits. Additionally, it frees up storage space for other (far away) origin servers.

The first step is to define an ACL for the local servers. You might want to use an address-based ACL, such as *dst*:

```
acl LocalServers dst 172.17.1.0/24
```

If the servers don't live on a single subnet, you might find it easier to create a *dstdomain* ACL:

```
acl LocalServers dstdomain .example.com
```

Next, you simply deny caching of those servers with a *no_cache* access rule:

```
no_cache deny LocalServers
```

The *no_cache* rules don't prevent your clients from sending these requests to Squid. There is nothing you can configure in Squid to stop such requests from coming. Instead, you must configure the user-agents themselves.

If you add a *no_cache* rule after Squid has been running for a while, the cache may contain some objects that match the new rule. Prior to Squid Version 2.5, these previously cached objects might be returned as cache hits. Now, however, Squid purges any cached response for a request that matches a *no_cache* rule.

Testing Access Controls

As your access control configuration becomes longer, it also becomes more complicated. I strongly encourage you to test your access controls before turning them loose on a production server. Of course, the first thing you should do is make sure that Squid can correctly parse your configuration file. Use the -k parse feature for this:

```
% squid -k parse
```

To further test your access controls, you may need to set up a fake Squid installation. One easy way to do that is compile another copy of the Squid source code with a different *$prefix* location. For example:

```
% tar xzvf squid-2.5.STABLE4.tar.gz
% cd squid-2.5.STABLE4
% ./configure --prefix=/tmp/squid ...
% make && make install
```

After installing, you need to edit the new *squid.conf* file and change a few directives. Change *http_port* if Squid is already running on the default port. For simple testing, create a single, small cache directory like this:

```
cache_dir ufs /tmp/squid/cache 100 4 4
```

If you don't want to recompile Squid again, you can also just create a new configuration file. The drawback to this approach is that you'll need to set all the log-file pathnames to the temporary location so that you don't overwrite the real files.

You can easily test some access controls with the squidclient program. For example, if you have a rule that depends on the origin server hostname (*dstdomain* ACL), or some part of the URL (*url_regex* or *urlpath_regex*), simply enter a URI that you would expect to be allowed or denied:

```
% squidclient -p 4128 http://blocked.host.name/blah/blah
```

or:

```
% squidclient -p 4128 http://some.host.name/blocked.ext
```

Certain aspects of the request are harder to control. If you have *src* ACLs that block requests from outside your network, you may need to actually test them from an external host. Testing *time* ACLs may be difficult unless you can change the clock on your system or stay awake long enough.

You can use squidclient's -H option to set arbitrary request headers. For example, use the following if you need to test a *browser* ACL.

```
% squidclient -p 4128 http://www.host.name/blah \
    -H 'User-Agent: Mozilla/5.0 (compatible; Konqueror/3)\r\n'
```

For more complicated request, with many headers, you may want to use the technique described in Chapter 16.

You might also consider developing a routine *cron* job that checks your ACLs for expected behavior and reports any anomalies. Here is a sample shell script to get you started:

```
#!/bin/sh
set -e

TESTHOST="www.squid-cache.org"

# make sure Squid is not proxying dangerous ports
#
ST=`squidclient 'http://$TESTHOST:25/' | head -1 | awk '{print $2}'`
if test "$ST" != 403 ; then
        echo "Squid did not block HTTP request to port 25"
fi


# make sure Squid requires user authentication
#
ST=`squidclient 'http://$TESTHOST/' | head -1 | awk '{print $2}'`
if test "$ST" != 407 ; then
        echo "Squid allowed request without proxy authentication"
fi


# make sure Squid denies requests from foreign IP addresses
# elsewhere we already created an alias 192.168.1.1 on one of
# the system interfaces
#
EXT_ADDR=192.168.1.1
ST=`squidclient -l $EXT_ADDR 'http://$TESTHOST/' | head -1 | awk '{print $2}'`
if test "$ST" != 403 ; then
        echo "Squid allowed request from external address $EXT_ADDR"
fi

exit 0
```

Exercises

- Define an ACL for each known type (*src*, *dst*, *ident*, etc.) and write a rule that uses all of them.

- Intentionally mistype the name of an ACL in one of your rules. Does **squid -k parse** catch the error? Does Squid start anyway?

- Write an *http_access* that uses slow ACLs, like *srcdomain* or *ident*. Time how long Squid takes to serve a request with and without the slow ACL checks.

CHAPTER 7
Disk Cache Basics

I'm going to talk a lot about disk storage and filesystems in this chapter. It is important to make sure you understand the difference between two related things: disk filesystems and Squid's storage schemes.

Filesystems are features of particular operating systems. Almost every Unix variant has an implementation of the Unix File System (UFS). It is also sometimes known as the Berkeley Fast File System (FFS). Linux's default filesystem is called *ext2fs*. Many operating systems also support newer filesystem technologies. These include names and acronyms such as *advfs*, *xfs*, and *reiserfs*.

Programs (such as Squid) interact with filesystems via a handful of system calls. These are functions such as open( ), close( ), read( ), write( ), stat( ), and unlink( ). The arguments to these system calls are either pathnames (strings) or file descriptors (integers). Filesystem implementation details are hidden from programs. They typically use internal data structures such as inodes, but Squid doesn't know about that.

Squid has a number of different storage schemes. The schemes have different properties and techniques for organizing and accessing cache data on the disk. Most of them use the filesystem interface system calls (e.g., open( ), write( ), etc.).

Squid has five different storage schemes: *ufs*, *aufs*, *diskd*, *coss*, and *null*. The first three use the same directory layout, and they are thus interchangeable. *coss* is an attempt to implement a new filesystem specifically optimized for Squid. *null* is a minimal implementation of the API: it doesn't actually read or write data to/from the disk.

 Due to a poor choice of names, "UFS" might refer to either the Unix filesystem or the Squid storage scheme. To be clear here, I'll write the filesystem as UFS and the storage scheme as *ufs*.

The remainder of this chapter focuses on the *squid.conf* directives that control the disk cache. This includes replacement policies, object removal, and freshness controls. For the most part, I'll only talk about the default storage scheme: *ufs*. We'll get to the alternative schemes and other tricks in the next chapter.

The cache_dir Directive

The *cache_dir* directive is one of the most important in *squid.conf*. It tells Squid where and how to store cache files on disk. The *cache_dir* directive takes the following arguments:

```
cache_dir scheme directory size L1 L2 [options]
```

Scheme

Squid supports a number of different storage schemes. The default (and original) is *ufs*. Depending on your operating system, you may be able to select other schemes. You must use the --enable-storeio=*LIST* option with ./configure to compile the optional code for other storage schemes. I'll discuss *aufs*, *diskd*, *coss*, and *null* in Chapter 8. For now, I'll only talk about the *ufs* scheme, which is compatible with *aufs* and *diskd*.

Directory

The *directory* argument is a filesystem directory, under which Squid stores cached objects. Normally, a *cache_dir* corresponds to a whole filesystem or disk partition. It usually doesn't make sense to put more than one cache directory on a single filesystem partition. Furthermore, I also recommend putting only one cache directory on each physical disk drive. For example, if you have two unused hard drives, you might do something like this:

```
# newfs /dev/da1d
# newfs /dev/da2d
# mount /dev/da1d /cache0
# mount /dev/da2d /cache1
```

And then add these lines to *squid.conf*:

```
cache_dir ufs /cache0 7000 16 256
cache_dir ufs /cache1 7000 16 256
```

If you don't have any spare hard drives, you can, of course, use an existing filesystem partition. Select one with plenty of free space, perhaps */usr* or */var*, and create a new directory there. For example:

```
# mkdir /var/squidcache
```

Then add a line like this to *squid.conf*:

```
cache_dir ufs /var/squidcache 7000 16 256
```

Size

The third *cache_dir* argument specifies the size of the cache directory. This is an upper limit on the amount of disk space that Squid can use for the *cache_dir*. Calculating an appropriate value can be tricky. You lose some space to filesystem overheads, and you must leave enough free space for temporary files and *swap.state* logs (see Chapter 13). I recommend mounting the empty filesystem and running df:

```
% df -k
Filesystem  1K-blocks    Used    Avail Capacity  Mounted on
/dev/da1d    3037766       8  2794737     0%     /cache0
/dev/da2d    3037766       8  2794737     0%     /cache1
```

Here you can see that the filesystem has about 2790 MB of available space. Remember that UFS reserves some "minfree" space, 8% in this case, which is why Squid can't use the full 3040 MB in the filesystem.

You might be tempted just to put 2790 on the *cache_dir* line. You might even to get away with it if your cache isn't very busy and if you rotate the log files often. To be safe, however, I recommend taking off another 10% or so. This extra space will be used by Squid's *swap.state* file and temporary files.

Note that the *cache_swap_low* directive also affects how much space Squid uses. I'll talk about the low and high watermarks in the "Disk Space Watermarks" section.

The bottom line is that you should initially be conservative about the size of your *cache_dir*. Start off with a low estimate and allow the cache to fill up. After Squid runs for a week or so with full cache directories, you'll be in a good position to re-evaluate the size settings. If you have plenty of free space, feel free to increase the cache directory size in increments of a few percent.

Inodes

Inodes are fundamental building blocks of Unix filesystems. They contain information about disk files, such as permissions, ownership, size, and timestamps. If your filesystem runs out of inodes, you can't create new files, even if it has space available. Running out of inodes is bad, so you may want to make sure you have enough before running Squid.

The programs that create new filesystems (e.g., *newfs* or *mkfs*) reserve some number of inodes based on the total size. These programs usually allow you to set the ratio of inodes to disk space. For example, see the -i option in the *newfs* and *mkfs* manpages. The ratio of disk space to inodes determines the mean file size the filesystem can support. Most Unix systems create one inode for each 4 KB, which is usually sufficient for Squid. Research shows that, for most caching proxies, the mean file size is about 10 KB. You may be able to get away with 8 KB per inode, but it is risky.

You can monitor your system's inode usage with df -i. For example:

```
% df -ik
Filesystem  1K-blocks      Used    Avail Capacity  iused    ifree  %iused  Mounted on
/dev/ad0s1a    197951     57114   125001     31%     1413    52345     3%  /
/dev/ad0s1f   5004533   2352120  2252051     51%   129175  1084263    11%  /usr
/dev/ad0s1e    396895      6786   358358      2%      205    99633     0%  /var
/dev/da0d     8533292   7222148   628481     92%   430894   539184    44%  /cache1
/dev/da1d     8533292   7181645   668984     91%   430272   539806    44%  /cache2
/dev/da2d     8533292   7198600   652029     92%   434726   535352    45%  /cache3
/dev/da3d     8533292   7208948   641681     92%   427866   542212    44%  /cache4
```

As long as the inode usage (%iused) is less than the space usage (Capacity), you're in good shape. Unfortunately, you can't add more inodes to an existing filesystem. If you find that you are running out of inodes, you need to stop Squid and recreate your filesystems. If you're not willing to do that, decrease the *cache_dir* size instead.

The relationship between disk space and process size

Squid's disk space usage directly affects its memory usage as well. Every object that exists on disk requires a small amount of memory. Squid uses the memory as an index to the on-disk data. If you add a new cache directory or otherwise increase the disk cache size, make sure that you also have enough free memory. Squid's performance degrades very quickly if its process size reaches or exceeds your system's physical memory capacity.

Every object in Squid's cache directories takes either 76 or 112 bytes of memory, depending on your system. The memory is allocated as *StoreEntry*, *MD5 Digest*, and *LRU policy node* structures. Small-pointer (i.e., 32-bit) systems, like those based on the Intel Pentium, take 76 bytes. On systems with CPUs that support 64-bit pointers, each object takes 112 bytes. You can find out how much memory these structures use on your system by viewing the Memory Utilization page of the cache manager (see Chapter 14).

Unfortunately, it is difficult to predict precisely how much additional memory is required for a given amount of disk space. It depends on the mean reply size, which typically fluctuates over time. Additionally, Squid uses memory for many other data structures and purposes. Don't assume that your estimates are, or will remain, correct. You should constantly monitor Squid's process size and consider shrinking the cache size if necessary.

L1 and L2

For the *ufs*, *aufs*, and *diskd* schemes, Squid creates a two-level directory tree underneath the cache directory. The L1 and L2 arguments specify the number of first- and second-level directories. The defaults are 16 and 256, respectively. Figure 7-1 shows the filesystem structure.

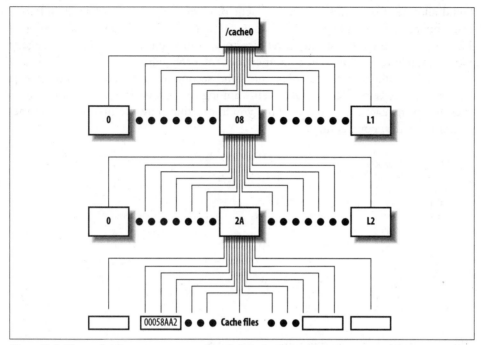

Figure 7-1. The cache directory structure for ufs-based storage schemes

Some people think that Squid performs better, or worse, depending on the particular values for L1 and L2. It seems to make sense, intuitively, that small directories can be searched faster than large ones. Thus, L1 and L2 should probably be large enough so that each L2 directory has no more than a few hundred files.

For example, let's say you have a cache directory that stores about 7000 MB. Given a mean file size of 10 KB, you can store about 700,000 files in this *cache_dir*. With 16 L1 and 256 L2 directories, there are 4096 total second-level directories. 700,000 ÷ 4096 leaves about 170 files in each second-level directory.

The process of creating swap directories with squid -z, goes faster for smaller values of L1 and L2. Thus, if your cache size is really small, you may want to reduce the number of L1 and L2 directories.

Squid assigns each cache object a unique *file number*. This is a 32-bit integer that uniquely identifies files on disk. Squid uses a relatively simple algorithm for turning file numbers into pathnames. The algorithm uses L1 and L2 as parameters. Thus, if you change L1 and L2, you change the mapping from file number to pathname. Changing these parameters for a nonempty *cache_dir* makes the existing files inaccessible. You should never change L1 and L2 after the cache directory has become active.

Squid allocates file numbers within a cache directory sequentially. The file number-to-pathname algorithm (e.g., `storeUfsDirFullPath( )`) is written so that each group of L2 files go into the same second-level directory. Squid does this to take advantage of locality of reference. This algorithm increases the probability that an HTML file and its embedded images are stored in the same second-level directory. Some people expect Squid to spread cache files evenly among the second-level directories. However, when the cache is initially filling, you'll find that only the first few directories contain any files. For example:

```
% cd /cache0; du -k
2164    ./00/00
2146    ./00/01
2689    ./00/02
1974    ./00/03
2201    ./00/04
2463    ./00/05
2724    ./00/06
3174    ./00/07
1144    ./00/08
1       ./00/09
1       ./00/0A
1       ./00/0B
...
```

This is perfectly normal and nothing to worry about.

Options

Squid has two scheme-independent *cache_dir* options: a read-only flag and a max-size value.

read-only

The read-only option instructs Squid to continue reading from the *cache_dir*, but to stop storing new objects there. It looks like this in *squid.conf*:

```
cache_dir ufs /cache0 7000 16 256 read-only
```

You might use this option if you want to migrate your cache storage from one disk to another. If you simply add one *cache_dir* and remove another, Squid's hit ratio decreases sharply. You can still get cache hits from the old location when it is read-only. After some time, you can remove the read-only cache directory from the configuration.

max-size

With this option, you can specify the maximum object size to be stored in the cache directory. For example:

```
cache_dir ufs /cache0 7000 16 256 max-size=1048576
```

Note that the value is in bytes. In most situations, you shouldn't need to add this option. If you do, try to put the *cache_dir* lines in order of increasing max-size.

Disk Space Watermarks

The *cache_swap_low* and *cache_swap_high* directives control the replacement of objects stored on disk. Their values are a percentage of the maximum cache size, which comes from the sum of all *cache_dir* sizes. For example:

```
cache_swap_low 90
cache_swap_high 95
```

As long as the total disk usage is below *cache_swap_low*, Squid doesn't remove cached objects. As the cache size increases, Squid becomes more aggressive about removing objects. Under steady-state conditions, you should find that disk usage stays relatively close to the *cache_swap_low* value. You can see the current disk usage by requesting the *storedir* page from the cache manager (see Chapter 14).

Note that changing *cache_swap_high* probably won't have a big impact on Squid's disk usage. In earlier versions of Squid, this parameter played a more important role; now, however, it doesn't.

Object Size Limits

You can control both the maximum and minimum size of cached objects. Responses larger than *maximum_object_size* aren't stored on disk. They are still proxied, however. The logic behind this directive is that you don't want a really big response to take up space better utilized by many small responses. The syntax is as follows:

```
maximum_object_size size-specification
```

Here are some examples:

```
maximum_object_size 100 KB
maximum_object_size 1 MB
maximum_object_size 12382 bytes
maximum_object_size 2 GB
```

Squid checks the response size in two different ways. If the reply includes a Content-Length header, Squid compares its value to the *maximum_object_size* value. If the content length is the larger of the two numbers, the object becomes immediately uncachable and never consumes any disk space.

Unfortunately, not every response has a Content-Length header. In this case, Squid writes the response to disk as data comes in from the origin server. Squid checks the object size again only when the response is complete. Thus, if the object's size reaches the *maximum_object_size* limit, it continues consuming disk space. Squid increments the total cache size only when it is done reading a response.

In other words, the active, or in-transit, objects don't contribute to the cache size value Squid maintains internally. This is good because it means Squid won't remove other objects in the cache, unless the object remains cachable and then contributes to the total cache size. However, it is also bad because Squid may run out of free disk space if the reply is very large. To reduce the chance of this happening, you should also use the *reply_body_max_size* directive. A response that reaches the *reply_body_max_size* limit is cut off immediately.

Squid also has a *minimum_object_size* directive. It allows you to place a lower limit on the size of cached objects. Responses smaller than this size aren't stored on disk or in memory. Note that this size is compared to the response's content length (i.e., the size of the reply body), which excludes the HTTP headers.

Allocating Objects to Cache Directories

When Squid wants to store a cachable response on disk, it calls a function that selects one of the cache directories. It then opens a disk file for writing on the selected directory. If, for some reason, the open() call fails, the response isn't stored. In this case, Squid doesn't try opening a disk file on one of the other cache directories.

Squid has two of these *cache_dir* selection algorithms. The default algorithm is called least-load; the alternative is round-robin.

The least-load algorithm, as the name implies, selects that cache directory that currently has the smallest workload. The notion of load depends on the underlying storage scheme. For the *aufs*, *coss*, and *diskd* schemes, the load is related to the number of pending operations. For *ufs*, the load is constant. For cases in which all *cache_dirs* have equal load, the algorithm uses free space and maximum object sizes as tiebreakers.

The selection algorithm also takes into account the max-size and read-only options. Squid skips a cache directory if it knows the object size is larger than the limit. It also always skips any read-only directories.

The round-robin algorithm also uses load measurements. It always selects the next cache directory in the list (subject to max-size and read-only), as long as its load is less than 100%.

Under some circumstances, Squid may fail to select a cache directory. This can happen if all *cache_dirs* are overloaded or if all have max-size limits less than the size of the object. In this case, Squid simply doesn't write the object to disk. You can use the cache manager to track the number of times Squid fails to select a cache directory. View the *store_io* page (see Chapter 14), and find the create.select_fail line.

Replacement Policies

The *cache_replacement_policy* directive controls the replacement policy for Squid's disk cache. Version 2.5 offers three different replacement policies: least recently used (LRU), greedy dual-size frequency (GDSF), and least frequently used with dynamic aging (LFUDA).

LRU is the default policy, not only for Squid, but for most other caching products as well. LRU is a popular choice because it is almost trivial to implement and provides very good performance. On 32-bit systems, LRU uses slightly less memory than the others (12 versus 16 bytes per object). On 64-bit systems, all policies use 24 bytes per object.

Over the years, many researchers have proposed alternatives to LRU. These other policies are typically designed to optimize a specific characteristic of the cache, such as response time, hit ratio, or byte hit ratio. While the research almost always shows an improvement, the results can be misleading. Some of the studies use unrealistically small cache sizes. Other studies show that as cache size increases, the choice of replacement policy becomes less important.

If you want to use the GDSF or LFUDA policies, you must pass the --enable-removal-policies option to the ./configure script (see Chapter 3). Martin Arlitt and John Dilley of HP Labs wrote the GDSF and LFUDA implementation for Squid. You can read their paper online at *http://www.hpl.hp.com/techreports/1999/HPL-1999-69.html*. My O'Reilly book, *Web Caching*, also talks about these algorithms.

The *cache_replacement_policy* directive is unique in an important way. Unlike most of the other *squid.conf* directives, the location of this one is significant. The *cache_replacment_policy* value is actually used when Squid parses a *cache_dir* directive. You can change the replacement policy for a *cache_dir* by setting the replacement policy beforehand. For example:

```
cache_replacement_policy lru
cache_dir ufs /cache0 2000 16 32
cache_dir ufs /cache1 2000 16 32
cache_replacement_policy heap GDSF
cache_dir ufs /cache2 2000 16 32
cache_dir ufs /cache3 2000 16 32
```

In this case, the first two cache directories use LRU replacement, and the second two use GDSF. This characteristic of the *replacement_policy* directive is important to keep in mind if you ever decide to use the *config* option of the cache manager (see Chapter 14). The cache manager outputs only one (the last) replacement policy value, and places it before all of the cache directories. For example, you may have these lines in *squid.conf*:

```
cache_replacement_policy heap GDSF
cache_dir ufs /tmp/cache1 10 4 4
```

```
cache_replacement_policy lru
cache_dir ufs /tmp/cache2 10 4 4
```

but when you select *config* from the cache manager, you get:

```
cache_replacement_policy lru
cache_dir ufs /tmp/cache1 10 4 4
cache_dir ufs /tmp/cache2 10 4 4
```

As you can see, the heap GDSF setting for the first cache directory has been lost.

Removing Cached Objects

At some point you may find it necessary to manually remove one or more objects from Squid's cache. This might happen if:

- One of your users complains about always receiving stale data.
- Your cache becomes "poisoned" with a forged response.
- Squid's cache index becomes corrupted after experiencing disk I/O errors or frequent crashes and restarts.
- You want to remove some large objects to free up room for new data.
- Squid was caching responses from local servers, and now you don't want it to.

Some of these problems can be solved by forcing a reload in a web browser. However, this doesn't always work. For example, some browsers display certain content types externally by launching another program; that program probably doesn't have a reload button or even know about caches.

You can always use the squidclient program to reload a cached object if necessary. Simply insert the -r option before the URI:

```
% squidclient -r http://www.lrrr.org/junk >/tmp/foo
```

If you happen to have a *refresh_pattern* directive with the ignore-reload option set, you and your users may be unable to force a validation of the cached response. In that case, you'll be better off purging the offending object or objects.

Removing Individual Objects

Squid accepts a custom request method for removing cached objects. The PURGE method isn't one of the official HTTP request methods. It is different from DELETE, which Squid forwards to an origin server. A PURGE request asks Squid to remove the object given in the URI. Squid returns either 200 (Ok) or 404 (Not Found).

The PURGE method is somewhat dangerous because it removes cached objects. Squid disables the PURGE method unless you define an ACL for it. Normally you should allow PURGE requests only from localhost and perhaps a small number of trusted hosts. The configuration may look like this:

```
acl AdminBoxes src 127.0.0.1 172.16.0.1 192.168.0.1
acl Purge method PURGE
http_access allow AdminBoxes Purge
http_access deny Purge
```

The squidclient program provides an easy way to generate PURGE requests. For example:

```
% squidclient -m PURGE http://www.lrrr.org/junk
```

Alternatively, you could use something else (such as a Perl script) to generate your own HTTP request. It can be very simple:

```
PURGE http://www.lrrr.org/junk HTTP/1.0
Accept: */*
```

Note that a URI alone doesn't uniquely identify a cached response. Squid also uses the original request method in the cache key. It may also use other request headers if the response contains a Vary header. When you issue a PURGE request, Squid looks for cached objects originally requested with the GET and HEAD methods. Furthermore, Squid also removes all variants of a response, unless you remove a specific variant by including the appropriate headers in the PURGE request. Squid removes only variants for GET and HEAD requests.

Removing a Group of Objects

Unfortunately, Squid doesn't provide a good mechanism for removing a bunch of objects at once. This often comes up when someone wants to remove all objects belonging to a certain origin server.

Squid lacks this feature for a couple of reasons. First, Squid would have to perform a linear search through all cached objects. This is CPU-intensive and takes a long time. While Squid is searching, your users can experience a performance degradation. Second, Squid keeps MD5s, rather than URIs, in memory. MD5s are one-way hashes, which means, for example, that you can't tell if a given MD5 hash was generated from a URI that contains the string "www.example.com." The only way to know is to recalculate the MD5 from the original URI and see if they match. Because Squid doesn't have the URI, it can't perform the calculation.

So what can you do?

You can use the data in *access.log* to get a list of URIs that might be in the cache. Then, feed them to squidclient or another utility to generate PURGE requests. For example:

```
% awk '{print $7}' /usr/local/squid/var/logs/access.log \
        | grep www.example.com \
        | xargs -n 1 squidclient -m PURGE
```

Removing All Objects

In extreme circumstances you may need to wipe out the entire cache, or at least one of the cache directories. First, you must make sure that Squid isn't running.

One of the easiest ways to make Squid forget about all cached objects is to overwrite the *swap.state* files. Note that you can't simply remove the *swap.state* files because Squid then scans the cache directories and opens all the object files. You also can't simply truncate *swap.state* to a zero-sized file. Instead, you should put a single byte there, like this:

```
# echo '' > /usr/local/squid/var/cache/swap.state
```

When Squid reads the *swap.state* file, it gets an error because the record that should be there is too short. The next read results in an end-of-file condition, and Squid completes the rebuild procedure without loading any object metadata.

Note that this technique doesn't remove the cache files from your disk. You've only tricked Squid into thinking that the cache is empty. As Squid runs, it adds new files to the cache and may overwrite the old files. In some cases, this might cause your disk to run out of free space. If that happens to you, you need to remove the old files before restarting Squid again.

One way to remove cache files is with rm. However, it often takes a very long time to remove all the files that Squid has created. To get Squid running faster, you can rename the cache directory, create a new one, start Squid, and remove the old one at the same time. For example:

```
# squid -k shutdown
# cd /usr/local/squid/var
# mv cache oldcache
# mkdir cache
# chown nobody:nobody cache
# squid -z
# squid -s
# rm -rf oldcache &
```

Another technique is to simply run newfs (or mkfs) on the cache filesystem. This works only if you have the *cache_dir* on its own disk partition.

refresh_pattern

The *refresh_pattern* directive controls the disk cache only indirectly. It helps Squid decide whether or not a given request can be a cache hit or must be treated as a miss. Liberal settings increase your cache hit ratio but also increase the chance that users receive a stale response. Conservative settings, on the other hand, decrease hit ratios and stale responses.

The *refresh_pattern* rules apply only to responses without an explicit expiration time. Origin servers can specify an expiration time with either the Expires header, or the Cache-Control: max-age directive.

You can put any number of *refresh_pattern* lines in the configuration file. Squid searches them in order for a regular expression match. When Squid finds a match, it uses the corresponding values to determine whether a cached response is fresh or stale. The *refresh_pattern* syntax is as follows:

```
refresh_pattern [-i] regexp min percent max [options]
```

For example:

```
refresh_pattern -i \.jpg$ 30 50% 4320 reload-into-ims
refresh_pattern -i \.png$ 30 50% 4320 reload-into-ims
refresh_pattern -i \.htm$ 0 20% 1440
refresh_pattern -i \.html$ 0 20% 1440
refresh_pattern -i . 5 25% 2880
```

The *regexp* parameter is a regular expression that is normally case-sensitive. You can make them case-insensitive with the -i option. Squid checks the *refresh_pattern* lines in order; it stops searching when one of the regular expression patterns matches the URI.

The *min* parameter is some number of minutes. It is, essentially, a lower bound on stale responses. A response can't be stale unless its time in the cache exceeds the minimum value. Similarly, *max* is an upper limit on fresh responses. A response can't be fresh unless its time in the cache is less than the maximum time.

Responses that fall between the minimum and maximum are subject to Squid's *last-modified factor* (LM-factor) algorithm. For such responses, Squid calculates the response age and the LM-factor and compares it to the *percent* value. The response age is simply the amount of time passed since the origin server generated, or last validated, the response. The resource age is the difference between the Last-Modified and Date headers. The LM-factor is the ratio of the response age to the resource age.

Figure 7-2 demonstrates the LM-factor algorithm. Squid caches an object that is 3 hours old (based on the Date and Last-Modified headers). With an LM-factor value of 50%, the response will be fresh for the next 1.5 hours, after which the object expires and is considered stale. If a user requests the cached object during the fresh period, Squid returns an unvalidated cache hit. For a request that occurs during the stale period, Squid forwards a validation request to the origin server.

It's important to understand the order that Squid checks the various values. Here is a simplified description of Squid's *refresh_pattern* algorithm:

- The response is stale if the response age is greater than the *refresh_pattern max* value.

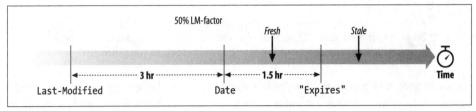

Figure 7-2. Calculating expiration times based on LM-factor

- The response is fresh if the LM-factor is less than the *refresh_pattern percent* value.
- The response is fresh if the response age is less than the *refresh_pattern min* value.
- Otherwise, the response is stale.

The *refresh_pattern* directive also has a handful of options that cause Squid to disobey the HTTP protocol specification. They are as follows:

override-expire

When set, this option causes Squid to check the *min* value before checking the Expires header. Thus, a non-zero *min* time makes Squid return an unvalidated cache hit even if the response is preexpired.

override-lastmod

When set, this option causes Squid to check the *min* value before the LM-factor percentage.

reload-into-ims

When set, this option makes Squid transform a request with a no-cache directive into a validation (If-Modified-Since) request. In other words, Squid adds an If-Modified-Since header to the request before forwarding it on. Note that this only works for objects that have a Last-Modified timestamp. The outbound request retains the no-cache directive, so that it reaches the origin server.

ignore-reload

When set, this option causes Squid to ignore the no-cache directive, if any, in the request.

Exercises

- Run **df** on your existing filesystems and calculate the ratio of inodes to disk space. If any of those partitions are used for Squid's disk cache, do you think you'll run out of space, or inodes first?
- Try to intentionally make Squid run out of disk space on a cache directory. How does Squid deal with this situation?

- Write a shell script to search the cache for given URIs and optionally remove them.
- Examine Squid's *store.log* and estimate the percentage of requests that are subject to the *refresh_pattern* rules.
- Can you think of any negative side effects of the `ignore-reload`, `override-expire`, and related options?

CHAPTER 8
Advanced Disk Cache Topics

Performance is one of the biggest concerns for Squid administrators. As the load placed on Squid increases, disk I/O is typically the primary bottleneck. The reason for this performance limitation is due to the importance that Unix filesystems place on consistency after a system crash.

By default, Squid uses a relatively simple storage scheme (*ufs*). All disk I/O is performed by the main Squid process. With traditional Unix filesystems, certain operations always block the calling process. For example, calling open( ) on the Unix Fast Filesystem (UFS) causes the operating system to allocate and initialize certain on-disk data structures. The system call doesn't return until these I/O operations complete, which may take longer than you'd like if the disks are already busy with other tasks.

Under heavy load, these filesystem operations can block the Squid process for small, but significant, amounts of time. The point at which the filesystem becomes a bottleneck depends on many different factors, including:

- The number of disk drives
- The rotational speed and seek time of your hard drives
- The type of disk drive interface (ATA, SCSI)
- Filesystem tuning options
- The number of files and percentage of free space

Do I Have a Disk I/O Bottleneck?

Web caches such as Squid don't usually come right out and tell you when disk I/O is becoming a bottleneck. Instead, response time and/or hit ratio degrade as load increases. The tricky thing is that response time and hit ratio may be changing for other reasons, such as increased network latency and changes in client request patterns.

Perhaps the best way to explore the performance limits of your cache is with a benchmark, such as Web Polygraph. The good thing about a benchmark is that you can fully control the environment and eliminate many unknowns. You can also repeat the same experiment with different cache configurations. Unfortunately, benchmarking often takes a lot of time and requires spare systems that aren't already being used.

If you have the resources to benchmark Squid, begin with a standard caching workload. As you increase the load, at some point you should see a significant increase in response time and/or a decrease in hit ratio. Once you observe this performance degradation, run the experiment again but with disk caching disabled. You can configure Squid never to cache any response (with the *null* storage scheme, see the later section "The null Storage Scheme"). Alternatively, you can configure the workload to have 100% uncachable responses. If the average response time is significantly better without caching, you can be relatively certain that disk I/O is a bottleneck at that level of throughput.

If you're like most people, you have neither the time nor resources to benchmark Squid. In this case, you can examine Squid's runtime statistics to look for disk I/O bottlenecks. The cache manager General Runtime Information page (see Chapter 14) gives you median response times for both cache hits and misses:

```
Median Service Times (seconds)  5 min    60 min:
        HTTP Requests (All):   0.39928  0.35832
        Cache Misses:          0.42149  0.39928
        Cache Hits:            0.12783  0.11465
        Near Hits:             0.37825  0.39928
        Not-Modified Replies:  0.07825  0.07409
```

For a healthy Squid cache, hits are significantly faster than misses. Your median hit response time should usually be 0.5 seconds or less. I strongly recommend that you use SNMP or another network monitoring tool to collect periodic measurements from your Squid caches (see Chapter 14). A significant (factor of two) increase in median hit response time is a good indication that you have a disk I/O bottleneck.

If you believe your production cache is suffering in this manner, you can test your theory with the same technique mentioned previously. Configure Squid not to cache any responses, thus avoiding all disk I/O. Then closely observe the *cache miss* response time. If it goes down, your theory is probably correct.

Once you've convinced yourself that disk throughput is limiting Squid's performance, you can try a number of things to improve it. Some of these require recompiling Squid, while others are relatively simple steps you can take to tune the Unix filesystems.

Filesystem Tuning Options

First of all, you should never use RAID for Squid cache directories. In my experience, RAID always degrades filesystem performance for Squid. It is much better to have a number of separate filesystems, each dedicated to a single disk drive.

I have found four simple ways to improve UFS performance for Squid. Some of these are specific to certain operating systems, such as BSD and Linux, and may not be available on your platform:

- Some UFS implementations support a *noatime* mount option. Filesystems mounted with *noatime* don't update the inode access time value for reads. The easiest way to use this option is to add it to the */etc/fstab* like this:

  ```
  # Device        Mountpoint    FStype  Options        Dump   Pass#
  /dev/ad1s1c     /cache0       ufs     rw,noatime     0      0
  ```

- Check your mount(8) manpage for the *async* option. With this option set, certain I/O operations (such as directory updates) may be performed asynchronously. The documentation for some systems notes that it is a dangerous flag. Should your system crash, you may lose the entire filesystem. For many installations, the performance improvement is worth the risk. You should use this option only if you don't mind losing the contents of your entire cache. If the cached data is very valuable, the *async* option is probably not for you.

- BSD has a feature called *soft updates*. Soft updates are BSD's alternative to journaling filesystems.[*] On FreeBSD, you can enable this option on an unmounted filesystem with the tunefs command:

  ```
  # umount /cache0
  # tunefs -n enable /cache0
  # mount /cache0
  ```

  You only have to run the tunefs once for each filesystem. Soft updates are automatically enabled on the filesystem again when your system reboots.

  On OpenBSD and NetBSD, you can use the *softdep* mount option:

  ```
  # Device        Mountpoint    FStype  Options        Dump   Pass#
  /dev/sd0f       /usr          ffs     rw,softdep     1      2
  ```

If you're like me, you're probably wondering what the difference is between the async option and soft updates. One important difference is that soft update code has been designed to maintain filesystem consistency in the event of a system crash, while the async option has not. This might lead you to conclude that async performs better than soft updates. However, as I show in Appendix D, the opposite is true.

---

[*] For further information, please see "Soft Updates: A Technique for Eliminating Most Synchronous Writes in the Fast File System" by Marshall Kirk McKusik and Gregory R. Ganger. *Proceedings of the 1999 USENIX Annual Technical Conference,* June 6–11, 1999, Monterey, California.

Previously, I mentioned that UFS performance, especially writing, depends on the amount of free space. Disk writes for empty filesystems are much faster than for full ones. This is one reason behind UFS's *minfree* parameter and space/time optimization tradeoffs. If your cache disks are full and Squid's performance seems bad, try reducing the *cache_dir* capacity values so that more free space is available. Of course, this reduction in cache size also decreases your hit ratio, but the response time improvement may be worth it. If you're buying the components for a new Squid cache, consider getting much larger disks than you need and using only half the space.

Alternative Filesystems

Some operating systems support filesystems other than UFS (or ext2fs). Journaling filesystems are a common alternative. The primary difference between UFS and journaling filesystems is in the way that they handle updates. With UFS, updates are made in-place. For example, when you change a file and save it to disk, the new data replaces the old data. When you remove a file, UFS updates the directory directly.

A journaling filesystem, on the other hand, writes updates to a separate journal, or log file. You can typically select whether to journal file changes, metadata changes, or both. A background process reads the journal during idle moments and applies the actual changes. Journaling filesystems typically recover much faster from crashes than UFS. After a crash, the filesystem simply reads the journal and commits all the outstanding changes.

The primary drawback of journaling filesystems is that they require additional disk writes. Changes are first written to the log and later to the actual files and/or directories. This is particularly relevant for web caches because they tend to have more disk writes than reads in the first place.

Journaling filesystems are available for a number of operating systems. On Linux, you can choose from ext3fs, reiserfs, XFS, and others. XFS is also available for SGI/IRIX, where it was originally developed. Solaris users can use the Veritas filesystem product. The TRU64 (formerly Digital Unix) Advanced Filesystem (advfs) supports journaling.

You can use a journaling filesystem without making any changes to Squid's configuration. Simply create and mount the filesystem as described in your operating system documentation. You don't need to change the *cache_dir* line in *squid.conf*. Use a command like this to make a reiserfs filesystem on Linux:

```
# /sbin/mkreiserfs /dev/sda2
```

For XFS, use:

```
# mkfs -t xfs -f /dev/sda2
```

Note that ext3fs is simply ext2fs with journaling enabled. Use the -j option to mke2fs when creating the filesystem:

```
# /sbin/mke2fs -j /dev/sda2
```

Refer to your documentation (e.g., manpages) for other operating systems.

The aufs Storage Scheme

The *aufs* storage scheme has evolved out of the very first attempt to improve Squid's disk I/O response time. The "a" stands for asynchronous I/O. The only difference between the default *ufs* scheme and *aufs* is that I/Os aren't executed by the main Squid process. The data layout and format is the same, so you can easily switch between the two schemes without losing any cache data.

aufs uses a number of thread processes for disk I/O operations. Each time Squid needs to read, write, open, close, or remove a cache file, the I/O request is dispatched to one of the thread processes. When the thread completes the I/O, it signals the main Squid process and returns a status code. Actually, in Squid 2.5, certain file operations aren't executed asynchronously by default. Most notably, disk writes are always performed synchronously. You can change this by setting ASYNC_WRITE to 1 in *src/fs/aufs/store_asyncufs.h* and recompiling.

The *aufs* code requires a *pthreads* library. This is the standard threads interface, defined by POSIX. Even though *pthreads* is available on many Unix systems, I often encounter compatibility problems and differences. The *aufs* storage system seems to run well only on Linux and Solaris. Even though the code compiles, you may encounter serious problem on other operating systems.

To use *aufs*, you must add a special ./configure option:

```
% ./configure --enable-storeio=aufs,ufs
```

Strictly speaking, you don't really need to specify *ufs* in the list of storeio modules. However, you might as well because if you try *aufs* and don't like it, you'll be able to fall back to the plain *ufs* storage scheme.

You can also use the --with-aio-threads=N option if you like. If you omit it, Squid automatically calculates the number of threads to use based on the number of *aufs* cache_dirs. Table 8-1 shows the default number of threads for up to six cache directories.

Table 8-1. Default number of threads for up to six cache directories

cache_dirs	Threads
1	16
2	26
3	32

Table 8-1. Default number of threads for up to six cache directories (continued)

cache_dirs	Threads
4	36
5	40
6	44

After you compile *aufs* support into Squid, you can specify it on a *cache_dir* line in *squid.conf*:

```
cache_dir aufs /cache0 4096 16 256
```

After starting Squid with *aufs* enabled, make sure everything still works correctly. You may want to run `tail -f store.log` for a while to make sure that objects are being swapped out to disk. You should also run `tail -f cache.log` and look for any new errors or warnings.

How aufs Works

Squid creates a number of thread processes by calling `pthread_create( )`. All threads are created upon the first disk activity. Thus, you'll see all the thread processes even if Squid is idle.

Whenever Squid wants to perform some disk I/O operation (e.g., to open a file for reading), it allocates a couple of data structures and places the I/O request into a queue. The thread processes have a loop that take I/O requests from the queue and executes them. Because the request queue is shared by all threads, Squid uses mutex locks to ensure that only one thread updates the queue at a given time.

The I/O operations block the thread process until they are complete. Then, the status of the operation is placed on a *done queue*. The main Squid process periodically checks the done queue for completed operations. The module that requested the disk I/O is notified that the operation is complete, and the request or response processing proceeds.

As you may have guessed, *aufs* can take advantage of systems with multiple CPUs. The only locking that occurs is on the request and result queues. Otherwise, all other functions execute independently. While the main process executes on one CPU, another CPU handles the actual I/O system calls.

aufs Issues

An interesting property of threads is that all processes share the same resources, including memory and file descriptors. For example, when a thread process opens a file as descriptor 27, all other threads can then access that file with the same descriptor number. As you probably know, file-descriptor shortage is a common problem with first-time Squid administrators. Unix kernels typically have two file-descriptor limits: per process and systemwide. While you might think that 256 file descriptors per process is plenty (because of all the thread processes), it doesn't work that way. In this case, all threads share that small number of descriptors. Be sure to increase your system's per-process file descriptor limit to 4096 or higher, especially when using *aufs*.

Tuning the number of threads can be tricky. In some cases, you might see this warning in *cache.log*:

```
2003/09/29 13:42:47| squidaio_queue_request: WARNING - Disk I/O overloading
```

It means that Squid has a large number of I/O operations queued up, waiting for an available thread. Your first instinct may be to increase the number of threads. I would suggest, however, that you decrease the number instead.

Increasing the number of threads also increases the queue size. Past a certain point, it doesn't increase *aufs*'s load capacity. It only means that more operations become queued. Longer queues result in higher response times, which is probably something you'd like to avoid.

Decreasing the number of threads, and the queue size, means that Squid can detect the overload condition faster. When a *cache_dir* is overloaded, it is removed from the selection algorithm (see Chapter 7). Then, Squid either chooses a different *cache_dir* or simply doesn't store the response on disk. This may be a better situation for your users. Even though the hit ratio goes down, response time remains relatively low.

Monitoring aufs Operation

The Async IO Counters option in the cache manager menu displays a few statistics relating to *aufs*. It shows counters for the number of open, close, read, write, stat, and unlink requests received. For example:

```
% squidclient mgr:squidaio_counts
...
ASYNC IO Counters:
Operation        # Requests
open              15318822
close             15318813
cancel            15318813
write                    0
read              19237139
stat                     0
unlink             2484325
check_callback   311678364
queue                    0
```

The cancel counter is normally equal to the close counter. This is because the close function always calls the cancel function to ensure that any pending I/O operations are ignored.

The write counter is zero because this version of Squid performs writes synchronously, even for *aufs*.

The check_callback counter shows how many times the main Squid process has checked the done queue for completed operations.

The queue value indicates the current length of the request queue. Normally, the queue length should be less than the number of threads × 5. If you repeatedly observe a queue length larger than this, you may be pushing Squid too hard. Adding more threads may help but only to a certain point.

The diskd Storage Scheme

diskd (short for disk daemons) is similar to *aufs* in that disk I/Os are executed by external processes. Unlike *aufs*, however, *diskd* doesn't use threads. Instead, interprocess communication occurs via message queues and shared memory.

Message queues are a standard feature of modern Unix operating systems. They were invented many years ago in AT&T's Unix System V, Release 1. The messages passed between processes on these queues are relatively small: 32–40 bytes. Each *diskd* process uses one queue for receiving requests from Squid and another queue for transmitting results back.

How diskd Works

Squid creates one *diskd* process for each *cache_dir*. This is different from *aufs*, which uses a large pool of threads for all *cache_dirs*. Squid sends a message to the corresponding *diskd* process for each I/O operation. When that operation is complete, the *diskd* process sends a status message back to Squid. Squid and the *diskd* processes preserve the order of messages in the queues. Thus, there is no concern that I/Os might be executed out of sequence.

For reads and writes, Squid and the *diskd* processes use a shared memory area. Both processes can read from, and write to, this area of memory. For example, when Squid issues a read request, it tells the *diskd* process where to place the data in memory. *diskd* passes this memory location to the read() system call and notifies Squid that the read is complete by sending a message on the return queue. Squid then accesses the recently read data from the shared memory area.

diskd (as with *aufs*) essentially gives Squid nonblocking disk I/Os. While the *diskd* processes are blocked on I/O operations, Squid is free to work on other tasks. This works really well as long as the *diskd* processes can keep up with the load. Because the main Squid process is now able to do more work, it's possible that it may overload the *diskd* helpers. The *diskd* implementation has two features to help out in this situation.

First, Squid waits for the *diskd* processes to catch up if one of the queues exceeds a certain threshold. The default value is 64 outstanding messages. If a *diskd* process gets this far behind, Squid "sleeps" a small amount of time and waits for it to complete some of the pending operations. This essentially puts Squid into a blocking I/O mode. It also makes more CPU time available to the *diskd* processes. You can configure this threshold by specifying a value for the Q2 parameter on a *cache_dir* line:

```
cache_dir diskd /cache0 7000 16 256 Q2=50
```

Second, Squid stops asking the *diskd* process to open files if the number of outstanding operations reaches another threshold. Here, the default value is 72 messages. If Squid would like to open a disk file for reading or writing, but the selected *cache_dir* has too many pending operations, the open request fails internally. When trying to open a file for reading, this causes a cache miss instead of a cache hit. When opening files for writing, it prevents Squid from storing a cachable response. In both cases the user still receives a valid response. The only real effect is that Squid's hit ratio decreases. This threshold is configurable with the Q1 parameter:

```
cache_dir diskd /cache0 7000 16 256 Q1=60 Q2=50
```

Note that in some versions of Squid, the Q1 and Q2 parameters are mixed-up in the default configuration file. For optimal performance, Q1 should be greater than Q2.

Compiling and Configuring diskd

To use *diskd*, you must add it to the --enable-storeio list when running ./configure:

```
% ./configure --enable-storeio=ufs,diskd
```

diskd seems to be portable since shared memory and message queues are widely supported on modern Unix systems. However, you'll probably need to adjust a few kernel limits relating to both. Kernels typically have the following variables or parameters:

MSGMNB
This is the maximum characters (octets) per message queue. With *diskd*, the practical limit is about 100 outstanding messages per queue. The messages that Squid passes are 32–40 octets, depending on your CPU architecture. Thus, MSGMNB should be 4000 or more. To be safe, I recommend setting this to 8192.

MSGMNI
This is the maximum number of message queues for the whole system. Squid uses two queues for each *diskd cache_dir*. If you have 10 disks, that's 20 queues. You should probably add even more in case other applications also use message queues. I recommend a value of 40.

MSGSSZ

This is the size of a message segment, in octets. Messages larger than this size are split into multiple segments. I usually set this to 64 so that the *diskd* message isn't split into multiple segments.

MSGSEG

This is the maximum number of message segments that can exist in a single queue. Squid normally limits the queues to 100 outstanding messages. Remember that if you don't increase MSGSSZ to 64 on 64-bit architectures, each message requires more than one segment. To be safe, I recommend setting this to 512.

MSGTQL

This is the maximum number of messages that can exist in the whole system. It should be at least 100 multiplied by the number of *cache_dirs*. I recommend setting it to 2048, which should be more than enough for as many as 10 cache directories.

MSGMAX

This is the maximum size of a single message. For Squid, 64 bytes should be sufficient. However, your system may have other applications that use larger messages. On some operating systems such as BSD, you don't need to set this. BSD automatically sets it to MSGSSZ × MSGSEG. On other systems you may need to increase the value from its default. In this case, you can set it to the same as MSGMNB.

SHMSEG

This is the maximum number of shared memory segments allowed per process. Squid uses one shared memory identifier for each *cache_dir*. I recommend a setting of 16 or higher.

SHMMNI

This is the systemwide limit on the number of shared memory segments. A value of 40 is probably enough in most cases.

SHMMAX

This is the maximum size of a single shared memory segment. By default, Squid uses about 409,600 bytes for each segment. Just to be safe, I recommend setting this to 2 MB, or 2,097,152.

SHMALL

This is the systemwide limit on the amount of shared memory that can be allocated. On some systems, SHMALL may be expressed as a number of pages, rather than bytes. Setting this to 16 MB (4096 pages) is enough for 10 *cache_dirs* with plenty remaining for other applications.

The diskd Storage Scheme | 117

To configure message queues on BSD, add these options to your kernel configuration file:[*]

```
# System V message queues and tunable parameters
options      SYSVMSG          # include support for message queues
options      MSGMNB=8192      # max characters per message queue
options      MSGMNI=40        # max number of message queue identifiers
options      MSGSEG=512       # max number of message segments per queue
options      MSGSSZ=64        # size of a message segment MUST be power of 2
options      MSGTQL=2048      # max number of messages in the system
options      SYSVSHM
options      SHMSEG=16        # max shared mem segments per process
options      SHMMNI=32        # max shared mem segments in the system
options      SHMMAX=2097152   # max size of a shared mem segment
options      SHMALL=4096      # max size of all shared memory (pages)
```

To configure message queues on Linux, add these lines to /etc/sysctl.conf:

```
kernel.msgmnb=8192
kernel.msgmni=40
kernel.msgmax=8192
kernel.shmall=2097152
kernel.shmmni=32
kernel.shmmax=16777216
```

Alternatively, or if you find that you need more control, you can manually edit include/linux/msg.h and include/linux/shm.h in your kernel sources.

For Solaris, add these lines to /etc/system and then reboot:

```
set msgsys:msginfo_msgmax=8192
set msgsys:msginfo_msgmnb=8192
set msgsys:msginfo_msgmni=40
set msgsys:msginfo_msgssz=64
set msgsys:msginfo_msgtql=2048
set shmsys:shminfo_shmmax=2097152
set shmsys:shminfo_shmmni=32
set shmsys:shminfo_shmseg=16
```

For Digital Unix (TRU64), you can probably add lines to the kernel configuration in the style of BSD, seen previously. Alternatively, you can use the sysconfig command. First, create a file called ipc.stanza like this:

```
ipc:
        msg-max = 2048
        msg-mni = 40
        msg-tql = 2048
        msg-mnb = 8192
        shm-seg = 16
        shm-mni = 32
        shm-max = 2097152
        shm-max = 4096
```

---

[*] OpenBSD is a little different. Use option instead of options, and specify the SHMMAX value in pages, rather than bytes.

Now, run this command and reboot:

```
# sysconfigdb -a -f ipc.stanza
```

After you have message queues and shared memory configured in your operating system, you can add the *cache_dir* lines to *squid.conf*:

```
cache_dir diskd /cache0 7000 16 256 Q1=72 Q2=64
cache_dir diskd /cache1 7000 16 256 Q1=72 Q2=64
...
```

If you forget to increase the message queue limits, or if you don't set them high enough, you'll see messages like this in *cache.log*:

```
2003/09/29 01:30:11| storeDiskdSend: msgsnd: (35) Resource temporarily unavailable
```

Monitoring diskd

The best way to monitor *diskd* performance is with the cache manager. Request the *diskd* page; for example:

```
% squidclient mgr:diskd
...
sent_count: 755627
recv_count: 755627
max_away: 14
max_shmuse: 14
open_fail_queue_len: 0
block_queue_len: 0

            OPS SUCCESS    FAIL
   open   51534   51530       4
 create   67232   67232       0
  close  118762  118762       0
 unlink   56527   56526       1
   read   98157   98153       0
  write  363415  363415       0
```

See Chapter 14 for a description of this output.

The coss Storage Scheme

The Cyclic Object Storage Scheme (*coss*) is an attempt to develop a custom filesystem for Squid. With the *ufs*-based schemes, the primary performance bottleneck comes from the need to execute so many open() and unlink() system calls. Because each cached response is stored in a separate disk file, Squid is always opening, closing, and removing files.

coss, on the other hand, uses one big file to store all responses. In this sense, it is a small, custom filesystem specifically for Squid. *coss* implements many of the functions normally handled by the underlying filesystem, such as allocating space for new data and remembering where there is free space.

Unfortunately, *coss* is still a little rough around the edges. Development of *coss* has been proceeding slowly over the last couple of years. Nonetheless, I'll describe it here in case you feel adventurous.

How coss Works

On the disk, each *coss cache_dir* is just one big file. The file grows in size until it reaches its maximum size. At this point, Squid starts over at the beginning of the file, overwriting any data already stored there. Thus, new objects are always stored at the "end" of this cyclic file.*

Squid actually doesn't write new object data to disk immediately. Instead, the data is copied into a 1-MB memory buffer, called a *stripe*. A stripe is written to disk when it becomes full. *coss* uses asynchronous writes so that the main Squid process doesn't become blocked on disk I/O.

As with other filesystems, *coss* also uses the *blocksize* concept. Back in Chapter 7, I talked about file numbers. Each cached object has a file number that Squid uses to locate the data on disk. For *coss*, the file number is the same as the block number. For example, a cached object with a swap file number equal to 112 starts at the 112th block in a *coss* filesystem. File numbers aren't allocated sequentially with *coss*. Some file numbers are unavailable because cached objects generally occupy more than one block in the *coss* file.

The *coss* block size is configurable with a *cache_dir* option. Because Squid's file numbers are only 24 bits, the block size determines the maximum size of a *coss* cache directory: size = block_size × 2^{24}. For example, with a 512-byte block size, you can store up to 8 GB in a *coss cache_dir*.

coss doesn't implement any of Squid's normal cache replacement algorithms (see Chapter 7). Instead, cache hits are "moved" to the end of the cyclic file. This is, essentially, the LRU algorithm. It does, unfortunately, mean that cache hits cause disk writes, albeit indirectly.

With *coss*, there is no need to unlink or remove cached objects. Squid simply forgets about the space allocated to objects that are removed. The space will be reused eventually when the end of the cyclic file reaches that place again.

Compiling and Configuring coss

To use *coss*, you must add it to the --enable-storeio list when running ./configure:

```
% ./configure --enable-storeio=ufs,coss ...
```

---

* The beginning is the location where data was first written; the end is the location where data was most recently written.

coss cache directories require a `max-size` option. Its value must be less than the stripe size (1 MB by default, but configurable with the `--enable-coss-membuf-size` option). Also note that you must omit the L1 and L2 values that are normally present for *ufs*-based schemes. Here is an example:

```
cache_dir coss /cache0/coss 7000 max-size=1000000
cache_dir coss /cache1/coss 7000 max-size=1000000
cache_dir coss /cache2/coss 7000 max-size=1000000
cache_dir coss /cache3/coss 7000 max-size=1000000
cache_dir coss /cache4/coss 7000 max-size=1000000
```

Furthermore, you can change the default *coss* block size with the `block-size` option:

```
cache_dir coss /cache0/coss 30000 max-size=1000000 block-size=2048
```

One tricky thing about *coss* is that the *cache_dir* directory argument (e.g., */cache0/coss*) isn't actually a directory. Instead, it is a regular file that Squid opens, and creates if necessary. This is so you can use raw partitions as *coss* files. If you mistakenly create the *coss* file as a directory, you'll see an error like this when starting Squid:

```
2003/09/29 18:51:42|  /usr/local/squid/var/cache: (21) Is a directory
FATAL: storeCossDirInit: Failed to open a coss file.
```

Because the *cache_dir* argument isn't a directory, you must use the *cache_swap_log* directive (see Chapter 13). Otherwise Squid attempts to create a *swap.state* file in the *cache_dir* directory. In that case, you'll see an error like this:

```
2003/09/29 18:53:38| /usr/local/squid/var/cache/coss/swap.state:
        (2) No such file or directory
FATAL: storeCossDirOpenSwapLog: Failed to open swap log.
```

coss uses asynchronous I/Os for better performance. In particular, it uses the `aio_read( )` and `aio_write( )` system calls. These may not be available on all operating systems. At this time, they are available on FreeBSD, Solaris, and Linux. If the *coss* code seems to compile okay, but you get a "Function not implemented" error message, you need to enable these system calls in your kernel. On FreeBSD, your kernel must have this option:

```
options         VFS_AIO
```

coss Issues

coss is still an experimental feature. The code has not yet proven stable enough for everyday use. If you want to play with and help improve it, be prepared to lose any data stored in a *coss cache_dir*. On the plus side, *coss*'s preliminary performance tests are very good. For an example, see Appendix D.

coss doesn't support rebuilding cached data from disk very well. When you restart Squid, you might find that it fails to read the *coss swap.state* files, thus losing any cached data. Furthermore, Squid doesn't remember its place in the cyclic file after a restart. It always starts back at the beginning.

coss takes a nonstandard approach to object replacement. This may cause a lower hit ratio than you might get with one of the other storage schemes.

Some operating systems have problems with files larger than 2 GB. If this happens to you, you can always create more, smaller *coss* areas. For example:

```
cache_dir coss /cache0/coss0 1900 max-size=1000000 block-size=128
cache_dir coss /cache0/coss1 1900 max-size=1000000 block-size=128
cache_dir coss /cache0/coss2 1900 max-size=1000000 block-size=128
cache_dir coss /cache0/coss3 1900 max-size=1000000 block-size=128
```

Using a raw disk device (e.g., */dev/da0s1c*) doesn't work very well yet. One reason is that disk devices usually require that I/Os take place on 512-byte block boundaries. Another concern is that direct disk access bypasses the systems buffer cache and may degrade performance. Many disk drives, however, have built-in caches these days.

The null Storage Scheme

Squid has a fifth storage scheme called *null*. As the name implies, this is more of a nonstorage scheme. Files that are "written" to a *null cache_dir* aren't actually written to disk.

Most people won't have any reason to use the *null* storage system. It's primarily useful if you want to entirely disable Squid's disk cache.[*] You can't simply remove all *cache_dir* lines from *squid.conf* because then Squid adds a default *ufs cache_dir*. The *null* storage system is also sometimes useful for testing and benchmarking Squid. Since the filesystem is typically the performance bottleneck, using the *null* storage scheme gives you an upper limit of Squid's performance on your hardware.

To use this scheme you must first specify it on the --enable-storeio list when running ./configure:

```
% ./configure --enable-storeio=ufs,null ...
```

You can then create a *cache_dir* of type null in *squid.conf*:

```
cache_dir /tmp null
```

It may seem odd that you need to specify a directory for the *null* storage scheme. However, Squid uses the directory name as a *cache_dir* identifier. For example, you'll see it in the cache manager output (see Chapter 14).

Which Is Best for Me?

Squid's storage scheme choices may seem a little overwhelming and confusing. Is *aufs* better than *diskd*? Does my system support *aufs* or *coss*? Will I lose my data if I use one of these fancy schemes? Is it okay to mix-and-match storage schemes?

---

[*] Some responses may still be cached in memory, however.

First of all, if your Squid is lightly used (say, less than five requests per second), the default *ufs* storage scheme should be sufficient. You probably won't see a noticeable performance improvement from the other schemes at this low request rate.

If you are trying to decide which scheme to try, your operating system may be a determining factor. For example, *aufs* runs well on Linux and Solaris but seems to have problems on other systems. The *coss* code uses functions that aren't available on certain operating systems (e.g., NetBSD) at this time.

It seems to me that higher-performing storage schemes are also more susceptible to data loss in the event of a system crash. This is the tradeoff for better performance. For many people, however, cached data is of relatively low value. If Squid's cache becomes corrupted due to a crash, you may find it easier to simply newfs the disk partition and let the cache fill back up from scratch. If you find it difficult or expensive to replace the contents of Squid's cache, you probably want to use one of the slow, but reliable, filesystems and storage schemes.

Squid certainly allows you to use different filesystems and storage schemes for each *cache_dir*. In practice, however, this is uncommon. You'll probably have fewer hassles if all cache directories are approximately the same size and use the same storage scheme.

Exercises

- Try to compile all possible storage schemes on your system.
- Run Squid with a separate *cache_dir* for each storage scheme you can get to compile.
- Run Squid with one or more *diskd cache_dir*s. Then run the **ipcs -o** command.

CHAPTER 9
Interception Caching

Interception caching is a popular technique for getting traffic to Squid without configuring any clients. Instead, you configure a router or switch to divert HTTP connections to the machine on which Squid is running. Squid's operating system is configured to accept the foreign packets and deliver them to the Squid process. To make HTTP interception work, you need to configure three separate components: a network device, Squid's operating system, and Squid itself.

This chapter begins with an overview of HTTP interception. I'll explain how it all works and define some terms so that the remaining sections make sense. I also explain the tradeoffs involved with HTTP interception.

Following that, I'll discuss your options for devices and configurations that can intercept client traffic. In particular, I cover Cisco policy routing, Cisco's WCCP, layer four switches, and running Squid on a host that also functions as a router or bridge.

Next, I'll show how to configure the operating system to handle the intercepted connections. This functionality is a feature of the IP packet filtering software, which varies from system to system. It is called *iptables* (Netfilter) on Linux; *ipfw* on FreeBSD; *pf* on OpenBSD; and *IPFilter* on NetBSD, Solaris, and other BSD variants.

Squid is the final component you need to configure. Fortunately, this is relatively straightforward because it doesn't depend on your operating system or network device.

I finish the chapter with a little checklist that may help you debug HTTP interception problems.

How It Works

Interception caching involves some network trickery, so it is helpful for you to understand what happens between the client and Squid. I'll use Figure 9-1 and the following sample tcpdump output to explain how the packets are intercepted as they flow through your network.

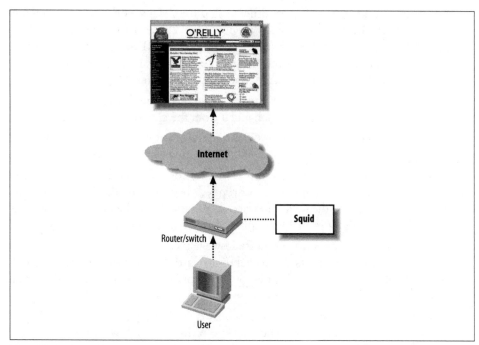

Figure 9-1. How HTTP interception works

1. The user-agent wants to request a resource, say */index.html* from an origin server, say *www.oreilly.com*. It needs the origin server's IP address, so it makes a DNS request:

```
Packet 1
TIME:   19:54:41.317310
UDP:    206.168.0.3.2459 -> 206.168.0.2.53
DATA:   .d..........www.oreilly.com.....
--------------------------------------------------------------------------
Packet 2
TIME:   19:54:41.317707 (0.000397)
UDP:    206.168.0.2.53 -> 206.168.0.3.2459
DATA:   .d..........www.oreilly.com.............PR.....%........PR.
        ....$........PR...ns1.sonic.net.........PR...ns2.Q........PR
        ...ns...M................h.............!.z.......b......
```

2. Now that it has the IP address, the user-agent initiates a TCP connection to the origin server on port 80:

```
Packet 3
TIME:   19:54:41.320652 (0.002945)
TCP:    206.168.0.3.3897 -> 208.201.239.37.80 Syn
DATA:   <No data>
```

3. The switch/router notices a TCP SYN packet with destination port 80. What happens next depends on the particular interception technology. In the case of layer four switches and policy routing, the device simply forwards the TCP

packet to Squid's datalink layer (Ethernet) address. This works only when Squid is directly attached to the network device. For WCCP, the router encapsulates the TCP packet into a GRE packet. Because the GRE packet has its own IP address, it can be routed through multiple subnets. In other words, WCCP doesn't require Squid to be directly attached to the router.

4. The Squid host's operating system receives the intercepted packet. For layer four switches, the TCP/IP packet is unchanged from the earlier explanation.

   If the packet is encapsulated with GRE, the host removes the outer IP and GRE headers and places the original TCP/IP packet on the input queue.

   Note that the Squid host receives an IP packet for a foreign address (the origin server's). Normally this packet is dropped because its destination address doesn't match any of the local interface addresses. To make the host accept the foreign packet, you must enable IP forwarding on most operating systems.

5. The client's TCP/IP packet is processed by the packet filtering code. The packet matches a rule that instructs the kernel to forward or divert this packet to Squid. Without this rule, the kernel simply forwards this packet on its way to the origin server, which isn't what you want.

   Note that the SYN packet's destination port is 80, but Squid may be listening on a different port, such as 3128. The packet filtering rules allow you to change the port number. You don't need to make Squid listen on port 80. You can't see this step with tcpdump because the diverted packet doesn't flow through the network interface code again.

   The packet filter's redirection rule is still necessary even if you have Squid listen on port 80. Simply making the port numbers match doesn't allow Squid to receive the intercepted packets. The redirection rule is the magic that delivers foreign packets to Squid.

6. Squid receives notification of the new connection, which it accepts. The kernel sends a SYN/ACK packet back to the client:

```
Packet 4
TIME:  19:54:41.320735 (0.000083)
TCP:   208.201.239.37.80 -> 206.168.0.3.3897 SynAck
DATA:  <No data>
```

   As you can see, the source address is the origin server's, even though this packet didn't reach the origin. The operating system simply copies and swaps the source and destination IP addresses from the SYN packet into the reply.

7. The user-agent receives the SYN/ACK packet, fully establishing the TCP connection. The user-agent now believes it is connected to the origin server, so it writes the HTTP request:

```
Packet 5
TIME:  19:54:41.323080 (0.002345)
TCP:   206.168.0.3.3897 -> 208.201.239.37.80 Ack
DATA:  <No data>
```

```
-------------------------------------------------------------------------
Packet 6
TIME:    19:54:41.323482 (0.000402)
TCP:     206.168.0.3.3897 -> 208.201.239.37.80 AckPsh
DATA:    GET / HTTP/1.0
         User-Agent: Wget/1.8.2
         Host: www.oreilly.com
         Accept: */*
         Connection: Keep-Alive
```

8. Squid receives the HTTP request. It uses the HTTP Host header to convert the partial URL into a full URL. In this case, you'll see *http://www.oreilly.com/* in the *access.log* file.

9. From this point on, Squid treats the request normally. As usual, cache hits are returned immediately. Cache misses are forwarded to the origin server.

10. Lastly, here is the response that Squid receives from the origin server:

```
Packet 8
TIME:    19:54:41.448391 (0.030030)
TCP:     208.201.239.37.80 -> 206.168.0.3.3897 AckPsh
DATA:    HTTP/1.0 200 OK
         Date: Mon, 29 Sep 2003 01:54:41 GMT
         Server: Apache/1.3.26 (Unix) PHP/4.2.1 mod_gzip/1.3.19.1a mo
         d_perl/1.27
         P3P: policyref="http://www.oreillynet.com/w3c/p3p.xml",CP="C
         AO DSP COR CURa ADMa DEVa TAIa PSAa PSDa IVAa IVDa CONo OUR
         DELa PUBi OTRa IND PHY ONL UNI PUR COM NAV INT DEM CNT STA P
         RE"
         Last-Modified: Sun, 28 Sep 2003 23:54:44 GMT
         ETag: "1b76bf-b910-3ede86c4"
         Accept-Ranges: bytes
         Content-Length: 47376
         Content-Type: text/html
         X-Cache: MISS from www.oreilly.com
         X-Cache: MISS from 10.0.0.1
         Connection: keep-alive
```

You don't want your switch/router to intercept the connections that Squid makes to origin servers. If that happens, Squid ends up talking to itself and can't satisfy any cache misses. The best way to avoid forwarding loops like this is to make sure that your users and Squid connect to separate interfaces on the switch/router. Whenever feasible, you should apply the interception rules to specific interfaces. Obviously, you should not enable interception on the interface that Squid uses.

Why (Not) Intercept?

Many organizations find interception caching attractive because they can't, or would rather not, configure all their user's web browsers. It's probably easier to perform a little network trickery on a single switch or router than it is to configure hundreds or thousands of workstations. As with many choices we face, interception caching is really a tradeoff. It brings both benefits and drawbacks. It may make your life easier, or more difficult.

The obvious benefit of interception caching is that all HTTP requests leaving your network automatically go through Squid. You don't need to worry about configuring any browsers or that users might disable their proxy settings. Interception caching puts you, the network administrator, in control of the HTTP traffic. You can change, add, or remove Squid caches from service without significantly interrupting your users' web surfing.

Most of the disadvantages surrounding HTTP interception are because this technique violates the TCP/IP standards. These protocols mandate that routers (and switches) forward TCP/IP packets to the host specified by the destination IP address. Diverting the packets to a caching proxy breaks the rules. The proxy accepts diverted connections under false pretense. User agents are tricked into believing they have established a TCP connection with the origin server.

This confusion causes a serious problem with older versions of Microsoft's Internet Explorer. The browser's Reload button is the easiest way to refresh an HTML page. When Explorer is configured to use a caching proxy, a reload request includes a Cache-Control: no-cache header to force a cache miss (or validation) and ensure that the response is up to date. Explorer omits this header when not explicitly configured for proxying. With interception caching, Explorer thinks it is connecting to the origin server anyway, and there is no need to send this header. Squid can't tell that the user pressed the Reload button in this case and may not validate the cached response. Squid's *ie_refresh* provides a partial workaround for this bug (see Appendix A). According to Microsoft, this problem has been corrected in Explorer Version 5.5, Service Pack 1.*

For similar reasons, you can't use HTTP proxy authentication in combination with interception caching. Because the client is unaware of the proxy, it doesn't send the necessary Proxy-Authorization header. Additionally, the 407 (Proxy Authorization Required) response code is inappropriate because the response should look like it came from the origin server, which would never send such a reply.

You also can't use RFC 1413 ident lookups (see Chapter 6) with interception. Squid can't bind a new TCP socket to the necessary IP address. The operating system cheats when forwarding the intercepted connection to Squid. However, it can't cheat when Squid wants to bind a new TCP socket to the foreign IP address. The address that it wants to bind to isn't really local, so the bind system call fails.

Interception caching is also incompatible with IP filtering designed to prevent address spoofing (See also RFC 2267: Network Ingress Filtering: Defeating Denial of

---

* See Microsoft support knowledge base article Q266121 for more (or less) information: *http://support. microsoft.com/support/kb/articles/Q266/1/21.ASP.*

Service Attacks Which Employ IP Source Address Spoofing). Consider the network shown in Figure 9-2. The router has two LAN interfaces: lan0 and lan1. The network administrator uses packet filters on the router to make sure that the internal hosts don't transmit packets with spoofed source addresses. The router forwards only packets with source addresses corresponding to the connected networks. The packet filter rules might look something like this:

```
# lan0
allow ip from 172.16.1.0/24 to any via lan0
deny ip from any to any via lan0
# lan1
allow ip from 10.0.0.0/16 to any via lan1
deny ip from any to any via lan1
```

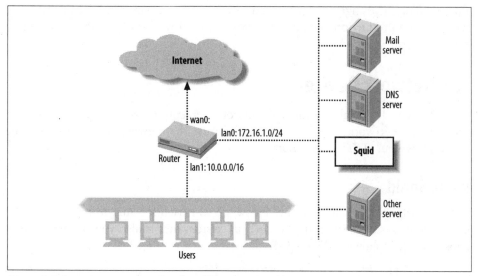

Figure 9-2. Interception caching breaks address spoofing filters

Now consider what happens when the router and Squid box on lan1 are configured to intercept HTTP connections coming from lan0. Squid pretends to be the origin server, which means that the TCP packets carrying response data from Squid back to the users have spoofed source addresses. These lan0 filter rules cause the router to deny these packets. To make interception caching work, the network administrator must remove the lan0 rules. This, in turn, leaves the network vulnerable to being the source of denial-of-service attacks.

As I explained in the previous section, clients must make DNS queries before opening a connection. This may be undesirable or difficult in certain firewall environments. A host whose HTTP traffic you want to intercept must be able to query the DNS. Clients that know they are using a proxy (due to manual configuration or proxy auto-configuration, for example) don't usually try to resolve hostnames.

Instead, they simply forward full URLs to Squid, and it becomes Squid's job to look up origin server IP addresses.

Another little problem is that Squid accepts connections for any destination IP address. Consider, for example, a web site that still has a DNS entry even though the site and server have been taken down. Squid accepts the TCP connection for this bogus site. The client believes the site is up and running, because it's connection is established. When Squid fails to connect to the origin server, it is forced to return an error message.

In case it's not clear, HTTP interception can be tricky and difficult to get working the first time. A number of different components must all work together and be correctly configured. Furthermore, it can be difficult to recreate the entire configuration from memory. I strongly encourage you to set up a test environment before attempting this on a production system. Once you get it all working, be sure to document every little step.

The Network Device

Now that you know all the ins and outs of interception caching, let's see how to actually make it work. We'll start by configuring the network devices that will be intercepting your HTTP connections.

Inline Squid

In this configuration, you don't need a switch or network router to intercept HTTP connections. Instead, Squid runs on a Unix system that is also your router (or perhaps bridge), as shown in Figure 9-3.

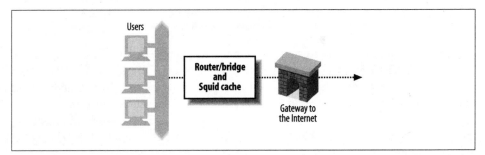

Figure 9-3. A system that combines routing and caching can easily intercept HTTP traffic

This configuration essentially skips the first three steps shown in the section "How It Works." The Squid host already receives the HTTP connection packets because it is the router for your network. If you are taking this approach, feel free to skip ahead to the "Operating System Tweaks" section.

Layer Four Switches

Many organizations use layer four switches specifically for their HTTP interception support. These products offer additional features as well, such as health checks and load balancing. I'll only cover interception here. For information on health checks and load balancing, see O'Reilly's *Server Load Balancing* and *Load Balancing Servers, Firewalls, and Caches* (John Wiley & Sons). The following subsections contain working-example configurations for a number of products and techniques.

Alteon/Nortel

The following configuration is from an ACEswitch 180 and Alteon's WebOS 8.0.21. The network setup is shown in Figure 9-4.

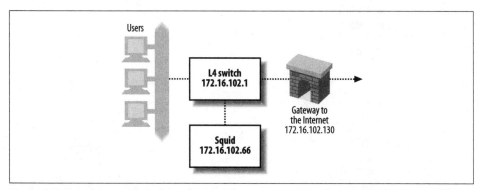

Figure 9-4. Sample network for layer four switch interception, for Alteon and Foundry examples

Clients are connected to port 1, the connection to the Internet is via port 2, and Squid is on port 3. The following lines are the relevant output of a /cfg/dump command on the switch. You don't necessarily need to type all of these lines. Furthermore, some of the commands may have changed for newer versions of Alteon's software. Note that Alteon calls this feature Web Cache Redirection (WCR). Here's the process, step by step:

1. First, you must give the Alteon switch an IP address. This seems necessary so that the switch can perform health checks with Squid:

   ```
   /cfg/ip/if 1
           ena
           addr 172.16.102.1
           mask 255.255.255.0
           broad 172.16.102.255
   ```

2. Alteon's WCR is a feature of its Server Load Balancing (SLB) configuration. Thus, you need to enable SLB features on the switch with this command:

   ```
   /cfg/slb
           on
   ```

3. Next, you define a real server with Squid's IP address:

```
/cfg/slb/real 1
        ena
        rip 172.16.102.66
```

4. You must also define a group and make the real server a member:

```
/cfg/slb/group 1
        health tcp
        add 1
```

5. The next step is to define two filters. The first filter matches HTTP connections—
   TCP packets with destination port 80—and redirects them to a server in group 1.
   The second filter matches all other packets and forwards them normally:

```
/cfg/slb/filt 1
        ena
        action redir
        sip any
        smask 0.0.0.0
        dip any
        dmask 0.0.0.0
        proto tcp
        sport any
        dport http
        group 1
        rport 0
/cfg/slb/filt 224
        ena
        action allow
        sip any
        smask 0.0.0.0
        dip any
        dmask 0.0.0.0
        proto any
```

6. The final step is to configure specific switch ports for SLB. On port 1, you enable
   client processing (this is where the clients connect), and add the two filters. On
   the second port you need only configure it for servers (i.e., the upstream Internet connection):

```
/cfg/slb/port 1
        client ena
        filt ena
        add 1
        add 224
/cfg/slb/port 2
        server ena
```

To verify that HTTP interception is configured and working correctly, you can use
the commands under the /stats/slb and /info/slb menus. The /info/slb/dump command is a quick and easy way to see the entire SLB configuration:

```
>> Main# /info/slb/dump
Real server state:
  1: 172.16.102.66, 00:c0:4f:23:d7:05, vlan 1, port 3, health 3, up

Virtual server state:

Redirect filter state:
  1: dport http, rport 0, group 1, health tcp, backup none
    real servers:
      1: 172.16.102.66, backup none, up

Port state:
  1: 0.0.0.0, client
     filt  enabled, filters: 1 224
  2: 0.0.0.0, server
     filt disabled, filters: empty
  3: 0.0.0.0
     filt disabled, filters: empty
```

In this output, notice that the switch says Squid is reachable via port 3 and that the health checks show Squid is up. You can also see that filter 1 has been applied to port 1, where the clients connect. In the Port state section, port 1 is designated as a place where clients connect, and port 2 is similarly marked as a server port.

The /stats/slb/real command shows a handful of statistics for the real server (i.e., Squid):

```
>> Main# /stats/slb/real 1
-------------------------------------------------------------------
Real server 1 stats:
Health check failures:            0
Current sessions:                41
Total sessions:                 760
Highest sessions:                55
Octets:                           0
```

Most of the statistics relate to the number of sessions (i.e., TCP connections). The Total sessions counter should increase if you execute the command again.

Lastly, the /stats/slb/group command shows almost the same information:

```
>> Main# /stats/slb/group 1
-------------------------------------------------------------------
Real server group 1 stats:
                         Current    Total Highest
Real IP address         Sessions Sessions Sessions          Octets
---- --------------- -------- ---------- -------- ---------------
   1 172.16.102.66         65     2004       90               0
---- --------------- -------- ---------- -------- ---------------
                          65     2004       90               0
```

This output would be more interesting if there was more than one real server in the group.

Foundry

The configuration in the following example comes from a ServerIron XL, running software version 07.0.07T12. As before, clients are on port 1, the Internet link is on port 2, and Squid is on port 3. However, that matters less for this particular configuration because you can enable HTTP interception globally. Foundry's name for interception caching is Transparent Cache Switching (TCS). Refer back to Figure 9-4 for this example.

The first step is to give the switch an IP address so it can perform health checks:

```
ip address 172.16.102.1 255.255.255.0
```

Foundry allows you to enable or disable TCS on particular ports. However, for the sake of simplicity, let's enable it globally:

```
ip policy 1 cache tcp http global
```

In this line, cache is a keyword that corresponds to the TCS feature. The next line defines a web cache. I've given it the name *squid1* and told the switch its IP address:

```
server cache-name squid1 172.16.102.66
```

The final step is to add the web cache to a cache group:

```
server cache-group 1
  cache-name squid1
```

If you're having problems getting the Foundry switch to divert connections, have a look at the show cache-group output:

```
ServerIron#show cache-group

Cache-group 1 has 1 members Admin-status = Enabled Active = 0
Hash_info: Dest_mask = 255.255.255.0 Src_mask = 0.0.0.0

Cache Server Name                   Admin-status Hash-distribution
squid1                              6            3

HTTP Traffic  From <-> to  Web-Caches

Name: squid1         IP: 172.16.102.66     State: 6   Groups =   1

                                  Host->Web-cache       Web-cache->Host
             State  CurConn TotConn Packets   Octets      Packets   Octets
Client       active 441     12390   188871    15976623    156962    154750098
Web-Server   active 193     11664   150722    151828731   175796    15853612
Total               634     24054   339593    167805354   332758    170603710
```

Some of this output is cryptic, but you can tell interception is working by repeating the command and watching the counters increase.

The show server real command provides almost the same information:

```
ServerIron#show server real squid1
Real Servers Info

Name : squid1                                   Mac-addr: 00c0.4f23.d705
IP:172.16.102.66   Range:1    State:Active      Wt:1     Max-conn:1000000
Src-nat (cfg:op):(off:off)    Dest-nat (cfg:op):(off:off)
squid1 is a TRANSPARENT CACHE in groups   1
Remote server    : No          Dynamic : No      Server-resets:0
Mem:server: 02009eae Mem:mac: 045a3714

Port    State   Ms CurConn TotConn Rx-pkts Tx-pkts Rx-octet  Tx-octet  Reas
----    -----   -- ------- ------- ------- ------- --------  --------  ----
http    active  0  855     29557   379793  471713  373508204 39425322  0
default active  0  627     28335   425106  366016  38408994  368496301 0

Server  Total      1482    57892   804899  837729  411917198 407921623 0
```

Finally, you can use the show logging command to see if the switch believes Squid is up or down:

```
ServerIron#show logging
...
00d00h11m51s:N:L4 server 172.16.102.66 squid1 port 80 is up
00d00h11m49s:N:L4 server 172.16.102.66 squid1 port 80 is down
00d00h10m21s:N:L4 server 172.16.102.66 squid1 port 80 is up
00d00h10m21s:N:L4 server 172.16.102.66 squid1 is up
```

Note that the ServerIron thinks the server is running on port 80. As you'll see later, my examples have Squid running on port 3128. The packet filtering rules actually change the packet's destination port from 80 to 3128. This has some interesting consequences for health checks, which I address later in the section "A comment on HTTP servers and health checks."

Extreme Networks

In this example, the hardware is a Summit1i, and the software is Version 6.1.3b11. Once again, the clients are on port 1, the Internet link is on port 2, and Squid is on port 3. The network configuration is shown in Figure 9-5.

The Extreme switch can intercept HTTP connections only for packets that it routes between subnets. In other words, if you use the Extreme switch in layer two mode (with a single VLAN), you can't divert traffic to Squid. To make HTTP interception work, you must configure separate VLANs for users, Squid, and the Internet:

```
configure Default delete port 1-8

create vlan Users
configure Users ip 172.16.102.1 255.255.255.192
configure Users add port 1

create vlan Internet
configure Internet ip 172.16.102.129 255.255.255.192
configure Internet add port 2
```

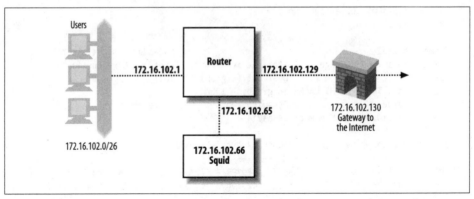

Figure 9-5. Sample network for intercepting with a router, for the Extreme and Cisco policy routing examples

```
create vlan Squid
configure Squid ip 172.16.102.65 255.255.255.192
configure Squid add port 3
```

The next step is to enable and configure routing in the switch:

```
enable ipforwarding
configure iproute add default 172.16.102.130
```

Lastly, you configure the switch to redirect HTTP connections to Squid:

```
create flow-redirect http tcp destination any ip-port 80 source any
configure http add next-hop 172.16.102.66
```

Cisco Arrowpoint

The following configuration is based on notes from an old test I ran. However, I don't have access to an arrowpoint switch now and can't verify that these lines are correct.

```
circuit VLAN1
  ip address 172.16.102.1 255.255.255.0

service pxy1
  type transparent-cache
  ip address 172.16.102.66
  port 80
  protocol tcp
  active

owner foo
  content bar
    add service pxy1
    protocol tcp
    port 80
    active
```

A comment on HTTP servers and health checks

I've set up these examples so that the router/switch forwards packets without changing the destination TCP port. The packet filtering rules that I'll cover in the section "Operating System Tweaks" change the destination port. An interesting problem arises when you also run an HTTP server on the Squid box.

To run an HTTP server on port 80 while running Squid on port 3128, your packet filter configuration must have a special rule that accepts TCP connections for the HTTP server. Otherwise, the connection gets diverted to Squid. The special rule is simple to construct. If the destination port is 80, and the destination address is the server's, accept the packet normally. All the intercepted packets have foreign destination addresses, so they won't match the special rule.

However, when the router/switch makes an HTTP health check, it connects to the server's IP address. Thus, the health-check packet matches the special rule and isn't diverted to Squid. The router/switch is checking the health of the wrong server. If the HTTP server is down, but Squid is up (or vice versa), the health check will be wrong.

If you find yourself in this situation, you have a few options:

- Don't run an HTTP server on the Squid host.
- Add a specific packet filtering rule that diverts TCP health check connections from the router/switch to Squid.
- Configure your router/switch to change the destination port to 3128.
- Disable layer four health checks.

Cisco Policy Routing

Policy routing isn't that different from what I've talked about with layer four switches. It is implemented in routing products made by Cisco and others. The primary difference is that policy routing doesn't include any health checking. Thus, if Squid becomes overloaded or fails entirely, the router continues to forward packets to Squid, rather than route them directly to origin servers. Policy routing requires that Squid be on one of the router's directly connected subnets.

In this example, I'm using a Cisco 7204 router running IOS Version 12.0(5)T. The network configuration is the same as the previous example, shown in Figure 9-5.

The first configuration step is to define an *access list* that matches port 80 packets coming from clients. You must make sure that port 80 packets coming from Squid aren't reintercepted. One way to do this is with a specific rule that denies packets coming from Squid, followed by a rule that allows all others:

```
access-list 110 deny tcp host 172.16.102.66 any eq www
access-list 110 permit tcp any any eq www
```

Alternatively, if Squid and your users are on different subnets, you can permit only those packets that originate from the client network:

```
access-list 110 permit tcp 10.102.0.0 0.0.255.255 any eq www
```

The next step is to define a *route map*. This is where you tell the router where to forward the intercepted packets:

```
route-map proxy-redirect permit 10
  match ip address 110
  set ip next-hop 172.16.102.66
```

Those commands say, "If the IP address matches access-list 110, forward the packet to 172.16.102.66." The 10 on the route-map line is a sequence number in case you have multiple route maps. The final step is to apply the route map to interfaces where your clients connect:

```
interface Ethernet0/0
  ip policy route-map proxy-redirect
```

IOS doesn't provide much in the way of debugging for policy routing. However, the show route-map command may be sufficient:

```
router#show route-map proxy-redirect
route-map proxy-redirect, permit, sequence 10
  Match clauses:
    ip address (access-lists): 110
  Set clauses:
    ip next-hop 172.16.102.66
  Policy routing matches: 730 packets, 64649 bytes
```

Web Cache Coordination Protocol

Cisco's answer to layer four switching technology (before they acquired Arrowpoint) is the Web Cache Coordination Protocol (WCCP).[*] WCCP is different from the typical layer four interception in a couple of ways.

First, intercepted packets are encapsulated with GRE (Generic Routing Encapsulation). This simply allows them to traverse subnets, which means Squid doesn't need to be directly connected to the router. Because they are encapsulated, the Squid host must unencapsulate them. Not all Unix systems have the code for unwrapping GRE packets.

The second difference is in how the router decides to spread the load among multiple caches. In fact, the router doesn't make this decision, the cache does. When a router has a group of WCCP-enabled caches, one nominates itself to be the leader. The leader decides how to spread the load and informs the router. This is an extra step that must occur before the router can redirect any connections.

---

[*] At various times it has also been called Web Cache Control Protocol.

Because WCCP uses GRE, the router may be forced to fragment large TCP packets from HTTP requests. Fortunately, this shouldn't occur very often because most HTTP requests are smaller than the Ethernet MTU size (1500 octets). The default TCP and IP packet headers are 20 octets each, which means an Ethernet frame can carry 1460 octets of actual data. GRE encapsulation adds 20 octets for the GRE header, plus another 20 for the second IP header. Thus a normal 1500-octet TCP/IP packet from the client becomes 1540 octets after encapsulation. This is too large to transmit in a single Ethernet frame, so the router fragments the original packet into two packets.

WCCPv1

The configuration examples in this section were tested on a Cisco 7204 running IOS Version 12.0(5)T. The network configuration is the same as shown in Figure 9-5.

First, enter these two lines in the IOS configuration to enable WCCP for the router:

```
ip wccp version 1
ip wccp web-cache
```

Second, you must enable WCCP on individual router interfaces. You should do this only on interfaces where HTTP packets leave the router. In other words, select interfaces that connect to origin servers or your Internet gateway:

```
interface Ethernet0/1
 ip address 172.16.102.129 255.255.255.192
 ip wccp web-cache redirect out
```

Be sure to save your configuration changes.

You may need to use an access list to prevent interception for certain web sites. You can also use the access list to prevent forwarding loops. For example:

```
! don't re-intercept connections coming from Squid:
access-list 112 deny   tcp host 172.16.102.66 any eq www

! don't intercept this broken web site
access-list 112 deny   tcp any 192.16.8.7 255.255.255.255 eq www

! allow other HTTP traffic
access-list 110 permit tcp any any eq www

ip wccp web-cache redirect-list 112
```

The router doesn't send any traffic to Squid until Squid announces itself to the router. I explain how to configure Squid for WCCP in the section "Configuring WCCPv1."

WCCPv2

The standard Squid distribution currently only supports WCCPv1. However, you can find a patch for WCCPv2 on the *http://devel.squid-cache.org/* site. This code is still experimental.

Note that the GRE packets sent from the router to Squid contain an additional four octets. WCCPv2 inserts a redirect header between the GRE header, and the encapsulated IP packet. You may need to modify your kernel code to account for this additional header.

Debugging

IOS provides a couple of commands to monitor and debug WCCP. The show ip wccp web-cache command provides some basic information:

```
router#show ip wccp web-cache
Global WCCP information:
    Router information:
        Router Identifier:                  172.16.102.129
        Protocol Version:                   1.0

    Service Identifier: web-cache
        Number of Cache Engines:            1
        Number of routers:                  1
        Total Packets Redirected:           1424
        Redirect access-list:               -none-
        Total Packets Denied Redirect:      0
        Total Packets Unassigned:           0
        Group access-list:                  -none-
        Total Messages Denied to Group:     0
        Total Authentication failures:      0
```

For a few more details, add the word detail to the end of the previous command:

```
router#show ip wccp web-cache detail
WCCP Cache-Engine information:
    IP Address:         172.16.102.66
    Protocol Version:   0.4
    State:              Usable
    Initial Hash Info:  00000000000000000000000000000000
                        00000000000000000000000000000000
    Assigned Hash Info: FFFFFFFFFFFFFFFFFFFFFFFFFFFFFFFF
                        FFFFFFFFFFFFFFFFFFFFFFFFFFFFFFFF
    Hash Allotment:     256 (100.00%)
    Packets Redirected: 1424
    Connect Time:       00:17:40
```

Here you can see Squid's IP address and state. If more than one cache speaks WCCP to the router, the hash assignment information should look different. Most likely, each cache receives an equal proportion of the hash buckets.

Note that the detailed output has a Protocol Version line with a different value than the first command. Unfortunately, the word "version" is overloaded. The show ip wccp web-cache command appears to report the WCCP protocol major version number (i.e., 1 or 2), while the detail version seems to be a different (perhaps internal, or minor version) number that matches the value of Squid's *wccp_version* directive.

Operating System Tweaks

You must enable certain networking features in your operating system to make interception caching work. First, you need to enable IP packet forwarding. This allows the operating system to receive packets with foreign destination addresses. Second, you must enable and configure optional code in the kernel that redirects the foreign packets to Squid.

Linux

The instructions in this section should work for the 2.4 series of Linux kernels. I used RedHat Linux 7.2 (kernel 2.4.7-10). If you are using an older or newer version, these may not work. I recommend searching the Squid FAQ and other places for updated or historical information.

In my tests with iptables, it wasn't necessary to enable IP forwarding. However, you may want to enable it initially and see if you can disable it after everything else is working. The best way to enable packet forwarding is to add this line to */etc/sysctl. conf*:

```
net.ipv4.ip_forward = 1
```

Most likely you'll need to make a new kernel before HTTP interception will work. See O'Reilly's *Running Linux* by Matt Welsh, Matthias Kalle Dalheimer, and Lar Kaufman, if you don't know how to configure and create a Linux kernel. When you configure the kernel, make sure these options are enabled:

```
o  General setup
      Networking support (CONFIG_NET=y)
      Sysctl support (CONFIG_SYSCTL=y)
o  Networking options
      Network packet filtering (CONFIG_NETFILTER=y)
      TCP/IP networking (CONFIG_INET=y)
      Netfilter Configuration
        Connection tracking (CONFIG_IP_NF_CONNTRACK=y)
        IP tables support (CONFIG_IP_NF_IPTABLES=y)
        Full NAT (CONFIG_IP_NF_NAT=y)
        REDIRECT target support (CONFIG_IP_NF_TARGET_REDIRECT=y)
o  File systems
      /proc filesystem support (CONFIG_PROC_FS=y)
```

Additionally, make sure this option isn't enabled:

```
o Networking options
    Fast switching (CONFIG_NET_FASTROUTE=n)
```

The code that redirects foreign packets to Squid is part of the Netfilter software. Here is a rule that sends the intercepted HTTP connections to Squid:

```
iptables -t nat -A PREROUTING -i eth0 -p tcp --dport 80 -j REDIRECT --to-port 3128
```

The Linux kernel maintains a number of different *tables*. The -t nat option indicates that we are modifying the Network Address Translation (NAT) table. In essence, we're using iptables to translate origin server TCP/IP addresses to Squid's local TCP/IP address.

Each iptables table has a number of *chains*. The -A PREROUTING option indicates that we are appending a rule to the built-in chain named PREROUTING. The PREROUTING chain applies only to packets entering the system from the outside network.

The next three options determine which packets match this rule. The -i eth0 option restricts the rule to packets received on the eth0 interface. The -p tcp option specifies TCP packets, and --dport 80 specifies packets with destination port equal to 80. If all three conditions are true, the packet matches the rule.

The -j REDIRECT option indicates the target, or action to take, for packets that match the rule. REDIRECT is a built-in target name that causes iptables to change the packet's destination address to 127.0.0.1. The --to-port 3128 option instructs iptables also to change the destination TCP port number to 3128.

If you are also running an HTTP server (such as Apache) on the Squid host, you must add another iptables rule. The additional rule is necessary to allow connections to your HTTP server. Otherwise, the REDIRECT rule causes iptables to send those connections to Squid on port 3128. You can use the -I option to insert a new rule at the top of the list:

```
iptables -t nat -I PREROUTING -i eth0 -p tcp -d 172.16.102.66 --dport 80 -j ACCEPT
```

Once you have all your iptables rules working correctly, be sure to save them with this command:

```
/sbin/service iptables save
```

This saves the current rules to */etc/sysconfig/iptables* so they get automatically loaded when you reboot.

Linux and WCCP

Version 2.4 of the Linux kernel comes with a GRE pseudo-interface. However, it doesn't work for decoding GRE-encapsulated packets from a WCCP session. The problem seems to be that the router sets the Protocol Type field to 0x883E for WCCP/GRE packets. Linux's GRE driver doesn't know what to do with these packets because it doesn't know about protocol type 0x883E.

You can try patching Linux's GRE module so that it works with WCCP. The Squid FAQ contains a link to such a patch. However, you'll probably find it easier to use the WCCP-specific module for Linux. You can find it at *http://www.squid-cache.org/WCCP-support/Linux/ip_wccp.c*.

You need to compile the *ip_wccp.c* file as a loadable kernel module. This can be a little tricky because the specific compiler options may change depending on your kernel version. One thing you can do is go to your kernel source directory, type make modules and watch the compiler commands scroll by. Then copy one of those commands and change the last argument to *ip_wccp.c*. Here are the commands that I used with the 2.4.7-10 Linux kernel:

```
% gcc -Wall -D__KERNEL__  -I/usr/src/linux-2.4.7-10/include  \
  -DMODULE -DMODVERSIONS -DEXPORT_SYMBAB \
  -include /usr/src/linux-2.4.7-10/include/linux/modversions.h \
  -O2 -c ip_wccp.c
```

The gcc command should leave you with an *ip_wccp.o* file in the current directory. The next step is to load that file into the kernel with the insmod command:

```
# insmod ip_wccp.o
```

Note that the *ip_wccp* module accepts GRE/WCCP packets from any source address. In other words, a malicious person might be able to send traffic to your Squid cache. If you use this module, you should also install an iptables rule to deny foreign GRE packets. For example:

```
# iptables -A INPUT -p gre -s 172.16.102.65 -j ACCEPT
# iptables -A INPUT -p gre -j DROP
```

Again, don't forget to save your working rules with the /sbin/service iptables save command.

FreeBSD

The examples in this section are based on FreeBSD-4.8 and should work for any later version of FreeBSD-4 and FreeBSD-5.

To enable IP packet forwarding, add this line to */etc/sysctl.conf*:

```
net.inet.ip.forwarding=1
```

You'll need a kernel with two special options enabled. If you don't know how to make a kernel, refer to Section 9 of the FreeBSD Handbook (*http://www.freebsd.org/handbook/index.html*). Edit your kernel config file and make sure these lines are present:

```
options      IPFIREWALL
options      IPFIREWALL_FORWARD
```

If the Squid box is in an unattended machine room, I also recommend using the `IPFIREWALL_DEFAULT_TO_ACCEPT` option. In case you mess up the firewall rules, you'll still be able to log in.

These `ipfw` commands tell the kernel to redirect intercepted connections to Squid:

```
/sbin/ipfw add allow tcp from 172.16.102.66 to any out
/sbin/ipfw add allow tcp from any 80 to any out
/sbin/ipfw add fwd 127.0.0.1,3128 tcp from any to any 80 in
/sbin/ipfw add allow tcp from any 80 to 172.16.102.66 in
```

The first rule matches packets originating from the Squid host. It ensures that outgoing TCP connections won't be redirected back to Squid.* The second rule matches TCP packets sent from Squid back to the clients. I've added it here in case you have additional `ipfw` rules later that would deny these packets. The third rule is the one that actually redirects incoming connections to Squid. The fourth rule matches packets coming back from origin servers to Squid. Again, this is in case you have subsequent deny rules.

If you're also running an HTTP server on the Squid host, you must add another rule that passes, rather than redirects, TCP packets destined for the origin server. The following rule goes before the `fwd` rule:

```
/sbin/ipfw add allow tcp from any to 172.16.102.66 80 in
```

FreeBSD typically stores `ipfw` rules in */etc/rc.firewall*. Once you get your rule set working properly, be sure to save them. Add this line to */etc/rc.conf* to make FreeBSD automatically run the */etc/rc.firewall* script when it boots:

```
firewall_enable="YES"
```

FreeBSD and WCCP

FreeBSD Version 4.8 and later have built-in support for GRE and WCCP. Earlier versions require patches, which you can still find at *http://www.squid-cache.org/WCCP-support/FreeBSD/*. The built-in implementation is much better, however, as it is written by real kernel gurus. You'll probably need to make a new kernel that supports GRE. Add this line to your kernel configuration:

```
pseudo-device    gre
```

For FreeBSD-5, use `device` instead of `pseudo-device`. Of course, you also need the `FIREWALL` options mentioned in the preceding section.

After installing and booting from the new kernel, you must configure a GRE tunnel to accept GRE packets from the router. For example:

```
# ifconfig gre0 create
# ifconfig gre0 172.16.102.66 172.16.102.65 netmask 255.255.255.255 up
```

---

* Although a misconfiguration on the switch/router may still reintercept these packets.

```
# ifconfig gre0 tunnel 172.16.102.66 172.16.102.65
# route delete 172.16.102.65
```

The ifconfig command adds a routing table entry for the router (172.16.102.65) over the gre0 interface. I found it necessary to delete that route so that Squid can talk to the router.

You may want or need to add an ipfw rule for the GRE packets coming from the router:

```
/sbin/ipfw add allow gre from 172.16.102.65 to 172.16.102.66
```

OpenBSD

The examples in this section are based on OpenBSD 3.3.

To enable packet forwarding, uncomment or add this line in */etc/sysctl.conf*:

```
net.inet.ip.forwarding=1
```

Now, configure the packet filter rules for interception by adding lines like these to */etc/pf.conf*:

```
rdr inet proto tcp from any to any port = www -> 127.0.0.1 port 3128
pass out proto tcp from 172.16.102.66 to any
pass out proto tcp from any port = 80 to any
pass in proto tcp from any port = 80 to 172.16.102.66
```

If you aren't already using OpenBSD's packet filter, you need to enable it with this line in */etc/rc.conf.local*:

```
pf=YES
```

OpenBSD and WCCP

First, tell the system to accept and process GRE and WCCP packets by adding these lines to */etc/sysctl.conf*:

```
net.inet.gre.allow=1
net.inet.gre.wccp=1
```

Then, configure a GRE interface with commands like these:

```
# ifconfig gre0 172.16.102.66 172.16.102.65 netmask 255.255.255.255 up
# ifconfig gre0 tunnel 172.16.102.66 172.16.102.65
# route delete 172.16.102.65
```

As with FreeBSD, I found it necessary to delete the route that is automatically added by ifconfig. Finally, depending on your packet filter configuration, you may need to add a rule that allows the GRE packets:

```
pass in proto gre from 172.16.102.65 to 172.16.102.66
```

IPFilter on NetBSD and Others

The examples in this section are based on NetBSD 1.6.1. They might also work on
Solaris, HP-UX, IRIX, and Tru64 since IPFilter runs on those systems as well.

To enable packet forwarding (on NetBSD), add this line to */etc/sysctl.conf*:

```
net.inet.ip.forwarding=1
```

Then, insert a line like this into the NAT (network address translation) configuration file, */etc/ipnat.conf*:

```
rdr fxp0 0/0 port 80 -> 172.16.102.66 port 3128 tcp
```

Your interface name may be different from fxp0 in this example.

NetBSD and WCCP

I was not able to make WCCP work with NetBSD, even after patching the GRE code
to accept WCCP packets. The problem seems to arise because the IPFilter rdr rule is
bound to a specific interface. Packets coming from the router go through NetBSD's
gre0 interface (where they are unencapsulated). However, packets going the other
way, back to the router, aren't encapsulated and don't go through the same network
interface. Therefore, the IPFilter code doesn't translate Squid's local IP address back
to the origin server's address.

Configure Squid

If you are using Linux 2.4 and iptables, you should probably use the --enable-
linux-netfilter option when you run (or re-run) ./configure. It enables some
Linux-specific code so that Squid can find the IP address of the origin server from
where the request was originally sent. Squid normally gets the origin server name
(and/or address) from the Host header. The --enable-linux-netfilter feature is necessary only for requests that don't have a Host header. Statistics show that almost all
requests have the Host header, so you may actually be able to get by without the
--enable-linux-netfilter option.

If you are using the IPFilter package (with NetBSD, Solaris, and others), you should
use the --enable-ipf-transparent option for the same reason. On OpenBSD, you
should use the --enable-pf-transparent option. Each time you run ./configure you
must recompile Squid, as described in Chapter 3.

After you get the ./configure options figured out, and Squid recompiled, you can
edit *squid.conf*. As a starting point, make sure the following directives are defined
with the given values:

```
httpd_accel_host virtual
httpd_accel_port 80
httpd_accel_uses_host_header on
```

```
httpd_accel_with_proxy on
httpd_accel_single_host off
```

The *httpd_accel_host* directive is the key. It instructs Squid to accept HTTP requests with partial URIs. The *httpd_accel_uses_host_header* directive is enabled so that Squid uses the Host header to reconstruct full URIs. The virtual keyword instructs Squid to put the origin server's IP address in the URL when the Host header is absent.

The *httpd_accel_with_proxy* directive controls whether or not Squid accepts both HTTP server (partial URI) requests, and proxy (full URI) requests. It should probably be enabled for interception caching. Squid may still work if *httpd_accel_with_proxy* is disabled as long as none of your clients are explicitly configured for Squid as a proxy.

The *httpd_accel_single_host* directive is normally disabled, but it was enabled by default in some earlier versions of Squid. I've listed it here to make sure that it is disabled for interception caching.

If you are intercepting more than just port 80, you may want to set *httpd_accel_port* to 0. See Appendix A for more information.

If you're not using WCCP, you should be ready to start sending intercepted traffic to Squid. Give it a try by surfing the Web with your browser or by making some test requests with squidclient. If you are using WCCP, there is just one more step that you must complete.

Configuring WCCPv1

The router doesn't send any traffic to Squid until Squid announces itself to the router. To make Squid do that, add these lines to your *squid.conf*:

```
wccp_router 172.16.102.65
wccp_version 4
```

Your router has many interfaces. Be sure to use the IP address of the interface closest to Squid. This is necessary because the WCCP messages coming from the router have the source IP address set to the address of the outgoing interface. Squid rejects WCCP messages if the source address doesn't match the *wccp_router* value.

The WCCPv1 document specifies 4 as the protocol version number. However, some users report that Cisco IOS 11.2 supports only Version 3. If you are using this version of IOS, change the version in *squid.conf*:

```
wccp_version 3
```

Debugging Problems

HTTP interception is complicated because many different devices must all work correctly together. To help you track down problems, here's a trouble-shooting check list:

Are client packets going through the router/switch?
> This should be obvious for simple networks. You can trace the cables and watch the activity lights blink. In a large, complex network, however, packets may be taking an alternate path. If your organization is large enough to have a network sniffer, you may want to observe the traffic on the link that should carry requests from web clients. A low-tech approach is to disconnect the link in question and see if it affects the client's web browsing.

Is the router/switch configured properly?
> You may want to double-check your router/switch configuration. If you configured specific interfaces, did you get the right ones?
>
> Is your new configuration actually *running* on the device? Perhaps the router/switch was rebooted before you could save the configuration. You may need to reboot before the changes take effect.

Can the switch/router talk to the Squid host?
> Can you ping Squid from the router/switch? Most layer four interception configurations require that the device and Squid be on the same subnet. Log into the router/switch, and make sure you can ping Squid's IP address.

Does the switch/router believe that Squid is up?
> Many traffic interception devices don't send traffic to Squid unless they know it's healthy. Use the debugging commands to view Squid's health status. You may find that a layer three health check (e.g., ICMP ping) is simpler than a layer four check (e.g., HTTP), and more likely to make the network device mark Squid as up.

Is Squid actually running?
> Double-check that Squid is really running, especially if the system has recently been rebooted.

Are packets arriving at the Squid host?
> You should be able to see intercepted TCP connections with tcpdump. Here's an example:
>
> ```
> # tcpdump -n -i eth0 port 80
> ```
>
> If you use WCCP, check for GRE packets coming from the router:
>
> ```
> # tcpdump -n -i eth0 ip proto gre
> ```
>
> If you don't see any output from tcpdump, the router/switch is probably not sending anything. In that case, return to the previous suggestions.

Note, if the device is using layer four health checks, you should see those in the tcpdump output. Health checks come from the router/switch IP address, so they should be easy to spot. If you see health checks, but no other traffic, it probably means the router/switch is interpreting Squid's reply as unhealthy. For example, the device may want to see a 200 (OK) response, but Squid returns an error, such as 401 (Unauthorized) or 404 (Not Found). You may want to run tail -f on the *access.log*.

Did you enable IP forwarding?

Double-check that Squid's operating system is configured to forward IP packets. If not, the host may drop intercepted packets because the destination IP address isn't local.

Did you configure the packet filter?

Make sure that the packet filter (i.e., ipfw, iptables, pf, etc.) is configured correctly. When everything is working well, you should be able to run the command periodically that displays the filtering rules and see the counters increase. For example:

```
# ipfw show 300 ; sleep 3; ipfw show 300
00300   86216 8480458 fwd 127.0.0.1,3128 tcp from any to any 80 in
00300   86241 8482240 fwd 127.0.0.1,3128 tcp from any to any 80 in
```

Note that in this example on FreeBSD, the packet and byte counters (second and third columns) are being incremented.

Is the loopback interface up and configured?

If you have a rule to forward/redirect packets to 127.0.0.1, make sure that the loopback (e.g., *lo0*, *lo*) interface is up and configured. If not, the kernel may simply skip the forward/redirect rule.

Are WCCP/GRE packets being unencapsulated correctly?

If you use WCCP, make sure that the GRE packets are being unencapsulated. If, for some reason, your system doesn't know what to do with GRE packets, it probably increments the "unknown/unsupported protocol" counter in netstat -s output:

```
# netstat -s | grep unknown
        46 packets for unknown/unsupported protocol
```

If your OS has a GRE interface, run netstat -i every so often and look for increasing packet counts:

```
# netstat -in | grep ^gre0
Name    Mtu Network       Address          Ipkts Ierrs  Opkts Oerrs  Coll
gre0   1476 <Link#4>                      304452     0      0     4     0
```

Also, try running tcpdump on the GRE interface:

```
# tcpdump -n -i gre0
```

Can Squid talk back to the clients?

You may have a situation in which the router/switch is able to send packets to Squid, but Squid can't send packets back to the clients. This can happen if your firewall filter rules reject those outgoing packets or if Squid just doesn't have a route to the client addresses. To check for this condition, run netstat -n and look for a lot of sockets in the SYN_RCVD state:

```
% netstat -n
Active Internet connections
Proto Recv-Q Send-Q  Local Address            Foreign Address          (state)
tcp4       0      0  10.102.129.246.80        10.102.0.1.36260         SYN_RCVD
tcp4       0      0  10.102.129.226.80        10.102.0.1.36259         SYN_RCVD
tcp4       0      0  10.102.128.147.80        10.102.0.1.36258         SYN_RCVD
tcp4       0      0  10.102.129.26.80         10.102.0.2.36257         SYN_RCVD
tcp4       0      0  10.102.129.29.80         10.102.0.2.36255         SYN_RCVD
tcp4       0      0  10.102.129.226.80        10.102.0.1.36254         SYN_RCVD
tcp4       0      0  10.102.128.117.80        10.102.0.1.36253         SYN_RCVD
tcp4       0      0  10.102.128.149.80        10.102.0.1.36252         SYN_RCVD
```

If you see this, use ping and traceroute to make sure that Squid has bidirectional communication with the clients.

Can Squid talk to origin servers?

Intercepted HTTP connections get stuck if Squid can't connect to origin servers. When this happens, netstat should show you a lot of connections in the SYN_ SENT state:

```
% netstat -n
Active Internet connections
Proto Recv-Q Send-Q  Local Address            Foreign Address          (state)
tcp4       0      0  172.16.102.66.5217       10.102.129.145.80        SYN_SENT
tcp4       0      0  172.16.102.66.5216       10.102.129.224.80        SYN_SENT
tcp4       0      0  172.16.102.66.5215       10.102.128.71.80         SYN_SENT
tcp4       0      0  172.16.102.66.5214       10.102.129.209.80        SYN_SENT
tcp4       0      0  172.16.102.66.5213       10.102.129.62.80         SYN_SENT
tcp4       0      0  172.16.102.66.5212       10.102.129.160.80        SYN_SENT
tcp4       0      0  172.16.102.66.5211       10.102.128.129.80        SYN_SENT
tcp4       0      0  172.16.102.66.5210       10.102.129.44.80         SYN_SENT
tcp4       0      0  172.16.102.66.5209       10.102.128.73.80         SYN_SENT
tcp4       0      0  172.16.102.66.5208       10.102.128.43.80         SYN_SENT
```

Again, use ping and traceroute to make sure that Squid can talk to origin servers.

Are outgoing connections being intercepted?

If Squid can ping origin servers, and you still see a lot of connections in the SYN_ SENT state, the router/switch may be intercepting Squid's outgoing TCP connections. In some cases, Squid can detect such forwarding loops, and it writes a warning message to *cache.log*. Such a forwarding loop can quickly exhaust all of Squid's file descriptors, which also generates a warning in *cache.log*.

If you suspect this problem, use the squidclient program to make some simple HTTP requests. For example, this command makes an HTTP request directly to the origin server:

```
% /usr/local/squid/bin/squidclient -p 80 -h slashdot.org /
```

If this command succeeds, you should see a bunch of ugly HTML from the Slashdot site on your screen. You can then try the same request through Squid:

```
% /usr/local/squid/bin/squidclient -r -p 3128 -h 127.0.0.1 http://slashdot.org/
```

Again, you should see some HTML on your screen. If not check for error messages in *cache.log*. If you see forwarding loop errors, you need to reconfigure your router/switch so that it allows Squid's outgoing connections to pass without being intercepted.

Exercises

- Try running Squid with a bogus *httpd_accel_host* value. For example:

  ```
  httpd_accel_host blah.blah.blah
  ```

  Does it still work, or do you get error messages?

- Disconnect Squid's network connection while your router/switch is diverting traffic to it. Does the network device bypass Squid? How long does it take to notice the problem?

- Repeat the same experiment, but this time kill the Squid process instead of unplugging the network cable.

- Enable Squid's user-agent log and see if you are intercepting any nonbrowser web traffic.

CHAPTER 10
Talking to Other Squids

For one reason or another, you may find that you want Squid to forward its cache misses to another cache or HTTP proxy. This is necessary, for example, if you are using Squid inside a large corporate network that has one or more firewalls protecting you from the outside world. If your caching service is actually a cluster of Squid caches, you probably want them to cooperate with each other to minimize duplication of cached responses. You can also use Squid as a *content router*—routing web traffic in different directions based on some aspect of the request. Or, perhaps you'd like to participate in an informal collection of caches to further improve response time and reduce wide-area network traffic.

Intercache communication is a complex undertaking, and Squid has numerous features and protocols to accomplish the task. After explaining some of the terminology and discussing the issues, I'll introduce the configuration file directives that control request routing. Following that I describe the nifty network measurement database.

Most likely, you'll use one or more of Squid's intercache protocols to assist in communicating with the other caches or proxies. The Internet Cache Protocol (ICP) is the oldest but not necessarily the best. It is widely implemented in non-Squid products, so you may need to use it for that reason alone. The newer protocols are Cache Digests, the Hypertext Caching Protocol (HTCP), and the Cache Array Routing Protocol (CARP).

There are many choices here, so I'll spend a bit of time explaining how everything works inside Squid.

Some Terminology

Caching hierarchy is the name generally given to a collection of caches (or proxies) that forward requests to one another. We say that the members of the hierarchy are *neighbors* or *peers*.

Neighbor caches have either a *parent* or *sibling* relationship. Topologically, parent caches are one level up in the hierarchy, while siblings are on the same level. The real difference is that parents can forward cache misses for their children. Siblings, on the other hand, aren't allowed to forward cache misses. This means that, before sending a request to a sibling, the originator should know that it will be a cache hit. Inter-cache protocols like ICP, HTCP, and Cache Digests can predict cache hits in neighbors. CARP, however, can't.

Sometimes, cache hierarchies aren't really hierarchical. Consider, for example, a group of five sibling caches. Because there are no parents or children, there is no sense of up or down. In this case, you could call it a *cache mesh*, or even an *array*, instead of a hierarchy.

Why (Not) Use a Hierarchy?

A neighbor cache improves performance by providing some extra fraction of requests as cache hits. In other words, some of the requests that are misses in your cache may be hits in the neighbor cache. If your cache can download these neighbor hits faster than from the origin server, the hierarchy should improve performance overall. The downside is that neighbor caches usually provide only a small percentage of requests as hits. About 5%, or maybe 10% if you're lucky, of your requests that are cache misses will be hits in a neighbor. In some cases, this small benefit doesn't justify the hassle of joining a hierarchy. In other cases, such as networks with poor or overutilized connectivity, hierarchies definitely improve performance for end users.

If you use Squid inside a firewalled network, you may need to configure the firewall proxy as a parent. In this case, Squid forwards every request to the firewall because it can't connect directly to outside origin servers. If you have some origin servers inside the firewall, you can instruct Squid to connect to them directly.

You can also use a hierarchy to send web traffic in different directions. This is sometimes called *application-layer routing*, or more recently, *content routing*. Consider, for example, a large organization with two Internet connections. Perhaps the second connection costs less, or has higher latency, than the other. This organization may want to use the second connection for low-priority traffic, such as downloading binaries, audio and video files, or other kinds of large transfers. Or, perhaps they want to send all HTTP traffic over one link, and non-HTTP traffic over the other. Or, perhaps certain users' traffic should go through the low-priority connection, while premium customers get to use the more expensive link. You can accomplish any of these scenarios with a hierarchy of caching proxies.

Trust is one of the most important issues for the members of a cache hierarchy. You must trust your neighbors to serve correct, unmodified responses. You must trust them with sensitive information, such as the URIs requested by your users. You must trust that they maintain secure and up-to-date systems to minimize the chances of unauthorized access and denials of service.

Another problem with hierarchies is the way that they normally propagate errors. When a neighbor cache experiences an error, such as an unreachable server, it generates an HTML page that explains the error and its origin. Your users may become confused if they get errors from neighbor caches outside the immediate organization. If the problem persists, they'll have a hard time finding an administrator who can help them.

Sibling relationships are subject to special problem, known as *false hits*. This occurs when Squid sends a request to a sibling, believing it will be a cache hit, but the sibling is unable to satisfy the request without contacting the origin server. False hits happen in a number of circumstances, but usually with a low probability. Furthermore, Squid and other HTTP proxies have features for automatically retrying such requests so that the user isn't even aware of the problem.

A *forwarding loop* is another problem sometimes seen in cache hierarchies. It occurs when Squid forwards a request somewhere, but that request comes back to Squid again, as shown in Figure 10-1.

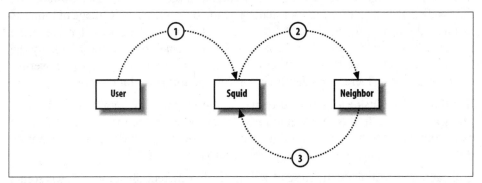

Figure 10-1. A forwarding loop

Forwarding loops typically happen when two caches consider each other parents. If you have such an arrangement, make sure that you use the *cache_peer_access* directive to prevent loops. For example, if the neighbor's IP address is 192.168.1.1, the following lines ensure Squid won't cause a forwarding loop:

```
acl FromNeighbor src 192.168.1.1
cache_peer_access the.neighbor.name deny FromNeighbor
```

Forwarding loops can also occur with HTTP interception, especially if the interception device is on the path between Squid and an origin server.

Squid detects forwarding loops by looking for its own hostname in the Via header. You may actually get false forwarding loops if two cooperating caches have the same hostname. The *unique_hostname* directive is useful in this situation. Note that if the

Via header is filtered out (e.g., with *headers_access*), Squid can't detect forwarding loops.

Telling Squid About Your Neighbors

The *cache_peer* directive defines your neighbor caches and tells Squid how to communicate with them:

```
cache_peer hostname type http-port icp-port [options]
```

The first argument is the neighbor's hostname, or IP address. You can safely use hostnames here because Squid doesn't block while resolving them. In fact, Squid periodically resolves the hostname in case the IP address changes while Squid is running. Neighbor hostnames must be unique: you can't have two neighbors with the same name, even if they have different ports.

The second argument specifies the type of neighbor cache. The choices are: *parent*, *sibling*, or *multicast*. Parent and sibling are straightforward. I'll talk about multicast in the later section "Multicast ICP."

The third argument is the neighbor's HTTP port number. It should correspond to the neighbor's *http_port* (or equivalent) setting. You must always specify a nonzero HTTP port number.

The fourth argument specifies either the ICP or HTCP port number. By default, Squid uses ICP to query other caches. That is, Squid sends ICP queries to the neighbor on the port given here. If you add the htcp option, Squid sends HTCP queries to this port instead. The default ICP port is 3130, and the default HTCP port is 4827. Make sure that you change the port number if you add the htcp option. Setting this port number to zero disables both ICP and HTCP. However, you should instead (or also) use the no-query option to disable these protocols.

cache_peer Options

The *cache_peer* directive has quite a few options. I'll describe some of them here, and the others in the sections relating to specific protocols.

proxy-only
> This option instructs Squid not to store any responses it receives from the neighbor. This is often useful when you have a cluster and don't want a resource to be stored on more than one cache.

weight=*n*
> This option is specific to ICP/HTCP. See the section "cache_peer options for ICP clients."

ttl=*n*
> This option is specific to multicast ICP. See the section "Multicast ICP."

no-query

> This option is specific to ICP/HTCP. See the section "cache_peer options for ICP clients."

default

> This option specifies the neighbor as a suitable choice in the absence of other hints. Squid normally prefers to forward a cache miss to a parent that is likely to have a cached copy of the particular resource. Sometimes Squid won't have any clues (e.g., if you disable ICP/HTCP with no-query). In these cases, Squid looks for a parent that has been marked as a default choice.

round-robin

> This option is a simple load-sharing technique. It makes sense only when you mark two or more parent caches as round-robin. Squid keeps a counter for each parent. When it needs to forward a cache miss, Squid selects the parent with the lowest counter.

multicast-responder

> This option is specific to multicast ICP. See the section "Multicast ICP."

closest-only

> This option is specific to ICP/HTCP. See the section "cache_peer options for ICP clients."

no-digest

> This option is specific to Cache Digests. See the section "Cache Digests."

no-netdb-exchange

> This option tells Squid not to request the neighbor's *netdb* database (see the section "The Network Measurement Database"). Note, this refers to the bulk transfer of the RTT measurements, not the inclusion of these measurements in ICP miss replies.

no-delay

> This option tells Squid to ignore any delay pools settings for requests to the neighbor. See Appendix C for more information on delay pools.

login=*credentials*

> This option instructs Squid to send HTTP authentication credentials to the neighbor. It has three different formats:
>
> login=*user:password*
>
>> This is the most commonly used form. It causes Squid to add the same username and password in every request going to the neighbor. Your users don't need to enter any authentication information.
>
> login=PASS
>
>> Setting the value to PASS causes Squid to pass the user's authentication credentials to the neighbor cache. It works only for HTTP basic authentication. Squid doesn't add or modify any authentication information.

If your Squid is configured to require proxy authentication (i.e., with a *proxy_auth* ACL), the neighbor cache must use the same username and password database. In other words, you should use the PASS form only for a group of caches owned and operated by a single organization. This feature is dangerous because Squid doesn't remove the authentication credentials from forwarded requests.

login=*:*password*

With this form, Squid changes the password, but not the username, in requests that it forwards. It allows the neighbor cache to identify individual users, but doesn't expose their passwords. This form is less dangerous than using PASS, but does have some privacy implications.

Use this feature with extreme caution. Even if you ignore the privacy issues, this feature may cause undesirable side effects with upstream proxies. For example, I know of at least one other caching product that only looks at the credentials of the first request on a persistent connection. It apparently assumes (incorrectly) that all requests on a single connection come from the same user.

connect-timeout=*n*

This option specifies how long Squid should wait when establishing a TCP connection to the neighbor. Without this option, the timeout is taken from the global *connect_timeout* directive, which has a default value of 120 seconds. By using a lower timeout, Squid gives up on the neighbor quickly and may try to send the request to another neighbor or directly to the origin server.

digest-url=*url*

This option is specific to Cache Digests. See the section "Cache Digests."

allow-miss

This option instructs Squid to omit the Cache-Control: only-if-cached directive for requests sent to a sibling. You should use this only if the neighbor has enabled the *icp_hit_stale* directive and isn't using a *miss_access* list.

max-conn=*n*

This option places a limit on the number of simultaneous connections that Squid can open to the neighbor. When this limit is reached, Squid excludes the neighbor from its selection algorithm.

htcp

This option designates the neighbor as an HTCP server. In other words, Squid sends HTCP queries, instead of ICP, to the neighbor. Note that Squid doesn't accept ICP and HTCP queries on the same port. When you add this option, don't forget to change the *icp-port* value as well. See the section "Configuring Squid for HTCP." HTCP support requires the --enable-htcp option when running ./configure.

```
carp-load-factor=f
```
This option makes the neighbor, which must be a parent, a member of a CARP array. The sum of all *f* values, for all parents, must equal 1. I cover CARP in the section "Cache Array Routing Protocol." CARP support requires the `--enable-carp` option when running `./configure`.

Neighbor State

Squid keeps a variety of statistics and state information about each of its neighbors. One of the most important is whether Squid thinks the neighbor is *alive* (up) or *dead* (down). The neighbor's alive/dead state affects many aspects Squid's selection procedures. The algorithm for determining the alive/dead state is a little bit complicated, so I'll go through it here. If you want to follow along in the source code, look at the `neighborUp( )` function.

Squid uses both TCP (HTTP) and UDP (ICP/HTCP) communication to determine the state. The TCP state defaults to alive, but changes to dead if 10 consecutive TCP connections fail. When this happens, Squid initiates probe connections, no more than once every *connect_timeout* time period (the global directive, not the *cache_peer* option). The state remains dead until one of the probe connections succeeds.

If the `no-query` option isn't set (meaning Squid is sending ICP/HTCP queries to the neighbor), the UDP layer communication also factors into the alive/dead algorithm. The UDP state defaults to alive, but changes to dead if Squid doesn't get any ICP/HTCP replies for a certain amount of time—the value of the *dead_peer_timeout* directive.

Squid also marks a neighbor dead if its hostname doesn't resolve to any IP addresses. When Squid determines a neighbor is dead, it writes an entry in *cache.log*. Here's an example:

```
2003/09/29 01:13:46| Detected DEAD Sibling: bo2.us.ircache.net/3128/3130
```

When communication with the neighbor is reestablished, Squid logs a message like this:

```
2003/09/29 01:13:49| Detected REVIVED Sibling: bo2.us.ircache.net/3128/3130
```

A neighbor's state affects neighbor-selection algorithms in the following ways:

- Squid doesn't expect to receive ICP/HTCP replies from dead neighbors. Squid sends ICP queries to dead neighbors no more than once each *dead_peer_timeout* interval. See Appendix A.
- A dead parent is excluded from the following algorithms: Cache Digests, round-robin parent, first up parent, default parent, and closest parent.
- CARP is special: any failed TCP connections (not the 10 required to become dead) excludes the parent from the CARP algorithm.

There is no way to force Squid to send HTTP requests to a dead neighbor. If all neighbors are dead, Squid will try connecting to the origin server. If you don't allow Squid to talk to the origin server (with *never_direct*, for example), Squid returns a cannot forward error message:

```
This request could not be forwarded to the origin server or to any
parent caches.  The most likely cause for this error is that:

  * The cache administrator does not allow this cache to make
    direct connections to origin servers, and
  * All configured parent caches are currently unreachable.
```

Altering the Relationship

The *neighbor_type_domain* directive allows you to change the relationship with your neighbor based on the origin server's hostname. This is useful, for example, if your neighbor is willing to serve cache hits for any request but misses only for certain nearby domains. The syntax is:

```
neighbor_type_domain neighbor.host.name relationship [!]domain ...
```

For example:

```
cache_peer squid.uk.web-cache.net sibling 3128 3130
neighbor_type_domain squid.uk.web-cache.net parent .uk
```

Of course, the *squid.uk.web-cache.net* cache in this example should utilize appropriate *miss_access* rules to enforce the sibling relationship for non-UK requests. Note that domain names are matched to hostnames as described in Chapter 6.

Restricting Requests to Neighbors

Many people who use hierarchical caching need to control or limit requests that Squid sends to its neighbors. Squid has seven different directives that affect request routing: *cache_peer_access*, *cache_peer_domain*, *never_direct*, *always_direct*, *hierarchy_stoplist*, *nonhierarchical_direct*, and *prefer_direct*.

cache_peer_access

The *cache_peer_access* directive defines an access list for a neighbor cache. That is, it determines which requests may, or may not, be sent to the neighbor.

You can use this, for example, to split the flow of FTP and HTTP requests. You can send all FTP URIs to one parent and all HTTP URIs to another:

```
cache_peer A-parent.my.org parent 3128 3130
cache_peer B-parent.my.org parent 3128 3130
acl FTP proto FTP
acl HTTP proto HTTP
```

```
cache_peer_access A-parent allow FTP
cache_peer_access B-parent allow HTTP
```

This configuration ensures that A-parent receives only requests for FTP URIs, while B-parent receives only requests for HTTP URIs. This includes ICP/HTCP queries as well.

You might also use *cache_peer_access* to enable or disable a neighbor cache during certain times of the day:

```
cache_peer A-parent.my.org parent 3128 3130
acl DayTime time 07:00-18:00
cache_peer_access A-parent.my.org deny DayTime
```

cache_peer_domain

The *cache_peer_domain* directive is an earlier form of *cache_peer_access*. Rather than using the full access control feature set, it only uses domain names in URIs. It is often used to partition a group of parent caches by domain name. For example, if you have a global intranet, you may want to send requests to caches located on each continent:

```
cache_peer europe-cache.my.org parent 3128 3130
cache_peer asia-cache.my.org    parent 3128 3130
cache_peer aust-cache.my.org    parent 3128 3130
cache_peer africa-cache.my.org parent 3128 3130
cache_peer na-cache.my.org      parent 3128 3130
cache_peer sa-cache.my.org      parent 3128 3130
cache_peer_domain europe-cache.my.org parent .ch .dk .fr .uk .nl .de .fi ...
cache_peer_domain asia-cache.my.org parent   .jp .kr .cn .sg .tw .vn .hk ...
cache_peer_domain aust-cache.my.org parent   .nz .au .aq ...
cache_peer_domain africa-cache.my.org parent .dz .ly .ke .mz .ma .mg ...
cache_peer_domain na-cache.my.org parent     .mx .ca .us ...
cache_peer_domain sa-cache.my.org parent     .br .cl .ar .co .ve ...
```

Of course, this scheme doesn't address the popular global top-level domains, such as *.com*.

never_direct

The *never_direct* directive is an access list for requests that must never be sent directly to an origin server. When a request matches this access list, it must be sent to a neighbor (usually parent) cache.

For example, if Squid is behind a firewall, it may be able to talk to your "internal" servers directly but must send all requests for external servers via the firewall proxy (a parent). You can tell Squid "never connect directly to sites outside the firewall." To do so, tell Squid what is inside the firewall:

```
acl InternalSites dstdomain .my.org
never_direct allow !InternalSites
```

The syntax is a little strange. `never_direct allow foo` means Squid will not go directly for requests that match "foo." Since the set of internal sites is easy to specify, I used the negation operator (!) to match external sites, which Squid must never directly contact.

Note that this example doesn't force Squid to connect directly to sites that match the *InternalSites* ACL. The *never_direct* access rule can only force Squid not to contact certain origin servers. You must use the *always_direct* rule to force direct connections to origin servers.

You must take care when using *never_direct* in combination with the other directives that control request routing. You can easily create an impossible situation. Here's an example:

```
cache_peer A-parent.my.org parent 3128 3130
acl COM dstdomain .com
cache_peer_access A-parent.my.org deny COM
never_direct allow COM
```

This configuration creates a contradiction because any request whose domain name ends with *.com* must go through a neighbor cache. However, I defined only one neighbor cache, and don't allow the *.com* requests to go there. When this happens, Squid emits the "cannot forward" error message mentioned earlier in the "Neighbor State" section.

always_direct

As you can probably guess, the list of `always_direct` rules tell Squid that some requests must be forwarded directly to the origin server. For example, many organizations want to keep their local traffic local. An easy way to do this is to define an IP address–based ACL and put it in the *always_direct* rule list:

```
acl OurNetwork src 172.16.3.0/24
always_direct allow OurNetwork
```

hierarchy_stoplist

Internally, Squid flags each client request as either hierarchical or nonhierarchical. A nonhierarchical request is one that is unlikely to result in a cache hit. For example, responses to POST requests are almost never cachable. Forwarding requests for uncachable objects to neighbors is a waste of resources when Squid can simply connect to the origin server.

Some of the rules for differentiating hierarchical and nonhierarchical requests are hardcoded in Squid. For example, the POST and PUT methods are always nonhierarchical. However, the *hierarchy_stoplist* directive allows you to customize the algorithm. It contains a list of strings that, when found in a URI, make the request nonhierarchical. The default list is:

```
hierarchy_stoplist ? cgi-bin
```

Thus, any request that contains a question mark or the cgi-bin string matches the stoplist and becomes nonhierarchical.

By default, Squid prefers to send nonhierarchical requests directly to origin servers. Because they are unlikely to result in cache hits, they are generally an extra burden on neighbor caches. However, the *never_direct* access control rules override *hierarchy_stoplist*. In particular, Squid:

- Never sends ICP/HTCP queries for nonhierarchical requests unless the request matches a *never_direct* rule
- Never sends ICP/HTCP queries to sibling caches for nonhierarchical requests
- Never looks in neighbor cache digests for nonhierarchical requests

nonhierarchical_direct

This directive controls the way that Squid forwards nonhierarchical (i.e., probably uncachable) requests. By default, Squid prefers to send nonhierarchical requests directly to origin servers. This is because such requests are unlikely to result in cache hits. I feel it is always better to get them directly from the origin server, rather than waste time looking for them in neighbor caches. If, for some reason, you want to route such requests through the hierarchy, disable this directive:

```
nonhierarchical_direct off
```

prefer_direct

This directive controls the way that Squid forwards hierarchical (i.e., probably cachable) requests. By default, Squid prefers to send such requests to a neighbor cache first and then directly to the origin server. You can reverse this behavior by enabling the directive:

```
prefer_direct on
```

In this way, your neighbor caches become a backup if communication with the origin server fails.

The Network Measurement Database

Squid's network measurement database (*netdb*) is designed to measure the proximity of origin servers. In other words, by querying this database, Squid knows how close it is to the origin server. The database includes ICMP round-trip time (RTT) measurements and hop counts. Squid normally uses only the RTT measurements but can also use the hop counts in some situations.

To enable *netdb*, you must configure Squid with the `--enable-icmp` option. You must also install the *pinger* program with superuser permissions, as described in Chapter 3. When everything is working correctly, you should see a message like this in *cache.log*:

```
2003/09/29 00:01:03| Pinger socket opened on FD 28
```

When *netdb* is enabled, Squid sends ICMP "pings" to origin servers. The ICMP messages are actually sent and received by the *pinger* program, which runs as *root*. Squid is careful not to send pings too frequently, which may annoy web site administrators. By default, Squid waits at least five minutes before sending another ping to the same host, or to any other host on the same /24 subnet. You can adjust the interval with the *netdb_ping_period* directive.

The ICMP pings are generally small in size (less than 100 bytes). Squid includes the origin server hostname in the payload of the ICMP message, along with a timestamp.

To reduce memory requirements, Squid aggregates the *netdb* data by /24 subnets. Squid assumes that all hosts within the subnet have similar RTT and hop-count measurements. This scheme also allows Squid to estimate the proximity of a new origin server when other servers in the subnet have already been measured.

Along with the RTT and hop-count measurements, Squid also stores a list of hostnames associated with the subnet. A typical record may look something like this:

```
Subnet 140.98.193.0
RTT    76.5
Hops   20.0
Hosts  services1.ieee.org
       www.spectrum.ieee.org
       www.ieee.org
```

The *netdb* measurements are primarily used by ICP and HTCP. When you enable the *query_icmp* directive in *squid.conf*, Squid sets a flag in the ICP/HTCP queries that it sends to neighbors. This flag is a request to include proximity measurements in the ICP/HTCP reply. If your neighbors also enabled *netdb*, their replies should include RTT and hop-count measurements if available. Note that Squid always sends ICP replies immediately. It doesn't wait for an ICMP measurement before replying to the query. See the section "ICP and netdb" for details on how ICP uses *netdb*.

Squid remembers the RTT values it learns from ICP/HTCP replies. These values may be used later to optimize forwarding decisions. Squid also supports a "bulk transfer" of *netdb* measurements via what is called *netdb exchange*. Squid periodically makes an HTTP request to a neighbor for its *netdb* data. You can disable these requests with the `no-netdb-exchange` option on the *cache_peer* line.

The *netdb_low* and *netdb_high* directives control the size of the measurement database. When the number of stored subnets reaches *netdb_high*, Squid deletes the least recently used entries until the count is less than *netdb_low*.

The *minimum_direct_hops* and *minimum_direct_rtt* directives instruct Squid to connect directly to origin servers that are no more than some number of hops, or milliseconds, away. Requests that meet this criteria are logged with CLOSEST_DIRECT in *access.log*.

The cache manager's *netdb* page displays the entire network measurement database, including values from neighbor caches. For example:

```
Network DB Statistics:
Network          recv/sent      RTT   Hops Hostnames
63.241.84.0        1/   1      25.0    9.0 www.xyzzy.com
    sd.us.ircache.net          21.5   15.0
    bo1.us.ircache.net         27.0   13.0
    pb.us.ircache.net          70.0   11.0
206.100.24.0       5/   5      25.0    3.0 wcarchive.cdrom.com ftp.cdrom.com
    uc.us.ircache.net          23.5   11.0
    bo1.us.ircache.net         27.7    7.0
    pb.us.ircache.net          35.7   10.0
    sd.us.ircache.net          72.9   10.0
146.6.135.0        1/   1      25.0   13.0 www.cm.utexas.edu
    bo1.us.ircache.net         32.0   11.0
    sd.us.ircache.net          55.0    8.0
216.234.248.0      2/   2      25.0    8.0 postfuture.com www1.123india.com
    pb.us.ircache.net          44.0   14.0
216.148.242.0      1/   1      25.0    9.0 images.worldres.com
    sd.us.ircache.net          25.2   15.0
    bo1.us.ircache.net         27.0   13.0
    pb.us.ircache.net          69.5   11.0
```

Here you can see that the server *www.xyzzy.com* has an IP address in the 63.241.84. 0/24 block. The RTT from this cache to the origin server is 25 milliseconds. The neighbor cache *sd.us.ircache.net* is a little closer, at 21.5 milliseconds.

Internet Cache Protocol

ICP is a lightweight object location protocol invented as a part of the Harvest project.[*] An ICP client sends a query message to one or more ICP servers, asking if they have a particular URI cached. Each server replies with an ICP_HIT, ICP_MISS, or other type of ICP message. The ICP client uses the information in the ICP replies to make a forwarding decision.

---

[*] For more information, see the following papers: "A Hierarchical Internet Object Cache," by Danzig, Chankhunthod, et al, *USENIX Annual Technical Conference, 1995*, and "The Harvest information discovery and access system," by C. Mic Bowman, Peter B. Danzig, Darren R. Hardy, Udi Manber, and Michael F. Schwartz, Proceedings of the Second International World Wide Web Conference.

In addition to predicting cache hits, ICP is also useful for providing hints about network conditions between Squid and the neighbor. ICP messages are similar to ICMP pings in this regard. By measuring the query/response round-trip time, Squid can estimate network congestion. In the extreme case, ICP messages may be lost, indicating that the path between the two is down or congested. From this, Squid decides to avoid the neighbor for that particular request.

Increased latency is perhaps the most significant drawback to using ICP. The query/response exchange takes some time. Caching proxies are supposed to decrease response time, not add more latency. If ICP helps us discover cache hits in neighbors, then it may lead to an overall reduction in response time. See the section "Putting It All Together" for a description of the query algorithm implemented in Squid.

ICP also suffers from a number of design deficiencies: security, scalability, false hits, and the lack of a request method. The protocol doesn't include any security features. In general, Squid can't verify that an ICP message is authentic; it relies on address-based access controls to filter out unwanted ICP messages.

ICP has poor scaling properties. The number of ICP messages (and bandwidth) grows in proportion to the number of neighbors. Unless you use some kind of partitioning scheme, this places a practical limit on the number of neighbors you can have. I don't recommend having more than five or six neighbors.

ICP queries contain only URIs, with no additional request headers. This makes it difficult to predict cache hits with perfect accuracy. An HTTP request may include additional headers (such as `Cache-Control: max-stale=N`) that turn a cache hit into a cache miss. These false hits are particularly awkward for sibling relationships.

Also missing from the ICP query message is the request method. ICP assumes that all queries are for `GET` requests. A caching proxy can't use ICP to locate cached objects for non-`GET` request methods.

You can find additional information about ICP by reading:

- My book *Web Caching* (O'Reilly)
- RFCs 2186 and 2187
- My article with kc claffy: "ICP and the Squid Web Cache" in the *IEEE Journal on Selected Areas in Communication*, April 1998
- *http://icp.ircache.net/*

Being an ICP Server

When you use the *icp_port* directive, Squid automatically becomes an ICP server. That is, it listens for ICP messages on the port you've specified, or port 3130 by default. Be sure to tell your sibling and/or child caches if you decide to use a nonstandard port.

By default, Squid denies all ICP queries. You must use the *icp_access* rule list to allow queries from your neighbors. It's usually easiest to do this with *src* ACLs. For example:

```
acl N1 src 192.168.0.1
acl N2 src 172.16.0.2
acl All src 0/0
icp_access allow N1
icp_access allow N2
icp_access deny All
```

Note that only ICP_QUERY messages are subject to the *icp_access* rules. ICP client functions, such as sending queries and receiving replies, don't require any special access controls. I also recommend that you take advantage of your operating system's packet filtering features (e.g., ipfw, iptables, and pf) if possible. Allow UDP messages on the ICP port from your trusted neighbors and deny them from all other hosts.

When Squid denies an ICP query due to the *icp_access* rules, it sends back an ICP_DENIED message. However, if Squid detects that more than 95% of the recent queries have been denied, it stops responding for an hour. When this happens, Squid writes a message in *cache.log*:

```
WARNING: Probable misconfigured neighbor at foo.web-cache.com
WARNING: 150 of the last 150 ICP replies are DENIED
WARNING: No replies will be sent for the next 3600 seconds
```

If you see this message, you should contact the administrator responsible for the misconfigured cache.

Squid was designed to answer ICP queries immediately. That is, Squid can tell whether or not it has a fresh, cached response by checking the in-memory index. This is also why Squid is a bit of a memory hog. When an ICP query comes in, Squid calculates the MD5 hash of the URI and looks for it in the index. If not found, Squid sends back an ICP_MISS message. If found, Squid checks the expiration time. If the object isn't fresh, Squid returns ICP_MISS. For fresh objects, Squid returns ICP_HIT.

By default, Squid logs all ICP queries (but not responses) to *access.log*. If you have a lot of busy neighbors, your log file may become too large to manage. Use the *log_icp_queries* directive to prevent logging of these queries. Although you'll lose the detailed logging for ICP, you can still get some aggregate stats via the cache manager (see Chapter 14).

If you have sibling neighbors, you'll probably want to use the *miss_access* directive to enforce the relationship. It specifies an access rule for cache misses. It is similar to *http_access* but is checked only for requests that must be forwarded. The default rule is to allow all cache misses. Unless you add some *miss_access* rules, any sibling cache can become a child cache and forward cache misses through your network connection, thus stealing your bandwidth.

Your *miss_access* rules can be relatively simple. Don't forget to include your local clients (i.e., web browsers) as well. Here's a simple example:

```
acl Browsers src 10.9.0.0/16
acl Child1 src 172.16.3.4
acl Child2 src 192.168.2.0/24
acl All src 0/0
miss_access allow Browsers
miss_access allow Child1
miss_access allow Child2
miss_access deny All
```

Note that I haven't listed any siblings here. The child caches are allowed to request misses through us, but the siblings are not. Their cache miss requests are denied by the deny All rule.

The icp_hit_stale directive

One of the problems with ICP is that it returns ICP_MISS for cached but stale responses. This is true even if the response is stale, but valid (such that a validation request returns "not modified"). Consider a simple hierarchy with a child and two parent caches. An object is cached by one parent but not the other. The cached response is stale, but unchanged, and needs validation. The child's ICP query results in two ICP_MISS replies. Not knowing that the stale response exists in the first parent, the child forwards its request to the second parent. Now the object is stored in both parents, wasting resources.

You might find the *icp_hit_stale* directive useful in this situation. It tells Squid to return an ICP_HIT for any cached object, even if it is stale. This is perfectly safe for parent relationships but can create problems for siblings.

Recall that in a sibling relationship, the client cache is only allowed to make requests that are cache hits. Enabling the *icp_hit_stale* directive increases the number of false hits because Squid must validate the stale responses. Squid normally handles false hits by adding the Cache-Control: only-if-cached directive to HTTP requests sent to siblings. If the sibling can't satisfy the HTTP request as a cache hit, it returns an HTTP 504 (Gateway Timeout) message instead. When Squid receives the 504 response, it forwards the request again, but only to a parent or the origin server.

It makes little sense to enable *icp_hit_stale* for sibling relationships if all the false hits must be reforwarded. This is where the ICP client's allow-miss option to *cache_peer* becomes useful. When the allow-miss option is set, Squid omits the only-if-cached directive in HTTP requests it sends to siblings.

If you enable *icp_hit_stale*, you also need to make sure that *miss_access* doesn't deny cache-miss requests from siblings. Unfortunately, there is no way to make Squid allow only cache-misses for cached, stale objects. Allowing cache misses for siblings also leaves your cache open to potential abuse. The administrator of the sibling cache may change it to a parent relationship without your knowledge or permission.

The ICP_MISS_NOFETCH feature

The command-line -Y option to Squid causes it to return ICP_MISS_NOFETCH, instead of ICP_MISS, while rebuilding the in-memory indexes. ICP clients that receive ICP_MISS_NOFETCH responses should not send HTTP requests for those objects. This reduces the load placed on Squid and allows the rebuild process to complete sooner.

The test_reachability directive

If you enable the *netdb* feature (see the section "The Network Measurement Database"), you might also be interested in enabling the *test_reachability* directive. The goal behind it is to accept only requests for origin servers Squid can reach. Enabling *test_reachability* causes Squid to return ICP_MISS_NOFETCH, instead of ICP_MISS, for origin server sites that don't respond to ICMP pings. This can help reduce the number of failed HTTP requests and increase the chance that the end user receives the data promptly. However, a significant percentage of origin server sites intentionally filter out ICMP traffic. For these, Squid returns ICP_MISS_NOFETCH even though an HTTP connection would succeed.

Enabling *test_reachability* also causes Squid to make *netdb* measurements in response to ICP queries. If Squid doesn't have any RTT measurements for the origin server in question, it sends out an ICMP ping (subject to the rate limiting mentioned previously).

Being an ICP Client

First, you must use the *cache_peer* directive to define your neighbor caches. See the section "Telling Squid About Your Neighbors."

Second, you must also use the *icp_port* directive, even if your Squid is only an ICP client. This is because Squid uses the same socket for sending and receiving ICP messages. It is perhaps a bad design decision in retrospect. If you are a client only, use *icp_access* to block queries. For example:

```
acl All src 0/0
icp_access deny All
```

Squid sends ICP queries to its neighbors for most requests by default. See the section "Putting It All Together" for a complete description of the way that Squid decides when, and when not, to query its neighbors.

After sending one or more queries, Squid waits some amount of time for ICP replies to arrive. If Squid receives an ICP_HIT from one of its neighbors, it forwards the request there immediately. Otherwise, Squid waits until all replies arrive or until a timeout occurs. The timeout is calculated dynamically, based on the following algorithm.

Squid knows the average round-trip time between itself and each neighbor, taken from recent ICP transactions. When querying a group of neighbors, Squid calculates the mean of all the neighbor ICP RTTs, and then doubles it. In other words, the query timeout is twice the mean of RTTs for each neighbor queried. Squid ignores neighbors that appear to be down when calculating the timeout.

In some cases, the algorithm doesn't work well, especially if you have neighbors with widely varying RTTs. You can change the upper limit on the timeout using the *maximum_icp_query_timeout* directive. Alternatively, you can make Squid always use a constant timeout value with the *icp_query_timeout* directive.

cache_peer options for ICP clients

weight=*n* allows you to weight parent caches artificially when using ICP/HTCP. It comes into play only when all parents report a cache miss. Normally, Squid selects the parent whose reply arrives first. In fact, it remembers which parent has the best RTT for the query. Squid actually divides the RTT by the weight, so that a parent with weight=2 is treated as if it's closer to Squid than it really is.

no-query disables ICP/HTCP for the neighbor. That is, your cache won't send any queries to the neighbor for cache misses. It is often used with the default option.

closest-only refers to one of Squid's *netdb* features. It instructs Squid to select the parent based only on *netdb* RTT measurements and not the order in which replies arrive. This option requires *netdb* at both ends.

ICP and netdb

As mentioned in the section "The Network Measurement Database," *netdb* is mostly used with ICP queries. In this section, we'll follow all the steps involved in this process.

1. A Squid cache, acting as an ICP client, prepares to send a query to one or more neighbors. If *query_icmp* is set, Squid sets the SRC_RTT flag in the ICP query. This informs the ICP server that Squid would like to receive an RTT measurement in the ICP reply.

2. The neighbor receives the query with the SRC_RTT flag set. If the neighbor is configured to make *netdb* measurements, it searches the database for the origin server hostname. Note that the neighbor doesn't query the DNS for the origin server's IP address. Thus, it finds a *netdb* entry only if that particular host has already been measured.

3. If the host exists in the *netdb* database, the neighbor includes the RTT and hop count in the ICP reply. The SRC_RTT flag is set in the reply to indicate the measurement is present.

4. When Squid receives the ICP reply with the SRC_RTT flag set, it extracts the RTT and hop count. These are added to the local *netdb* so that, in the future, Squid knows the approximate RTT from the neighbor to the origin server.

5. An ICP_HIT reply causes Squid to forward the HTTP request immediately. If, on the other hand, Squid receives only ICP_MISS replies, it selects the parent with the smallest (nonzero) measured RTT to the origin server. The request is logged to *access.log* with CLOSEST_PARENT_MISS.

6. If none of the parent ICP_MISS replies contain RTT values, Squid selects the parent whose ICP reply arrived first. In this case, the request is logged with FIRST_PARENT_MISS. However, if the closest-only option is set for a parent cache, Squid never selects it as a "first parent." In other words, the parent is selected only if it is the closest parent to the origin server.

Multicast ICP

As you already know, ICP has poor scaling properties. The number of messages is proportional to the number of neighbors. Because Squid sends identical ICP_QUERY messages to each neighbor, you can use multicast to reduce the number of messages transmitted on the network. Rather than send *N* messages to *N* neighbors, Squid sends one message to a multicast address. The multicast routing infrastructure makes sure each neighbor receives a copy of the message. See the book *Interdomain Multicast Routing: Practical Juniper Networks and Cisco Systems Solutions* by Brian M. Edwards, Leonard A. Giuliano, and Brian R. Wright (Addison Wesley) for more information on the inner workings of multicast.

Note that ICP replies are always sent via unicast. This is because ICP replies may be different (e.g., hit versus miss) and because the unicast and multicast routing topologies may differ. Because ICP is also used to indicate network conditions, an ICP reply should follow the same path an HTTP reply takes. The bottom line is that multicast only reduces message counts for queries.

Historically, I've found multicast infrastructure unstable and unreliable. It seems to be a low priority for many ISPs. Even though it works one day, something may break a few days or weeks later. You're probably safe using multicast entirely within your own network, but I don't recommend using it for ICP on the public Internet.

Multicast ICP server

A multicast ICP server joins one or more multicast group addresses to receive messages. The *mcast_groups* directive specifies these group addresses. The values must be multicast IP addresses or hostnames that resolve to multicast addresses. The IPv4 multicast address range is 224.0.0.0–239.255.255.255. For example:

```
mcast_groups 224.11.22.45
```

An interesting thing about multicast is that hosts, rather than applications, join a group. When a host joins a multicast group, it receives all packets that are transmitted to that group. This means that you need to be a little bit careful when selecting a multicast group to use for ICP. You don't want to select an address that's already being used by another application. When this kind of group overlap occurs, the two groups become joined and receive each other's traffic.

Multicast ICP client

Multicast ICP clients transmit queries to one or more multicast group addresses. Thus, the hostname argument of the *cache_peer* line must be, or resolve to, a multicast address. For example:

```
cache_peer 224.0.14.1 multicast 3128 3130 ttl=32
```

The HTTP port number (e.g., 3128) is irrelevant in this case because Squid never makes HTTP connections to a multicast neighbor.

Realize that multicast groups don't have any access controls. Any host can join any multicast group address. This means that, unless you're careful, others may be able to receive the multicast ICP queries sent by your Squid. IP multicast has two ways to prevent packets from traveling too far: TTLs and administrative scoping. Because ICP queries may carry sensitive information (i.e., URIs that your users access), I recommend using an administratively scoped address and properly configured routers. See RFC 2365 for more information.

The ttl=n option is for multicast neighbors only. It is the multicast TTL value to use for ICP queries. It controls how far away the ICP queries can travel. The valid range is 0–128. A larger value allows the multicast queries to travel farther, and possibly be intercepted by outsiders. Use a lower number to keep the queries close to the source and within your network.

Multicast ICP clients must also tell Squid about the neighbors that will be responding to queries. Squid doesn't blindly trust any cache that happens to send an ICP reply. You must tell Squid about legitimate, trusted neighbors. The multicast-responder option to *cache_peer* identifies such neighbors. For example, if you know that 172.16.2.3 is a trusted neighbor on the multicast group, you should add this line to *squid.conf*:

```
cache_peer 172.16.3.2 parent 3128 3130 multicast-responder
```

You can, of course, use a hostname instead of an IP address. ICP replies from foreign (unlisted) neighbors are ignored, but logged in *cache.log*.

Squid normally expects to receive an ICP reply for each query that it sends. This changes, however, with multicast because one query may result in multiple replies. To account for this, Squid periodically sends out "probes" on the multicast group address. These probes tell Squid how many servers are out there listening. Squid counts the number of replies that arrive within a certain amount of time. That amount of time is given by the *mcast_icp_query_timeout* directive. Then, when Squid sends a real ICP query to the group, it adds this count to the number of ICP replies to expect.

Multicast ICP example

Since multicast ICP is tricky, here's another example. Let's say your ISP has three parent caches that listen on a multicast address for ICP queries. The ISP needs only one line in its configuration file:

```
mcast_groups 224.0.14.255
```

The configuration for you (the child cache) is a little more complicated. First, you must list the multicast neighbor to which Squid should send queries. You must also list the three parent caches with their unicast addresses so that Squid accepts their replies:

```
cache_peer 224.0.14.225 multicast 3128 3130 ttl=16
cache_peer parent1.yourisp.net parent 3128 3130 multicast-responder
cache_peer parent2.yourisp.net parent 3128 3130 multicast-responder
cache_peer parent3.yourisp.net parent 3128 3130 multicast-responder
mcast_icp_query_timeout 2 sec
```

Keep in mind that Squid never makes HTTP requests to `multicast` neighbors, and it never sends ICP queries to `multicast-responder` neighbors.

Cache Digests

One of the most common complaints about ICP is the additional delay added for each request. In many cases, Squid waits for all ICP replies to arrive before making a forwarding decision. Squid's Cache Digest feature offers similar functionality but without per-request network delays.

Cache Digests are based on a technique first published by Pei Cao, called Summary Cache. The fundamental idea is to use a Bloom filter to represent the cache contents. Neighboring caches download each other's Bloom filters, or digests in this terminology. Then, they can query the digest to determine whether or not a particular URI is in the neighbor's cache.

Compared to ICP, Cache Digests trade time for space. Whereas ICP queries incur time penalties (latency), digests incur space (memory, disk) penalties. In Squid, a neighbor's digest is stored entirely in memory. A typical digest requires about 625 KB of memory for every million objects.

The Bloom filter is an interesting data structure that provides lossy encoding of a collection of items. The filter itself is simply a large array of bits. Given a Bloom filter (and the parameters used to generate it), you can find, with some uncertainty, if a particular item is in the collection. In Squid, items are URIs, and the digest is sized at

5 bits per cached object. For example, you can represent the collection of 1,000,000 cached objects with a filter of 5,000,000 bits, or 625,000 bytes.

Due to their nature, Bloom filters aren't a perfect representation of the collection. They sometimes incorrectly indicate that a particular item is present in the collection because two or more items may turn on the same bit. In other words, the filter can indicate that object X is in the cache, even though X was never cached or requested. These false positives occur with a certain probability you can control by adjusting the parameters of the filter. For example, increasing the number of bits per object decreases the false positive probability. See my O'Reilly book, *Web Caching,* for many more details about Cache Digests.

Configuring Squid for Cache Digests

First of all, you must compile Squid with the Cache Digest code enabled. Simply add the `--enable-cache-digests` option when running `./configure`. Taking this step causes two things to happen when you run Squid:

- Your Squid cache generates a digest of its own contents. Your neighbors may request this digest if they are also configured to use Cache Digests.
- Your Squid requests a Cache Digest from each of its neighbors.

If you don't want to request digests for a particular neighbor, use the `no-digest` option on the *cache_peer* line. For example:

```
cache_peer neighbor.host.name parent 3128 3130 no-digest
```

Squid stores its own digest under the following URL: *http://my.host.name:port/squid-internal-periodic/store_digest*. When Squid requests a neighbor's digest, it simply requests *http://neighbor.host.name:port/squid-internal-periodic/store_digest*. Obviously, this naming scheme is specific to Squid. If you have a non-Squid neighbor that supports Cache Digests, you may need to tell your Squid that the neighbor's digest has a different address. The `digest-url=url` option to *cache_peer* allows you to configure the URL for the neighbor's Cache Digest. For example:

```
cache_peer neighbor.host.name parent 3128 3130 digest-url=http://blah/digest
```

squid.conf has a number of directives that control the way in which Squid generates its own Cache Digest. First, the *digest_generation* directive controls whether or not Squid generates a digest of its cache. You might want to disable digest generation if your cache is a child to a parent, but not a parent or sibling to any other caches. The remaining directives control low-level underlying details of digest generation. You should change them only if you fully understand the Cache Digest implementation.

The *digest_bits_per_entry* determines the size of the digest. The default value is 5. Increasing the value results in larger digests (consuming more memory and bandwidth) and lower false-hit probabilities. A lower setting results in smaller digests and more false hits. I feel that the default setting is a very nice tradeoff. A setting of 3 or lower has too many false hits to be useful, and a setting of 8 or higher simply wastes bandwidth.

Squid uses a two-step process to create a cache digest. First, it builds the cache digest data structure. This is basically a large Bloom filter and small header that contains the digest parameters. Once the data structure is filled, Squid creates a cached HTTP response for the digest. This simply involves prepending some HTTP headers and storing the response on disk with the other cached responses.

A Cache Digest represents a snapshot in time of the cache's contents. The *digest_rebuild_period* controls how frequently Squid rebuilds the digest data structure (but not the HTTP response). The default is once per hour. More frequent rebuilds mean Squid's digest is more up to date, at the expense of higher CPU utilization. The rebuild procedure is relatively CPU-intensive. Your users may experience a slow-down while Squid rebuilds its digest.

The *digest_rebuild_chunk_percentage* directive controls how much of the cache to add to the digest each time the rebuild procedure is called. The default is 10%. During each invocation of the rebuild function, Squid adds some percentage of the cache to the digest. Squid doesn't process user requests while this function runs. After adding the specified percentage, the function reschedules itself and then exits so that Squid can process normal HTTP requests. After processing pending requests, Squid returns to the rebuild function and adds another chunk of the cache to the digest. Decreasing this value should give better response time to your users, while increasing the total time needed to rebuild the digest.

The *digest_rewrite_period* directive controls how often Squid creates an HTTP response from the digest data structure. In most cases, this should match the *digest_rebuild_period* value. The default is one hour. The rewrite procedure consists of numerous calls to a function that simply appends some amount of the digest data structure to the cache entry (as though Squid were reading an origin server response from the network). Each time this function is called, Squid appends *digest_swapout_chunk_size* bytes of the digest.

Hypertext Caching Protocol

HTCP and ICP have many common characteristics, although HTCP is broader in scope and generally more complex. Both use UDP for transport, and both are per-request protocols. However, HTCP addresses a number of problems with ICP, namely:

- An ICP query contains only a URI, without even a request method. HTCP queries contain full HTTP request headers.

- ICP provides no security. HTCP has optional message authentication via shared secret keys, although it isn't yet implemented in Squid. Neither protocol supports encrypted messages.

- ICP uses a simple, fixed-sized binary message format that is difficult to extend. HTCP uses a complex, variable-sized binary message format.

HTCP supports four basic opcodes:

TST
> Tests for the presence of a cached response

SET
> Tells a neighbor to update cached object headers

CLR
> Tells a neighbor to remove an object from its cache

MON
> Monitors a neighbor cache's activity

In Squid, only the TST opcode is currently implemented. This book won't cover the others.

The primary advantage of using HTCP over ICP is fewer false hits. HTCP has fewer false hits because the query messages include full HTTP request headers, including any Cache-Control requirements from the client. The primary disadvantages are that HTCP queries are larger, and they require additional CPU processing to generate and parse. Measurements indicate that HTCP queries are about six times larger than ICP queries, due to the presence of HTTP request headers. However, Squid's HTCP replies are typically smaller than ICP replies.

HTCP is documented as an experimental protocol in RFC 2756. For more information about the message format, see the RFC at *http://www.htcp.org* or my O'Reilly book, *Web Caching*.

Configuring Squid for HTCP

To use HTCP, you must configure Squid with the --enable-htcp option. With this option enabled, Squid becomes an HTCP server by default. The *htcp_port* specifies the HTCP port number, which defaults to 4827. Setting the port to 0 disables the HTCP server mode.

To become an HTCP client, you need to add the htcp option to a *cache_peer* line. When you add this option, Squid always sends HTCP messages, instead of ICP, to the neighbor. You can't use both HTCP and ICP with a single neighbor. The ICP port number field actually becomes an HTCP port number, so you need to change that as well. For example, let's say you want to convert an ICP neighbor to HTCP. Here's the neighbor configured for ICP:

```
cache_peer neighbor.host.name parent 3128 3130
```

To switch over to HTCP, the line becomes:

```
cache_peer neighbor.host.name parent 3128 4827 htcp
```

Sometimes people forget to change the port number, and they end up sending HTCP messages to the ICP port. When this happens, Squid writes warnings to *cache.log*:

```
2003/09/29 02:28:55| WARNING: Unused ICP version 23 received from 64.216.111.20:4827
```

Squid doesn't currently log HTCP queries as it does for ICP queries. HTCP queries aren't tracked in the client_list page either. However, when you enable HTCP for a peer, the cache manager server_list page (see Chapter 14) shows the count and percentage of HTCP replies that were hits and misses:

```
Histogram of PINGS ACKED:
      Misses     5085  98%
      Hits         92   2%
```

Note that none of the current Squid versions support HTCP authentication yet.

Cache Array Routing Protocol

CARP is an algorithm that partitions *URI-space* among a group of caching proxies. In other words, each URI is assigned to one of the caches. CARP maximizes hit ratios and minimizes duplication of objects among the group of caches. The protocol consists of two major components: a Routing Function and a Proxy Array Membership Table. Unlike ICP, HTCP, and Cache Digests, CARP can't predict whether a particular request will be a cache hit. Thus, you can't use CARP with siblings—only parents.

The basic idea behind CARP is that you have a group, or array, of parent caches to handle all the load from users or child caches. A cache array is one way to handle ever-increasing loads. You can add more array members whenever you need more capacity. CARP is a deterministic algorithm. That is, the same request always goes to the same array member (as long as the array size doesn't change). Unlike ICP and HTCP, CARP doesn't use query messages.

Another interesting thing about CARP is that you have the choice to deploy it in a number of different places. For example, one approach is to make all user-agents execute the CARP algorithm. You could probably accomplish this with a Proxy Auto-Configuration (PAC) function, written in JavaScript (see Appendix F). However, you're likely to have certain web agents on your network that don't implement or support PAC files. Another option is to use a two-level cache hierarchy. The lower level (child caches) accept requests from all user-agents, and they execute the CARP algorithm to select the parent cache for each request. However, unless your network is very large, many caches can be more of a burden than a benefit. Finally, you can also implement CARP within the array itself. That is, user-agents connect to a random member of the cache array, but each member forwards cache misses to another member of the array based on the CARP algorithm.

CARP was designed to be better than a simple hashing algorithm, which typically works by applying a hash function, such as MD5, to URIs. The algorithm then calculates the modulus for the number of array members. It might be as simple as this pseudocode:

```
N = MD5(URI) % num_caches;
next_hop = Caches[N];
```

This technique uniformly spreads the URIs among all the caches. It also provides a consistent mapping (maximizing cache hits), as long as the number of caches remains constant. When caches are added or removed, however, this algorithm changes the mapping for most of the URIs.

CARP's Routing Function improves on this technique in two ways. First, it allows for unequal sharing of the load. For example, you can configure one parent to receive twice as many requests as another. Second, adding or removing array members minimizes the fraction of URIs that get reassigned.

The downside to CARP is that it is relatively CPU-intensive. For each request, Squid calculates a "score" for each parent. The request is sent to the parent cache with the highest score. The complexity of the algorithm is proportional to the number of parents. In other words, CPU load increases in proportion to the number of CARP parents. However, the calculations in CARP have been designed to be faster than, say, MD5, and other cryptographic hash functions.

In addition to the load-sharing algorithm, CARP also has a protocol component. The Membership Table has a well-defined structure and syntax so that all clients of a single array can have the same configuration. If some clients are configured differently, CARP becomes less useful because not all clients send the same request to the same parent. Note that Squid doesn't currently implement the Membership Table feature.

Squid's CARP implementation is lacking in another way. The protocol says that if a request can't be forwarded to the highest-scoring parent cache, it should be sent to the second-highest-scoring member. If that also fails, the application should give up. Squid currently uses only the highest-scoring parent cache.

CARP was originally documented as an Internet Draft in 1998, which is now expired. It was developed by Vinod Valloppillil of Microsoft and Keith W. Ross of the University of Pennsylvania. With a little searching, you can still find the old document out there on the Internet. You may even be able to find some documentation on the Microsoft sites. You can also find more information on CARP in my O'Reilly book *Web Caching*.

Configuring Squid for CARP

To use CARP in Squid, you must first run the `./configure` script with the `--enable-carp` option. Next, you must add `carp-load-factor` options to the *cache_peer* lines for parents that are members of the array. The following is an example.

```
cache_peer neighbor1.host.name parent 3128 0 carp-load-factor=0.3
cache_peer neighbor2.host.name parent 3128 0 carp-load-factor=0.3
cache_peer neighbor3.host.name parent 3128 0 carp-load-factor=0.4
```

Note that all carp-load-factor values must add up to 1.0. Squid checks for this condition and complains if it finds a discrepancy. Additionally, the *cache_peer* lines must be listed in order of increasing load factor values. Only recent versions of Squid check that this condition is true.

Remember that CARP is treated somewhat specially with regard to a neighbor's alive/dead state. Squid normally declares a neighbor dead (and ceases sending requests to it) after 10 failed connections. In the case of CARP, however, Squid skips a parent that has one or more failed connections. Once Squid is working with CARP, you can monitor it with the *carp* cache manager page. See Chapter 14 for more information.

Putting It All Together

As you probably realize by now, Squid has many different ways to decide how and where requests are forwarded. In many cases, you can employ more than one protocol or technique at a time. Just by looking at the configuration file, however, you'd probably have a hard time figuring out how Squid uses the different techniques in combination. In this section I'll explain how Squid actually makes the forwarding decision.

Obviously, it all starts with a cache miss. Any request that is satisfied as an unvalidated cache hit doesn't go through the following sequence of events.

The goal of the selection procedure is to create a list of appropriate next-hop locations. A next-hop location may be a neighbor cache or the origin server. Depending on your configuration, Squid may select up to three possible next-hops. If the request can't be satisfied by the first, Squid tries the second, and so on.

Step 1: Determine Direct Options

The first step is to determine if the request may, must, or must not be sent directly to the origin server. Squid evaluates the *never_direct* and *always_direct* access rule lists for the request. The goal is to set a flag to one of three values: DIRECT_YES, DIRECT_MAYBE, or DIRECT_NO. This flag later determines whether Squid should, or should not, try to select a neighbor cache for the request. Squid checks the following conditions in order. If any condition is true, it sets the direct flag and proceeds to the next step. If you're following along in the source code, this step corresponds to the beginning of the peerSelectFoo( ) function:

1. Squid looks at the *always_direct* list first. If the request matches this list, the direct flag is set to DIRECT_YES.

---

2. Squid looks at the *never_direct* list next. If the request matches this list, the direct flag is set to DIRECT_NO.

3. Squid has a special check for requests that appear to be looping. When Squid detects a forwarding loop, it sets the direct flag to DIRECT_YES to break the loop.

4. Squid checks the *minimum_direct_hops* and *minimum_direct_rtt* settings, but only if you've enabled *netdb*. If the measured hop count or round-trip time is lower than the configured values, Squid sets the direct flag to DIRECT_YES.

5. If none of the previous conditions are true, Squid sets the direct flag to DIRECT_MAYBE.

If the direct flag is set to DIRECT_YES, the selection process is complete. Squid forwards the request directly to the origin server and skips the remaining steps in this section.

Step 2: Neighbor Selection Protocols

Here Squid uses one of the hierarchical protocols to select a neighbor cache. As before, once Squid selects a neighbor in this step, it exits the routine and proceeds to Step 3. This step roughly corresponds to the peerGetSomeNeighbor( ) function:

1. Squid examines the neighbor's Cache Digests. If it indicates a hit, that neighbor is placed on the next-hop list.

2. Squid tries CARP if enabled. CARP always succeeds (i.e., selects a parent), unless the *cache_peer_access* or *cache_peer_domain* rules forbid communication with any of the parent caches for a particular request.

3. Squid checks *netdb* measurements (if enabled) for a "closest parent." If Squid knows that the round-trip time from one or more parents to the origin server is less than its own RTT to the origin server, Squid selects the parent with the least RTT. For this to happen, the following conditions must be met:

   - Both your Squid and the parent cache(s) must have enabled *netdb* measurements.

   - *query_icmp* must be enabled in your configuration file.

   - The origin server must respond to ICMP pings.

   - The parent(s) must have previously measured the RTT to the origin server and returned those measurements in ICP/HTCP replies, or through a *netdb* exchange.

4. Squid sends ICP/HTCP queries as the last resort. Squid loops through all neighbors and checks a number of conditions. Squid doesn't query a neighbor if:

   - The direct flag is DIRECT_MAYBE and the request is nonhierarchical (see the section "hierarchy_stoplist"). Because Squid is allowed to go directly to the origin server, it doesn't bother the neighbor with this request, which is likely to be uncachable.

- The direct flag is DIRECT_NO, the neighbor is a sibling, and the request is nonhierarchical. Because Squid is forced to use a neighbor, it only queries parents, which can always handle a cache miss.

- The *cache_peer_access* or *cache_peer_domain* rules forbid sending this request to the neighbor.

- The neighbor's no-query flag is set, or its ICP/HTCP port number is zero.

- The neighbor is a multicast responder.

Squid counts how many queries it sends and calculates how many replies to expect. If it expects at least one reply, the rest of the next-hop selection procedure is postponed until the replies arrive, or a timeout occurs. Squid expects to receive replies from neighbors that are alive, but not neighbors that are dead (see the section "Neighbor State").

Step 2a: ICP/HTCP Reply Processing

If Squid sends out any ICP or HTCP queries, it waits for some number of replies. Just after transmitting the queries, Squid knows how many replies to expect and the maximum amount of time to wait for them. Squid expects a reply from every alive neighbor queried. If you're using multicast, Squid adds the current group size estimate to the expected reply count. While waiting for replies, Squid schedules a timeout, in case one or more of the replies don't arrive.

When Squid receives an ICP/HTCP reply from a neighbor, it takes the following actions:

1. If the reply is a hit, Squid forwards the request to that neighbor immediately. Any replies arriving after this point are ignored.

2. If the reply is a miss, and it is from a sibling, it is ignored.

3. Squid doesn't immediately act on ICP/HTCP misses from parents. Instead, it remembers which parents meet the following criteria:

The closest-parent miss
> If the reply includes a *netdb* RTT measurement, Squid remembers the parent that has the least RTT to the origin server.

The first-parent miss
> Squid remembers the parent that had the first reply. In other words, the parent with least RTT to your cache. Two *cache_peer* options affect this part of the algorithm: weight=N and closest-only.

> The weight=N option makes a parent closer than it really is. When calculating RTTs, Squid divides the actual RTT by this artificial weight. Thus you

can give higher preference to certain parents by increasing their weight value.

The closest-only option disables the first-parent miss feature for a neighbor cache. In other words, Squid selects a parent (based on ICP/HTCP miss replies) only if that parent is the closest to the origin server.

4. If Squid receives the expected number of replies (all misses), or if the timeout occurs, it selects the closest-parent miss neighbor if set. Otherwise, it selects the first-parent miss neighbor if set.

Squid may not receive any ICP/HTCP replies from parent caches, either because they weren't queried or because the network dropped some packets. In this case, Squid relies on the secondary parent (or direct) selection algorithm described in the next section.

If the ICP/HTCP query timeout occurs before receiving the expected number of replies, Squid prepends the string TIMEOUT_ to the result code in *access.log*.

Step 3: Secondary Parent Selection

This step is a little tricky. Remember that if the direct flag is DIRECT_YES, Squid never executes this step. If the flag is DIRECT_NO, Squid calls the getSomeParent( ) function (described subsequently) to select a backup parent, in case Step 2 failed to select one. Following that, Squid adds to the list all parents it believes are alive. Thus, it tries all possible parent caches before returning an error message to the user.

In the case of DIRECT_MAYBE, Squid adds both a parent cache, and the origin server. The order, however, depends on the *prefer_direct* setting. If *prefer_direct* is enabled, Squid inserts the origin server into the list first. Next, Squid calls getSomeParent( ) if the request is hierarchical or if the *nonhierarchical_direct* directive is disabled. Finally, Squid adds the origin server last if *prefer_direct* is disabled.

The getSomeParent( ) function selects one of the parents based on the following criteria. In each case, the parent must be alive and allowed to handle the request according to the *cache_peer_access* and *cache_peer_domain* rules:

- The first parent with the default *cache_peer* option
- The parent with the round-robin *cache_peer* option that has the lowest request count
- The first parent that is known to be alive

Retrying

Occasionally, Squid's attempt to forward a request to an origin server or neighbor may fail for one reason or another. This is why Squid creates a list of appropriate next-hop locations during the neighbor selection procedure. When one of the following types of errors occurs, Squid can retry the request at the next server in the list:

- Network congestion or other errors can cause a "connection timeout."
- The origin server or neighbor cache may be temporarily unavailable, causing a "connection refused" error.
- A sibling may return a 504 (Gateway Timeout) error if the request would cause a cache miss.
- A neighbor may return an "access denied" error message if the two caches have a mismatch in access control policies.
- A read error may occur on an established connection before Squid reads the HTTP message body.
- There may be race conditions with persistent connections.

Squid's algorithm for retrying failed requests is relatively aggressive. It is better for Squid to keep trying (causing some extra delay), rather than return an error to the user.

How Do I ...

New Squid users often ask the same, or similar, questions about getting Squid to forward requests in the right way. Here I'll show you how to configure Squid for some common scenarios.

Send All Requests Through Another Proxy?

You simply need to define a parent and tell Squid it isn't allowed to connect directly to origin servers. For example:

```
cache_peer parent.host.name parent 3128 0
acl All src 0/0
never_direct allow All
```

The drawback to this configuration is that Squid can't forward cache misses if the parent goes down. If that happens, your users receive the "cannot forward" error message.

Send All Requests Through Another Proxy Unless It's Down?

Try this configuration:

```
nonhierarchical_direct off
prefer_direct off
cache_peer parent.host.name parent 3128 0 default no-query
```

Or, if you'd like to use ICP with the other proxy:

```
nonhierarchical_direct off
prefer_direct off
cache_peer parent.host.name parent 3128 3130 default
```

With this configuration, Squid forwards all cache misses to the parent as long as it is alive. Using ICP should cause Squid to detect a dead parent quickly, but at the same time may incorrectly declare the parent dead on occasion.

Make Sure Squid Doesn't Use Neighbors for Some Requests?

Define an ACL to match the special request:

```
cache_peer parent.host.name parent 3128 0
acl Special dstdomain special.server.name
always_direct allow Special
```

In this case, cache misses for requests in the *special.server.name* domain are always sent to the origin server. Other requests may, or may not, go through the parent cache.

Send Some Requests Through a Parent to Bypass Local Filters?

Some ISPs (and other organizations) have upstream providers that force HTTP traffic through a filtering proxy (perhaps with HTTP interception). You might be able to get around their filters if you can use a different proxy beyond their network. Here's how you can send only special requests to the far-away proxy:

```
cache_peer far-away-parent.host.name parent 3128 0
acl BlockedSites dstdomain www.censored.com
cache_peer_access far-away-parent.host.name allow BlockedSites
never_direct allow BlockedSites
```

Exercises

- Toggle your *prefer_direct* and/or *nonhierarchical_direct* settings and look for any changes in the *access.log*.
- Enable *netdb* and view the *netdb* cache manager page after Squid has been running for a while.
- If using ICP or HTCP, count the percentage of requests that experienced a timeout waiting for replies to arrive.
- If you used --enable-cache-digests and have a reasonably full cache, disable the *digest_generation* directive and note any change in memory usage.

- Use your operating system's packet filters to block ICP or HTCP messages to your neighbors. How quickly does Squid change their state from alive to dead, and back again?

## CHAPTER 11

Redirectors

A *redirector* is an external process that rewrites URIs from client requests. For example, although a user requests the page *http://www.example.com/page1.html*, a redirector can change the request to something else, such as *http://www.example.com/page2.html*. Squid fetches the new URI automatically, as though the client originally requested it. If the response is cachable, Squid stores it under the new URI.

The redirector feature allows you to implement a number of interesting things with Squid. Many sites use them for access controls, removing advertisements, local mirrors, or even working around browser bugs.

One of the nice things about using a redirector for access control is that you can send the user to a page that explains exactly why her request is denied. You may also find that a redirector offers more flexibility than Squid's built-in access controls. As you'll see shortly, however, a redirector doesn't have access to the full spectrum of information contained in a client's request.

Many people use a redirector to filter out web page advertisements. In most cases, this involves changing a request for a GIF or JPEG advertisement image into a request for a small, blank image, located on a local server. Thus, the advertisement just "disappears" and doesn't interfere with the page layout.

So in essence, a redirector is really just a program that reads a URI and other information from its input and writes a new URI on its output. Perl and Python are popular languages for redirectors, although some authors use compiled languages such as C for better performance.

The Squid source code doesn't come with any redirector programs. As an administrator, you are responsible for writing your own or downloading one written by someone else. The first part of this chapter describes the interface between Squid and a redirector process. I also provide a couple of simple redirector examples in Perl. If you're interested in using someone else's redirector, rather than programming your own, skip ahead to the "The Redirector Pool" section.

The Redirector Interface

A redirector receives data from Squid on *stdin* one line at a time. Each line contains the following four tokens separated by whitespace:

- Request-URI
- Client IP address and fully qualified domain name
- User's name, via either RFC 1413 ident or proxy authentication
- HTTP request method

For example:

```
http://www.example.com/page1.html 192.168.2.3/user.host.name jabroni GET
```

The Request-URI is taken from the client's request, including query terms, if any. Fragment identifier components (e.g., the # character and subsequent text) are removed, however.

The second token contains the client IP address and, optionally, its fully qualified domain name (FQDN). The FQDN is set only if you enable the *log_fqdn* directive or use a *srcdomain* ACL element. Even then, the FQDN may be unknown because the client's network administrators didn't properly set up the reverse pointer zones in their DNS. If Squid doesn't know the client's FQDN, it places a hyphen (-) in the field. For example:

```
http://www.example.com/page1.html 192.168.2.3/- jabroni GET
```

The client ident field is set if Squid knows the name of the user behind the request. This happens if you use proxy authentication, *ident* ACL elements, or enable *ident_lookup_access*. Remember, however, that the *ident_lookup_access* directive doesn't cause Squid to delay request processing. In other words, if you enable that directive, but don't use the access controls, Squid may not yet know the username when writing to the redirector process. If Squid doesn't know the username, it displays a -. For example:

```
http://www.example.com/page1.html 192.168.2.3/- - GET
```

Squid reads back one token from the redirector process: a URI. If Squid reads a blank line, the original URI remains unchanged.

A redirector program should never exit until end-of-file occurs on *stdin*. If the process does exit prematurely, Squid writes a warning to *cache.log*:

```
WARNING: redirector #2 (FD 18) exited
```

If 50% of the redirector processes exit prematurely, Squid aborts with a fatal error message.

Handling URIs That Contain Whitespace

If the Request-URI contains whitespace, and the *uri_whitespace* directive is set to allow, any whitespace in the URI is passed to the redirector. A redirector with a simple parser may become confused in this case. You have two options for handling whitespace in URIs when using a redirector.

One option is to set the *uri_whitespace* directive to anything except allow. The default setting, strip, is probably a good choice in most situations because Squid simply removes the whitespace from the URI when it parses the HTTP request. See Appendix A for information on the other values for this directive.

If that isn't an option, you need to make sure the redirector's parser is smart enough to detect the extra tokens. For example, if it finds more than four tokens in the line received from Squid, it can assume that the last three are the IP address, ident, and request method. Everything before the third-to-last token comprises the Request-URI.

Generating HTTP Redirect Messages

When a redirector changes the client's URI, it normally doesn't know that Squid decided to fetch a different resource. This is, in all likelihood, a gross violation of the HTTP RFC. If you want to be nicer, and remain compliant, there is a little trick that makes Squid return an HTTP redirect message. Simply have the redirector insert 301:, 302:, 303:, or 307:, before the new URI.

For example, if a redirector writes this line on its *stdout*:

```
301:http://www.example.com/page2.html
```

Squid sends a response like this back to the client:

```
HTTP/1.0 301 Moved Permanently
Server: squid/2.5.STABLE4
Date: Mon, 29 Sep 2003 04:06:23 GMT
Content-Length: 0
Location: http://www.example.com/page2.html
X-Cache: MISS from zoidberg
Proxy-Connection: close
```

Some Sample Redirectors

Example 11-1 is a very simple redirector written in Perl. Its purpose is to send HTTP requests for the *squid-cache.org* site to a local mirror site in Australia. If the requested URI looks like it is for *www.squid-cache.org* or one of its mirror sites, this script outputs a new URI with the hostname set to *www1.au.squid-cache.org*.

A common problem first-time redirector writers encounter is *buffered I/O*. Note that here I make sure *stdout* is unbuffered.

Example 11-1. A simple redirector in Perl

```perl
#!/usr/bin/perl -wl
$|=1;    # don't buffer the output
while (<>) {
        ($uri,$client,$ident,$method) = ();
        ($uri,$client,$ident,$method) = split;
        next unless ($uri =~ m,^http://.*\.squid-cache\.org(\S*),);
        $uri = "http://www1.au.squid-cache.org$1";
} continue {
        print "$uri";
}
```

Example 11-2 is another, somewhat more complicated, example. Here I make a feeble attempt to deny requests when the URI contains "bad words." This script demonstrates an alternative way to parse the input fields. If I don't get all five required fields, the redirector returns a blank line, leaving the request unchanged.

This example also gives preferential treatment to some users. If the ident string is equal to "BigBoss," or comes from the 192.168.4.0 subnet, the request is passed through. Finally, I use the 301: trick to make Squid return an HTTP redirect to the client. Note, this program is neither efficient nor smart enough to correctly deny so-called bad requests.

Example 11-2. A slightly less simple redirector in Perl

```perl
#!/usr/bin/perl -wl
$|=1;    # don't buffer the output

$DENIED = "http://www.example.com/denied.html";
&load_word_list();

while (<>) {
        unless (m,(\S+) (\S+)/(\S+) (\S+) (\S+),) {
                $uri = '';
                next;
        }
        $uri = $1;
        $ipaddr = $2;
        #$fqdn = $3;
        $ident = $4;
        #$method = $5;
        next if ($ident eq 'TheBoss');
        next if ($ipaddr =~ /^192\.168\.4\./);
        $uri = "301:$DENIED" if &word_match($uri);
} continue {
        print "$uri";
}

sub load_word_list {
        @words = qw(sex drugs rock roll);
}
```

Example 11-2. A slightly less simple redirector in Perl (continued)

```
sub word_match {
        my $uri = shift;
        foreach $w (@words) { return 1 if ($uri =~ /$w/); }
        return 0;
}
```

For more ideas about writing your own redirector, I recommend reading the source code for the redirectors mentioned in the section "Popular Redirectors."

The Redirector Pool

A redirector can take an arbitrarily long time to return its answer. For example, it may need to make a database query, search through long lists of regular expressions, or make some complex computations. Squid uses a pool of redirector processes so that they can all work in parallel. While one is busy, Squid hands a new request off to another.

For each new request, Squid examines the pool of redirector processes in order. It submits the request to the first idle process. If your request rate is very low, the first redirector may be able to handle all requests itself.

You can control the size of the redirector pool with the *redirect_children* directive. The default value is five processes. Note that Squid doesn't dynamically increase or decrease the size of the pool depending on the load. Thus, it is a good idea to be a little liberal. If all redirectors are busy, Squid queues pending requests. If the queue becomes too large (bigger than twice the pool size), Squid exits with a fatal error message:

```
FATAL: Too many queued redirector requests
```

In this case, you need to increase the size of the redirector pool or change something so that the redirectors can process requests faster. You can use the cache manager's *redirector* page to find out if you have too few, or too many redirectors running. For example:

```
% squidclient mgr:redirector
...
Redirector Statistics:
program: /usr/local/squid/bin/myredir
number running: 5 of 5
requests sent: 147
replies received: 142
queue length: 2
avg service time: 953.83 msec

        #      FD     PID  # Requests    Flags    Time  Offset Request
        1      10   35200         46     AB       0.902      0 http://...
        2      11   35201         29     AB       0.401      0 http://...
        3      12   35202         25     AB       1.009      1 cache_o...
```

```
4     14    35203        25    AB      0.555      0 http://...
5     15    35204        21    AB      0.222      0 http://...
```

If, as in this example, you see that the last redirector has almost as many requests as the second to last, you should probably increase the size of the redirector pool. If, on the other hand, you see many redirectors with no requests, you can probably decrease the pool size.

Configuring Squid

The following five *squid.conf* directives control the behavior of redirectors in Squid.

redirect_program

The *redirect_program* directive specifies the command line for the redirector program. For example:

```
redirect_program /usr/local/squid/bin/my_redirector -xyz
```

Note, the redirector program must be executable by the Squid user ID. If, for some reason, Squid can't execute the redirector, you should see an error message in *cache. log.** For example:

```
ipcCreate: /usr/local/squid/bin/my_redirector: (13) Permission denied
```

Due to the way Squid works, the main Squid process may be unaware of problems executing the redirector program. Squid doesn't detect the error until it tries to write a request and read a response. It then prints:

```
WARNING: redirector #1 (FD 6) exited
```

Thus, if you see such a message for the first request sent to Squid, check *cache.log* closely for other errors, and make sure the program is executable by Squid.

redirect_children

The *redirect_children* directive specifies how many redirector processes Squid should start. For example:

```
redirect_children 20
```

Squid warns you (via *cache.log*) when all redirectors are simultaneously busy:

```
WARNING: All redirector processes are busy.
WARNING: 1 pending requests queued.
```

---

* This message appears only in *cache.log*, and not on *stdout,* if you use the -d option, or in syslog, if you use the -s option.

If you see this warning, you should increase the number of child processes and restart (or reconfigure) Squid. If the queue size becomes twice the number of redirectors, Squid aborts with a fatal message.

Don't attempt to disable Squid's use of the redirectors by setting *redirect_children* to 0. Instead, simply remove the *redirect_program* line from *squid.conf*.

redirect_rewrites_host_header

Squid normally updates a request's Host header when using a redirector. That is, if the redirector returns a new URI with a different hostname, Squid puts the new hostname in the Host header. If you use Squid as a surrogate (see Chapter 15), you might want to disable this behavior by setting the *redirect_rewrites_host_header* directive to off:

```
redirect_rewrites_host_header off
```

redirector_access

Squid normally sends every request through a redirector. However, you can use the *redirector_access* rules to send certain requests through selectively. The syntax is identical to *http_access*:

```
redirector_access allow|deny [!]ACLname ...
```

For example:

```
acl Foo src 192.168.1.0/24
acl All src 0/0
redirector_access deny Foo
redirector_access allow All
```

In this case, Squid skips the redirector for any request that matches the *Foo* ACL.

redirector_bypass

If you enable the *redirector_bypass* directive, Squid bypasses the redirectors when all of them are busy. Normally, Squid queues pending requests until a redirector process becomes available. If this queue grows too large, Squid exits with a fatal error message. Enabling this directive ensures that Squid never reaches that state.

The tradeoff, of course, is that some user requests may not be redirected when the load is high. If that's all right with you, simply enable the directive with this line:

```
redirector_bypass on
```

Popular Redirectors

As I already mentioned, the Squid source code doesn't include any redirectors. However, you can find a number of useful third-party redirectors linked from the *Related Software* page on *http://www.squid-cache.org*. Here are some of the more popular offerings:

Squirm

http://squirm.foote.com.au/

Squirm comes from Chris Foote. It is written in C and distributed as source code under the GNU General Public License (GPL). Squirm's features include:

- Being very fast with minimal memory usage
- Full regular expression pattern matching and replacement
- Ability to apply different redirection lists to different client groups
- Interactive mode for testing on the command line
- Fail-safe mode passes requests through unchanged in the event that configuration files contain errors
- Writing debugging, errors, and more to various log files

Jesred

http://www.linofee.org/~elkner/webtools/jesred/

Jesred comes from Jens Elkner. It is written in C, based on Squirm, and also released under the GNU GPL. Its features include:

- Being faster than Squirm, with slightly more memory usage
- Ability to reread its configuration files while running
- Full regular expression pattern matching and replacement
- Fail-safe mode passes requests through unchanged in the event that configuration files contain errors
- Optionally logging rewritten requests to a log file

squidGuard

http://www.squidguard.org/

squidGuard comes from Pål Baltzersen and Lars Erik Håland at Tele Danmark Inter-Nordia. It is released under the GNU GPL. The authors also make sure squidGuard compiles easily on modern Unix systems. Their site contains a lot of good documentation. Here are some of squidGuard's features:

- Highly configurable; you can apply different rules to different groups of clients or users and at different times or days
- URI substitution, not just replacement, à la sed
- printf-like substitutions allow passing parameters to CGI scripts for customized messages
- Supportive of the 301/302/303/307 HTTP redirect status code feature for redirectors
- Selective logging for rewrite rule sets

At the squidGuard site, you can also find a blacklist of more than 100,000 sites categorized as porn, aggressive, drugs, hacking, ads, and more.

AdZapper

http://www.zip.com.au/~cs/adzap/index.html

AdZapper is a popular redirector because it specifically targets removal of advertisements from HTML pages. It is a Perl script written by Cameron Simpson. AdZapper can block banners (images), pop-up windows, flash animations, page counters, and web bugs. The script includes a list of regular expressions that match URIs known to contain ads, pop-ups, etc. Cameron updates the script periodically with new patterns. You can also maintain your own list of patterns.

Exercises

- Write a redirector that never changes the requested URI and configure Squid to use it.
- While running **tail -f cache.log**, kill Squid's redirector processes one by one until something interesting happens.
- Download and install one of the redirectors mentioned in the previous section.

CHAPTER 12
Authentication Helpers

I originally talked about proxy authentication in Chapter 6. However, I only explained how to write access control rules that use proxy authentication. Here, I'll show you how to select and configure the particular authentication helpers.

Recall that Squid supports three methods for gathering authentication credentials from users: Basic, Digest, and NTLM. These methods specify how Squid receives the username and password from a client. From a security standpoint, Basic authentication is extremely weak. Digest and NTLM are significantly stronger. For each method, Squid provides some authentication modules, or helper processes, which actually validate the credentials.

All of the authentication helpers that I mention here are included in the Squid source code distribution. You can compile them with ./configure options that match their directory names. For example:

```
% ls helpers/basic_auth
LDAP                    NCSA                    getpwnam
MSNT                    PAM                     multi-domain-NTLM
Makefile                SASL                    winbind
Makefile.am             SMB
Makefile.in             YP

% ./configure --enable-basic-auth-helpers=LDAP,NCSA ...
```

Helper programs are normally installed in the *$prefix/libexec* directory.

As with redirectors, Squid uses a pool of authentication helper processes. A request for authentication is sent to the first idle helper. When all authenticator processes are busy, Squid queues pending requests. If the queue becomes too large, Squid exits with a fatal error message. In most cases, Squid caches authentication results. This reduces the load on the helper processes and improves response time.

Configuring Squid

The *auth_param* directive controls every aspect of configuring Squid's authentication helpers. The different methods (Basic, Digest, NTLM) have some things in common, and some unique parameters. The first argument following *auth_param* must be one of basic, digest, or ntlm. I'll cover this directive in detail for each authentication scheme later in the chapter.

In addition to *auth_param*, Squid has two more directives that affect proxy authentication. You can use the *max_user_ip* ACL to prevent users from sharing their username and password with others. If Squid detects the same username coming from too many different IP addresses, the ACL is a match and you can deny the request. For example:

```
acl FOO max_user_ip 2
acl BAR proxy_auth REQUIRED
http_access deny FOO
http_access allow BAR
```

In this case, if a user submits requests from three or more different IP addresses, Squid denies the request. The *authenticate_ip_ttl* directive controls how long Squid remembers the source IP addresses for each user. A smaller TTL makes it easier for users with frequently changing IP addresses. You can use larger TTLs in an environment where users have the same IP address for long periods of time.

HTTP Basic Authentication

Basic authentication is the simplest and least secure that HTTP has to offer. It essentially transmits user passwords as cleartext, although they are encoded into printable characters. For example, if the user types her name as Fannie and her password as FuRpAnTsClUb, the user-agent first combines the two into a single string, with name and password separated by a colon:

```
Fannie:FuRpAnTsClUb
```

Then it encodes this string with base64 encoding, as defined in RFC 2045. It looks like this in the HTTP headers:

```
Authorization: Basic RmFubmllOkZ1UnBBblRzQ2xVYgo=
```

Anyone who happens to capture your users' HTTP requests can easily get both the username and password:

```
% echo RmFubmllOkZ1UnBBblRzQ2xVYgo= | /usr/local/lib/python1.5/base64.py -d
Fannie:FuRpAnTsClUb
```

As required by the HTTP/1.1 RFC, Squid doesn't forward "consumed" authorization credentials to other servers. In other words, if the credentials are for access to Squid, the Authorization header is removed from outgoing requests.*

You'll notice that some of the Basic authenticators can be configured to check the system password file. Because Basic credentials aren't encrypted, it is a bad idea to combine login passwords with cache access passwords. If you choose to use the *getpwnam* authenticator, make sure you fully understand the implications of having your users' passwords transmitted in the clear across your network.

HTTP Basic authentication supports the following *auth_param* parameters:

- auth_param basic program *command*
- auth_param basic children *number*
- auth_param basic realm *string*
- auth_param basic credentialsttl *time-specification*

The program parameter specifies the command, including arguments, for the helper program. In most cases, this will be the pathname to one of the authentication helper programs that you compiled. By default, they live in */usr/local/squid/libexec*.

The children parameter tells Squid how many helper processes to use. The default value is 5, which is a good starting point if you don't know how many Squid needs to handle the load. If you specify too few, Squid warns you with messages in *cache.log*.

The realm parameter is the authentication realm string that the user-agent should present to the user when prompting for a username and password. You can use something simple, such as "access to the Squid caching proxy."

The credentialsttl parameter specifies the amount of time that Squid internally caches authentication results. A larger value reduces the load on the external authenticator processes, but increases the amount of time until Squid detects changes to the authentication database. Note, this only affects positive results (i.e., successful validations). Negative results aren't cached inside Squid. The default TTL value is two hours.

Here is a complete example:

```
auth_param basic program /usr/local/squid/libexec/pam_auth
auth_param basic children 10
auth_param basic realm My Awesome Squid Cache
auth_param basic credentialsttl 1 hour

acl KnownUsers proxy_auth REQUIRED
http_access allow KnownUsers
```

Next I will discuss the Basic authentication helper programs that come with Squid.

* Unless you configure a peer with the login=PASS option.

NCSA

```
./configure --enable-basic-auth-helpers=NCSA
```

The NCSA authentication helper is relatively popular due to its simplicity and history. It stores usernames and passwords in a single text file, similar to the Unix */etc/passwd* file. This password file format was originally developed as a part of the NCSA HTTP server project.

You pass the path to the password file as the program's single command-line argument in *squid.conf*:

```
auth_param basic program /usr/local/squid/libexec/ncsa_auth
    /usr/local/squid/etc/passwd
```

You can use the htpasswd program that comes with Apache to create and update the password file. Also, you can download it from *http://www.squid-cache.org/htpasswd/*. From that page, you can also download the chpasswd CGI script, which allows users to change their own passwords if necessary.

LDAP

```
./configure --enable-basic-auth-helpers=LDAP
```

The LDAP helper interfaces to a Lightweight Directory Access Protocol server. The OpenLDAP libraries and header files must be installed before you can compile the squid_ldap_auth helper. You can find OpenLDAP at *http://www.openldap.org/*.

The squid_ldap_auth program requires at least two arguments: the base distinguished name (DN) and the LDAP server hostname. For example:

```
auth_param basic program /usr/local/squid/libexec/squid_ldap_auth
    -b "ou=people,dc=example,dc=com"  ldap.example.com
```

The LDAP helper has a Unix manual page that describes all of its options and parameters. However, Squid's manual pages aren't normally installed when you run make install. You can read the manual page by locating it in the source tree and manually running nroff. For example:

```
% cd helpers/basic_auth/LDAP
% nroff -man squid_ldap_auth.8 | less
```

MSNT

```
./configure --enable-basic-auth-helpers=MSNT
```

The MSNT authenticator interfaces to a Microsoft NT domain database via the Server Message Block (SMB) protocol. It uses a small configuration file, named *msntauth.conf*, which must be placed in the *$prefix/etc* or --sysconfidr directory.

You can specify up to five NT domain controllers in the configuration file. For example:

```
server pdc1_host bdc1_host my_nt_domain
server pdc2_host bdc2_host another_nt_domain
```

By default, the MSNT authenticator allows any user validated by the server. However, it also has the ability to allow or deny specific usernames. If you create an *allowusers* file, only the users listed there are allowed access to Squid. You might want to use this feature if you have a large number of users on the NT server, but only a small number who are allowed to use the cache. Alternatively, you can create a *denyusers* file. Any user listed in that file is automatically denied access, even before checking the *allowusers* file.

Alternatively, you can allow or deny specific usernames by placing them in the proxy_auth ACL as described in Chapter 6.

For additional documentation, see the *README.html* file in the *helpers/basic_auth/ MSNT* directory.

Multi-domain-NTLM

```
./configure --enable-basic-auth-helpers=multi-domain-NTLM
```

The multi-domain-NTLM authenticator is similar to MSNT. Both send queries to a Windows NT domain database. Whereas MSNT queries up to five domain controllers, the multi-domain-NTLM authenticator requires users to insert the NT domain name before their username, like this:

```
ntdomain\username
```

The multi-domain-NTLM helper program is a relatively short Perl script. It relies on the Authen::SMB package from CPAN (*http://www.cpan.org*). If you don't hardcode the domain controller hostnames in the Perl script, it utilizes the nmblookup program from the Samba package (*www.samba.org*) to discover them automatically.

The Perl script is named *smb_auth.pl*. It might look like this in *squid.conf*:

```
auth_param basic program /usr/local/squid/libexec/smb_auth.pl
```

Documentation for multi-domain-NTLM is thin, but if you understand Perl, you should be able to figure it out by reading the code.

PAM

```
./configure --enable-basic-auth-helpers=PAM
```

In a sense, Pluggable Authentication Modules (PAM) are the glue between authentication methods (e.g., one-time passwords, kerberos, smart cards) and applications requiring authentication services (e.g., ssh, ftp, imap). Your system's */etc/pam.conf* file describes which methods to use for each application.

To use Squid's PAM authentication helper, you need to add "squid" as a service in the */etc/pam.conf* file and specify which PAM modules to use. For example, to use the Unix password file on FreeBSD, you might put this in *pam.conf*:

```
squid auth required pam_unix.so try_first_pass
```

 To check the Unix password database, the pam_auth process must run as root. This is a security risk and you must manually make the executable setuid root. If pam_auth doesn't run as root, and it is configured to check the Unix password database, every request for authentication fails.

The PAM authenticator is documented with a manual page that you can find in the *helpers/basic_auth/PAM* directory.

SASL

```
./configure --enable-basic-auth-helpers=SASL
```

The Simple Authentication and Security Layer (SASL) is an IETF proposed standard, documented in RFC 2222. It is a protocol for negotiating security parameters for connection-based protocols (e.g., FTP, SMTP, HTTP). However, the SASL authenticator is similar to the PAM authenticator. It interfaces with a third-party library to query a number of different authentication databases.

Specifically, Squid's SASL authenticator requires the Cyrus SASL library developed by Carnegie Mellon University. You can find it at *http://asg.web.cmu.edu/sasl/*.

You can configure the SASL authenticator to check the traditional password file, the PAM system, or any of the other databases supported by CMU's library. For further information, see the *README* file in the *helpers/basic_auth/SASL* directory.

SMB

```
./configure --enable-basic-auth-helpers=SMB
```

SMB is another authenticator for Microsoft Windows databases. The authenticator itself is a C program. That program executes a shell script each time it talks to the Windows domain controller. The shell script contains commands from the Samba package. Thus, you'll need to install Samba before using the SMB authenticator.

The SMB authenticator program, smb_auth takes the Windows domain name as an argument. For example:

```
auth_param basic program /usr/local/squid/libexec/smb_auth -W MYNTDOMAIN
```

You can list multiple domains by repeating the -W option. For full documentation, see *http://www.hacom.nl/~richard/software/smb_auth.html*.

YP

```
./configure --enable-basic-auth-helpers=YP
```

The YP authenticator checks a system's "Yellow Pages" (a.k.a. NIS) directory. To use it with Squid, you need to provide the NIS domain name and the name of the password database, usually passwd.byname on the authenticator command line:

```
auth_param basic program /usr/local/squid/libexec/yp_auth my.nis.domain passwd.byname
```

The yp_auth program is relatively simple, but doesn't have any documentation.

getpwnam

```
./configure --enable-basic-auth-helpers=getpwnam
```

This authenticator is simply an interface to the getpwnam( ) function found in the C library on Unix systems. The getpwnam( ) function looks in the system password file for a given username. If you use YP/NIS, getpwnam( ) checks those databases as well. On some operating systems, it may also utilize the PAM system. You can use this authenticator if your cache users have login accounts on the system where Squid is running. Alternatively, you could set up "nologin" accounts in the password file for your cache users.

winbind

```
./configure --enable-basic-auth-helpers=winbind
```

Winbind is a feature of the Samba suite of software. It allows Unix systems to utilize Windows NT user account information. The *winbind* authenticator is a client for the Samba winbindd daemon. You must have Samba installed and the winbindd daemon running before you can use this authenticator.

The name of the *winbind* Basic authenticator is *wb_basic_auth*. It typically looks like this in *squid.conf*:

```
auth_param basic program /usr/local/squid/libexec/wb_basic_auth
```

The Basic Auth API

The interface between Squid and a Basic authenticator is quite simple. Squid sends usernames and passwords to the authenticator process, separated by a space and terminated by a newline. The authenticator reads the username and password pairs on *stdin*. After checking the credentials, the authenticator writes either OK or ERR to *stdout*.

Any "URL-unsafe" characters are encoded according to the RFC 1738 rules. Thus, the name "jack+jill" becomes "jack%2bjill". Squid accepts usernames and passwords that contain whitespace characters. For example "a password" becomes "a%20password". The authenticator program should be prepared to handle whitespace and other special characters after decoding the name and password.

You can easily test a Basic authenticator on the command line. Simply run the authenticator program in a terminal window and enter usernames and passwords. Or, you can do it like this:

```
% echo "bueller pencil" | ./ncsa_auth /tmp/passwd
OK
```

Here is a simple template authenticator written in Perl:

```
#!/usr/bin/perl -wl

use URI::Escape;

$|=1;                    # don't buffer stdout
while (<>) {
    ($u,$p) = split;
    $u = uri_unescape($u);
    $p = uri_unescape($p);
    if (&valid($u,$p)) {
        print "OK";
    } else {
        print "ERR";
    }
}

sub valid {
    my $user = shift;
    my $pass = shift;
    ...
}
```

HTTP Digest Authentication

Digest authentication is designed to be significantly more secure than Basic. It makes extensive use of cryptographic hash functions and other tricks. Essentially, instead of sending a cleartext password, the user-agent sends a "message digest" of the password, username, and other information. (See RFC 2617 and O'Reilly's *HTTP: The Definitive Guide* for more information.)

HTTP Digest authentication supports the following *auth_param* parameters:

- auth_param digest program *command*
- auth_param digest children *number*

- `auth_param digest realm` *string*
- `auth_param digest nonce_garbage_interval` *time-specification*
- `auth_param digest nonce_max_duration` *time-specification*
- `auth_param digest nonce_max_count` *number*
- `auth_param digest nonce_strictness on|off`

The `program`, `children`, and `realm` parameters are the same as for Basic authentication. All of the unique parameters relate to Digest authentication's use of something called *nonce*.

A nonce is a special string of data, which changes occasionally. During the authentication process, the server (Squid in this case) provides a nonce value to the client. The client uses the nonce value when generating the digest. Without the nonce data, an attacker could simply intercept and replay the digest values to gain access to Squid.

The `nonce_garbage_interval` parameter tells Squid how often to clean up the nonce cache. The default value is every 5 minutes. A very busy cache with many Digest authentication clients may benefit from more frequent nonce garbage collection.

The `nonce_max_duration` parameter specifies how long each nonce value remains valid. When a client attempts to use a nonce value older than the specified time, Squid generates a 401 (Unauthorized) response and sends along a fresh nonce value so the client can re-authenticate. The default value is 30 minutes. Note that any captured `Authorization` headers can be used in a replay attack until the nonce value expires. Setting the `nonce_max_duration` too low, however, causes Squid to generate 401 responses more often. Each 401 response essentially wastes the user's time as the client and server renegotiate their authentication credentials.

The `nonce_max_count` parameter places an upper limit on how many times a nonce value may be used. After the specified number of requests, Squid returns a 401 (Unauthorized) response and a new nonce value. The default is 50 requests.

Nonce counts are another feature designed to prevent replay attacks. Squid sends `qop=auth` in its 401 responses. This causes user-agents to include a nonce count in their requests, and to use the nonce count when generating the digest itself. Nonce count values must always increase over time. A decreasing nonce count indicates a replay attack. However, the counts may increase, but skip some values, for example: 5,6,8,9. The `nonce_strictness` parameter determines what Squid does in this case. If set to on, Squid returns a 401 response if a nonce count doesn't equal the previous nonce count plus one. If set to `off`, Squid allows gaps in the nonce count values.

Here is a complete example:

```
auth_param digest program /usr/local/squid/libexec/digest_pw
auth_param digest children 8
auth_param digest realm Access to Squid
auth_param digest nonce_garbage_interval 10 minutes
```

```
auth_param digest nonce_max_duration 45 minutes
auth_param digest nonce_max_count 100
auth_param digest nonce_strictness on

acl KnownUsers proxy_auth REQUIRED
http_access allow KnownUsers
```

Next I will discuss the Digest authentication helper programs that come with Squid.

password

```
./configure --enable-auth=digest --enable-digest-auth-helpers=password
```

This is a simple, reference implementation of Digest authentication for Squid. It demonstrates how to write a Digest-based authentication helper. This code simply reads usernames and passwords from a plaintext file. The format of this file is as follows:

```
username:password
```

The password file pathname is the single argument to the *digest_pw_auth* program. For example:

```
auth_param digest program /usr/local/squid/libexec/digest_pw_auth
        /usr/local/squid/etc/digest_passwd
auth_param digest realm Some Nifty Realm
```

Squid doesn't provide any tools to maintain a password file in this format. If you choose to use Digest authentication, you must manage the file on your own, perhaps with a text editor or Perl scripts.

Digest Authentication API

If you'd like to write your own Digest authentication helper, you need to understand the communication between Squid and the helper process. The exchange is similar to that for Basic authentication, albeit a little more complicated.

The first difference is that Squid writes the username and realm string, rather than username and password, to the helper process. These strings are quoted and separated by a colon. For example:

```
"bobby":"Tom Landry Middle School"
```

The second difference is that the helper process returns an MD5 digest string, rather than OK, if the username is valid. As with Basic authentication, the helper process writes ERR if the user doesn't exist or if the input from Squid is unparseable for some reason.

The helper returns an MD5 digest with the username, realm, and password. The three strings are concatenated together and separated by colons:

```
username:realm:password
```

Remember that the password isn't sent in the HTTP request. Rather, the helper retrieves the user's password from a database (like the plaintext file used by the *password* helper). For example, let's say that Bobby's password is CapeRs. The helper process receives the username and realm from Squid, gets the password from its database, and calculates an MD5 checksum of this string:

```
bobby:Tom Landry Middle School:CapeRs
```

The Squid source code includes a library function, DigestCalcHA1( ), which implements this calculation. We can test all this in a terminal window to see what the helper returns:

```
% echo 'bobby:CapeRs' > /tmp/pw
% echo bogus_input | digest_pw_auth /tmp/pw
ERR
% echo "nouser":"some realm" | digest_pw_auth /tmp/pw
ERR
% echo '"bobby":"Tom Landry Middle School"' | digest_pw_auth /tmp/pw
c7ca3efda238c65b2d48684a51baa90e
```

Squid stores this MD5 checksum and uses it in other parts of the Digest authentication algorithm. Note that the checksum only changes when the user changes his password. In Squid's current Digest implementation, these checksums are kept in memory as long as the user remains active. If the user is inactive for *authenticate_ttl* seconds, the MD5 checksum may be removed from Squid's memory. Upon the next request from that user, Squid asks the external helper process to calculate it again.

Microsoft NTLM Authentication

NTLM* is a proprietary connection authentication protocol from Microsoft. A number of groups, including the Squid developers, have reverse-engineered the protocol from what little information is available and by examining network traffic. You can find some technical details at *http://www.innovation.ch/java/ntlm.html*.

NTLM uses a three-way handshake to authenticate a connection. First, the client sends its request with a couple of identifiers. Second, the server sends back a challenge message. Third, the client sends its request again with a response to the challenge. At this point, the connection is authenticated and any further requests on the same connection don't require any challenge/response information. If the connection is closed, the client and server must repeat the entire three-way handshake. Persistent connections help reduce this overhead for NTLM.

NTLM uses cryptographic hash functions and nonce values, similar to Digest authentication, although experts believe NTLM is weaker.

NTLM authentication supports the following *auth_param* parameters:

---

* NTLM apparently stands for "NT LanMan" or perhaps "NT Lan Manager."

- `auth_param ntlm program` *command*
- `auth_param ntlm children` *number*
- `auth_param ntlm max_challenge_reuses` *number*
- `auth_param ntlm max_challenge_lifetime` *time-specification*

The program and children parameters are the same as for Basic and Digest authentication. The remaining parameters determine how often Squid may reuse a single challenge token.

The `max_challenge_reuses` parameter specifies how many times a challenge token may be reused. The default value is 0, so that challenges are never reused. Increasing this value may reduce the computational load on Squid and the NTLM helper processes, at the risk of weakening the protocol's security.

Similarly, the `max_challenge_lifetime` parameter places a time limit on challenge reuses, even if the `max_challenge_reuses` count has not been reached. The default value is 60 seconds.

Here is a complete example:

```
auth_param ntlm program /usr/local/squid/libexec/ntlm_auth foo\bar
auth_param ntlm children 12
auth_param ntlm max_challenge_reuses 5
auth_param ntlm max_challenge_lifetime 2 minutes

acl KnownUsers proxy_auth REQUIRED
http_access allow KnownUsers
```

Squid comes with the following NTLM authentication helper programs:

SMB

```
./configure --enable-auth=ntlm --enable-ntlm-auth-helpers=SMB
```

The Server Message Block (SMB) authenticator for NTLM is similar to those for Basic authentication. Your users can simply supply their Windows NT domain, username, and password. This authenticator can load balance between multiple domain controllers. The domain and controller names go on the command line:

```
auth_param ntlm program /usr/local/squid/libexec/ntlm_auth
    domain\controller [domain\controller ...]
```

winbind

```
./configure --enable-auth=ntlm --enable-ntlm-auth-helpers=winbind
```

This authenticator is similar to *winbind* for Basic authentication. Both require that you have the Samba winbindd daemon installed and running. The name of the winbind Basic authenticator is *wb_nltm_auth*. It typically looks like this in *squid.conf*:

```
auth_param basic program /usr/local/squid/libexec/wb_ntlm_auth
```

NTLM Authentication API

The communication between Squid and an NTLM authenticator is much more complicated than for Basic and Digest. One reason is that each helper process actually creates its own challenge. Thus, helpers become "stateful" and Squid must remember which connections belong to which helpers.

Squid and the helper processes use a handful of two-character codes to indicate what they are sending. Those codes are as follows:

YR   Squid sends this to a helper when it needs a new challenge token. This is always the first communication between the two processes. It may also occur at any time that Squid needs a new challenge, due to the *auth_param* max_challenge_ lifetime and max_challenge_uses parameters. The helper should respond with a TT message.

TT *challenge*
   A helper sends this message back to Squid and includes a challenge token. It is sent in response to a YR request. The challenge is base64-encoded, as defined by RFC 2045.

KK *credentials*
   Squid sends this to a helper when it wants to authenticate a user's credentials. The helper responds with either AF, NA, BH, or LD.

AF *username*
   The helper sends this message back to Squid when the user's authentication credentials are valid. The helper sends the username with this message because Squid doesn't try to decode the NTLM Authorization header.

NA *reason*
   The helper sends this message back to Squid when the user's credentials are invalid. It also includes a "reason" string that Squid can display on an error page.

BH *reason*
   The helper sends this message back to Squid when the validation procedure fails. This might happen, for example, when the helper process is unable to communicate with a Windows NT domain controller. Squid rejects the user's request.

LD *username*
   This helper-to-Squid response is similar to BH, except that Squid allows the user's request. Like AF, it returns the username. To use this feature, you must compile Squid with the --enable-ntlm-fail-open option.

Since this protocol is relatively complicated, you'll probably be better off to start with one of the two skeleton authenticators included in the Squid source distribution. The no_check helper is written in Perl, and fakeauth is written in C. You can find them in the *helpers/ntlm_auth* directory.

External ACLs

As of Version 2.5, Squid includes a new feature known as *external ACLs*. These are ACL elements that are implemented in external helper processes. You instruct Squid to write certain information to the helper, which then responds with either OK or ERR. Refer to Chapter 6 for a description of the *external_acl_type* syntax. Here, I'll only discuss the particular external ACL helper programs that come with the Squid source code.

ip_user

```
./configure --enable-external-acl-helpers=ip_user
```

This helper reads usernames and client IP addresses as input. It checks the two values against a configuration file to decide whether or not the combination is valid. To use this ACL helper, you would add lines like this to *squid.conf*:

```
external_acl_type ip_user_helper %SRC %LOGIN
    /usr/local/squid/libexec/ip_user -f /usr/local/squid/etc/ip_user.conf
acl AclName external ip_user_helper
```

%SRC is replaced with the client's IP address and %LOGIN is replaced with the username for each request. The *ip_user.conf* configuration file has the following format:

```
ip_addr[/mask]          user|@group|ALL|NONE
```

For example:

```
127.0.0.1               ALL
192.168.1.0/24          bob
10.8.1.0/24             @lusers
172.16.0.0/16           NONE
```

This configuration file causes ip_user to return OK for any request coming from 127.0.0.1, for Bob's requests coming from the 192.168.1.0/24 network, for any name in the *luser* group when the request comes from the 10.8.1.0/24 network, and returns ERR for any request from the 172.16.0.0/16 network. It also returns ERR for any address and username pair that doesn't appear in the list.

ldap_group

```
./configure --enable-external-acl-helpers=ldap_group
```

This helper determines whether or not a user belongs to a particular LDAP group. You specify the LDAP group names on the *acl* line. It might look like this in your configuration file:

```
external_acl_type ldap_group_helper %LOGIN /usr/local/squid/libexec/squid_ldap_group
    -b "ou=people,dc=example,dc=com"  ldap.example.com
acl AclName external ldap_group_helper GroupRDN ...
```

Note that you must have the OpenLDAP (*http://www.openldap.org*) libraries installed on your system to compile the squid_ldap_group helper program.

unix_group

```
./configure --enable-external-acl-helpers=unix_group
```

This helper looks for usernames in the Unix group database (e.g., */etc/group* file). You specify the groups to check on the helper command line as follows:

```
external_acl_type unix_group_helper %LOGIN
    /usr/local/squid/libexec/check_group -g group1 -g group2 ...
acl AclName external unix_group_helper
```

Alternatively, you can specify groups on the *acl* line. This allows you to use the same helper for different groups:

```
external_acl_type unix_group_helper %LOGIN /usr/local/squid/libexec/check_group
acl AclName1 external unix_group_helper group1 ...
acl AclName2 external unix_group_helper group2 ...
```

wbinfo_group

```
./configure --enable-external-acl-helpers=wbinfo_group
```

This helper is a short Perl script that utilizes the wbinfo program from the Samba package. wbinfo is a client for the winbindd daemon. The script expects a single Unix group name following the username on each request. Thus, you must put a group name on the *acl* line:

```
external_acl_type wbinfo_group_helper %LOGIN /usr/local/squid/libexec/wbinfo_group.pl
acl AclName external wbinfo_group_helper group
```

winbind_group

```
./configure --enable-external-acl-helpers=winbind_group
```

This helper, written in C, also queries a winbindd server about group membership of Windows NT usernames. It is based on the winbind helpers for Basic and NTLM authentication. You can specify multiple group names on the *acl* command line:

```
external_acl_type winbind_group_helper %LOGIN /usr/local/squid/libexec/wb_check_group
acl AclName external winbind_group_helper group1 group2 ...
```

Write Your Own

The external ACL interface offers a lot of flexibility. Chances are you can use it to implement almost any access control check not supported by the built-in methods. Writing an external ACL is a two-step process. First, you must decide what request information the helper program needs to make a decision. Place the appropriate keywords on an *external_acl_type* line, along with the pathname to the helper program. For example, if you want to write an external ACL helper that uses the client's IP address, the user's name, and the value of the Host header, you would write something like:

```
external_acl_type MyAclHelper %SRC %LOGIN %{Host}
    /usr/local/squid/libexec/myaclhelper
```

The second step is to write the myaclhelper program. It must read the request tokens on stdin, make its decision, then write either OK or ERR to stdout. Continuing with the previous example, this Perl script illustrates how to do it:

```
#!/usr/bin/perl -wl
require 'shellwords.pl';
$|=1;
while (<>) {
    ($ip,$name,$host) = &shellwords;
    if (&valid($ip,$name,$host)) {
        print "OK";
    } else {
        print "ERR";
    }
}

sub valid {
    my $ip = shift;
    my $name = shift;
    my $host = shift;
    ...
}
```

Refer to Chapter 6 for the list of tokens (%SRC, %LOGIN, etc.) that you can pass from Squid to the helper. Note that when a token contains whitespace, Squid wraps it in double quotes. As the example shows, you can use Perl's *shellwords* library to parse quoted tokens easily.

Of course, to utilize the external ACL, you must reference it in an *acl* line. The ACL element is a match whenever the external helper returns OK.

The external ACL helper interface allows you to pass additional information from the helper to Squid (on the OK/ERR line). These take the form of *keyword=value* pairs. For example:

```
OK user=hank
```

Currently, the only keywords that Squid knows about are error and user. If the user value is set, Squid uses it in the *access.log*. The error value isn't currently used by Squid.

Exercises

- Write a fake helper for Basic authentication that always returns either OK or ERR.

- Use tcpdump or ethereal to capture some HTTP requests. Decode the authorization credentials.

- If you're using NTLM, capture some HTTP requests and attempt a replay attack.

- Kill Squid's authentication helper processes one-by-one while running **tail -f cache.log**.

- Find out what happens to your favorite NTLM-based authenticator when it can't communicate with the NT domain controller.

## CHAPTER 13

Log Files

Log files are the primary sources of persistent information about Squid's operation. In other words, they provide a record of what Squid has been doing. This includes URIs requested by users, objects that have been saved to disk, and various warnings and errors. When Squid appears to be malfunctioning, you'll want to check the log files first. By the end of this chapter, you'll know how to interpret and manage all of Squid's various log files.

Depending on your configuration, Squid maintains, at most, seven log files. The three primary files are: *cache.log*, *access.log*, and *store.log*. Two optional log files, *useragent.log* and *referer.log*, are similar to *access.log* but contain additional information. I'll also talk about the *swap.state* and *netdb_state* files. These are databases, used by Squid when it restarts.

Note that the filenames, such as *access.log*, are the default values. You can change most of the log file names with various *squid.conf* directives.

The following list contains a brief description of each log file:

cache.log
> This log file contains human-oriented, informational messages about Squid's operation. The filename is defined by the *cache_log* directive. Under normal conditions, the file grows by about 10–100 KB per day.

access.log
> This log file contains an entry for every HTTP and (optionally) ICP transaction made by Squid's clients. The filename is defined by the *cache_access_log* directive. It grows at a rate of 100–200 bytes per transaction.

store.log
> This log file contains low-level information about objects that enter and leave the cache. The filename is defined by the *cache_store_log* directive. It grows at a rate of about 150 bytes per transaction.

referer.log

> This optional log file contains HTTP `Referer`* headers for each client request. You must enable referer logging with the `--enable-referer-log` option when running `./configure`. The filename is defined by the *referer_log* directive. It grows at a rate of about 80 bytes per transaction.

useragent.log

> This optional log file contains HTTP `User-Agent` headers for each client request. You must enable user-agent logging with the `--enable-useragent-log` option when running `./configure`. The filename is defined by the *useragent_log* directive. It grows at a rate of about 75 bytes per transaction.

swap.state

> These files contain internal metadata about the objects stored on disk. Squid uses them to reconstruct the cache upon startup. By default, they are located in the *cache_dir* directories. However, you can change the location with the *cache_swap_log* directive. They grow at a rate of 100 bytes per cache miss.

netdb_state

> This file holds the contents of the Network Measurement Database (see Chapter 10). It is always located in the first *cache_dir* directory. Its size is determined by the *netdb_high* value.

If Squid receives an error while writing a log file, it doesn't silently continue. Instead, it exits with a fatal error message to get your attention. Make sure that you periodically rotate the log files, as described in the later section "Rotating the Log Files," to reduce the possibility of filling your disks. For the same reason, I also recommend placing your log files on a partition separate from any of your cache directories.

cache.log

cache.log contains various messages such as information about Squid's configuration, warnings about possible performance problems, and serious errors. Here is some sample *cache.log* output:

```
2003/09/29 12:09:45| Starting Squid Cache version 2.5.STABLE4 for i386-unknown-
freebsd4.8...
2003/09/29 12:09:45| Process ID 18990
2003/09/29 12:09:45| With 1064 file descriptors available
2003/09/29 12:09:45| Performing DNS Tests...
2003/09/29 12:09:45| Successful DNS name lookup tests...
2003/09/29 12:09:45| DNS Socket created at 0.0.0.0, port 1154, FD 5
2003/09/29 12:09:45| Adding nameserver 24.221.192.5 from /etc/resolv.conf
2003/09/29 12:09:45| Adding nameserver 24.221.208.5 from /etc/resolv.conf
2003/09/29 12:09:45| helperOpenServers: Starting 5 'redirector.pl' processes
```

---

* No, this isn't a typo. "Referer" has been historically misspelled by HTTP developers.

```
2003/09/29 12:09:45| Unlinkd pipe opened on FD 15
2003/09/29 12:09:45| Swap maxSize 10240 KB, estimated 787 objects
2003/09/29 12:09:45| Target number of buckets: 39
2003/09/29 12:09:45| Using 8192 Store buckets
2003/09/29 12:09:45| Max Mem  size: 8192 KB
2003/09/29 12:09:45| Max Swap size: 10240 KB
2003/09/29 12:09:45| Rebuilding storage in /usr/local/squid/var/cache (CLEAN)
2003/09/29 12:09:45| Using Least Load store dir selection
2003/09/29 12:09:45| Set Current Directory to /usr/local/squid/var/cache
2003/09/29 12:09:45| Loaded Icons.
2003/09/29 12:09:45| Accepting HTTP connections at 0.0.0.0, port 3128, FD 16.
2003/09/29 12:09:45| Accepting ICP messages at 0.0.0.0, port 3130, FD 17.
2003/09/29 12:09:45| WCCP Disabled.
2003/09/29 12:09:45| Ready to serve requests.
```

Each *cache.log* entry starts with a timestamp showing when the message was generated. The very first entry in this sample reports the Squid version (2.5.STABLE4) and a string identifying the operating system for which Squid was configured (i386-unknown-freebsd4.8). The process ID (18990) follows. Many *cache.log* entries may look cryptic (Target number of buckets: 39). In most cases, under normal conditions, you can ignore entries you don't understand. On the other hand, you may want to look over essential configuration details such as name-server addresses or HTTP server address. This sample output ends with a statement that Squid is ready to serve requests. At this point, Squid can accept HTTP connections from clients.

Usually, the *cache.log* file grows slowly. However, an unusual HTTP transaction or similar event may cause Squid to emit a debugging message. If such an event happens often (e.g., a DoS attack, a new virus, or sudden disk failure), the log file may grow quickly. Rotating log files reduces the chance that you'll run out of disk space.

Major errors and abnormal conditions are likely to be reported in *cache.log*. I recommend archiving these logs so that it is possible to go back and find the first occurrence of an unusual event. When describing a particular Squid problem on the mailing list or a similar forum, the relevant lines from *cache.log* may be very useful. You may also want to increase debugging levels for some sections so that others can better understand and fix your problem.

Debugging Levels

The *debug_options* directive controls the level of detail for *cache.log* messages. The default value (ALL,1) is usually the best choice. At higher levels, the unimportant messages make it harder to find the important ones. Refer to Chapter 16 for a thorough description of the *debug_options* directive.

Note that debugging at the highest levels (9 or 10) may add thousands of lines for each request, quickly consuming disk space and significantly degrading Squid's performance.

You can use Squid's -X command-line option to enable full debugging for all sections. This mode is particularly useful if Squid refuses to start, and the debugging levels in *squid.conf* are insufficient to diagnose the problem. This is also a good way to enable full debugging of the configuration file parser, before it gets to the *debug_options* directive. You should never use the -X when Squid is operating properly.

You can use Squid's -k debug command-line option to enable full debugging immediately on a running Squid process. This command operates as a toggle: the first invocation turns on full debugging, and the second invocation turns it off. See Chapter 5 for a general discussion about the -k option.

As I already mentioned, full debugging generates an overwhelming amount of data. This can make Squid, and the operating system, very slow. In extreme cases, you may find your terminal session becomes unresponsive after executing the first squid -k debug command. Locking yourself out while Squid is spitting megabytes of *cache.log* entries per second is an unpleasant experience. I find the following trick useful to get a compact, five-second debugging snapshot with less risk:

```
% squid -k debug; sleep 5; squid -k debug
```

Forwarding cache.log Messages to the System Log

To have Squid send copies of *cache.log* messages to the system log, use the -s command-line option. Only messages with debugging levels 0 and 1 are forwarded. Level 0 messages are logged with syslog level LOG_WARNING. Level 1 messages use syslog level LOG_NOTICE. All messages use the LOCAL4 syslog facility. Here is one way to configure syslogd so that these messages are saved:

```
local4.warning                    /var/log/squid.log
```

Using syslog in addition to *cache.log* is especially handy when you maintain several Squid boxes. You can configure each local syslog daemon to forward these messages to a central host and enjoy a unified view of all caches in one location. For example, you might use this entry in */etc/syslogd.conf*:

```
local4.notice                     @192.168.45.1
```

Dumping cache.log Messages to Your Terminal

The -d level command-line option instructs Squid to dump *cache.log* messages to your terminal (i.e., *stderr*). The level argument specifies the maximum level for messages that are dumped. Note that you'll see only messages that would appear in *cache.log*, subject to the *debug_options* setting. For example, if you have *debug_options ALL,1*, and run squid -d2, you won't see any level 2 debugging messages.

The -d level and -N options are most useful for debugging Squid problems or quickly testing a change to the configuration file. They allow you to start Squid easily and see the *cache.log* messages. This option may also be useful when Squid starts from cron or a similar facility that automatically captures a program's standard error output and reports it back to the user. For example, you may have a cron job that automatically reconfigures the running Squid process:

```
15 */4 * * * /usr/local/squid/sbin/squid -d1 -k reconfigure
```

access.log

Squid saves key information about HTTP transactions in *access.log*. This file is line-based, such that each line corresponds to one client request. Squid records the client IP address (or hostname), requested URI, response size, and other information.

Squid records all HTTP accesses in *access.log*, except for those that disconnect before sending any data. Squid also records all ICP (but not HTCP) transactions unless you disable them with the *log_icp_queries* directive. The later section "Configuration Directives That Affect access.log" describes the other *squid.conf* directives that affect the access log.

The default *access.log* format contains 10 fields. Here are some examples, with long lines split and indented:

```
1066037222.011   126389 9.121.105.207 TCP_MISS/503 1055
        GET http://home.gigigaga.com/n8342133/Miho.DAT.019 -
        DIRECT/203.187.1.180 -
1066037222.011    19120 12.83.179.11 TCP_MISS/200 359
        GET http://ads.x10.com/720x300/Z2FtZ3J1ZXRpbmcxLmRhd/7/AMG -
        DIRECT/63.211.210.20 text/html
1066037222.011    34173 166.181.33.71 TCP_MISS/200 559
        GET http://coursesites.blackboard.com:8081/service/collab/../1010706448190/ -
        DIRECT/216.200.107.101 application/octet-stream
1066037222.011    19287 41.51.105.27 TCP_REFRESH_MISS/200 500
        GET http://fn.yam.com/include/tsemark/show.js -
        DIRECT/210.59.224.59 application/x-javascript
1066037222.011    19395 41.51.105.27 TCP_MISS/304 274
        GET http://fnasp.yam.com/image/coin3.gif -
        DIRECT/211.72.254.133 -
1066037222.011    19074 30.208.85.76 TCP_CLIENT_REFRESH_MISS/304 197
        GET http://ads.icq.com/content/B0/0/..bC6GygEYNeHGjBUin5Azfe68m5hD1jLk$/aol -
        DIRECT/64.12.184.121 -
1066037222.011    19048 12.83.179.11 TCP_MISS/200 261
        GET http://ads.adsag.com/js.ng/...ne&cat=friendship&subcat=girltalk -
        DIRECT/209.225.54.119 application/x-javascript
1066037222.118      106 41.51.105.27 TCP_HIT/200 536
        GET http://rcm-images.amazon.com/images/G/01/rcm/privacy.gif -
        NONE/- image/gif
1066037222.352    19475 27.34.49.248 TCP_MISS/200 12387
        GET http://espanol.geocities.com/lebastias/divulgacion/budismo-tarot.html -
        DIRECT/209.1.225.139 text/html
1066037222.352      132 144.157.100.17 TCP_MISS/504 1293
        GET http://ar.atwola.com/image/93101912/aol -
        NONE/- -
```

Here are the definitions for all fields:

1: timestamp

> The completion time of the request, expressed as the number of seconds since the Unix epoch (Thu Jan 1 00:00:00 UTC 1970), with millisecond resolution. Squid uses this format, instead of something more human-friendly, to simplify the work of various log file processing programs.
>
> You can use a simple Perl command to convert the Unix timestamps into local time. For example:

```
perl -pe 's/^\d+\.\d+/localtime($&)/e;' access.log
```

2: response time

> For HTTP transactions, this field indicates how much time it took to process the request. The timer starts when Squid receives the HTTP request and stops when the response has been fully delivered. The response time is given in milliseconds.
>
> The response time is usually 0 for ICP queries. This is because Squid answers ICP queries very quickly. Furthermore, Squid doesn't update the process clock between receiving an ICP query and sending the reply.
>
> While time values are reported with millisecond resolution, the precision of those entries is probably about 10 milliseconds. Timing becomes even less precise when Squid is heavily loaded.

3: client address

> This field contains the client's IP address, or hostname if you enable *log_fqdn*. For security or privacy reasons, you may want to mask a part of client's address out using the *client_netmask* directive. However, that also makes it impossible to group requests coming from the same client.

4: result/status codes

> This field consists of two tokens separated by a slash. The first token, result code, classifies the protocol and the result of a transaction (e.g., TCP_HIT or UDP_DENIED). These are Squid-specific codes, defined in the later section "access.log Result Codes." The codes that begin with TCP_ refer to HTTP requests, while UDP_ refers to ICP queries.
>
> The second token is the HTTP response status code (e.g, 200, 304, 404, etc.). The status code normally comes from the origin server. In some cases, however, Squid may be responsible for selecting the status code. These codes, defined by the HTTP RFC, are summarized later in Table 13-1.

5: transfer size

> This field indicates the number of bytes transferred to the client. Strictly speaking, it is the number of bytes that Squid told the TCP/IP stack to send to the client. Thus, it doesn't include overheads from TCP/IP headers. Also note that the transfer size is normally larger than the response's Content-Length. This value includes the HTTP response headers, while Content-Length does not.

These properties make the transfer size field useful for approximate bandwidth usage analysis but not for exact HTTP entity size calculations. If you need to know a response's Content-Length, you can find it in the *store.log* file.

6: *request method*

This field contains the request method. Because Squid clients may use ICP or HTTP, the request method is either HTTP- or ICP-specific. The most common HTTP request method is GET. ICP queries are always logged with ICP_QUERY. See Chapter 6 for a list of HTTP methods Squid knows about.

7: *URI*

This field contains the URI from the client's request. The vast majority of logged URIs are actually URLs (i.e., they have hostnames).

Squid uses a special format for certain failures. These are cases when Squid can't parse the HTTP request or otherwise determine the URI. Instead of a URI/URL, you'll see a string such as "error:invalid-request." For example:

```
1066036250.603 310 192.0.34.70 NONE/400 1203 GET error:invalid-request - NONE/- -
```

Also in this field look out for whitespace characters in the URI. Depending on your *uri_whitespace* setting, Squid may print the URI in the log file with whitespace characters. When this happens, the tools that read *access.log* files may become confused by the extra fields.

When logging, Squid strips all URI characters after the first question mark unless the *strip_query_terms* directive is disabled.

8: *client identity*

Squid can determine a user's identity in two different ways. One is with the RFC 1413 ident protocol; the other is from HTTP authentication headers.

Squid attempts ident lookups based on the *ident_lookup_access* rules, if any (see Chapter 6). Alternatively, if you use proxy authentication (or regular server authentication in surrogate mode), Squid places the given username in this field. If both methods provide Squid with a username, and you're using the native *access.log* format, the HTTP authentication name is logged, and the RFC 1413 name is ignored. The common log file format has separate fields for both names.

9: *peering code/peerhost*

The peering information consists of two tokens, separated by a slash. It is relevant only for requests that are cache misses. The first token indicates how the next hop was chosen. The second token is the address of that next hop. The peering codes are listed in the "access.log Peering Codes" section.

When Squid sends a request to a neighbor cache, the peerhost address is the neighbor's hostname. If the request is sent directly to the origin server, however, Squid writes the origin server's IP address or its hostname if *log_ip_on_direct* is disabled. The value NONE/- indicates that Squid didn't forward this request to any other servers.

10: content type

> The final field of the default, native *access.log* is the content type of the HTTP response. Squid obtains the content type value from the response's Content-Type header. If that header is missing, Squid uses a hyphen (-).

If you enable the *log_mime_headers* directive, Squid appends two additional fields to each line:

11: HTTP request headers

> Squid encodes the HTTP request headers and prints them between a pair of square brackets. The brackets are necessary because Squid doesn't encode space characters. The encoding scheme is a little strange. Carriage return (ASCII 13) and newline (ASCII 10) are printed as \r and \n, respectively. Other non-printable characters are encoded with the RFC 1738 style, such that Tab (ASCII 9) becomes %09.

12: HTTP response headers

> Squid encodes the HTTP response headers and prints them between a pair of square brackets. Note that these are the headers sent to the client, which may be different from headers received from the origin server.

Squid writes to *access.log* only after the entire response has been sent to the client. This allows Squid to include both request and response information in the log file. However, transactions that take minutes, or even hours, to complete aren't visible in *access.log* at the time of the request. When these types of transactions present a performance or policy concern, the *access.log* may be unable help you. Instead, use the cache manager to view a list of pending transactions (see Chapter 14).

access.log Result Codes

The following labels may appear in the fourth field of the *access.log* file in response to HTTP requests:

TCP_HIT

> Squid found a likely fresh copy of the requested resource and sent it immediately to the client.

TCP_MISS

> Squid didn't have a cached copy of the requested resource.

TCP_REFRESH_HIT

> Squid found a likely stale copy of the requested resource and sent a validation request to the origin server. The origin server sent a 304 (Not Modified) response, indicating that Squid's copy is still fresh.

TCP_REF_FAIL_HIT

> Squid found a likely stale copy of the requested resource and sent a validation request to the origin server. However, the origin server failed to respond or sent

a response that Squid didn't understand. In any case, Squid sent the cached (and likely stale) copy to the client.

TCP_REFRESH_MISS

Squid found a likely stale copy of the requested resource and sent a validation request to the origin server. The server responded with new content, indicating the cached response was indeed stale.

TCP_CLIENT_REFRESH_MISS

Squid found a copy of the requested resource, but the client's request included a Cache-Control: no-cache directive. Squid forwarded the client's request to the origin server, forcing a cache validation.

TCP_IMS_HIT

The client sent a validation request, and Squid found a more recent, and likely fresh, copy of the requested resource. Squid sent the newer content to the client, without contacting the origin server.

TCP_SWAPFAIL_MISS

Squid found a valid copy of the requested resource but failed to load it from disk. Squid then sent the request to the origin server as though it were a cache miss.

TCP_NEGATIVE_HIT

When a request to an origin server results in an HTTP error, Squid may cache the response anyway. Repeated requests for these resources, within a short amount of time, result in negative hits. The *negative_ttl* directive controls the amount of time these errors may be cached. Also note that errors are cached only in memory and never written to disk. The following HTTP status codes may be negatively cached, subject to additional constraints: 204, 305, 400, 403, 404, 405, 414, 500, 501, 502, 503, 504.

TCP_MEM_HIT

Squid found a valid copy of the requested resource in the memory cache and sent it immediately to the client. Note that this doesn't accurately represent all responses served from memory. For example, responses that are cached in memory, but require validation, are logged with TCP_REFRESH_HIT, TCP_REFRESH_MISS, etc.

TCP_DENIED

The client's request was denied, due to either the *http_access* or *http_reply_access* rules. Note that requests denied by *http_access* have NONE/- in the ninth field, whereas those denied by *http_reply_access* have a valid entry.

TCP_OFFLINE_HIT

When *offline_mode* is enabled, Squid returns cache hits for almost any cached response, without considering its freshness.

TCP_REDIRECT

A redirector program told Squid to generate an HTTP redirect to a new URI (see Chapter 11). Normally, Squid doesn't log these redirects. To do so, you must manually define the LOG_TCP_REDIRECTS preprocessor directive before compiling Squid.

NONE

Unclassified result used for certain errors, such as invalid hostnames.

The following labels may appear in the fourth field of the *access.log* file in response to ICP queries:

UDP_HIT

Squid found a likely fresh copy of the requested resource in the cache.

UDP_MISS

Squid didn't find a likely fresh copy of the requested resource in the cache. If the same object is requested via HTTP, it would probably be a cache miss. Compare with UDP_MISS_NOFETCH.

UDP_MISS_NOFETCH

Like UDP_MISS, except that this also indicates Squid's reluctance to handle the corresponding HTTP request. If you use the -Y command-line option, Squid returns this, instead of UDP_MISS, while rebuilding its in-memory indexes at startup.

UDP_DENIED

The ICP query is denied due to the *icp_access* rules. If more than 95% of the ICP replies to a client are UDP_DENIED, and the client database is enabled (see Appendix A), Squid stops sending any ICP replies to the client for an hour. When this happens you'll also see a warning in *cache.log*.

UDP_INVALID

Squid received an invalid query (e.g., truncated message, invalid protocol version, whitespace in the URI, etc.). Squid sent an ICP_INVALID reply back to the client.

HTTP Response Status Codes

Table 13-1 lists the numerical HTTP response codes and reason phrases. Note that Squid and other HTTP agents care only about the numeric value. The reason phrase is purely informational and doesn't affect the meaning of the response. For each status code, I also provide a reference to the particular section in RFC 2616 that describes it. Note that status codes 0 and 600 are nonstandard values used by Squid, and aren't mentioned in the RFC.

Table 13-1. HTTP response status codes

Code	Reason phrase	RFC 2616 section
0	No Response Received (Squid-specific)	N/A
1xx	Informational	10.1

Table 13-1. HTTP response status codes (continued)

Code	Reason phrase	RFC 2616 section
100	Continue	10.1.1
101	Switching Protocols	10.1.2
2xx	Successful	10.2
200	OK	10.2.1
201	Created	10.2.2
202	Accepted	10.2.3
203	Non-Authoritative Information	10.2.4
204	No Content	10.2.5
205	Reset Content	10.2.6
206	Partial Content	10.2.7
3xx	Redirection	10.3
300	Multiple Choices	10.3.1
301	Moved Permanently	10.3.2
302	Found	10.3.3
303	See Other	10.3.4
304	Not Modified	10.3.5
305	Use Proxy	10.3.6
306	(Unused)	10.3.7
307	Temporary Redirect	10.3.8
4xx	Client Error	10.4
400	Bad Request	10.4.1
401	Unauthorized	10.4.2
402	Payment Required	10.4.3
403	Forbidden	10.4.4
404	Not Found	10.4.5
405	Method Not Allowed	10.4.6
406	Not Acceptable	10.4.7
407	Proxy Authentication Required	10.4.8
408	Request Timeout	10.4.9
409	Conflict	10.4.10
410	Gone	10.4.11
411	Length Required	10.4.12
412	Precondition Failed	10.4.13
413	Request Entity Too Large	10.4.14
414	Request-URI Too Long	10.4.15
415	Unsupported Media Type	10.4.16

Table 13-1. HTTP response status codes (continued)

Code	Reason phrase	RFC 2616 section
416	Requested Range Not Satisfiable	10.4.17
417	Expectation Failed	10.4.18
5xx	Server Error	10.5
500	Internal Server Error	10.5.1
501	Not Implemented	10.5.2
502	Bad Gateway	10.5.3
503	Service Unavailable	10.5.4
504	Gateway Timeout	10.5.5
505	HTTP Version Not Supported	10.5.6
6xx	Proxy Error	N/A
600	Unparseable Response Headers (Squid-specific)	N/A

You'll see status code 0 in the *access.log* if Squid doesn't receive any response from the origin server. You'll see status code 600 if Squid received a response but couldn't find any HTTP headers. In a small fraction of cases, certain origin servers send only the response body and omit any headers.

access.log Peering Codes

The following codes may appear in the ninth field of the *access.log*. Refer to Chapter 10 for a description of how Squid selects the next-hop for cache misses.

NONE
> This indicates that Squid didn't communicate with any other servers (neighbors, origin) for this request. You'll see it in association with various types of cache hits, denied requests, cache manager requests, errors, and all ICP queries.

DIRECT
> Squid forwarded the request directly to the origin server. The second half of the field shows the origin server's IP address, or hostname if you've disabled *log_ip_on_direct*.

SIBLING_HIT
> Squid sent the request to this sibling cache after the sibling returned an ICP or HTCP hit.

PARENT_HIT
> Squid sent the request to this parent cache after the parent returned an ICP or HTCP hit.

DEFAULT_PARENT
> Squid selected this parent because it was marked as default on the *cache_peer* line in *squid.conf*.

FIRST_UP_PARENT

Squid forwarded the request to this parent because it is the first parent in the list known to be alive.

FIRST_PARENT_MISS

Squid forwarded the request to the parent cache that was first to respond with an ICP/HTCP miss message. In other words, for this particular ICP/HTCP query, at this particular time, the selected parent had the best round-trip time. Note that measured RTTs may be artificially adjusted by the weight option to the *cache_peer* directive.

CLOSEST_PARENT_MISS

Squid selected this parent because it reports the lowest RTT to the origin server. This occurs only if both caches have *netdb* enabled (see Chapter 10), and the origin server (or other servers on its subnet) returns ICMP pings.

CLOSEST_PARENT

This is similar to CLOSEST_PARENT_MISS, except that the RTT measurements don't come from the ICP/HTCP reply messages. Instead, they come from older measurements saved by Squid, such as the netdb exchange feature.

CLOSEST_DIRECT

Squid forwarded the request to the origin server based on *netdb* measurements. This happens if any of these conditions occur:

- The RTT between Squid and the origin server is less than the configured *minimum_direct_rtt* value.

- The measured number of router hops between Squid and the origin server is less than the configured *minimum_direct_hops* value.

- The RTT values returned in ICP/HTCP replies indicate that Squid is closer to the origin server than any of its neighbors.

ROUNDROBIN_PARENT

Squid forwarded the request to this parent because the round-robin option was set, and it had the lowest usage counter.

CD_PARENT_HIT

Squid forwarded the request to this parent based on the Cache Digest algorithm (see Chapter 10).

CD_SIBLING_HIT

Squid forwarded the request to this sibling based on the Cache Digest algorithm.

CARP

Squid selected this parent based on the Cache Array Routing Protocol algorithm (see Chapter 10).

ANY_PARENT

Squid selected this parent as a last resort because none of the other methods resulted in a viable next-hop.

Note that most of these codes may be preceded by TIMEOUT_ to indicate that a timeout occurred while waiting for ICP/HTCP replies. For example:

```
1066038165.382    345 193.233.46.21 TCP_MISS/200 2836
            GET http://www.caida.org/home/images/home.jpg
            TIMEOUT_CLOSEST_DIRECT/213.219.122.19 image/jpeg
```

You can adjust the timeout with the *icp_query_timeout* directive.

Configuration Directives That Affect access.log

Following are the configuration file directives that affect the *access.log* in one way or another.

log_icp_queries

This directive, enabled by default, causes Squid to log all ICP queries. If you're running a busy parent cache, this may make your *access.log* files huge. To save space, disable this directive:

```
log_icp_queries off
```

If you disable ICP query logging, I suggest that you monitor the number of queries, either through the cache manager or with SNMP.

emulate_httpd_log

The *access.log* file has two formats: common and native. The common format is the same as most HTTP servers (e.g., Apache) use. It contains less information than Squid's native format. However, you might want to use the common log-file format if you use Squid as a surrogate (see Chapter 15). The common format may also be useful if you have log-file analysis tools that know how to parse it. Use this directive to enable the common format:

```
emulate_httpd_log on
```

See the site *http://www.w3.org/Daemon/User/Config/Logging.html#common-logfile-format,* for a description of this format.

log_mime_hdrs

Use the *log_mime_hdrs* directive to make Squid log the HTTP request and response headers:

```
log_mime_headers on
```

When enabled, Squid appends the request and response headers to *access.log*. This adds two fields to each line. Each field is surrounded by square brackets to make parsing easier. Certain characters are encoded to keep the log file readable. Table 13-2 shows the encoding scheme.

Table 13-2. Character encoding rules for HTTP headers in access.log

Character	Encoding
Newline	\n
Carriage return	\r
Backslash	\\
[	%5b
]	%5d
%	%25
ASCII 0–31	%xx (hexadecimal value)
ASCII 127–255	%xx (hexadecimal value)

log_fqdn

By default, Squid puts client IP addresses in the *access.log*. You can record hostnames, when available, by enabling this directive:

```
log_fqdn on
```

This causes Squid to make reverse DNS lookups for the client's address when it receives a request. If an answer is available by the time the request is complete, Squid places it in the third field.

ident_lookup_access

This access rule list determines whether or not Squid makes an RFC 1413 ident query for the client's TCP connection. By default, Squid doesn't issue ident queries. To enable this feature, simply add one or more rules:

```
acl All src 0/0
ident_lookup_access allow All
```

If an answer is available by the time the request is complete, Squid places it in the eighth field. If you are also using HTTP authentication, that username is written instead of the ident answer.

log_ip_on_direct

When Squid forwards a cache miss to an origin server, it records the origin server's IP address in the ninth field. You can disable this directive so that Squid writes the hostname instead:

```
log_ip_on_direct off
```

In this case, the hostname comes from the URI. If the URI contains an IP address, Squid doesn't convert it to a hostname.

client_netmask

This directive exists to provide some level of privacy for your users. Rather than logging the entire client IP address, you can mask off some bits. For example:

```
client_netmask 255.255.255.0
```

With this setting, all client IP addresses in *access.log* have 0 as the last octet:

```
1066036246.918     35 163.11.255.0 TCP_IMS_HIT/304 266 GET http://...
1066036246.932     16 163.11.255.0 TCP_IMS_HIT/304 266 GET http://...
1066036247.616    313 140.132.252.0 TCP_MISS/200 1079 GET http://...
1066036248.598  44459 140.132.252.0 TCP_MISS/500 1531 GET http://...
1066036249.230     17 170.210.173.0 TCP_IMS_HIT/304 265 GET http://...
1066036249.752   2135 140.132.252.0 TCP_MISS/200 50230 GET http://...
1066036250.467      4 170.210.173.0 TCP_IMS_HIT/304 265 GET http://...
1066036250.762    102 163.11.255.0 TCP_IMS_HIT/304 265 GET http://...
1066036250.832     20 163.11.255.0 TCP_IMS_HIT/304 266 GET http://...
1066036251.026     74 203.91.150.0 TCP_CLIENT_REFRESH_MISS/304 267 GET http://...
```

strip_query_terms

This directive is another privacy feature. It removes query terms from URIs before logging them. If your log files somehow fall into the wrong hands, they won't be able to find any usernames and passwords. When this directive is enabled, all characters after a question mark (?) are removed. For example, a URI like this:

```
http://auto.search.msn.com/response.asp?MT=www.kimo.com.yw&srch=3&prov=&utf8
```

is logged like this:

```
http://auto.search.msn.com/response.asp?
```

uri_whitespace

Earlier, I mentioned the problem with whitespace appearing in some URIs. The RFCs state that URIs must not contain whitespace, but in reality it happens all too often. The *uri_whitespace* directive dictates how Squid should handle such cases. The allowed settings are: strip (default), deny, allow, encode, and chop. Of these, strip, encode, and chop ensure that the URI field doesn't contain any whitespace (thus adding more fields to *access.log*).

The allow setting allows the request to pass through Squid unmodified. It is likely to cause trouble for redirectors and log file parsers. The deny setting, on the other hand, causes Squid to deny the request. The user receives an error message, but the request is still written to *access.log* with the whitespace characters.

If you set it to encode, Squid changes the whitespace characters to their RFC 1738 equivalents. This is probably what the user-agent should have done in the first place. The chop setting causes Squid to cut off the URI at the first whitespace character.

The default setting is strip, which makes Squid remove the whitespace characters from the URI. It ensures that your log-file parsers and redirectors will be happy, but it might break certain things, such as improperly encoded search engine queries.

buffered_logs

By default, Squid disables buffering for the *cache.log* file, which allows you to run tail -f and watch log file entries appear in real time. If you think this will cause an unnecessary overhead, you can disable buffering:

```
buffered_logs off
```

However, it probably doesn't matter unless you are running Squid with full debugging. Note that this option affects only *cache.log*. The others always use unbuffered writes.

access.log Analysis Tools

The *access.log* file contains a wealth of information, much more than you can see by just browsing through it. In order to get the big picture view, you'll need to use a third-party log-file analysis package. You can find a long list of them linked from the Squid web page, or by going directly to *http://www.squid-cache.org/Scripts/*.

One of the most popular tools is Calamaris—a Perl script that parses the log file and generates either text or HTML-based reports. It provides a breakdown of traffic by request method, client IP address, origin server domain name, content types, filename extensions, reply size, and more. Calamaris also reports on ICP query traffic and even understands log files from other caching products. Check it out by visiting *http://calamaris.cord.de/*.

Squeezer, and its derivative, Squeezer2, are Squid-specific analysis tools. They provide many statistics that can help you understand Squid's performance, especially when you have neighbors. Both generate HTML pages as output. Visit the *Logfile Analysis* page on the *squid-cache.org* site for links to these programs.

Webalyzer is another good utility. It is designed to be fast and produces HTML pages with tables and bar charts. It was originally designed for origin server access logs. Although it can parse Squid's logs, it doesn't report on such things as hit ratios and response times. It also uses some terms differently than I do. For example, Webalyzer calls any request a "hit," which isn't the same as a cache hit. It also makes a distinction between "pages" and "files." For more information, visit the Webalyzer home page at *http://www.mrunix.net/webalyzer/*.

store.log

The *store.log* is a record of Squid's decisions to store and remove objects from the cache. Squid creates an entry for each object it stores in the cache, each uncachable object, and each object that is removed by the replacement policy. The log file covers both in-memory and on-disk caches.

The *store.log* provides the following you can't get from *access.log*:

- Whether or not a particular response was cached.
- The file number for cached objects. For UFS-based storage schemes, you can convert this to a pathname and examine the contents of the cache file.
- The response's content length: the Content-Length value, and the actual body length.
- Values for the Date, Last-Modified, and Expires headers.
- The response's cache key (i.e., MD5 hash value).

As you can see, this is mostly low-level information you won't need on a daily basis. Unless you do sophisticated analyses, or wish to debug a problem, you can probably get by without the *store.log*. You can disable it with a special setting:

```
cache_store_log none
```

As with other log files, Squid appends new *store.log* entries to the end of the file. A given URI may appear in the file more than once. For example, it gets cached, then released, then cached again. Only the most recent entry reflects the object's current status.

The *store.log* is text-based and looks something like this:

```
1067299212.411 RELEASE -1 FFFFFFFF A5964B32245AC98592D83F9B6EA10B8D 206
    1067299212 1064287906 -1 application/octet-stream 6840/6840
    GET http://download.windowsupdate.com/msdownload/update/v3-19990518/cab...
1067299212.422 SWAPOUT 02 0005FD5F 6F34570785CACABC8DD01ABA5D73B392 200
    1067299210 1057899600 -1 image/gif 1125/1125
    GET http://forum.topsportsnet.com/shfimages/nav_members1.gif
1067299212.641 RELEASE -1 FFFFFFFF B0616CB4B7280F67672A40647DD08474 200
    1067299212 -1 -1 text/html -1/67191
    GET http://www.tlava.com/
1067299212.671 RELEASE -1 FFFFFFFF 5ECD93934257594825659B596D9444BC 200
    1067299023 1034873897 1067299023 image/jpeg 3386/3386
    GET http://ebiz0.ipixmedia.com/abc/ebiz/_EBIZ_3922eabf57d44e2a4c3e7cd234a...
1067299212.786 RELEASE -1 FFFFFFFF B388F7B766B307ADEC044A4099946A21 200
    1067297755 -1 -1 text/html -1/566
    GET http://www.evenflowrocks.com/pages/100303pic15.cfm
1067299212.837 RELEASE -1 FFFFFFFF ABC862C7107F3B7E9FC2D7CA01C8E6A1 304
    1067299212 -1 1067299212 unknown -1/0
    GET http://ebiz0.ipixmedia.com/abc/ebiz/_EBIZ_3922eabf57d44e2a4c3e7cd234a...
1067299212.859 RELEASE -1 FFFFFFFF 5ED2726D4A3AD83CACC8A01CFDD6082B 304
    1066940882 1065063803 -1 application/x-javascript -1/0
    GET http://www.bellsouth.com/scripts/header_footer.js
```

Each entry contains the following 13 fields:

1: *timestamp*

The timestamp when the event took place, expressed as seconds since the Unix epoch with millisecond resolution.

2: *action*

The action taken on the object. This field has three possible values: SWAPOUT, RELEASE, and SO_FAIL.

- A SWAPOUT occurs when Squid successfully completes saving the object data to disk. Some objects, such as those that are negatively cached, are kept in memory, but not on disk. Squid doesn't make a *store.log* entry for them.

- A SO_FAIL entry indicates that Squid could not completely save the object to disk. Most likely it means that the storage scheme implementation refused to open a new disk file for writing.

- A RELEASE occurs when Squid removes an object from the cache, or decides that the response isn't cachable in the first place.

3: *directory number*

The directory number is a 7-bit index to the list of cache directories that's written as a decimal number. For objects that aren't saved to disk, this field contains the value -1.

4: *file number*

The file number is a 25-bit identifier used internally by Squid. It is written as an 8-character hexadecimal number. The UFS-based storage schemes have an algorithm for mapping file numbers to pathnames (see the later section "Mapping File Numbers to Pathnames").

Objects that aren't saved to disk don't have a valid file number. For these, the file number field contains FFFFFFFF. This value appears only for RELEASE and SO_FAIL entries.

5: *cache key*

Squid uses MD5 hash values for the primary index to locate cached objects. The key is based on the request method, URI, and possibly other information.

You might be able to use the cache key to match up *store.log* entries. Note, however, that an object's cache key can change. This happens, for example, whenever Squid logs a TCP_REFRESH_MISS request in *access.log*. It looks like this:

```
1065837334.045 SWAPOUT ... 554BACBD2CB2A0C38FF9BF4B2239A9E5 ... http://blah
1066031047.925 RELEASE ... 92AE17121926106EB12FA8054064CABA ... http://blah
1066031048.074 SWAPOUT ... 554BACBD2CB2A0C38FF9BF4B2239A9E5 ... http://blah
```

So what's going on? The object is originally cached under one key (554B...). Some time later, Squid receives another request for the object and forwards a validation request to the origin server. When the response comes back with new content, Squid changes the cache key of the old object (to 92AE...) so that it can give the new object the correct key (554B...). The old object is then removed, and the new object is saved to disk.

6: status code

This field shows the HTTP status code of the response, just like *access.log*. See Table 13-1 for a list of status codes.

7: date

The value of the Date header in the HTTP response, expressed as seconds since the Unix epoch. The value -1 indicates an unparseable Date header, and -2 means the header was entirely absent.

8: last-modified

The value of the Last-Modified header in the HTTP response, expressed as seconds since the Unix epoch. The value -1 indicates an unparseable Last-Modified header, and -2 means the header was entirely absent.

9: expires

The value of the Expires header in the HTTP response, expressed as seconds since the Unix epoch. The value -1 indicates an unparseable Expires header, and -2 means the header was entirely absent.

10: content-type

The value of the Content-Type header in the HTTP response, excluding any media-type parameters. Squid inserts the value unknown if the Content-Type is missing.

11: content-length/size

This field contains two numbers, separated by a slash. The first is the value of the Content-Length header. A -1 indicates the Content-Length header is absent. The second is the actual size of the HTTP message body. You can use these two numbers to identify partially received responses and origin servers that incorrectly calculate the content length. In most cases, the two numbers are the same.

12: method

The HTTP request method for the object, as in *access.log*.

13: URI

The final field is the requested URI, as in *access.log*. This field also has the whitespace problem mentioned in the previous section. However, it is less worrisome here because you can safely ignore any extra fields.

For many of the RELEASE entries, you'll see question marks (?) for the last eight fields. This is because most of those field values come from what Squid calls the MemObject structure. This structure is present only for objects that have just been received, or are being stored entirely in memory. Most of the objects in Squid's cache don't have a MemObject because they exist only on disk. For these, Squid puts question marks in the fields with missing information.

Mapping File Numbers to Pathnames

If you find you need to examine a particular cache file, you can, with some effort, turn a file number into a pathname. You'll also need the directory number, and L1 and L2 values. In the Squid source code, the storeUfsDirFullPath( ) function does this. You can find it in the *src/fs/ufs/store_dir_ufs.c* file. This short Perl program mimics the current algorithm:

```perl
#!/usr/bin/perl
$L1 = 16;
$L2 = 256;
while (<>) {
    $filn = hex($_);
    printf("%02X/%02X/%08X\n",
        (($filn / $L2) / $L2) % $L1,
        ($filn / $L2) % $L2,
        $filn);
}
```

And here's how you can use it:

```
% echo 000DCD06 | ./fileno-to-pathname.pl
0D/CD/000DCD06
```

To find this file in the *N*th *cache_dir*, simply go to the corresponding directory and list or view the file:

```
% cd /cache2
% ls -l 0D/CD/000DCD06
-rw------- 1 squid  squid  391 Jun  3 12:40 0D/CD/000DCD06
% less 0D/CD/000DCD06
```

referer.log

The optional *referer.log* contains Referer header values from client requests. To use this feature, you must run ./configure with the --enable-referer-log option. You must also enter a pathname for the *referer_log* directive. For example:

```
referer_log /usr/local/squid/var/logs/referer.log
```

Set the filename to none if you want to disable referer logging.

The Referer header normally contains the URI from which the request was obtained (see Section 14.36 of RFC 2616). For example, when a web browser issues a request for an embedded image, the Referer header is set to the URI of the (HTML) page containing the images. It is also set when you click on an HTML link. Some web site operators use Referer values to find so-called dead links. You may find *referer.log* particularly useful if you use Squid as a surrogate.

The *referer.log* has a simple format, with only four fields. Here are a few examples:

```
1068047502.377 3.0.168.206
    http://www.amazon.com/exec/obidos/search-handle-form/002-7230223-8205634
```

```
       http://www.amazon.com/exec/obidos/ASIN/0596001622/qid=1068047396/sr=2-1/...
1068047503.109 3.0.168.206
       http://www.amazon.com/exec/obidos/ASIN/0596001622/qid=1068047396/sr=2-1/...
       http://g-images.amazon.com/images/G/01/gourmet/gourmet-segway.gif
1068047503.196 3.0.168.206
       http://www.amazon.com/exec/obidos/ASIN/0596001622/qid=1068047396/sr=2-1/...
       http://g-images.amazon.com/images/G/01/marketing/cross-shop/arnold/appar...
1068047503.198 3.0.168.206
       http://www.amazon.com/exec/obidos/ASIN/0596001622/qid=1068047396/sr=2-1/...
       http://g-images.amazon.com/images/G/01/marketing/cross-shop/arnold/appar...
1068047503.825 3.0.168.206
       http://www.amazon.com/exec/obidos/ASIN/0596001622/qid=1068047396/sr=2-1/...
       http://images.amazon.com/images/P/B00005R8BC.01.TZZZZZZZ.jpg
1068047503.842 3.0.168.206
       http://www.amazon.com/exec/obidos/ASIN/0596001622/qid=1068047396/sr=2-1/...
       http://images.amazon.com/images/P/0596001622.01._PE_PI_SCMZZZZZZZ_.jpg
```

Note that requests that lack a Referer header aren't logged. The four fields are as follows:

1: *timestamp*
> The time of the request, expressed as the number of seconds since Unix epoch with millisecond resolution.
>
> Note that, unlike *access.log*, a *referer.log* entry is made as soon as Squid receives the complete request. Thus, the *referer.log* entry occurs before the *access.log*, which waits for the end of the response.

2: *client address*
> The same as the client address in *access.log*. The *log_fqdn* and *client_netmask* directives affect this log file as well.

3: *referer*
> The value of the Referer header from the client's request. Note that the referer value might have whitespace (or any other) characters. Squid doesn't encode the value before writing to *referer.log*.

4: *URI*
> The URI that the client is requesting. It matches the URI in *access.log*.

useragent.log

The optional *useragent.log* contains User-Agent header values from client requests. To use this feature, you must supply the --enable-useragent-log option when running ./configure. You also must enter a pathname for the *useragent_log* directive. For example:

```
useragent_log /usr/local/squid/var/logs/useragent.log
```

The User-Agent header normally contains a description of the agent that made the request. In most cases, the description is simply a list of product names with optional version information. You should be aware that applications can easily provide false user-agent information. Modern user-agents provide a way to customize the description. Even Squid can alter the User-Agent header in forwarded requests.

The *useragent.log* format is relatively simple. It looks like this:

```
3.0.168.206 [05/Nov/2003:08:51:43 -0700]
    "Mozilla/5.0 (compatible; Konqueror/3; FreeBSD)"
3.0.168.207 [05/Nov/2003:08:52:18 -0700]
    "Opera/7.21 (X11; FreeBSD i386; U) [en]"
4.241.144.204 [05/Nov/2003:08:55:11 -0700]
    "Mozilla/5.0 (Macintosh; U; PPC Mac OS X; en-us) AppleWebKit/103u (KHTM..."
3.0.168.206 [05/Nov/2003:08:51:43 -0700]
    "Java1.3.1_01"
64.68.82.28 [05/Nov/2003:08:52:50 -0700]
    "Googlebot/2.1 (http://www.googlebot.com/bot.html)"
3.0.168.205 [05/Nov/2003:08:52:50 -0700]
    "WebZIP/4.1 (http://www.spidersoft.com)"
4.241.144.201 [05/Nov/2003:08:52:50 -0700]
    "Mozilla/4.0 (compatible; MSIE 5.0; Windows 98; DigExt; Hotbar 3.0)"
3.0.168.206 [05/Nov/2003:08:54:40 -0700]
    "Bookmark Renewal Check Agent [http://www.bookmark.ne.jp/] (Version 2.0..."
```

Unlike the other log files, it has just three fields:

1: *client address*

The same as the client address in *access.log*. The *log_fqdn* and *client_netmask* directives affect this log file as well.

2: *timestamp*

Unlike the other log files, which represent the time as seconds since the Unix epoch, this one uses a human-readable format. It is the HTTP common log-file format timestamp, which looks like this:

```
[10/Jun/2003:22:38:36 -0600]
```

Note that the square brackets delimit the timestamp, which includes a space character. Also note that, like *referer.log*, these entries are created as soon as Squid receives the complete request.

3: *user-agent*

The value of the User-Agent header. These strings almost always contain whitespace. Squid doesn't encode User-Agent values before writing them in this log file.

swap.state

A *swap.state* file is a journal of objects that have been added to, and removed from, a cache directory. Each *cache_dir* has its own *swap.state* file. When Squid starts up, it reads the *swap.state* files to rebuild its in-memory indexes of cached objects. These files are a relatively critical part of Squid's operation.

By default, each *swap.state* file is located in its corresponding cache directory. Thus, each state file automatically stays with each *cache_dir*. This is important if you ever decide to reorder your *cache_dir* lines or if you remove one or more from the list.

If you prefer to put them in a different location, you can use the *cache_swap_log* directive:

```
cache_swap_log /usr/local/squid/var/logs/swap.state
```

In this case, Squid creates a *swap.state* file for each directory by appending a numeric suffix. For example, if you have four cache directories, Squid creates the following:

```
/usr/local/squid/var/logs/swap.state.00
/usr/local/squid/var/logs/swap.state.01
/usr/local/squid/var/logs/swap.state.02
/usr/local/squid/var/logs/swap.state.03
```

In this situation, if you add, remove, or rearrange *cache_dir* lines, you may need to rename the *swap.state* files manually to keep everything consistent.

Technically, the *swap.state* format is storage scheme-dependent. However, all storage schemes use the same format in the current versions of Squid. The *swap.state* file uses a fixed-size (48-byte) binary format. Fields are written in host-byte order and are thus not necessarily portable between different operating systems. Table 13-3 describes the fields of a *swap.state* entry.

Table 13-3. swap.state entry fields

Name	Size, in bytes	Description
op	1	Operation on the entry: added (1) or deleted (2).
file number	4	Same as the fourth field of *store.log*, except it is stored in binary.
timestamp	4	A timestamp corresponding to the time when the response was generated or last validated. Taken from the Date header for responses that have one. Stored as the number of seconds since the Unix epoch.
lastref	4	A timestamp corresponding to the most recent access to the object.
expires	4	The object's expiration time, taken from an Expires header or Cache-Control max-age directive.
last-modified	4	The object's Last-Modified value.
swap file size	4	The amount of space the object occupies on disk. This includes HTTP headers and other Squid-specific meta-information.
refcount	2	The number of times this object has been requested.
flags	2	Various internal flags used by Squid.
key	16	The MD5 hash of the corresponding URI. Same as the key in *store.log*, except this one is stored in binary.

Rotating the Log Files

Squid always appends new entries to its log files. If your cache is busy, some of these files can become very large after a few days. Some operating systems even place limits on the size of a file (e.g., 2 GB) and return an error for writes beyond that size. To keep your log files manageable, and Squid happy, you must regularly rotate them.

Squid has a built-in feature for rotating log files. You can invoke it with the `squid -k rotate` command. You then tell Squid how many old copies of each file to keep with the *logfile_rotate* directive. For example, if you set it to 7, you'll have eight versions of each log file: the current file and seven old ones.

Old log files are renamed with numeric extensions. For example, when you execute a rotation, Squid renames *log.6* to *log.7*, then *log.5* to *log.6*, and so on. The current *log* becomes *log.0*, and Squid creates a new, empty file named *log*.

Each time you execute `squid -k rotate`, Squid rotates the following files: *cache.log*, *access.log*, *store.log*, *useragent.log* (if enabled), and *referer.log* (if enabled). Squid also creates up-to-date versions of the *swap.state* files. Note, however, that *swap.state* isn't archived with numeric extensions.

Squid doesn't rotate the log files automatically. The best way to make it happen is with a daily cron job. For example:

```
0 0 * * * /usr/local/squid/sbin/squid -k rotate
```

If you'd rather write your own scripts to manage the log files, Squid has a special mode that you'll find useful. Simply set the *logfile_rotate* directive to 0. Then, when you run `squid -k rotate`, Squid simply closes the current log files and opens new ones. This is very useful when the operating system allows you to rename files opened by another process. The following shell script illustrates the idea:

```
#!/bin/sh
set -e

yesterday_secs=`perl -e 'print time -43200'`
yesterday_date=`date -r $yesterday_secs +%Y%m%d`

cd /usr/local/squid/var/logs

# rename the current log file without interrupting the logging process
mv access.log access.log.$yesterday_date

# tell Squid to close the current logs and open new ones
/usr/local/squid/sbin/squid -k rotate

# give Squid some time to finish writing swap.state files
sleep 60

mv access.log.$yesterday_date /archive/location/
gzip -9 /archive/location/access.log.$yesterday_date
```

Privacy and Security

Squid's log files, especially *access.log*, contain a record of users' activities and, hence, are subject to privacy concerns. As the Squid administrator, you should take every precaution to keep the log files safe and secure. One of the best ways to do that is limit the number of people who have access to the system on which Squid runs. If that isn't possible, carefully examine the file and directory permissions to make sure they can't be viewed by untrusted or unauthorized users.

You can also help protect your users' privacy by taking advantage of the *client_netmask* and *strip_query_terms* directives. The former makes it harder to identify individual users in the *access.log*; the latter removes URI query terms that may contain personal information. See the earlier section "Configuration Directives That Affect access.log" for more information.

You may also want to develop a policy for keeping old log files. Obviously *access.log* helps keep users accountable for their activities, but how far back would you ever need to go searching for something? A week? A year? What would you do if presented with a court order to hand over your log files for the last three months?

If you like to keep historical data for a long time, perhaps you can make the log files anonymous or somehow reduce the dataset. If you are interested only in which URIs were accessed, but not by whom, you can extract only that field from *access.log*. This not only makes the file smaller, it also reduces the risk of a privacy violation. Another technique is to randomize the client IP addresses. In other words, create a filter that maps real IP addresses to fake ones, such that the same real address is always changed to the same fake address. If you are using RFC 1413 identification or HTTP authentication, consider making those fields anonymous as well.

Exercises

- Configure Squid so that it doesn't create any log files, except for the *swap.state* file(s).
- Write a simple Perl or awk script to calculate your cache hit ratio from *access.log*.
- How does an "access denied" response appear in the *access.log*?
- Does *store.log* have the same number of, more, or fewer, entries than *access.log*?
- Take a file number from *store.log* and find the corresponding file in the disk cache. Examine the file and make sure you've found the correct response.
- Develop and implement a policy for archiving old cache log files. Consider where and how they will be stored, for how long, and who has permission to access them.

## CHAPTER 14

Monitoring Squid

How can you tell if Squid is performing well? Does Squid have enough memory, bandwidth, and disk space? When the Internet seems slow, is it Squid's fault or a problem somewhere else? Is the operating system giving enough resources to Squid? Is someone trying to abuse or hack into my proxy? You can find the answers to these, and many more, questions in this chapter. Squid provides information about itself in three different ways: *cache.log* messages, the *cache manager*, and an SNMP MIB.

Squid writes various messages to *cache.log* as it runs. Most of these are abnormal events of one sort or another. Unfortunately, Squid isn't always smart enough to differentiate serious problems from those that can be safely ignored. Even so, *cache.log* is a good place to start when investigating a Squid problem.

The cache manager and SNMP interfaces allow you to query Squid for a variety of data. The cache manager, which has its own shortcomings, probably provides the most information in current versions of Squid. It has a TCP socket-based interface and tries to generate output suitable for both human and computer processing. The bulk of this chapter is devoted to explaining all the information available from the cache manager.

Squid supports SNMP as well. Unfortunately, the data available through SNMP is only a subset of the cache-manager information. Additionally, the Squid MIB has not evolved much over the years; it's essentially unchanged since its first incarnation. I'll explain how to make Squid process SNMP queries and describe all objects in the current MIB.

cache.log Warnings

This is one of the first places you should look whenever you perceive a problem with Squid. During normal operation, you'll find various warnings and informational messages that may or may not indicate a problem. I covered the mechanics of *cache.log* back in Chapter 13. Here, I'll go over a few of the warning messages you might see in your log file.

The *high_response_time_warning* directive makes Squid print a warning whenever the median response time exceeds a threshold. The value is in milliseconds and is disabled by default. If you add this line to *squid.conf*:

```
high_response_time_warning 1500
```

Squid will print the following warning if the median response time, measured over a 1-minute interval, exceeds 1.5 seconds:

```
2003/09/29 03:17:31| WARNING: Median response time is 2309 milliseconds
```

Before setting this directive, you should have a good idea of Squid's normal response time levels. If you set it too low, you'll get false alarms. In this particular example, it means that half of your user's requests take more than 2.3 second to complete. High response times may be caused by local problems, such as running out of file descriptors, or by remote problems, such as a severely congested Internet link.

The *high_page_fault_warning* directive is similar. It causes Squid to emit a warning if the number of page faults per minute exceeds a given value. A high page-fault rate usually indicates that the Squid process can't fit entirely in memory and must be swapped out to disk. This swapping severely impacts Squid's performance, so you should remedy the situation as soon as possible, as I'll discuss in Chapter 16.

Squid uses the Unix getrusage( ) function to get page fault counts. On some operating systems (e.g., Solaris), the page fault counter represents something besides swapping. Therefore, the *high_page_fault_warning* may cause false alarms on those systems.

The *high_memory_warning* directive is also similar to the previously mentioned warnings. In this case, it checks the size of the Squid process; if it exceeds the threshold, you get the warning in *cache.log*. On some operating systems, the process size can only grow and never shrink. Therefore, you'll constantly get this warning until Squid shuts down.

Process size information comes from either the mallinfo( ), mstats( ), or sbrk( ) functions. If these are unavailable on your operating system, the *high_memory_warning* warning won't work.

Squid has a number of other hardcoded warnings you may see in *cache.log*:

DNS lookup for 'neighbor.host.name' failed!
This occurs whenever Squid fails to look up the IP address for a cache neighbor. Squid refreshes the neighbor addresses every hour or so. As long as the neighbor's address is unknown, Squid doesn't send any traffic there.

`Detected DEAD Sibling: neighbor.host.name/3128/3130`
Squid logs this message when it believes it can't communicate with a neighbor cache. This happens, for example, when too many consecutive ICP queries go unacknowledged. See Chapter 10 for more information.

`95% of replies from 'neighbor.host.name' are UDP_DENIED`
This message indicates that a neighbor cache is refusing to answer Squid's queries. It probably means that you are sending queries to the neighbor without their permission. If they are using address-based access controls, and you have recently changed your address, they won't know about the change. Squid refuses to send any more queries to the neighbor after detecting this condition.

`Probable misconfigured neighbor at 192.168.121.5`
This occurs when you have an unauthorized cache client sending you ICP or HTCP queries. The best thing to do in this case is try to find out the person or organization responsible for the given address. Ask why they are querying your cache.

`Forwarding loop detected for:`
Recall that a forwarding loop occurs when a single request flows through Squid a second time. The request's `Via` header contains a list of all proxies that have seen the request. If Squid detects its own name in the `Via` list, it emits the forwarding loop warning and sends the request directly to the origin server. See Chapter 10 for an explanation of forwarding loops.

`Closing client 192.168.121.5 connection due to lifetime timeout`
The *client_lifetime* directive places an upper limit on the duration for a single HTTP request. Squid warns you when such a request is terminated because it may indicate someone is abusing your cache with very long-lived connections, for example, by downloading infinitely long objects.

As you can see, *cache.log* provides only notification of abnormal events. For periodic monitoring, you need something else. The cache manager is perhaps the best choice, even though its interface is less than perfect.

The Cache Manager

The Cache Manager is an interface to Squid for receiving information about various components. It is accessed via normal HTTP requests with a special protocol name: `cache_object`. A full cache manager URL looks like *cache_object://cache.host.name/ info*. Squid provides two easy ways to access the cache manager information: the command-line `squidclient` program[*] or the `cachemgr.cgi` CGI program.

---

[*] In older versions of Squid, it was called just `client`.

The `squidclient` utility is a simple HTTP client, with a few special features for use with Squid. For example, you can use a shortcut to request the cache manager pages. Rather than typing a long URL like this:

```
% squidclient cache_object://cache.host.name/info
```

you can use this shorter version:

```
% squidclient mgr:info
```

`squidclient` is a convenient way to quickly see some of the cache manager pages. It's also useful when you need to save the cache manager output to disk for later analysis. However, some pages, such as the memory utilization table, are difficult to read in a terminal window. They are really designed to be formatted as an HTML page and viewed with your web browser. In that case, you may want to use `cachemgr.cgi`.

To use `cachemgr.cgi`, you must have an HTTP server that can execute the program. You can use an existing server or install one alongside Squid if you prefer. Keep in mind that the cache manager has only weak security (cleartext passwords). If the HTTP server is on a different host, you need to add its IP address to a cache manager access list (see the section "Cache Manager Access Controls"). You may also want to add access controls to the HTTP server so that others can't access `cachemgr.cgi`.

If you use Apache, I recommend making a special *cgi-bin* directory so you can protect `cachemgr.cgi` with access controls. For example, create a new directory, and copy the binary to it:

```
# mkdir /usr/local/apache/squid-cgi
# cp /usr/local/squid/libexec/cachemgr.cgi /usr/local/apache/squid-cgi
# chmod 755 /usr/local/apache/squid-cgi/cachemgr.cgi
```

Now, add a *ScriptAlias* line to Apache's *httpd.conf*:

```
ScriptAlias /squid-cgi/ "/usr/local/apache/squid-cgi/"
```

Finally, create an *.htaccess* file in the *squid-cgi* directory that contains access controls. To allow requests from only one IP address, use something like this:

```
Allow from 192.168.4.2
Deny from all
```

Once `cachemgr.cgi` is installed, simply enter the appropriate URL into your web browser. For example:

```
http://www.server.name/squid-cgi/cachemgr.cgi
```

If the CGI program is working, you should see a page with four fields. See Figure 14-1 for an example. The *Cache Host* field contains the name of the host on which Squid is running—*localhost* by default. You can set it with the `--enable-cachemgr-hostname` option when running `./configure`. Similarly, *Cache Port* contains the TCP port number to which Squid listens for requests. It's 3128 by default and can be changed with the `--enable-cachemgr-port` option. The *Manager name* and *Password* fields are for access to protected pages, which I'll talk about shortly.

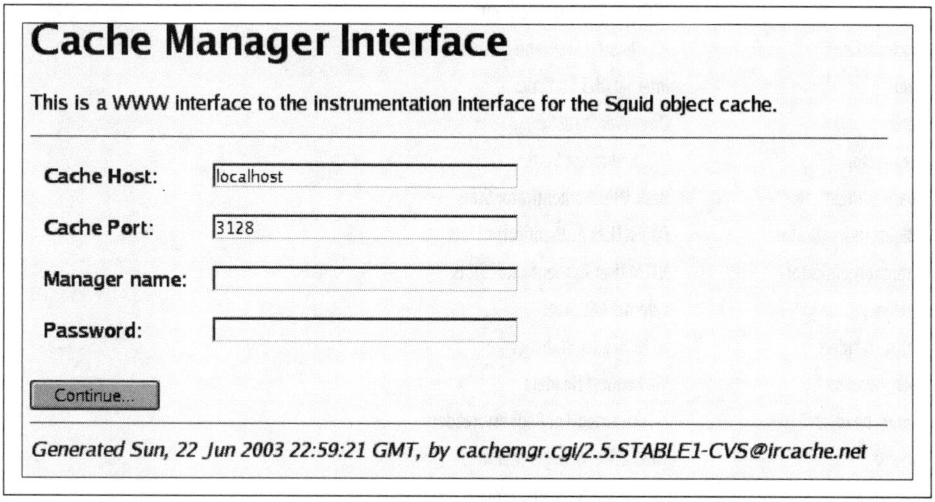

Cache Manager Interface

This is a WWW interface to the instrumentation interface for the Squid object cache.

Cache Host: `localhost`

Cache Port: `3128`

Manager name:

Password:

Continue...

Generated Sun, 22 Jun 2003 22:59:21 GMT, by cachemgr.cgi/2.5.STABLE1-CVS@ircache.net

Figure 14-1. The cachemgr.cgi login screen

After clicking on the *Continue...* button, you should see a list of all cache manager pages currently available. The following section describes the various pages, some of which are available only when you enable certain features at compile time.

Cache Manager Pages

This section describes the cache manager pages, in the same order in which they appear in the menu. Each section title has both the page name (for use with `squidclient`), followed by its description. Descriptions that contain an asterisk indicate pages that are disabled by default, unless you configure a password for them. Table 14-1 shows the table of contents and the section number for each page.

Table 14-1. Cache manager pages

Short name	Description
leaks	Memory Leak Tracking
mem	Memory Utilization
cbdata	Callback Data Registry Contents
events	Event Queue
squidaio_counts	Async IO Function Counters
diskd	DISKD Stats
config	Current Squid Configuration*
comm_incoming	comm_incoming( ) Stats

Table 14-1. Cache manager pages (continued)

Short name	Description
ipcache	IP Cache Stats and Contents
fqdncache	FQDN Cache Stats and Contents
idns	Internal DNS Statistics
dns	Dnsserver Statistics
redirector	URL Redirector Stats
basicauthenticator	Basic User Authenticator Stats
digestauthenticator	Digest User Authenticator Stats
ntlmauthenticator	NTLM User Authenticator Stats
external_acl	External ACL Stats
http_headers	HTTP Header Statistics
via_headers	Via Request Headers
forw_headers	X-Forwarded-For Request Headers
menu	This Cache Manager Menu
shutdown	Shut Down the Squid Process*
offline_toggle	Toggle offline_mode Setting*
info	General Runtime Information
filedescriptors	Process File Descriptor Allocation
objects	All Cache Objects
vm_objects	In-Memory and In-Transit Objects
openfd_objects	Objects with Swapout Files Open
io	Server-Side Network read( ) Size Histograms
counters	Traffic and Resource Counters
peer_select	Peer Selection Algorithms
digest_stats	Cache Digest and ICP Blob
5min	5 Minute Average of Counters
60min	60 Minute Average of Counters
utilization	Cache Utilization
histograms	Full Histogram Counts
active_requests	Client-Side Active Requests
store_digest	Store Digest
storedir	Store Directory Stats
store_check_cachable_stats	storeCheckCachable( ) Stats
store_io	Store IO Interface Stats
pconn	Persistent Connection Utilization Histograms
refresh	Refresh Algorithm Statistics
delay	Delay Pool Levels

Table 14-1. Cache manager pages (continued)

Short name	Description
forward	Request Forwarding Statistics
client_list	Cache Client List
netdb	Network Measurement Database
asndb	AS Number Database
carp	CARP Information
server_list	Peer Cache Statistics
non_peers	List of Unknown Sites Sending ICP Messages

leaks: Memory Leak Tracking

This page is available only with the ./configure --enable-leakfinder option and is intended for developers trying to track down memory leaks. The page shows each memory pointer being tracked and where and when it was most recently referenced. See the Squid Programmer's Guide (*http://www.squid-cache.org/Doc/Prog-Guide/*) for more information about Squid's leak-finder feature.

mem: Memory Utilization

The memory utilization page shows a large table of numbers. Each row corresponds to a different pool of memory. The pools have names like acl_list and MemObject. Much of this information is of interest to developers only. However, a few columns are worth mentioning here.

> It is important to keep in mind that this table doesn't represent all the memory allocated by Squid. Some memory allocations aren't tracked and don't appear in the table. Thus, the *Total* row may be much less than Squid's actual memory usage.

The impact column shows each pool's contribution to the total amount of memory allocated. Usually, the StoreEntry, MD5 digest, and LRU policy node pools take up most of the memory.

If you are a developer, you can use this page to look for memory leaks. The column labeled high (hrs) shows the amount of time elapsed since the pool reached its maximum size. A small value in this column may indicate that memory for that pool isn't being freed correctly.

You can also use this page to find out if certain features, such as *netdb*, the *ipcache*, and *client_db* consume too much memory. For example, the ClientInfo pool is associated with the *client_db* feature. The memory utilization page shows you how much memory you can save if you disable *client_db* in *squid.conf*.

cbdata: Callback Data Registry Contents

The Callback Data Registry is an internal Squid programming feature for managing memory pointers. Currently, this cache manager page doesn't provide much useful information, apart from the number of active *cbdata* pointers being tracked. In earlier Squid versions, the *cbdata* feature was implemented differently and this page provided some information to developers debugging their code.

events: Event Queue

Squid maintains an event queue for a number of tasks that must occur separately from user requests. Perhaps the most important of these is the periodic task that maintains the disk cache size. Every second or so, this task runs and looks for cache files to remove. On this page, you can see all tasks currently scheduled for execution. Most likely, you'll not find this very interesting unless you are hacking the source code.

squidaio_counts: Async IO Function Counters

This page is available only with the ./configure --enable-storeio=aufs option. It shows counters for the number of open, close, read, write, stat, and unlink requests received. For example:

```
ASYNC IO Counters:
Operation       # Requests
open            15318822
close           15318813
cancel          15318813
write                  0
read            19237139
stat                   0
unlink           2484325
check_callback 311678364
queue                  0
```

The cancel counter is normally equal to the close counter. This is because the close function always calls the cancel function to ensure that any pending I/O operations are ignored.

The write counter is zero because this version of Squid performs writes synchronously, even for *aufs*.

The check_callback counter shows how many times the main Squid process has checked the done queue for completed operations.

The queue value indicates the current length of the request queue. Normally, the queue length should be less than the number of threads × 5. If you repeatedly observe a queue length larger than this, you may be pushing Squid too hard. Adding more threads may help, but only to a certain point.

---

diskd: DISKD Stats

This page is available only with the ./configure --enable-storeio=diskd option. It provides various statistics relating to the *diskd* storage scheme.

The sent_count and recv_count lines are counters for the number of I/O requests sent between Squid and the group of *diskd* processes. The two numbers should be very close to each other and could possibly be equal. The difference indicates how many requests are currently outstanding.

The max_away value indicates the largest number of outstanding requests. Similarly, the max_shmuse counter indicates the maximum number of shared memory blocks in use at once. These two values are reset (to zero) each time you request this page. Thus, if you wait longer between requests for this page, these maximum counters are likely to be larger.

The open_fail_queue_len counter indicates the number of times that the *diskd* code decided to return failure in response to a request to open a file because the message queue exceeded its configured limit. In other words, this is the number of times a *diskd* queue reached the Q1 limit. Similarly, block_queue_len shows how many times the Q2 limit has been reached. See the descriptions of Q1 and Q2 in Chapter 8.

The *diskd* page also shows how many requests Squid sent to the *diskd* processes for each of the six I/O operations: open, create, close, unlink, read, and write. It also shows how many times each operation succeeded or failed. Note, these counters are incremented only for requests sent. The open_fail_queue_len check occurs earlier, and in that case, Squid doesn't send a request to a *diskd* process.

config: Current Squid Configuration*

This option dumps Squid's current configuration in the *squid.conf* format. Thus, if you ever accidentally remove the configuration file, you can recover it from the running Squid process. By saving the output to a file, you can also compare (e.g., with the diff command) the running configuration to the saved configuration. Note, however, that comments and blank lines aren't preserved.

This option reveals potentially sensitive information, so it's available only with a password. You must add a cache manager password for the *config* option with the *cachemgr_passwd* directive. See the section "Cache Manager Access Controls" for specifics. Additionally, these cache manager passwords aren't displayed in this output.

comm_incoming: comm_incoming( ) Stats

This page provides low-level network I/O information to developers and Squid wizards. The loop that checks for activity on file descriptors is called comm_poll( ). Over the years, this function has become increasingly complicated in order to improve Squid's performance. One of those performance improvements relates to how often Squid checks certain network sockets relative to the others.

For example, the incoming HTTP socket is where Squid accepts new client connections. This socket tends to be busier than a normal data socket because each new connection comes through the incoming socket. To provide good performance, Squid makes an extra effort to check the incoming socket more frequently than the others.

At the top of the *comm_incoming* page, you'll see three incoming interval numbers: one each for ICP, DNS, and HTTP. The interval is the number of normal I/O events that Squid handles before checking the incoming socket again. For example, if incoming_dns_interval is set to 140, Squid checks the incoming DNS socket after 140 I/Os on normal connections. Unless your Squid is very busy, you'll probably see 256 for all incoming intervals.

The page also contains three histograms that show how many events occur for each incoming function call. Normally, the majority of the histogram counts occur in the low values. In other words, functions such as comm_select_http_incoming( ) usually handle between one and four events.

ipcache: IP Cache Stats and Contents

The IP cache contains cached results of hostname-to-address lookups. This cache manager page displays quite a lot of information. At the top of this page you'll see a handful of statistics like these:

```
IPcache Entries: 10034
IPcache Requests: 1066445
IPcache Hits: 817880
IPcache Negative Hits: 6846
IPcache Misses: 200497
```

In this example, you can see that the IP cache contains slightly more than 10,000 entries (hostnames). Since Squid was started, there have been 1,066,445 name-to-address requests, 817,880 of which were cache hits. This is a cache hit ratio of 77%. An IP cache negative hit occurs when Squid receives a subsequent request for a hostname that it recently failed to resolve. Rather than retry the DNS lookup immediately, Squid assumes it will fail again and returns an error message to the user.

Following these brief statistics, you'll see a long list of the IP cache contents. For each hostname in the cache, Squid prints six fields:

- The hostname itself
- Flags: N for negatively cached entries and H if the addresses came from the local *hosts* file, rather than the DNS
- The number of seconds since the hostname was last requested or used
- The number of seconds until the cached entry expires

- The number of IP addresses known for the host, and, in parentheses, the number of BAD addresses
- A list of IP addresses and whether each is OK or BAD

Here is a short sample (formatted to fit the page):

```
Hostname                Flg lstref   TTL  N
ads.x10.com                    9      110  1( 0)   63.211.210.20-OK
us.rd.yahoo.com              640     -340  4( 0) 216.136.232.150-OK
                                                 216.136.232.147-OK
                                                 216.136.232.149-OK
                                                 216.136.232.148-OK
www.movielodge.com          7143    -2161  1( 0)   66.250.223.36-OK
shell.windows.com          10865    -7447  2( 1)  207.46.226.48-BAD
                                                 207.46.248.237-OK
www.surf3.net             126810   -40415  1( 0)  212.74.112.95-OK
```

The list is sorted by the time since last reference. Recently referenced names are at the top of the list, and unused (about to be removed) names are at the bottom.

IP addresses are marked OK by default. An address is marked BAD when Squid receives an error or timeout during a TCP connection attempt. Subsequent IP cache requests don't return BAD addresses. If all the host's addresses become BAD, Squid resets them all back to OK.

fqdncache: FQDN Cache Stats and Contents

The FQDN cache is similar to the IP cache, except that it stores address-to-hostname lookups. Another difference is that the FQDN cache doesn't mark hostnames as OK or BAD.

Your FQDN cache may be empty, unless you enable the *log_fqdn* directive, use domain-based ACLs (such as *srcdomain*, *dstdomain*, *srcdom_regex*, and *dstdom_regex*), or use a redirector.

idns: Internal DNS Statistics

Squid contains an internal DNS client implementation, which is enabled by default. Disabling internal DNS with the --disable-internal-dns option also disables this page. Here is some sample output:

```
Internal DNS Statistics:

The Queue:
                      DELAY SINCE
    ID   SIZE SENDS FIRST SEND LAST SEND
   ------ ---- ----- ---------- ---------
   001876   44    1      0.010     0.010
   001875   44    1      0.010     0.010
```

```
Nameservers:
IP ADDRESS       # QUERIES # REPLIES
--------------- --------- ---------
192.168.19.124      4889      4844
192.168.19.190        91        51
192.168.10.2          73        39

Rcode Matrix:
RCODE ATTEMPT1 ATTEMPT2 ATTEMPT3
    0     6149        4        2
    1        0        0        0
    2       38       34       32
    3        0        0        0
    4        0        0        0
    5        0        0        0
```

The Internal DNS page contains three tables. First, you'll see the queue of unanswered queries. Unfortunately, you can't see the contents of the query (the hostname or IP address). Instead, Squid prints the ID, size, number of transmissions, and elapsed times for each query. You should see relatively few queries in the queue. If you see a lot relative to your total traffic rate, make sure your DNS servers are functioning properly.

The second table (Nameservers) shows how many queries have been sent to, and replies received from, each DNS server. Squid always queries the first server in the list first. Second (and third, etc.) servers are queried only when the previous server times out for a given query. If you see zero replies from the first address, make sure a server is actually running at that address.

Finally, you'll see a table of DNS response codes versus number of attempts. The cell for response code 0 and ATTEMPT1 should have the highest count. Response code 0 indicates success, while others are different types of errors (see RFC 1035 for their descriptions). You may see some smaller numbers for response code 0 in the columns for ATTEMPT2 and ATTEMPT3. This shows the cases when retransmitting a query, after initially receiving an error, resulted in a successful reply. Note that Squid retries only response code 2 (server failure) errors.

dns: Dnsserver Statistics

This cache manager page is available only when you use the --disable-internal-dns option. In this case, Squid uses a number of external dnsserver processes to perform DNS lookups. The dnsserver program is one of a number of helper processes Squid can use. The other types of helpers are redirectors, authenticators, and external ACLs. All Squid's helpers have cache manager pages that display the same statistics. For example:

```
Dnsserver Statistics:
number running: 5 of 5
requests sent: 3001
replies received: 3001
```

```
queue length: 0
avg service time: 23.10 msec

    #    FD    PID  # Requests    Flags     Time  Offset Request
    1     6  20110         128    AB       0.293       0 www.nlanr.net
    2     7  20111          45    A        0.000       0 (none)
    3     8  20112           4    A        0.000       0 (none)
    4     9  20113           0    A        0.000       0 (none)
    5    10  20114           0    A        0.000       0 (none)
```

The number running line shows how many helper processes are running and how many should be running. The *dns_children* directive specifies how many dnsserver processes to use. The two numbers should match, but they may not if a helper process dies unexpectedly or if some processes could not be started. Recall that when you reconfigure a running Squid instance, all the helpers are killed and restarted. See the discussion in Appendix A.

The requests sent and replies received values display the number of requests sent to (and responses received from) the helpers since Squid started. The difference between these two, if any, should correspond to the number of outstanding requests.

The queue length line shows how many requests are queued, waiting for one of the helpers to become free. The queue length should usually be zero. If not, you should add more helpers to reduce delays for your users.

The avg service time line shows the running average service time for all helpers. Your particular value may depend on numerous factors, such as your network bandwidth and processing power.

The next section displays a table of statistics for the running dnsserver processes. The FD column shows the file descriptor for the socket between Squid and each dnsserver process. Similarly, the PID column shows each helper's process ID number.

The # Requests column shows how many requests have been sent to each helper. These numbers are zeroed each time you reconfigure Squid, so they many not add up to the total number of requests sent, as shown earlier. Note that Squid always chooses the first idle helper in the list, so the first process should receive the largest number of requests. The last few processes may not receive any requests at all.

The Flags column shows a few flags describing the state of the helper process. You should normally see A (for Alive) in each column. Occasionally, when the helper process is handling a request, you'll see B (for Busy).

The Time column displays the amount of time elapsed (in seconds) for the current, or last, request. Offset shows how many bytes of the response message Squid has read on the socket. This is almost always zero. Finally, the Request column shows the request that was sent to the helper process. In this case, it is either a hostname or an IP address.

redirector: URL Redirector Stats

The Redirector Stats page is available only if you are using a redirector (see Chapter 11). The format of this page is identical to *Dnsserver Statistics*, described earlier.

basicauthenticator: Basic User Authenticator Stats

This page is available only with the ./configure --enable-auth=basic option and when you define a Basic authenticator with the *auth_param basic program* directive. The format of this page is identical to *Dnsserver Statistics*, described earlier.

digestauthenticator: Digest User Authenticator Stats

This page is available only with the ./configure --enable-auth=digest option and when you define a Digest authenticator with the *auth_param digest program* directive. The format of this page is identical to *Dnsserver Statistics*, described earlier.

ntlmauthenticator: NTLM User Authenticator Stats

This page is available only with the ./configure --enable-auth=ntlm option and when you define a NTLM authenticator with then *auth_param ntlm program* directive. The format of this page is similar to *Dnsserver Statistics*, described earlier, with a few additions.

The table of helper processes includes an extra column: # Deferred Requests. NTLM requires "stateful" helpers because the helper processes themselves generate the challenges. Squid receives a challenge from a helper, sends that challenge to a user, and receives a response. Squid must send the user's challenge response back to the same helper for validation. For this protocol to work, Squid must defer some messages to be sent to a helper until the helper is ready to accept them.

These helpers also have two new flags: R (reserved or deferred) and P (placeholder). The R flag is set when the helper has at least one deferred request waiting. The P flag is set when Squid is waiting for the NTLM helper to generate a new challenge token.

external_acl: External ACL Stats

This page displays helper statistics for your external ACLs. If you don't have any *external_acl_type* lines in *squid.conf*, this page will be empty. Otherwise, Squid displays the statistics for each external ACL. The format is the same as for the *Dnsserver Statistics*.

http_headers: HTTP Header Statistics

This page displays a number of tables containing statistics about HTTP headers. It contains up to four sections: HTCP reply stats (if HTCP is enabled), HTTP request stats, HTTP reply stats, and a final section called HTTP Fields Stats. The HTCP reply statistics refer to HTCP replies received by your cache. The HTTP request section refers to HTTP requests either sent or received by your cache. Similarly, the HTTP reply section refers to replies either sent or received by Squid.

The first three sections have the same format. Each section contains three tables: Field type distribution, Cache-control directives distribution, and Number of fields per header distribution.

The Field type distribution table shows the number of times that each header value occurs and the percentage of cases in which it occurs. For example, in Table 14-2 you can see that the Accept header occurs in 98% of HTTP requests.

Table 14-2. Sample Field type distribution values for HTTP requests

ID	Name	Count	#/header
0	Accept	1416268	0.98
1	Accept-Charset	322077	0.22
2	Accept-Encoding	709715	0.49
3	Accept-Language	1334736	0.92
...	...	...	...

Unfortunately, these (and the following) statistics are tricky because they don't correspond one-to-one for client requests. For example, Squid may report 1,416,268 Accept headers in requests but only 800,542 client requests. This happens because Squid creates more than one HTTP header data structure for each request. In the case of HTTP replies, it seems that Squid may create up to four separate header structures, depending on the circumstances.

The Cache-Control directives distribution is similar, but applies only to the values of the Cache-Control header. Table 14-3 shows some of the possible field values.

Table 14-3. Sample Cache-Control directives distribution values for HTTP requests

ID	Name	Count	#/cc_field
0	public	6866	0.02
1	private	69783	0.24
2	no-cache	78252	0.27
3	no-store	9878	0.03
4	no-transform	168	0.00
5	must-revalidate	10983	0.04
6	proxy-revalidate	2480	0.01
7	max-age	165034	0.56
8	s-maxage	4995	0.02
9	max-stale	0	0.00

Table 14-3. Sample Cache-Control directives distribution values for HTTP requests (continued)

ID	Name	Count	#/cc_field
10	only-if-cached	0	0.00
11	Other	9149	0.03

The `Number of fields per header distribution` table shows how many headers occur in each request or reply. Usually, you should see something like a normal distribution with a peak around 10–13 headers per request or response.

Finally, this page ends with a table labeled `Http Fields Stats (replies and requests)`. For each header, this table shows three values: `#alive`, `%err`, and `%repeat`.

The `#alive` column shows how many instances of this header are currently stored in memory. HTTP headers are kept in memory for both active requests/responses and for completed objects stored in the memory cache.

The `%err` column shows the percentage of times Squid encountered an error while parsing this header. Common errors include incorrect date formats for `Date`, `Expires`, `Last-Modified`, and similar headers. The value `-1` indicates no errors.

The `%repeat` column indicates the number of times that a particular header is repeated in a single request or response. These aren't errors because HTTP allows headers to be repeated.

via_headers: Via Request Headers

This page is available only with the `./configure --enable-forw-via-db` option. The information in this page is intended to help cache administrators understand where client requests come from. When enabled, Squid counts the number of times each unique `Via` header occurs in client requests.

The `Via` header contains a list of downstream proxies that have forwarded the request so far. When a proxy forwards a request, it should append its hostname and other identifying information to the `Via` header. With the information in this database, you can, in theory, reconstruct the hierarchy of proxies forwarding requests through yours.

Squid prints the `Via` database entries in a random order. The output may look something like this:

```
   4 1.0 proxy.firekitten.org:3128 (squid/2.5.STABLE1)
   1 1.0 xnsproxy.dyndns.org:3128 (squid/2.5.PRE3-20020125)
1751 1.0 nt04.rmtcc.cc.oh.us:3128 (Squid/2.4.STABLE6),
        1.0 tasksmart.rmtcc.cc.oh.us:3128 (Squid/2.4.STABLE7)
 137 1.0 reg3.bdg.telco.co.id:8080 (Squid/2.2.STABLE5),
        1.0 c1.telco.co.id:8080 (Squid/2.4.STABLE6),
        1.0 cache2.telco.co.id:8080 (Squid/2.4.STABLE1)
```

```
 53 1.0 IS_GW_312:3128 (Squid/2.4.STABLE6)
 60 1.0 proxy.kiltron.net:3128 (Squid/2.4.STABLE7)
815 1.1 DORM
```

In this example, Squid received 1751 requests that previously passed through two other proxies (*nt04* and *tasksmart*). Note that only proxies add a Via header. Requests from user-agents usually don't have the header and, therefore, aren't counted in this database.

As you can see, the Via headers reveal some semiprivate information, such as hostnames, port numbers, and software versions. Please take care to respect the privacy of your users if you enable this feature.

The Via database is stored entirely in memory and is lost if Squid restarts. The database is cleared whenever you rotate the log files (see Chapter 13).

forw_headers: X-Forwarded-For Request Headers

This page is available only with the ./configure --enable-forw-via-db option. It is similar to the *via_headers* page, except that it displays the accumulation of X-Forwarded-For headers.

X-Forwarded-For is a nonstandard HTTP header that originated with the Squid project. Its value is a list of client IP addresses. In other words, when Squid receives and forwards a request, it appends the client's IP address to this header. It is similar to Via because the header grows each time a proxy passes the request on towards the origin server.

The *forw_headers* output is similar to *via_headers*. Each line begins with an integer, followed by a header value. The integer indicates how many times that particular X-Forwarded-For value was received. For example:

```
  1 10.37.1.56, 10.1.83.8
  3 10.3.33.77, 10.1.83.8
569 116.120.203.54
 21 10.65.18.200, 10.1.83.120
 31 116.120.204.6
  5 10.1.92.7, 10.1.83.120
  1 10.3.65.122, 10.3.1.201, 10.1.83.8
  2 10.73.73.51, 10.1.83.120
  1 10.1.68.141, 10.1.83.8
  3 10.1.92.7, 10.1.83.122
```

As with *via_headers*, this database is also stored in memory and is lost if Squid exits. The database is cleared each time you rotate Squid's log files.

menu: This Cache Manager Menu

This page simply displays a listing of the other cache manager pages. You can use it if you forget the name of a page or if you want to know if certain optional pages are available. When using cachemgr.cgi, each item in the menu is a clickable link.

shutdown: Shut Down the Squid Process*

This is one of the few cache manager functions that doesn't simply display some information. Rather, this "page" allows you to shut down Squid remotely. To allow shutdown via the cache manager, you must assign it a password with the *cachemgr_passwd* (see the section "Cache Manager Access Controls") directive in *squid.conf*. Without a password, the shutdown operation is disabled (but you can still use squid -k shutdown).

Because the cache manager has very weak security—passwords are sent in cleartext—I don't recommend enabling this operation.

offline_toggle: Toggle offline_mode Setting*

This is another function that allows you to control Squid, rather than simply receive information. It also requires a password (see the section "Cache Manager Access Controls") in order to become active.

Each time you request this page, Squid toggles the *offline_mode* setting. Squid reports the new setting on your screen and in *cache.log*.

info: General Runtime Information

This page provides a lot of basic information about the way that Squid is operating. It is a good starting point for using the cache manager and for tracking down performance problems.

At the top, you'll see the release version (e.g., Version 2.5.STABLE4) and two timestamps: the starting and current times. For example:

```
Squid Object Cache: Version 2.5.STABLE4
Start Time:     Mon, 22 Sep 2003 03:10:37 GMT
Current Time:   Mon, 13 Oct 2003 10:25:16 GMT
```

Following that, you'll see seven different sections. The first section, Connection information, displays a few statistics about the number and rate of connections, and the number of cache clients:

```
Connection information for squid:
        Number of clients accessing cache:     386
        Number of HTTP requests received:       12997469
        Number of ICP messages received:        16302149
        Number of ICP messages sent:    16310714
        Number of queued ICP replies:   0
        Request failure ratio:   0.00
        Average HTTP requests per minute since start:   423.7
        Average ICP messages per minute since start:    1063.2
        Select loop called: 400027445 times, 4.601 ms avg
Number of clients accessing cache
```

    Here, "client" actually means IP address. Squid assumes that each client has a unique IP address.

Number of HTTP requests received

The total number of HTTP requests since Squid was started.

Number of ICP messages received

The total number of ICP messages received since Squid was started. Note, received messages includes both queries and responses. These values don't include HTCP messages, however.

Number of ICP messages sent

The total number of ICP messages sent since Squid was started. Note, received messages includes both queries and responses. Doesn't include HTCP messages. Most likely, your sent and received counts will be about the same.

Number of queued ICP replies

ICP messages are sent over UDP. The sendto( ) system call rarely fails, but if it does, Squid queues the ICP message for retransmission. This counter shows how many times an ICP message was queued for retransmission. Most likely, you'll see 0 here.

Request failure ratio

The failure ratio is a moving average ratio between the number of failed and successful requests. In this context, a failed request is caused by either a DNS error, TCP connection error, or network read error. When this ratio exceeds 1.0— meaning Squid returns more errors than successful responses— Squid goes into hit-only mode. In this mode, Squid returns ICP_MISS_NOFETCH instead of ICP_MISS. Thus, your neighbor caches that use ICP won't forward cache misses to you until the problem goes away.

Average HTTP requests per minute since start

This value is simply the number of HTTP requests divided by the amount of time Squid has been running. This average doesn't reflect short-term variations in load. To get a better instantaneous load measurement, use the *5min* or *60min* page.

Average ICP messages per minute since start

The number of ICP queries received by Squid divided by the amount of time that it has been running.

Select loop called

This number is probably meaningful only to Squid developers. It represents the number of times the select( ) (or poll( )) function has been called and the average time between calls. During normal operation, the time between calls should be in the 1–100 millisecond range.

The Cache information section displays hit ratio and cache size statistics:

```
Cache information for squid:
        Request Hit Ratios:     5min: 22.6%, 60min: 25.8%
        Byte Hit Ratios:        5min: 24.6%, 60min: 38.7%
        Request Memory Hit Ratios:      5min: 0.7%, 60min: 1.4%
```

```
Request Disk Hit Ratios:       5min: 6.0%, 60min: 12.4%
Storage Swap size:      41457489 KB
Storage Mem size:         10180 KB
Mean Object Size:         14.43 KB
Requests given to unlinkd:       0
```

Request Hit Ratios

Here, and on subsequent lines, you'll see two hit ratio numbers: one for the last five minutes, and one for the last hour. These values are simply the percentage of HTTP requests that result in a cache hit. Here, hits include cases in which Squid validates a cached response and receives a 304 (Not Modified) reply.

Byte Hit Ratios

Squid calculates byte hit ratio by comparing the number of bytes received from origin servers (or neighbors) to the number of bytes sent to clients. When received bytes are less than sent bytes, the byte hit ratio is positive. However, it is possible to see a negative byte hit ratio. This might occur, for example, if you have a lot of clients that abort their request before receiving the entire response.

Request Memory Hit Ratios

These values represent the percentage of all cache hits that were served from memory. Or, more accurately, the percentage of all hits (not requests!) logged as TCP_MEM_HIT.

Request Disk Hit Ratios

Similarly, these values represent the percentage of "plain" cache hits served from disk. In particular, these values are the percentage of all hits logged as TCP_HIT. You'll see that the memory and disk hit percentages don't add up to 100%. This is because the other cases (such as TCP_IMS_HIT, etc.) aren't included in either disk or memory hits.

Storage Swap size

The amount of data currently cached on disk. It is always expressed in kilobytes. To compensate for space wasted in partial blocks at the end of files, Squid rounds up file sizes to the nearest filesystem block size.

Storage Mem size

The amount of data currently cached in memory. It is always expressed in kilobytes and is always a multiple of Squid's memory page size: 4 KB.

Mean Object Size

Simply the storage swap size divided by the number of cached objects. You should set the configuration directive *store_avg_object_size* close to the actual value reported here. Squid uses the configured value for a number of internal estimates.

Requests given to unlinkd

The unlinkd process handles file deletion external to Squid (depending on your configuration). This value simply shows how many files Squid has asked unlinkd to remove. It is zero when unlinkd isn't used.

The Median Service Times section displays the median of various service time (or response time) distributions. You'll see a value for the last five minutes and for the last hour. All values are in seconds. Squid uses the median, rather than the mean, because these distributions often have heavy tails that can significantly skew the mean value. The output looks like this:

```
Median Service Times (seconds)  5 min    60 min:
          HTTP Requests (All):  0.19742  0.15048
                Cache Misses:   0.22004  0.17711
                  Cache Hits:   0.05951  0.04047
                   Near Hits:   0.37825  0.14252
        Not-Modified Replies:   0.01309  0.01387
                 DNS Lookups:   0.05078  0.03223
                 ICP Queries:   0.00000  0.07487
```

HTTP Requests (All)

These are the median response times for all HTTP requests taken together. For an HTTP request, the timer starts as soon as Squid receives the request and ends when Squid writes the last byte of the response. Thus, this time also includes DNS lookups (if any), and ICP queries to upstream neighbors (if you have them) for cache misses.

Cache Misses

This line shows the response time for cache misses only. Unless your cache hit ratio is close to 50%, the cache miss response time is close to (but a little larger than) the overall response time.

Cache Hits

The cache hit response time includes only requests logged as TCP_HIT, TCP_MEM_HIT, and TCP_OFFLINE_HIT. These are unvalidated cache hits served directly from Squid, without any communication to the origin server. Thus, your cache hit response time should be significantly less than the miss time. You should keep track of this value over time; if it climbs too high, your disk filesystem may be a performance bottleneck.

Near Hits

A near hit is a validated cache hit. It corresponds to TCP_REFRESH_HIT in *access. log*. For these, Squid contacts the origin server (or parent cache), which adds some latency to the response time. The server's response is a small 304 (Not Modified) message. Thus, the near hit response time is typically in between cache hits and cache misses.

Not-Modified Replies

This line shows the response times for requests logged as TCP_IMS_HIT. This occurs when the client sends a conditional (a.k.a. validation) request, and Squid serves a response without contacting the origin server. The name "not-modified" is somewhat misleading for this category because the status code received by the client isn't necessarily 304. For example, the client may send an If-modified-since request, and Squid has a fresh, cached response with a more recent modification time. Squid knows that its response is fresh and that the client's copy is stale. In this case, the client receives a 200 (OK) reply with the new object data.

DNS Lookups

The DNS service time shows how long it takes, on average, to query the DNS. This includes both name-to-address and address-to-name lookups. It doesn't include IP- and FQDN-cache hits, however. DNS queries can be a significant source of latency. If you experience performance problems with Squid, be sure to check this value. If you see a high median service time (i.e., around five seconds), make sure your primary DNS server (usually listed in *letc/resolv.conf*) is up and running.

ICP Queries

The ICP query time represents the elapsed time between an ICP query and response that causes Squid to select the corresponding neighbor as the next hop. Thus, it includes only requests logged as PARENT_HIT, SIBLING_HIT, FIRST_PARENT_MISS, and CLOSEST_PARENT_MISS. This value may not be a good estimate of the overall ICP response time because ICP query/response transactions that don't result in Squid selecting a neighbor are ignored. Due to a bug in Squid Versions 2.5.STABLE1 and earlier, ICP response time statistics aren't collected, and these values always appear as 0.

The Resource usage section includes a few statistics relating to CPU and memory usage:

```
Resource usage for squid:
        UP Time:        1840478.681 seconds
        CPU Time:         70571.874 seconds
        CPU Usage:      3.83%
        CPU Usage, 5 minute avg:        1.33%
        CPU Usage, 60 minute avg:       4.41%
        Process Data Segment Size via sbrk(): 342739 KB
        Maximum Resident Size: 345612 KB
        Page faults with physical i/o: 65375
```

UP Time

This line simply shows the amount of time this Squid process has been running. It is expressed in seconds.

CPU Time

The amount of CPU time used by Squid, also in seconds. This value comes from the getrusage( ) system call, which might not be available on all operating systems.

CPU Usage

This section has three CPU Usage lines. The first is the CPU Time value divided by the UP Time value. It is a long-term average CPU usage measurement. The next two lines show the CPU usage for the last five minutes and the last hour.

Process Data Segment Size via sbrk( )

This line offers an estimate of Squid's process size. sbrk( ) is a low-level system call used by the memory allocation library (malloc( )). The sbrk( ) technique provides only an estimate, which usually differs from values reported by programs such as ps and top. When the sbrk( ) value is greater than the Maximum Resident Size (discussed next), the Squid process is probably page faulting, and performance may be degrading.

Maximum Resident Size

This is another estimate of memory usage and process size. The maximum resident set size (RSS) value comes from the getrusage( ) system call. Although the definition of RSS may vary between operating systems, you can think of it as the maximum amount of physical memory used by the process at any one time. Squid's process size may be larger than the RSS, in which case some parts of the process are actually swapped to disk.

Page faults with physical i/o

This value also comes from getrusage( ). A *page fault* occurs when the operating system must read a page of the process's memory from disk. This usually happens when the Squid process becomes too large to fit entirely in memory, or when the system has other programs competing for memory. Squid's performance suffers significantly when page faults occur. You probably won't notice any problems as long as the page-faults rate is an order of magnitude lower than the HTTP request rate.

You'll see a section called Memory usage for squid via mstats( ) if your system has the mstats( ) function. In particular, you'll have this function if the GNU malloc library (*libgnumalloc.a*) is installed. Squid reports two statistics from mstats( ):

```
Memory usage for squid via mstats():
        Total space in arena:  415116 KB
        Total free:            129649 KB 31%
```

Total space in arena

This represents the total amount of memory allocated to the process. It may be similar to the value reported by sbrk( ). Note that this value only increases over time.

Total free

This represents the amount of memory allocated to the process but not currently in use by Squid. For example, if Squid frees up some memory, it goes into this category. Squid can later reuse that memory, perhaps for a different data structure, without increasing the process size. This value fluctuates up and down over time.

The Memory accounted for section contains a few tidbits about Squid's internal memory management techniques:

```
Memory accounted for:
        Total accounted:       228155 KB
```

```
memPoolAlloc calls: 2282058666
memPoolFree calls: 2273301305
```

Total accounted

Squid keeps track of some, but not nearly all, of the memory allocated to it. This value represents the total size of all data structures accounted for. Unfortunately, it is typically only about two-thirds of the actual memory usage. Squid uses a significant amount of memory in ways that make it difficult to track properly.

memPoolAlloc calls

memPoolAlloc( ) is the function through which Squid allocates many fixed-size data structures. This line shows how many times that function has been called.

memPoolFree calls

memPoolFree( ) is the companion function through which Squid frees memory allocated with memPoolAlloc( ). In a steady-state condition, the two values should increase at the same rate and their difference should be roughly constant over time. If not, the code may contain a bug that frees pooled memory back to the malloc library.

The File descriptor usage section shows how many file descriptors are available to Squid and how many are in use:

```
File descriptor usage for squid:
        Maximum number of file descriptors:   7372
        Largest file desc currently in use:    151
        Number of file desc currently in use:  105
        Files queued for open:                   0
        Available number of file descriptors: 7267
        Reserved number of file descriptors:   100
        Store Disk files open:                   0
```

Maximum number of file descriptors

This is the limit on open file descriptors for the squid process. This should be the same value reported by ./configure when you compiled Squid. If you don't see at least 1024 here, you should probably go back and recompile Squid after reading Chapter 3.

Largest file desc currently in use

This is the highest file descriptor currently open. Its value isn't particularly important but should be within 15–20% of the next line (number currently in use). This value is more useful for developers because it corresponds to the first argument of the select( ) system call.

Number of file desc currently in use

The number of currently open descriptors is an important performance metric. In general, Squid's performance decreases as the number of open descriptors increases. The kernel must work harder to scan the larger set of descriptors for activity. Meanwhile, each file descriptor waits longer (on average) to be serviced.

Files queued for open

This value will always be zero, unless you are using the *aufs* storage scheme (see Chapter 8). It shows how many file-open requests have been dispatched to the thread processes but have not yet returned. *aufs* is the only storage scheme in which disk file descriptors are opened asynchronously.[*]

Available number of file descriptors

The number of available descriptors is the maximum, minus the number currently open and the number queued for open. It represents the amount of breathing room Squid has to handle more load. When the available number gets close to the reserved number (next line), Squid stops accepting new connections so that existing transactions continue receiving service.

Reserved number of file descriptors

The number of reserved file descriptors starts out at the lesser of 100 or 25% of the maximum. Squid refuses new client connections if the number of available (free) descriptors reaches this limit. It is increased if Squid encounters an error while trying to create a new TCP socket. In this case, you'll see a message in *cache.log*:

```
Reserved FD adjusted from 100 to 150 due to failures
```

Store Disk files open

This counter shows the number of disk files currently open for reading or writing. It is always zero if you are using the *diskd* storage scheme because disk files are opened by the diskd processes, rather than Squid itself. If you use the *max_open_disk_fds* directive in *squid.conf*, Squid stops opening more cache files for reading or writing when it reaches that limit. If your filesystem is a bottleneck, this is a simple way to sacrifice a few cache hits for stable performance.

The Internal Data Structures section gives a quick overview of how many objects are in the cache and how many are on disk or in memory. You can find more detail about Squid's data structure allocations in the *mem* page (see the previous section "mem: Memory Utilization"). This section has a few stats:

```
Internal Data Structures:
        2873586 StoreEntries
           1336 StoreEntries with MemObjects
           1302 Hot Object Cache Items
        2873375 on-disk objects
```

StoreEntries

This represents the number of objects cached by Squid. Each object in the cache uses one StoreEntry structure.

---

[*] *diskd* also opens files asynchronously, but those file descriptors belong to the diskd processes, not the squid process.

StoreEntries with MemObjects
> MemObject is the data structure used for objects currently being requested and for objects stored in the memory cache.

Hot Object Cache Items
> The Hot Object Cache is another name for the memory cache (see Appendix B). These objects are stored entirely in memory (as well as on disk). This number should always be less than the number of entries with MemObjects.

on-disk objects
> This counter shows how many objects are currently stored on disk. The counter is incremented when the entire object has been successfully written. Thus, this number isn't necessarily equal to the number of StoreEntries minus the number of Hot Objects.

filedescriptors: Process File Descriptor Allocation

This page displays a table of all file descriptors currently opened by Squid. It looks like this:

```
File Type    Tout Nread    * Nwrite * Remote Address    Description
---- ------  ---- -------- -------- ----------------- ----------------------------
   3 File    0        0        0                       /usr/local/squid/logs/cache.log
   6 File    0        0  2083739                       /usr/local/squid/logs/access.log
  12 Pipe    0        0        0                       unlinkd -> squid
  13 File    0        0  2485913                       /usr/local/squid/logs/store.log
  15 Pipe    0        0        0                       squid -> unlinkd
  16 Socket  24  220853*    1924 65.200.216.110.80     http://downloads.mp3.com/
  18 Pipe    0        0        0                       squid -> diskd
  19 Socket 179     476*    1747 202.59.16.30.4171     http://ads.vesperexchange.com/
  21 Pipe    0        0        0                       squid -> diskd
  22 Socket  20  158783*     998 210.222.20.8.80       http://home.hanmir.com/a
  24 Pipe    0        0        0                       squid -> diskd
  25 Socket   1       0       0* 210.222.20.8.80       http://home.hanmir.com/b
  26 Socket   0 9048307* 1578290 .0                    DNS Socket
  27 Pipe    0        0        0                       squid -> diskd
  28 Socket   0       0       0* 66.28.234.77.80       http://updates.hotbar.com/
  29 Socket   0       0*      0  .0                    HTTP Socket
  30 Pipe    0        0        0                       squid -> diskd
  31 Socket   0      93     1126 127.0.0.1.3434        ncsa_auth #1
  32 Socket   0       3       31 127.0.0.1.3438        ncsa_auth #3
  33 Socket   0       0        0 127.0.0.1.3440        ncsa_auth #4
  34 Socket 164    8835* 1070222* 212.47.19.52.2201    http://www.eyyubyaqubov.com/
  35 Socket 177    6137*  249899* 212.47.19.25.3044    http://files10.rarlab.com/
  36 Socket   0       0        0 127.0.0.1.3442        ncsa_auth #5
  37 Socket   7  158783*     774 210.222.20.8.80       http://home.hanmir.com/c
  38 Socket 166    1000*  148415* 202.17.13.8.5787     http://home.hanmir.com/d
```

The table has seven columns:

File

This is simply the file descriptor number. The list always starts with 3 because descriptors 0, 1, and 2 are reserved for *stdin*, *stdout*, and *stderr*. Any other gaps in the list represent closed descriptors.

Type

The type field contains one of the following values: *File*, *Pipe*, or *Socket*. The *File* type is used both for files storing cached responses and for log files, such as *cache.log* and *access.log*. The *Pipe* type represents kernel pipes used for interprocess communication. The *Socket* type is also occasionally used for interprocess communication, but it's mostly used for HTTP (and FTP) connections to clients and servers.

Tout

This is the general-purpose timeout value for the descriptor. It is expressed in minutes. *Files* and *Pipes* usually don't have a timeout, so this value is zero. For *Sockets*, however, if this number of minutes go by without any activity on the descriptor, Squid calls a timeout function.

Nread

This is where Squid reports the number of bytes read from the descriptor. An asterisk (*) after the number means Squid has a function (a read handler) registered to read additional data, if there is some available.

Nwrite

This column shows the number of bytes written to the descriptor. Again, the asterisk (*) indicates that a write handler is present for the descriptor. You can usually tell if a given socket is connected to a client or to a server by comparing the number of bytes read and written. Because requests are normally smaller than responses, a server connection has a higher Nread count than Nwrite. The opposite is true for client connections.

Remote Address

For *Sockets*, this field shows the remote TCP address of the connection. The format is similar to what you would find in netstat -n output: an IP address followed by the TCP port number.

Description

The description field indicates the descriptor's use. For *Files*, you'll see a pathname; for *Pipes*, a description to what the pipe is connected; and for *Sockets*, a URI, or at least the first part of it. A description such as web.icq.com idle connection indicates an idle persistent connection to an origin server. Similarly, Waiting for next request is an idle client-side persistent connection.

By default, the File Descriptor page isn't password-protected. However, you may want to give it a password because it contains some sensitive and, perhaps, personally identifiable information.

objects: All Cache Objects

Requesting this page results in a list of all objects in the cache. Be careful with this page because it can be extremely long. Furthermore, it contains low-level information that is probably useful only to developers.

For each cached object, Squid prints a sequence of lines, most of which look like this:

```
KEY FF1F6736BCC167A4C3F93275A126C5F5
        STORE_OK      NOT_IN_MEMORY SWAPOUT_DONE PING_NONE
        CACHABLE,DISPATCHED,VALIDATED
        LV:1020824321 LU:1020824671 LM:1020821288 EX:-1
        0 locks, 0 clients, 1 refs
        Swap Dir 0, File 0X010AEE
```

The first line shows the cache key—a 128-bit MD5 checksum of the URI. The same MD5 checksum appears in *store.log* and in the metadata at the beginning of each response cached on disk.

The second line shows four state variables of the StoreEntry data structure: *store_status*, *mem_status*, *swap_status*, and *ping_status*. Refer to the Squid source code if you'd like more information about them.

The third line is a list of the StoreEntry flags that are set. Search the source code for *e->flags* for more information.

The fourth line shows the values of four timestamps: last-validation, last-use, last-modification, and expiration. The last-modification and expiration timestamps are taken from the origin server's HTTP response. The others are maintained by Squid.

The fifth line shows a few counters: locks, clients, and references. An entry with locks can't be removed. The clients counter shows how many clients are currently receiving data for this object. The refs counter shows how many times the object has been requested.

The sixth line shows the object's index to the on-disk storage. Each object has a 7-bit swap directory index and a 25-bit file number. Each storage scheme has a function to map these numbers into pathnames.

vm_objects: In-Memory and In-Transit Objects

This page is similar to All Cache Objects, except that it displays only objects that have a MemObject data structure. In other words, objects that are currently being requested or are stored in the memory cache. These objects are displayed like this:

```
KEY 5107D49BA7F9C6BA9559E006D6DDC4B2
        GET http://www.rpgplanet.com/ac2hq/cartography/dynamic/LinvakMassif.jpg
        STORE_PENDING NOT_IN_MEMORY SWAPOUT_WRITING PING_DONE
        CACHABLE,DISPATCHED,VALIDATED
        LV:1043286120 LU:1043286122 LM:1036015230 EX:-1
        4 locks, 1 clients, 1 refs
```

```
Swap Dir 1, File 00X31BD9
inmem_lo: 184784
inmem_hi: 229840
swapout: 229376 bytes queued
swapout: 229509 bytes written
Client #0, 1533a1018
        copy_offset: 217552
        seen_offset: 217552
        copy_size: 4096
        flags:
```

As you can see, many of the lines are the same. However, the in-memory objects have a few additional lines. Directly following the cache key (MD5 checksum), Squid prints the request method and URI.

The inmem_lo and inmem_hi lines are byte offsets of the HTTP reply. They indicate the section of object data currently in memory. In most cases, the difference between these two should be less than the value of the *maximum_object_size_in_memory* directive.

The swapout: bytes queued line shows the offset for how many bytes have been given to the storage layer for writing. For objects in the SWAPOUT_DONE state, this value is the same as the object size. If the state is SWAPOUT_WRITING, Squid also shows the bytes written line, which indicates how many bytes have been successfully stored on disk.

If one or more clients are currently receiving the response, you'll see a section for each of them (Client #0 in this example). For each client, Squid reports another pair of offset values. The first, copy_offset, is the starting point for the last time the client-side asked for data from the storage system. The second, seen_offset, is the point at which the response data has been sent to the client. Note that copy_offset is always greater than or equal to seen_offset. The copy_size indicates the maximum amount of data the client can receive from the storage system.

openfd_objects: Objects with Swapout Files Open

The format of this page is the same as for In-Memory and In-Transit Objects. The objects reported on this page should all be in the SWAPOUT_WRITING state. The page is primarily useful to developers when trying to track down file-descriptor leaks.

io: Server-Side Network read( ) Size Histograms

This page displays a histogram for each of the following four server-side protocols: HTTP, FTP, Gopher, and WAIS. The histograms show how many bytes each read( ) call received. The information is primarily useful to developers for tuning buffer sizes and other aspects of the source code.

The bins of the histogram are logarithmic to accommodate the large scale of read sizes. Here is an example:

```
HTTP I/O
number of reads: 9016088
Read Histogram:
    1-    1:      3082  0%
    2-    2:       583  0%
    3-    4:       905  0%
    5-    8:      2666  0%
    9-   16:     16690  0%
   17-   32:     88046  1%
   33-   64:     19712  0%
   65-  128:    116655  1%
  129-  256:    749259  8%
  257-  512:    633075  7%
  513- 1024:    903145 10%
 1025- 2048:   3664862 41%
 2049- 4096:   1643747 18%
 4097- 8192:    789796  9%
 8193-16384:     99476  1%
16385-32768:     30059  0%
```

In this case, you can see that the bin for 1025–2048 bytes is the most popular. When reading from an HTTP server, Squid got between 1025 and 2048 bytes per read 41% of the time.

counters: Traffic and Resource Counters

Squid maintains a data structure of counters. Actually, it is an array of counters. Squid shifts the array every 60 seconds and calculates 1-, 5-, and 60-minute averages from this array. This page is simply a dump of the current counter values in a format more suitable for computer processing than for reading by humans. The counters are as follows:

sample_time
>   The sample time is actually the time of the last shift, rather than the current time. The sample time is always within 60 seconds of the current time.

client_http.requests
>   The number of HTTP requests received from clients.

client_http.hits
>   The number of cache hits in response to client requests. A hit is any transaction logged with one of the TCP_HIT codes in *access.log*.

client_http.errors
>   The number of client transactions that resulted in an error.

`client_http.kbytes_in`

The amount of traffic (in kilobytes) received from clients in their requests. This is measured at the HTTP layer and doesn't include TCP, IP, and other packet headers.

`client_http.kbytes_out`

The amount of traffic (in kilobytes) sent to clients in responses. Also measured at the HTTP layer.

`client_http.hit_kbytes_out`

The amount of traffic sent to clients in responses that are cache hits. Keep in mind that some cache hits are 304 (Not Modified) responses.

`server.all.requests`

The number of requests forwarded to origin servers (or neighbor caches) for all server-side protocols (HTTP, FTP, Gopher, etc.).

`server.all.errors`

The number of server-side requests (all protocols) that resulted in some kind of error.

`server.all.kbytes_in`

The amount of traffic (in kilobytes) read from the server-side for all protocols.

`server.all.kbytes_out`

The amount of traffic written to origin servers and/or neighbor caches for server-side requests.

`server.http.requests`

The number of server-side requests to HTTP servers, including neighbor caches.

`server.http.errors`

The number of server-side HTTP requests that resulted in an error.

`server.http.kbytes_in`

The amount of traffic read from HTTP origin servers and neighbor caches.

`server.http.kbytes_out`

The amount of traffic written to HTTP origin servers and neighbor caches.

`server.ftp.requests`

The number of requests sent to FTP servers.

`server.ftp.errors`

The number of requests sent to FTP servers that resulted in an error.

`server.ftp.kbytes_in`

The amount of traffic read from FTP servers, including control channel traffic.

`server.ftp.kbytes_out`

The amount of traffic written to FTP servers, including control channel traffic.

server.other.requests

    The number of "other" server-side requests. Currently, the other protocols are Gopher, WAIS, and SSL.

server.other.errors

    The number of Gopher, WAIS, and SSL requests that resulted in an error.

server.other.kbytes_in

    The amount of traffic read from Gopher, WAIS, and SSL servers.

server.other.kbytes_out

    The amount of traffic written to Gopher, WAIS, and SSL servers.

icp.pkts_sent

    The number of ICP messages sent to neighbors. This includes both queries and replies but doesn't include HTCP messages.

icp.pkts_recv

    The number of ICP messages received from neighbors, including both queries and replies.

icp.queries_sent

    The number of ICP queries sent to neighbors.

icp.replies_sent

    The number of ICP replies sent to neighbors.

icp.queries_recv

    The number of ICP queries received from neighbors.

icp.replies_recv

    The number of ICP replies received from neighbors.

icp.query_timeouts

    The number of times that Squid timed out waiting for ICP replies to arrive.

icp.replies_queued

    The number of times Squid queued an ICP message after the initial attempt to send failed. See the section "info: General Runtime Information."

icp.kbytes_sent

    The amount of traffic sent in all ICP messages, including both queries and replies.

icp.kbytes_recv

    The amount of traffic received in all ICP messages, including both queries and replies.

icp.q_kbytes_sent

    The amount of traffic sent to neighbors in ICP queries.

icp.r_kbytes_sent

    The amount of traffic sent to neighbors in ICP replies.

icp.q_kbytes_recv
  The amount of traffic received from neighbors in ICP queries.

icp.r_kbytes_recv
  The amount of traffic received from neighbors in ICP replies.

icp.times_used
  The number of times ICP resulted in the selection of a neighbor as the next-hop for a cache miss.

cd.times_used
  The number of times Cache Digests resulted in the selection of a neighbor as the next-hop for a cache miss.

cd.msgs_sent
  The number of Cache Digest messages sent to neighbors.

cd.msgs_recv
  The number of Cache Digest messages received from neighbors.

cd.memory
  The amount of memory (in kilobytes) used by enabling the Cache Digests' feature.

cd.local_memory
  The amount of memory (in kilobytes) used to store Squid's own Cache Digest.

cd.kbytes_sent
  The amount of traffic sent to neighbors in Cache Digest messages.

cd.kbytes_recv
  The amount of traffic received from neighbors in Cache Digest messages.

unlink.requests
  The number of unlink requests given to the (optional) unlinkd process.

page_faults
  The number of (major) page faults as reported by getrusage( ).

select_loops
  The number of times Squid called select( ) or poll( ) in the main I/O loop.

cpu_time
  The amount of CPU time (in seconds) accumulated, as reported by getrusage( ).

wall_time
  The amount of human time (in seconds) elapsed since Squid was started.

swap.outs
  The number of objects (swap files) saved to disk.

swap.ins
  The number of objects (swap files) read from disk.

```
swap.files_cleaned
```
The number of orphaned cache files removed by the periodic cleanup procedure.
```
aborted_requests
```
The number of server-side HTTP requests aborted due to client-side aborts.

peer_select: Peer Selection Algorithms

This page contains a lot of low-level detail about cache digests that I won't discuss. Most of the numbers are meaningful only to the developers that originally wrote the Cache Digest implementation.

However, at the end of this page is a little table that compares Algorithm usage:

```
Algorithm usage:
Cache Digest:      27 ( 24%)
Icp:               84 ( 76%)
Total:            111 (100%)
```

In this example, you can see that Squid sent 111 requests to one of its neighbors: 27 are due to Cache Digests and 84 are due to ICP. In this context, ICP also includes HTCP.

digest_stats: Cache Digest and ICP Blob

This page is actually just a concatenation of the following other cache manager pages:

- Traffic and Resource Counters
- 5 Minute Average of Counters
- Full Histogram Counts
- Peer Selection Algorithms
- Store Digest

Its only purpose is to enable developers to take a snapshot of a number of statistics with a single request.

5min: 5 Minute Average of Counters

This page shows a five-minute average of the data in the Traffic and Resource Counters page. In addition to the counters mentioned in the section "counters: Traffic and Resource Counters," this page also contains the following values:

```
client_http.all_median_svc_time
```
The median service (response) time for all client requests from the last five minutes.
```
client_http.miss_median_svc_time
```
The median service time for cache misses from the last five minutes.

client_http.nm_median_svc_time

The five-minute median service time for requests logged as TCP_IMS_HIT. See "Not-Modified Replies" in the "info: General Runtime Information" section.

client_http.nh_median_svc_time

The five-minute median service time for Near Hits (TCP_REFRESH_HIT requests).

client_http.hit_median_svc_time

The five-minute median service time for unvalidated cache hits.

icp.query_median_svc_time

The five-minute median service time for ICP queries sent by Squid (how long it takes for the neighbors to reply to our queries).

icp.reply_median_svc_time

The five-minute median service time for ICP queries received by Squid (how long it takes Squid to reply to its neighbor's queries). ICP processing normally occurs faster than the process clock is updated, so this value is always zero.

dns.median_svc_time

The five-minute median service time for DNS queries.

select_fds

The mean rate at which the main I/O loop scans file descriptors with select( ) or poll( ). Note: a low number doesn't necessarily indicate poor performance. It may just be that Squid often has no work to do.

average_select_fd_period

The mean number of seconds required to scan a file descriptor in the main I/O loop.

median_select_fds

The five-minute median number of ready file descriptors each time Squid calls select( ) or poll( ) (the median of the select( )/poll( ) return value). Unfortunately, this value is almost always zero because Squid's functions for calculating the median don't work very well with the select_fds histogram, in which 0 and 1 are the most common values.

syscalls.selects

The five-minute mean rate of calls to select( )/poll( ). If Squid is using poll( ) on your system, the variable is called *syscalls.polls*. This value may be a little larger than *select_loops*, because the latter only includes calls in the main I/O loop.

syscalls.disk.opens

The five-minute mean rate of open( ) calls for disk files.

syscalls.disk.closes

The five-minute mean rate of close( ) calls for disk files.

syscalls.disk.reads

The five-minute mean rate of read( ) calls for disk files.

syscalls.disk.writes
> The five-minute mean rate of write( ) calls for disk files.

syscalls.disk.seeks
> The five-minute mean rate of seek( ) calls for disk files. Probably zero unless you are using *aufs*, which always calls seek( ) before reading.

syscalls.disk.unlinks
> The five-minute mean rate of unlink( ) (or, in some cases, truncate( )) calls for disk files.

syscalls.sock.accepts
> The five-minute mean rate of accept( ) calls for network sockets.

syscalls.sock.sockets
> The five- minute mean rate of socket( ) calls for network sockets.

syscalls.sock.connects
> The five-minute mean rate of connect( ) calls for network sockets.

syscalls.sock.binds
> The five-minute mean rate of bind( ) calls for network sockets.

syscalls.sock.closes
> The five-minute mean rate of close( ) calls for network sockets.

syscalls.sock.reads
> The five-minute mean rate of read( ) calls for network sockets.

syscalls.sock.writes
> The five-minute mean rate of write( ) calls for network sockets.

syscalls.sock.recvfroms
> The five-minute mean rate of recvfrom( ) calls for network sockets. Used for UDP-based protocols, such as DNS, ICP, HTCP, and some interprocess communication.

syscalls.sock.sendtos
> The five-minute mean rate of sendto( ) calls for network sockets. Used for UDP-based protocols, such as DNS, ICP, HTCP, and some interprocess communication.

60min: 60 Minute Average of Counters

This page shows a 60-minute average of the data in the Traffic and Resource Counters page. The descriptions are identical to those for the 5 Minute Average of Counters page, except the measurements are taken over one hour.

utilization: Cache Utilization

This page displays averages of the counters (see Traffic and Resource Counters and 5 Minute Average of Counters) over various time spans. The same values are reported for 5-minute, 15-minute, 1-hour, 8-hour, 1-day, and 3-day intervals.

This page, with a poorly chosen name, exists primarily so that developers can take a quick snapshot of statistics for testing purposes.

histograms: Full Histogram Counts

This page displays the current histogram values (since Squid was started) for a number of measurements:

- `client_http.all_svc_time`
- `client_http.miss_svc_time`
- `client_http.nm_svc_time`
- `client_http.nh_svc_time`
- `client_http.hit_svc_time`
- `icp.query_svc_time`
- `icp.reply_svc_time`
- `dns.svc_time`
- `select_fds_hist`

These are the same measurements described in the section "5min: 5 Minute Average of Counters," except that here Squid gives the full histogram, instead of the mean or median.

Depending on the type of histogram, you may see two or three columns. The first column is the bin number and lower bound on the bin value. The second column is the number of counts for that bin. The optional third column is the number of counts divided by the "size" of the bin. The last column is probably only interesting for log-based histograms, in which the bin size isn't constant.

active_requests: Client-Side Active Requests

This page shows a list of currently active client-side requests. The list is sorted starting with the most recent, and ending with the oldest requests. The information given here is primarily useful to developers. A typical entry looks like this:

```
Connection: 0x84ecd10
        FD 132, read 1273, wrote 12182
        FD desc: http://www.squid-cache.org/Doc/FAQ/FAQ.html
        in: buf 0xa063000, offset 0, size 4096
        peer: 206.168.0.9:1058
        me: 192.43.244.42:3128
```

```
        nrequests: 3
        defer: n 0, until 0
uri http://www.squid-cache.org/Doc/FAQ/FAQ.html
log_type TCP_MISS
out.offset 0, out.size 0
req_sz 392
entry 0x960c680/3B49762ABF444D80B6465552F6CFAD4C
old_entry 0x0/N/A
start 1066036250.669955 (2.240814 seconds ago)
```

Connection

>   The internal memory address of the connection structure.

FD

>   The file descriptor for the TCP connection, followed by the number of bytes read and written.

FD desc

>   A short description of the socket, usually a URI. This is the same as in the "file-descriptors: Process File Descriptor Allocation" section.

in

>   The internal memory location of the input buffer, the offset at which Squid will place data after the next read( ) call, and the size of the input buffer.

peer

>   The remote socket address of the TCP connection. You can correlate this value with what you see in netstat -n output.

me

>   The local socket address of the TCP connection.

nrequests

>   The number of HTTP requests received on this connection. A value greater than 1 indicates persistent connection reuse.

defer

>   Indicates whether Squid is postponing reads on the socket.

uri

>   The URI from the client's request. Unlike FD desc, this one isn't truncated.

log_type

>   The cache status code that appears in *access.log* when this transaction is complete.

out.offset

>   The offset, relative to the start of the HTTP reply message, in which the client side has requested data from the storage system.

out.size

>   The number of response bytes written to the client.

req_sz
: The size of the client's HTTP request. Note, for persistent connections, this refers only to the current request.

entry
: The memory address and MD5 hash of the corresponding StoreEntry structure.

old_entry
: For validation requests, this is the memory address and MD5 hash of the cached response StoreEntry.

start
: The time at which Squid began processing this request.

store_digest: Store Digest

This page is available only with the ./configure --enable-cache-digests option. It displays a few statistics about Squid's own cache digest. It looks like this:

```
store digest: size: 620307 bytes
        entries: count: 324806 capacity: 992490 util: 33%
        deletion attempts: 0
        bits: per entry: 5 on: 1141065 capacity: 4962456 util: 23%
        bit-seq: count: 1757902 avg.len: 2.82
        added: 324806 rejected: 611203 ( 65.30 %) del-ed: 0
        collisions: on add: 0.08 % on rej: 0.07 %
```

size
: The number of bytes that the digest occupies in memory.

entries count
: The number of cached objects entered into the digest.

entries capacity
: The target capacity for the digest. Note, this isn't a hard limit, but rather an estimate for optimally sizing the digest.

entries util
: The percentage of entries added compared to the capacity.

deletion attempts
: Squid doesn't currently support deletion of cache digest entries, so this is always zero.

bits per entry
: The number of bits that each item turns on. The same as the *digest_bits_per_entry* value from *squid.conf*.

bits on
: The number of bits that have been turned on so far.

bits capacity
: The total number of bits in the digest. Equal to the digest size multiplied by eight.

bit-seq count

> The number of same-bit sequences in the digest. For example, the pattern 110100011111 has 5 sequences of 1s and 0s.

bit-seq avg.len

> The mean length of same-bit sequences.

added

> The number of entries added to the digest since it was created.

rejected

> The number of entries not added to the digest. An entry may not be added because it isn't cachable, is too large, stale, or about to become stale, etc.

del-ed

> Squid doesn't currently support deletion of cache digest entries, so this is always zero.

collisions on add

> This is the percentage of additions that didn't turn on any new bits. Recall that Bloom filters have the property that two or more entries may turn on the same bit.

collisions on rej

> This is the percentage of rejected additions that wouldn't have turned on any new bits.

storedir: Store Directory Stats

This page displays some statistics from the storage system. First, you'll see a few global values. For example:

```
Store Directory Statistics:
Store Entries        : 2873564
Maximum Swap Size    : 46080000 KB
Current Store Swap Size: 41461672 KB
Current Capacity     : 90% used, 10% free
```

Store Entries

> The number of StoreEntry objects. Most, but not necessarily all, of these are for on-disk objects.

Maximum Swap Size

> The sum of all *cache_dir* sizes.

Current Store Swap Size

> The total amount of cached data currently stored on disk. Note that Squid rounds response sizes (e.g., 1722 bytes) up to the nearest multiple filesystem block size (e.g., 2048 bytes) when incrementing and decrementing this value.

Current Capacity

> The percentage of the maximum disk space currently in use. The percentage in use should normally stay below the *cache_swap_high* value.

Next, you'll see a section for each *cache_dir*. It looks something like this:

```
Store Directory #1 (diskd): /cache1
FS Block Size 1024 Bytes
First level subdirectories: 16
Second level subdirectories: 64
Maximum Size: 15360000 KB
Current Size: 13823996 KB
Percent Used: 90.00%
Filemap bits in use: 958439 of 2097152 (46%)
Filesystem Space in use: 14030485/17370434 KB (81%)
Filesystem Inodes in use: 959440/4340990 (22%)
Flags: SELECTED
Pending operations: 0
Removal policy: lru
LRU reference age: 23.63 days
```

Store Directory #

> The directory number, type, and pathname.

FS Block Size

> The filesystem block size, determined by the statfs( ) or statvfs( ) system calls. If these functions aren't available or return an error, the block size defaults to 2048 bytes.

The next few lines are actually storage scheme-dependent. For the most part, *ufs*, *aufs*, and *diskd* are very similar and all report the same statistics.

First level subdirectories

> The number of first-level subdirectories you told Squid to use on the *cache_dir* line.

Second level subdirectories

> The number of second-level subdirectories you told Squid to use on the *cache_dir* line.

Maximum Size

> The maximum allowed size for this cache directory.

Current Size

> The amount of disk space currently in use.

Percent Used

> The percentage of *cache_dir* space currently in use.

Filemap bits in use

> Squid uses a bitmap to keep track of file numbers that are allocated and free. This line shows the number and percentage of bits in use. The filemap grows automatically as needed, so don't worry if it shows up as 99% full.

Filesystem Space in use

> These numbers come from the statfs( )/statvfs( ) system calls. These should be the same values as you'd see from the df command. Squid doesn't use these numbers, other than to report them here for your information. Note that these

values may be larger than Current Size, especially if the partition is used for more than Squid's cache.

Filesystem Inodes in use
These numbers also come from statfs( )/statvfs( ). They are present to remind you that running out of inodes is just as bad as running out of free space. Unfortunately, if you run out of inodes, you'll probably be forced to newfs the partition.

Flags
Possible values include SELECTED and READ-ONLY. The SELECTED flag means that this particular *cache_dir* was most recently selected by the cache directory selection algorithm (see Chapter 7). The READ-ONLY flag means that the cache directory has been marked read-only in the configuration file (see Chapter 7).

Pending operations
This line appears only for *diskd* cache directories. It shows the number of I/O requests dispatched to the diskd process that have not yet been acknowledged.

That's the end of the scheme-specific data. The remaining lines are specific to the *cache_dir* replacement algorithm:

Removal policy
Possible values include lru (the default) or heap. Note that for heap, you won't see the algorithm name (LFU, GDSF, or LRU).

LRU reference age
If the removal policy is lru, you'll also see this line. It shows the age of the oldest object in the LRU list.

store_check_cachable_stats: storeCheckCachable( ) Stats

This page displays a table of counters from the storeCheckCachable( ) function. It is called for most responses, just before Squid attempts to open a disk file for writing.

 Squid knows that some responses can't be cached, based entirely on the request. These responses aren't included in the storeCheckCachable( ) statistics.

The table includes the following lines:

no.not_entry_cachable
The ENTRY_CACHABLE flag was cleared for some reason.

no.release_request
The RELEASE_REQUEST flag was set while reading the response. This may be due to an error (such as receiving a partial response) or to the rules of the transfer protocol.

In some versions of Squid, this counter is always zero because the storeReleaseRequest() function always clears the ENTRY_CACHABLE bit, causing such objects to be counted as no.not_entry_cachable instead.

no.wrong_content_length
The actual content length doesn't match the Content-Length header value.

In some versions of Squid, this counter is always zero because storeReleaseRequest() is always called if the response size doesn't match the expected content length.

no.negative_cached
The ENTRY_NEGCACHED flag was set. See the description for TCP_NEGATIVE_HIT in Chapter 13.

no.too_big
The response body was larger than the *maximum_object_size* value.

no.too_small
The response body was smaller than the *minimum_object_size* value.

no.private_key
The response has a private cache key, indicating that it can't be shared with other users.

no.too_many_open_files
The Squid process was low on free file descriptors.

no.too_many_open_fds
Squid had more than *max_open_disk_fds* opened at one time.

yes.default
The response was cachable because it did not meet any of the preceding criteria.

store_io: Store IO Interface Stats

This short table contains four lines related to allocating disk storage for a new response. For example:

```
Store IO Interface Stats
create.calls 2825670
create.select_fail 0
create.create_fail 0
create.success 2825670
```

create.calls
The number of calls to the function that creates a new disk file.

create.select_fail
The number of times that the create operation failed because the *cache_dir* selection algorithm did not select a cache directory. The default selection algorithm, least-load, fails if it thinks all cache directories are too busy.

```
create.create_fail
```
The number of times that the create operation failed at the storage layer. This may happen if the open( ) call returns an error or if the storage system (e.g., *diskd*) elects to not open a disk file for some reason (e.g., overload condition).

```
create.success
```
The number of times the create operation succeeded.

pconn: Persistent Connection Utilization Histograms

This page displays two histograms. The first is for client-side persistent connection usage. For example:

```
Client-side persistent connection counts:

    req/
    conn      count
    ----   ---------
      0       74292
      1    14362705
      2     3545955
      3     2068486
      4     1411423
      5     1030023
      6      778722
      7      603649
      8      474592
      9      376154
     10      301396
```

On the left is the number of requests per connection. On the right is the number of times a client connection had that many requests. Most likely, you'll see that one request/connection has the highest count and that the counts decrease as the number of requests/connection increases.

The second table has the same information, but for server-side HTTP connections. You should see the same sort of pattern here, with one request/connection having the highest count.

refresh: Refresh Algorithm Statistics

The *refresh* page shows a few tables relating to the freshness of cached objects. Internally, Squid keeps track of the way different modules use the refresh functions. The first table shows how many calls each module has made. The really interesting data is contained in the remaining tables, however.

The HTTP histogram shows the breakdown of freshness checks for client HTTP requests. For example:

```
HTTP histogram:
Count   %Total  Category
    0     0.00  Fresh: request max-stale wildcard
    0     0.00  Fresh: request max-stale value
```

```
173984     9.76  Fresh: expires time not reached
462757    25.97  Fresh: refresh_pattern last-mod factor percentage
    42     0.00  Fresh: refresh_pattern min value
     0     0.00  Fresh: refresh_pattern override expires
     0     0.00  Fresh: refresh_pattern override lastmod
  5521     0.31  Stale: response has must-revalidate
     0     0.00  Stale: changed reload into IMS
     0     0.00  Stale: request has no-cache directive
470912    26.43  Stale: age exceeds request max-age value
455073    25.54  Stale: expires time reached
 65612     3.68  Stale: refresh_pattern max age rule
144706     8.12  Stale: refresh_pattern last-mod factor percentage
  3274     0.18  Stale: by default
1781881  100.00  TOTAL
```

Note, the rules aren't necessarily evaluated in the order in which they appear in the table. Here's what each line means:

Fresh: request max-stale wildcard

Squid considers the cached response fresh because the request includes a max-stale directive without any value. For example:

```
GET /blah... HTTP/1.1
Cache-control: max-stale
```

According to RFC 2616: "If no value is assigned to max-stale, then the client is willing to accept a stale response of any age."

Fresh: request max-stale value

Squid considers the cached response fresh because the request includes a max-stale directive with a particular value, which is larger than the amount of time since the object expired.

Fresh: expires time not reached

Squid considers the cached response fresh because its expiration time has not yet been reached.

Fresh: refresh_pattern last-mod factor percentage

Squid considers the cached response fresh because it matches one of the refresh_pattern rules and has a last-modified factor (LM-factor) value that's less than that specified by the rule. See Chapter 7.

Fresh: refresh_pattern min value

Squid considers the cached response fresh because it matches one of the refresh_pattern rules and its age is less than the min value specified by the rule. See Chapter 7.

Fresh: refresh_pattern override expires

Squid considers the cached response fresh because it matched one of the refresh_pattern rules with the override-expire option. This option causes Squid to give precedence to the refresh_pattern minimum value over the object's expiration time. Note: using the override-expire option is a violation of RFC 2616.

Fresh: refresh_pattern override lastmod
: Squid considers the cached response fresh because it matched one of the refresh_pattern rules with the override-lastmod option. This option causes Squid to give precedence to the refresh_pattern minimum value over the LM-factor value. Note: using the override-lastmod option is a violation of RFC 2616.

Stale: response has must-revalidate
: Squid considers the cached response stale because it contains a Cache-Control: must-revalidate directive.

Stale: changed reload into IMS
: Squid considers the cached response stale because it matches one of the refresh_pattern rules with the reload-into-ims option. With this option, Squid turns a request with Cache-Control: no-cache (or similar) into a cache validation. Note: using the reload-into-ims option is a violation of RFC 2616.

Stale: request has no-cache directive
: Squid considers the cached response stale because the request contains a Cache-Control: no-cache directive.

Stale: age exceeds request max-age value
: Squid considers the cached response stale because the request has a max-age directive, which is less than the response's age.

Stale: expires time reached
: Squid considers the cached response stale because its expiration time has been reached.

Stale: refresh_pattern max age rule
: Squid considers the cached response stale because it matches one of the *refresh_pattern* rules, and its age is greater than the max value specified by the rule.

Stale: refresh_pattern last-mod factor percentage
: Squid considers the cached response stale because it matches one of the *refresh_pattern* rules, and its LM-factor value is greater than the factor specified by the rule.

Stale: by default
: Squid considers the cached response stale by default, because it didn't meet any of the other criteria.

Following the HTTP histogram, you'll see the same data for ICP, HTCP, Cache Digests, and On Store.

The On Store table represents freshness checks for responses that are coming into Squid's cache (i.e., cachable misses). Note, however, that Squid does store stale responses (as long as they have a cache validator). Don't be alarmed if you see some stale responses in the On Store histogram.

delay: Delay Pool Levels

This page displays the Delay Pool statistics. Squid has three classes of pools (1, 2, 3) and three types of buckets (aggregate, individual, and network). A class 1 pool has only an aggregate bucket, a class 2 pool has both aggregate and individual, and a class 3 pool has all three.

An aggregate bucket looks like this:

```
Aggregate:
        Max: 16384
        Restore: 4096
        Current: 6144
```

The values are all in bytes. Max is the size of the bucket, which is the number of bytes the bucket can hold. Restore is the number of bytes added to the bucket each second. Current is the number of bytes currently in the bucket. If nobody uses the bytes, the bucket fills until it reaches the maximum size.

An individual bucket is almost the same:

```
Individual:
        Max: 20000
        Restore: 5000
        Current: 1:18760 9:4475 14:20000
```

The only difference is that the Current line displays a number of different values, one for each host number. The *host number* is defined as the last octet of an IPv4 address. In this example, the host numbers are 1, 9, and 14. In a class 2 delay pool, the host numbers from different networks share the same bucket. For example, 192.168.0.1 and 192.168.44.1 both share the bucket for host number 1. In a class 3 pool, however, each network number (third octet) has its own array of individual buckets. Thus, for a class 3 pool, the individual buckets appear this way:

```
Individual:
        Max: 20000
        Rate: 5000
        Current [Network 0]: 1:12000
        Current [Network 44]: 1:17000
```

A network bucket (for class 3 pools only) is similar as well:

```
Network:
        Max: 30000
        Rate: 15000
        Current: 0:3912 7:30000
```

In this case, the Current line shows the current level for each network number (third octet). See Appendix C for more information about Delay Pools.

forward: Request Forwarding Statistics

The table on this page shows how many attempts were made to forward each request, with their results. Upon receiving some status codes, Squid gives up immediately. For others, however, Squid keeps trying. Each row of the table is a different HTTP status code (200, 401, 404, etc.). Each column is the number of forwarding attempts. The value in each cell is how many requests were forwarded that many times, resulting in the corresponding status code. This information helps developers understand whether or not it makes sense to retry a request after receiving certain types of responses. Here is an example:

Status	try#1	try#2	try#3	try#4	try#5	try#6	try#7	try#8	try#9	try#10
0	1	0	0	0	0	0	0	0	0	0
200	3970083	111015	51185	29002	18242	12097	8191	6080	4490	6140
201	57	0	0	0	0	0	0	0	0	0
202	162	0	0	0	0	0	0	0	0	0
204	1321	11	0	0	0	0	0	0	0	0
206	624288	453	25	9	4	3	0	1	0	0
207	147	0	0	0	0	0	0	0	0	0
300	23	0	0	0	0	0	0	0	0	0
301	23500	25	2	0	0	0	1	0	0	0
302	339332	3806	153	26	6	4	2	3	0	1
303	101	1	0	0	0	0	0	0	0	0
304	772831	3510	125	21	7	8	8	5	3	2
307	7	0	0	0	0	0	0	0	0	0
400	529	1	0	0	0	0	0	0	0	0
401	1559	0	0	0	0	0	0	0	0	0
403	5098	30	1	1	0	0	0	0	0	0
404	100800	216	25	6	7	1	2	4	1	5
405	1	0	0	0	0	0	0	0	0	0

...

A value of 29,002 in the cell under try#4 and in the row for status 200 means that there were 29,002 times when Squid finally got a successful response after 4 forwarding attempts. If you look at the table, you may see some unknown status codes. Squid keeps track of all status codes up to 600, even those it doesn't know about. See Table 13-1 for the list of codes that Squid does know about.

client_list: Cache Client List

The cache client list shows a handful of statistics for each client IP address accessing Squid, which looks like this:

```
Address: 206.168.0.9
Name: 206.168.0.9
Currently established connections: 0
    ICP Requests 59000
        UDP_HIT                 1609    3%
        UDP_MISS               57388   97%
        UDP_INVALID                3    0%
    HTTP Requests 11281
        TCP_HIT                  656    6%
        TCP_MISS                3464   31%
        TCP_REFRESH_HIT         4477   40%
        TCP_REFRESH_MISS         767    7%
        TCP_CLIENT_REFRESH_M     397    4%
```

```
TCP_IMS_HIT              1082   10%
TCP_SWAPFAIL_MISS           7    0%
TCP_NEGATIVE_HIT           13    0%
TCP_MEM_HIT               418    4%
```

The Address line, obviously, shows the client's IP address. Name is the same, unless you have *log_fqdn* enabled, and the DNS reports a name for the address. The Currently established connections line shows how many HTTP connections are currently open between the client and Squid.

If the client has sent any ICP queries, you'll see a breakdown of the results here. In this example, only 3% of this client's ICP queries were hits. Note, this page doesn't currently include HTCP result statistics. Finally, you'll see a breakdown of HTTP request result codes.

The client database consumes a fair amount of memory, especially if you have a large number of client IP addresses accessing Squid. You can disable the database entirely, thus conserving memory, with the *client_db* directive. Also note that there is no way to clear the counters or to remove entries while Squid is running.

netdb: Network Measurement Database

This page is available only with the ./configure --enable-icmp option (see Chapter 10). On this page you'll find quite a lot of IP addresses, hostnames, packet counters, and RTT values. It looks something like this:

```
Network DB Statistics:
Network          recv/sent     RTT  Hops Hostnames
165.123.34.0       7/  7      12.7   8.6 onlinebooks.library.upenn.edu
                                         www.library.upenn.edu
                                         digital.library.upenn.edu
      rtp.us.ircache.net      17.0  11.0
      sj.us.ircache.net       71.0  17.3
209.202.204.0      4/  4      12.8  10.0 adbuyer3.lycos.com
      rtp.us.ircache.net      20.6  15.0
      sj.us.ircache.net       77.6  15.0
63.151.139.0      17/ 17      12.8   9.0 www.originlab.com
      sj.us.ircache.net       80.0  12.0
209.68.20.0       23/ 23      12.8  11.7 www6.tomshardware.com www.guestbook.nu
      rtp.us.ircache.net      34.9  15.1
      sj.us.ircache.net       73.9  14.7
```

Each /24 network is listed, in order of increasing round-trip time. You can see how many ICMP pings have been sent and received, the average RTT, and the estimated router hop-count. The Hostnames field shows the hostnames that resolve to addresses within the /24 network. If Squid has ICMP measurements from its neighbors for the network, those are printed as well. In this example, the local cache is closer to all the networks than its neighbors (*rtp.us.ircache.net* and *sj.us.ircache.net*).

asndb: AS Number Database

Although this page is always available, it contains interesting data only if you are using one of the Autonomous System (AS) ACLs, such as *src_as* or *dst_as*.

When you use an AS-based ACL, Squid queries the Routing Arbiter database (*whois. ra.net*) to discover the IP networks associated with the AS number. The results of those queries are displayed on this page. The output looks like this:

```
        Address    AS Numbers
   128.98.0.0/16   7
   146.80.0.0/16   7
   192.5.28.0/24   7
   192.5.29.0/24   7
   192.5.30.0/24   7
 192.107.178.0/24  7
 192.135.183.0/24  5637
 194.61.177.0/24   7
 194.61.180.0/24   7
 194.61.183.0/24   7
 194.83.162.0/24   7
```

carp: CARP Information

This page is available only with the ./configure --enable-carp option and if you have some CARP parents configured. Squid displays a table of all CARP parents, which looks like this:

```
        Hostname     Hash  Multiplier    Factor     Actual
 bo1.us.ircache.net  f142425b  0.894427  0.400000  0.527950
 bo2.us.ircache.net  12180f04  1.118034  0.600000  0.472050
```

Hash is the neighbor's hash value from the CARP algorithm. Multiplier is another value used by the algorithm. Factor is taken from the carp-load-factor option on the *cache_dir* line in *squid.conf*. Actual is the actual distribution of requests among the CARP parents. Ideally, it should match the Factor value.

server_list: Peer Cache Statistics

This page displays various counters and statistics for your neighbor caches. For example:

```
Sibling     : pa.us.ircache.net/3128/4827
Flags       : htcp
Address[0]  : 192.6.19.203
Status      : Up
AVG RTT     : 14 msec
OPEN CONNS  : 19
LAST QUERY  :       4 seconds ago
LAST REPLY  :       4 seconds ago
PINGS SENT  :    9119
PINGS ACKED:    9115 100%
FETCHES     :    109   1%
```

```
IGNORED    :    9114 100%
Histogram of PINGS ACKED:
        Misses     9114 100%
        Hits          1   0%
keep-alive ratio: 100%
```

Type

The first line shows the neighbor type (parent, sibling, or multicast group), followed by the hostname and port numbers. The first port number is for HTTP requests, while the second is for ICP or HTCP.

Flags

Here you'll see any of the *cache_peer* options that you may have specified, such as no-query, closest-only, and more. See Chapter 10 for the complete list.

Address[ ]

This line displays the IP address(es) associated with the hostname. The number in brackets is the number of addresses. Squid stores up to 10 addresses for each neighbor.

Status

The status line indicates whether Squid thinks the neighbor is Up or Down. See Chapter 10.

AVG RTT

This is the running average RTT for ICP/HTCP queries to the neighbor.

OPEN CONNS

This is the number of HTTP connections currently open to the neighbor.

LAST QUERY

This indicates the amount of time since Squid last sent an ICP/HTCP query to the neighbor.

LAST REPLY

This indicates the amount of time since Squid last received an ICP/HTCP reply from the neighbor.

PINGS SENT

The number of ICP/HTCP queries sent to the neighbor.

PINGS ACKED

The number of ICP/HTCP replies received back from the neighbor.

FETCHES

The number of HTTP requests sent to the neighbor. The percentage is based on the PINGS ACKED number. Unfortunately, the FETCHES number counts requests forwarded for any reason (ICP, HTCP, Cache Digests, default parent, etc.). Thus, the percentage doesn't always make sense and may be higher than 100%.

IGNORED

The number of ICP/HTCP replies ignored. The most common reason that Squid ignores an ICP/HTCP reply is that it is too late.

Histogram of PINGS ACKED
> Here you'll see a breakdown of ICP/HTCP results. For ICP neighbors, Squid prints the ICP status codes (ICP_HIT, ICP_MISS, etc.). For HTCP neighbors, the only categories are Hits and Misses.

keep-alive ratio
> This shows the percentage of times that Squid wanted an HTTP connection to be persistent, and the neighbor agreed. Note, this doesn't indicate anything about whether the connection was actually reused, only that both sides agreed that it could be.

non_peers: List of Unknown Sites Sending ICP messages

This page shows a list of clients that send unauthorized ICP (but not HTCP) queries. The list is the same format as the *Cache Client List* page.

Cache Manager Access Controls

The cache manager interface provides a lot of information. Much of it is sensitive and should be kept private. For example, the *Cache Client List* reveals the IP addresses of users, the *Process Filedescriptor Allocation* page shows URIs currently being requested, and the *Current Squid Configuration* displays the values from *squid. conf*, including passwords and access control rules. To keep unwanted visitors from browsing the cache manager pages, you must carefully configure access to it.

http_access

All cache manager requests use the pseudo-protocol scheme cache_object. The best way to protect the cache manager is restrict the IP addresses allowed to make cache_ object requests. The default *squid.conf* contains these lines:

```
acl Manager proto cache_object
acl Localhost src 127.0.0.1/255.255.255.255
http_access allow Manager Localhost
http_access deny Manager
```

Thus, cache manager requests from the local host (127.0.0.1) are allowed, but all others are denied. If you have additional trusted hosts, you may want to add them to the access rules also. Make sure these lines are at the top of your *http_access* rules.

cachemgr_passwd

You may also want to modify the default *cachemgr_passwd* settings. Some of the cache manager pages require a password, so you won't be able to view those until you add one. For example, if you want to use the *Current Squid Configuration* page, you must assign it a password:

```
cachemgr_passwd JeckCy config
```

You can have a number of different passwords, but each action may have only one password. You may want to use a different password for less sensitive pages:

```
cachemgr_passwd byDroth filedescriptors client_list netdb
```

To disable a cache manager action, use disable as the password:

```
cachemgr_passwd disable netdb
```

To enable the sensitive actions without requiring a password, use none:

```
cachemgr_passwd none offline_toggle
```

If you want to give the same password to all actions, use the keyword all:

```
cachemgr_passwd Knoujush all
```

When using the command-line cache manager interface (e.g., squidclient), put an @ sign and the password after the action name. For example:

```
squidclient mgr:objects@byDroth | less
```

Note that cache manager passwords aren't printed when you request the *Current Squid Configuration* page (see the section "config: Current Squid Configuration*").

cachemgr.cgi

If you use cachemgr.cgi, the IP address of your HTTP server must be able to make cache manager requests to Squid. This opens up a back-door security hole. Anyone who can execute the CGI program on your server will be able to view the cache manager pages. The passwords described earlier can help, but you may also want to install access controls on your HTTP server so that only certain people can execute cachemgr.cgi.

The main cachemgr.cgi page has a form with *Username* and *Password* fields. The username is purely informational. If you have multiple administrators in your organization, each person can enter their own name for auditing purposes.

If you leave the password field blank, the password-protected pages are disabled. Entering a password activates links for those pages. cachemgr.cgi is stateless, so the password must be included as a URI parameter in links. Furthermore, the password encoding scheme isn't very sophisticated and trivial to break. Because many applications (such as Squid!) log the URIs of HTTP requests, your cache-manager password may be logged or even observed by an untrusted third party. If you really want to keep your cache manager passwords secret, never use them with cachemgr.cgi or from any remote system.

Reasons to Dislike the Cache Manager

The cache manager interface leaves much to be desired. It has a very unpolished feel. Novice administrators will probably find it difficult to use and understand. One of the first problems you might notice is that the menu (or table of contents) is unorganized. There is no logical order or grouping. The first items in the list provide low-level information primarily meant for developers. Currently, the order is determined by the initialization sequence in the source code.

The output is often ugly. The cachemgr.cgi program renders very bland-looking HTML pages. There are no icons or graphics of any kind. Furthermore, many of the pages are simply presented as unformatted text. cachemgr.cgi doesn't do much more than format tab-delimited lines as HTML tables and put <A> tags around some URIs. Some of the cache manager pages are structured so that the output can be easily parsed by computer programs, rather than humans.

By today's standards, the cache manager has very weak security. You are essentially forced to use address-based controls and cleartext passwords. If you allow cache manager requests only from *localhost*, and your system security is good, you'll be relatively safe.

Squid-RRD

I personally use the cache manager to populate a number of RRDTool databases (*http://www.rrdtool.com/*). RRDTool is nice package for storing and displaying time-series data. It allows you to archive data at different time scales (e.g., days, weeks, months, years) in a database that doesn't grow in size over time.

I use a Perl script that runs every five minutes from cron. It issues cache manager requests for a number of pages and extracts the values that I am interested in. These values are stored in the RRD files.

RRDTool also generates nice-looking graphs, from either a CGI script or standalone program. I use the CGI program and check the graphs at least daily. See Figure 14-2 for some samples from one of my own Squid boxes.

You can find my scripts and instructions for integrating the cache manager and RRD-Tool at *http://www.squid-cache.org/~wessels/squid-rrd/*.

Using SNMP

Squid has a built-in SNMP agent that you can query with various SNMP client tools. It allows you to collect a few basic statistics from Squid. Unfortunately, the Squid MIB has not evolved much since its initial implementation. Many of the parameters that you'd like to monitor aren't available through the SNMP MIB. Perhaps this will be rectified in a future version.

To enable SNMP in Squid, use the --enable-snmp option when running ./configure and recompile if necessary. Squid uses UDP port 3401 for SNMP by default. You can use a different port by setting the *snmp_port* directive.

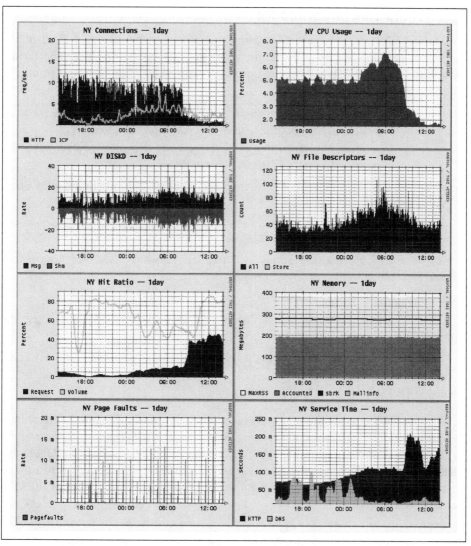

Figure 14-2. Some sample RRD graphs from RRDTool and cache manager data

Use the *snmp_access* access list and *snmp_community* ACL type to define an access policy for the SNMP agent. For example:

```
acl Snmppublic snmp_community public
acl Adminhost src 192.168.1.1
snmp_access allow Adminhost Snmppublic
```

In this case, Squid accepts SNMP requests from 192.168.1.1 with the community name set to public.

Using snmpwalk and snmpget

The NET-SNMP package (*http://net-snmp.sourceforge.net/*) provides a good implementation of the snmpwalk and snmpget command-line tools for Unix. The former walks through an SNMP MIB tree, displaying every value, while the latter prints the value for a single MIB object.

After installing NET-SNMP, copy the Squid MIB file to the directory where the utilities can find it. By default, this is the */usr/local/share/snmp/mibs* directory:

```
# cp squid-2.5.STABLE4/src/mib.txt /usr/local/share/snmp/mibs/SQUID-MIB.txt
# chmod 644 /usr/local/share/snmp/mibs/SQUID-MIB.txt
```

You should then be able to use the snmpget command. Note that Squid is an SNMPv1 agent:

```
% snmpget -v 1 -c public -m SQUID-MIB localhost:3401 cacheDnsSvcTime.5
SQUID-MIB::cacheDnsSvcTime.5 = INTEGER: 44
```

If you want to see the entire Squid MIB tree, use snmpwalk. The -Cc option tells snmpwalk to ignore nonincreasing OIDs:

```
% snmpwalk -v 1 -c public -m SQUID-MIB -Cc localhost:3401 squid | less
```

If you can't get the Squid MIB installed so that snmpwalk sees it, you can use the numeric OID value instead:

```
% snmpwalk -v 1 -c public -m SQUID-MIB -Cc localhost:3401 .1.3.6.1.4.1.3495.1 | less
```

The Squid MIB

In this section, I provide a brief description for each OID in the Squid MIB, which lives in the global MIB tree under *iso.org.dod.internet.private.enterprises.nlanr.squid*, or .1.3.6.1.4.1.3495.1. The full MIB names, such as *cachePerf.cacheProtoStats.cacheMedianSvcTable.cacheMedianSvcEntry.cacheHttpMissSvcTime.60*, take up too much space on the page. Instead, I'll just use the last nonnumeric component of the OID name, which is unique.

cacheSysVMsize
> The amount of memory (in kilobytes) currently used to store in-memory objects. For example:
> ```
> SQUID-MIB::cacheSysVMsize = INTEGER: 10224
> ```

cacheSysStorage
> The amount of disk space (in kilobytes) currently used to store on-disk objects. For example:
> ```
> SQUID-MIB::cacheSysStorage = INTEGER: 19347723
> ```

cacheUptime
> The amount of time (number of seconds) since Squid was started.
> ```
> SQUID-MIB::cacheUptime = Timeticks: (33239630) 3 days, 20:19:56.30
> ```

cacheAdmin

The email address, or name, of the cache administrator. For example:

```
SQUID-MIB::cacheAdmin = STRING: wessels@bo2.us.ircache.net
```

cacheSoftware

The name of the application. For example:

```
SQUID-MIB::cacheSoftware = STRING: squid
```

cacheVersionId

The application's version identification. For example:

```
SQUID-MIB::cacheVersionId = STRING: "2.5.STABLE4"
```

cacheLoggingFacility

The current debugging levels, from the *debug_options* directive. For example:

```
SQUID-MIB::cacheLoggingFacility = STRING: ALL,1
```

cacheMemMaxSize

The value of the *cache_mem* directive, in megabytes. For example:

```
SQUID-MIB::cacheMemMaxSize = INTEGER: 10
```

cacheSwapMaxSize

The total amount of disk storage, in megabytes, taken from the sum of all *cache_dir* lines. For example:

```
SQUID-MIB::cacheSwapMaxSize = INTEGER: 21000
```

cacheSwapHighWM

The high watermark percentage for disk storage, taken from the *cache_swap_high* directive. For example:

```
SQUID-MIB::cacheSwapHighWM = INTEGER: 95
```

cacheSwapLowWM

The low watermark percentage for disk storage, taken from the *cache_swap_low* directive. For example:

```
SQUID-MIB::cacheSwapLowWM = INTEGER: 90
```

cacheSysPageFaults

The number of page faults for the Squid process since it was started. (See "Page faults with physical i/o" in the section "info: General Runtime Information.") For example:

```
SQUID-MIB::cacheSysPageFaults = Counter32: 9
```

cacheSysNumReads

The number of times this process called read( ) on HTTP sockets connected to origin servers and neighbor caches. For example:

```
SQUID-MIB::cacheSysNumReads = Counter32: 15941979
```

cacheMemUsage

The amount of memory allocated by the memory pooling routines. Not the same as the total memory used by Squid. (See "Total accounted" in the section "info: General Runtime Information.") For example:

```
SQUID-MIB::cacheMemUsage = INTEGER: 143709
```

cacheCpuTime

The amount of CPU time, in seconds, accumulated by the Squid process. For example:

```
SQUID-MIB::cacheCpuTime = INTEGER: 79313
```

cacheCpuUsage

The mean CPU utilization, as a percentage, since Squid was started. Unfortunately, since this value is an integer, any graphs that you make will be "quantized." For example:

```
SQUID-MIB::cacheCpuUsage = INTEGER: 23
```

cacheMaxResSize

The maximum resident set size, in kilobytes, for the Squid process. (See "Maximum Resident Size" in the section "info: General Runtime Information.") For example:

```
SQUID-MIB::cacheMaxResSize = INTEGER: 219128
```

cacheNumObjCount

The total number of objects currently in the cache. For example:

```
SQUID-MIB::cacheNumObjCount = Counter32: 1717181
```

cacheCurrentLRUExpiration

Current versions of Squid don't have a global LRU expiration age value, so this is always reported as zero. For example:

```
SQUID-MIB::cacheCurrentLRUExpiration = Timeticks: (0) 0:00:00.00
```

cacheCurrentUnlinkRequests

The number of files given to the external unlinkd process for removal. Note that Squid doesn't use unlinkd with the *diskd* and *aufs* storage schemes. For example:

```
SQUID-MIB::cacheCurrentUnlinkRequests = Counter32: 0
```

cacheCurrentUnusedFDescrCnt

The current number of available (unused) file descriptors. For example:

```
SQUID-MIB::cacheCurrentUnusedFDescrCnt = Gauge32: 7253
```

cacheCurrentResFileDescrCnt

The number of reserved file descriptors. (See "Reserved number of file descriptors" in the section "info: General Runtime Information.") For example:

```
SQUID-MIB::cacheCurrentResFileDescrCnt = Gauge32: 100
```

cacheProtoClientHttpRequests

The total number of HTTP requests received from cache clients. For example:

```
SQUID-MIB::cacheProtoClientHttpRequests = Counter32: 7277019
```

cacheHttpHits

The number of client requests that were cache hits. For example:

```
SQUID-MIB::cacheHttpHits = Counter32: 2526484
```

cacheHttpErrors

The number of client requests that resulted in an error. For example:

```
SQUID-MIB::cacheHttpErrors = Counter32: 0
```

cacheHttpInKb

The amount of network traffic, in kilobytes, read from cache clients. For example:

```
SQUID-MIB::cacheHttpInKb = Counter32: 4231883
```

cacheHttpOutKb

The amount of network traffic, in kilobytes, written to cache clients. For example:

```
SQUID-MIB::cacheHttpOutKb = Counter32: 56894945
```

cacheIcpPktsSent

The number of ICP messages (both queries and replies) sent to neighbors. For example:

```
SQUID-MIB::cacheIcpPktsSent = Counter32: 5296120
```

cacheIcpPktsRecv

The number of ICP messages (both queries and replies) received from neighbors. For example:

```
SQUID-MIB::cacheIcpPktsRecv = Counter32: 5271238
```

cacheIcpKbSent

The amount of network traffic, in kilobytes, used for ICP messages sent to neighbors, not including UDP and IP headers. For example:

```
SQUID-MIB::cacheIcpKbSent = Counter32: 428112
```

cacheIcpKbRecv

The amount of network traffic, in kilobytes, used for ICP messages received from neighbors, not including UDP and IP headers. For example:

```
SQUID-MIB::cacheIcpKbRecv = Counter32: 447762
```

cacheServerRequests

The number of requests forwarded to origin servers and neighbor caches. For example:

```
SQUID-MIB::cacheServerRequests = INTEGER: 5338305
```

cacheServerErrors

The number of errors received from origin servers and neighbor caches. Currently unimplemented and always reported as zero. For example:

```
SQUID-MIB::cacheServerErrors = INTEGER: 0
```

cacheServerInKb

The amount of network traffic, in kilobytes, read from origin servers and neighbor caches. For example:

```
SQUID-MIB::cacheServerInKb = Counter32: 49196559
```

cacheServerOutKb

The amount of network traffic, in kilobytes, written to origin servers and neighbor caches. For example:

```
SQUID-MIB::cacheServerOutKb = Counter32: 3404717
```

cacheCurrentSwapSize

The amount of disk space, in kilobytes, currently in use by Squid. Compare to cacheSysStorage. For example:

```
SQUID-MIB::cacheCurrentSwapSize = Counter32: 19347723
```

cacheClients

The number of clients that sent HTTP requests to Squid since it was started. For example:

```
SQUID-MIB::cacheClients = Counter32: 498
```

cacheMedianTime.X

These OIDs report the time intervals, in minutes, over which median values are computed for subsequent OIDs. The value is the same as the last number of the OID. For example:

```
SQUID-MIB::cacheMedianTime.1 = INTEGER: 1
SQUID-MIB::cacheMedianTime.5 = INTEGER: 5
SQUID-MIB::cacheMedianTime.60 = INTEGER: 60
```

cacheHttpAllSvcTime.X

The 1-, 5-, and 60-minute median service time values, in milliseconds, for all client HTTP requests. For example:

```
SQUID-MIB::cacheHttpAllSvcTime.1 = INTEGER: 78
SQUID-MIB::cacheHttpAllSvcTime.5 = INTEGER: 70
SQUID-MIB::cacheHttpAllSvcTime.60 = INTEGER: 56
```

cacheHttpMissSvcTime.X

The 1-, 5-, and 60-minute median service time values for cache misses. For example:

```
SQUID-MIB::cacheHttpMissSvcTime.1 = INTEGER: 114
SQUID-MIB::cacheHttpMissSvcTime.5 = INTEGER: 87
SQUID-MIB::cacheHttpMissSvcTime.60 = INTEGER: 74
```

cacheHttpNmSvcTime.X

The 1-, 5-, and 60-minute median service time values for requests logged as TCP_ IMS_HIT. (See "Not-Modified Replies" in the section "info: General Runtime Information.") For example:

```
SQUID-MIB::cacheHttpNmSvcTime.1 = INTEGER: 12
SQUID-MIB::cacheHttpNmSvcTime.5 = INTEGER: 34
SQUID-MIB::cacheHttpNmSvcTime.60 = INTEGER: 32
```

cacheHttpHitSvcTime.X

The 1-, 5-, and 60-minute median service time values for cache hits, logged as TCP_HIT. For example:

```
SQUID-MIB::cacheHttpHitSvcTime.1 = INTEGER: 45
SQUID-MIB::cacheHttpHitSvcTime.5 = INTEGER: 45
SQUID-MIB::cacheHttpHitSvcTime.60 = INTEGER: 40
```

cacheIcpQuerySvcTime.X

The 1-, 5-, and 60-minute service time values for ICP queries sent by Squid (the time elapsed between sending your query and receiving a neighbor's reply). For example:

```
SQUID-MIB::cacheIcpQuerySvcTime.1 = INTEGER: 0
SQUID-MIB::cacheIcpQuerySvcTime.5 = INTEGER: 0
SQUID-MIB::cacheIcpQuerySvcTime.60 = INTEGER: 3563
```

cacheIcpReplySvcTime.X

The 1-, 5-, and 60-minute median service time values for ICP queries received by Squid. In current implementations, these are always zero because processing occurs faster than the process clock is updated. For example:

```
SQUID-MIB::cacheIcpReplySvcTime.1 = INTEGER: 0
SQUID-MIB::cacheIcpReplySvcTime.5 = INTEGER: 0
SQUID-MIB::cacheIcpReplySvcTime.60 = INTEGER: 0
```

cacheDnsSvcTime.X

The 1-, 5-, and 60-minute median service time values for Squid's DNS queries. For example:

```
SQUID-MIB::cacheDnsSvcTime.1 = INTEGER: 40
SQUID-MIB::cacheDnsSvcTime.5 = INTEGER: 42
SQUID-MIB::cacheDnsSvcTime.60 = INTEGER: 42
```

cacheRequestHitRatio.X

Squid's cache hit ratio (percentage) over the last 1, 5, and 60 minutes. For example:

```
SQUID-MIB::cacheRequestHitRatio.1 = INTEGER: 16
SQUID-MIB::cacheRequestHitRatio.5 = INTEGER: 18
SQUID-MIB::cacheRequestHitRatio.60 = INTEGER: 22
```

cacheRequestByteRatio.X

Squid's byte hit ratio (percentage) over the last 1, 5, and 60 minutes. For example:

```
SQUID-MIB::cacheRequestByteRatio.1 = INTEGER: 73
SQUID-MIB::cacheRequestByteRatio.5 = INTEGER: 43
SQUID-MIB::cacheRequestByteRatio.60 = INTEGER: 34
```

cacheIpEntries

The number of entries in Squid's IP (name-to-address) cache. For example:

```
SQUID-MIB::cacheIpEntries = Gauge32: 10033
```

cacheIpRequests

The number of requests received by Squid's IP cache. For example:

```
SQUID-MIB::cacheIpRequests = Counter32: 8195627
```

cacheIpHits

The number of lookups that were hits in the IP cache. For example:

```
SQUID-MIB::cacheIpHits = Counter32: 6040658
```

If the ratio of hits to requests is less than 60–75%, you may want to increase the size of your IP cache.

cacheIpPendingHits
>   Always zero in the current implementation. For example:

```
SQUID-MIB::cacheIpPendingHits = Gauge32: 0
```

>   Older versions of Squid had the notion of IP cache hits for outstanding queries.

cacheIpNegativeHits
>   The number of lookups that were negative hits in the IP cache. Certain failed queries may be negatively cached for an amount of time determined by the *negative_dns_ttl* directive. For example:

```
SQUID-MIB::cacheIpNegativeHits = Counter32: 49433
```

cacheIpMisses
>   The number of IP cache misses. For example:

```
SQUID-MIB::cacheIpMisses = Counter32: 1807438
```

cacheBlockingGetHostByName
>   Always zero in the current implementation. For example:

```
SQUID-MIB::cacheBlockingGetHostByName = Counter32: 0
```

>   Older versions occasionally called the gethostbyname( ) function if the IP cache couldn't provide an answer.

cacheAttemptReleaseLckEntries
>   Always zero in the current implementation. Older versions would, in some cases, want to release locked IP cache entries. For example:

```
SQUID-MIB::cacheAttemptReleaseLckEntries = Counter32: 0
```

cacheFqdnEntries
>   The number of entries in the FQDN (address-to-name) cache. For example:

```
SQUID-MIB::cacheFqdnEntries = Gauge32: 1
```

cacheFqdnRequests
>   The number of requests to the FQDN cache. For example:

```
SQUID-MIB::cacheFqdnRequests = Counter32: 0
```

cacheFqdnHits
>   The number of FQDN cache requests satisfied as hits. For example:

```
SQUID-MIB::cacheFqdnHits = Counter32: 0
```

cacheFqdnPendingHits
>   Always zero in the current implementation. For example:

```
SQUID-MIB::cacheFqdnPendingHits = Gauge32: 0
```

cacheFqdnNegativeHits
>   The number of FQDN requests satisfied as negative cache hits. For example:

```
SQUID-MIB::cacheFqdnNegativeHits = Counter32: 0
```

cacheFqdnMisses
>   The number of FQDN cache misses. For example:

```
SQUID-MIB::cacheFqdnMisses = Counter32: 0
```

cacheBlockingGetHostByAddr

Always zero in the current implementation. For example:

```
SQUID-MIB::cacheBlockingGetHostByAddr = Counter32: 0
```

cacheDnsRequests

The number of DNS queries made by Squid. This counter is reset each time you reconfigure the running Squid process. For example:

```
SQUID-MIB::cacheDnsRequests = Counter32: 3262
```

cacheDnsReplies

The number of DNS replies received by Squid. This counter is reset each time you reconfigure the running Squid process. For example:

```
SQUID-MIB::cacheDnsReplies = Counter32: 2440
```

cacheDnsNumberServers

When using internal DNS (the default), this OID reports the number of nameservers that Squid knows about. For external DNS, it reports the number of (running) dnsserver helper processes. For example:

```
SQUID-MIB::cacheDnsNumberServers = Counter32: 2
```

cachePeerName.A.B.C.D

This, and the next group of OIDs, come from the list of neighbor caches. (See the section "server_list: Peer Cache Statistics.) These OIDs are indexed by the IPv4 address of the peer. This particular OID returns the neighbor cache's hostname. For example:

```
SQUID-MIB::cachePeerName.192.203.230.19 = STRING: sv.us.ircache.net
```

cachePeerAddr.A.B.C.D

This is the IP address of the peer, which, of course, you already know from the OID itself. For example:

```
SQUID-MIB::cachePeerAddr.192.203.230.19 = IpAddress: 192.203.230.19
```

cachePeerPortHttp.A.B.C.D

This is the neighbor cache's HTTP port number. For example:

```
SQUID-MIB::cachePeerPortHttp.192.203.230.19 = INTEGER: 3128
```

cachePeerPortIcp.A.B.C.D

This is the neighbor cache's ICP or HTCP port number. For example:

```
SQUID-MIB::cachePeerPortIcp.192.203.230.19 = INTEGER: 3130
```

cachePeerType.A.B.C.D

The type of the neighbor: 1 for sibling, 2 for parent, and 3 for multicast. For example:

```
SQUID-MIB::cachePeerType.192.203.230.19 = INTEGER: 1
```

cachePeerState.A.B.C.D

The state of the peer: 1 for up, 0 for down. (See Chapter 10.) For example:

```
SQUID-MIB::cachePeerState.192.203.230.19 = INTEGER: 1
```

cachePeerPingsSent.A.B.C.D

> The number of ICP/HTCP queries sent to the neighbor. For example:
>
> ```
> SQUID-MIB::cachePeerPingsSent.192.203.230.19 = Counter32: 924
> ```

cachePeerPingsAcked.A.B.C.D

> The number of ICP/HTCP queries received from the neighbor. For example:
>
> ```
> SQUID-MIB::cachePeerPingsAcked.192.203.230.19 = Counter32: 901
> ```

cachePeerFetches.A.B.C.D

> The number of HTTP requests sent to the neighbor. (See the discussion about FETCHES in "server_list: Peer Cache Statistics.") For example:
>
> ```
> SQUID-MIB::cachePeerFetches.192.203.230.19 = Counter32: 34
> ```

cachePeerRtt.A.B.C.D

> The average round-trip time for ICP/HTCP queries to this peer. For example:
>
> ```
> SQUID-MIB::cachePeerRtt.192.203.230.19 = INTEGER: 26
> ```

cachePeerIgnored.A.B.C.D

> The number of ICP/HTCP replies that Squid ignored. (See the discussion about IGNORED in "server_list: Peer Cache Statistics.") For example:
>
> ```
> SQUID-MIB::cachePeerIgnored.192.203.230.19 = Counter32: 201
> ```

cachePeerKeepAlSent.A.B.C.D

> The number of HTTP requests sent to the neighbor with a request to keep the connection open. For example:
>
> ```
> SQUID-MIB::cachePeerKeepAlSent.192.203.230.19 = Counter32: 34
> ```

cachePeerKeepAlRecv.A.B.C.D

> The number of HTTP replies received from the neighbor with a request to keep the connection open. For example:
>
> ```
> SQUID-MIB::cachePeerKeepAlRecv.192.203.230.19 = Counter32: 34
> ```

cacheClientAddr.A.B.C.D

> The cacheClientAddr OIDs come from the same database as the *Cache Client List* (see the section "client_list: Cache Client List"). This particular OID's value is the IPv4 address, just like the last four octets of the OID itself. For example:
>
> ```
> SQUID-MIB::cacheClientAddr.206.168.0.9 = IpAddress: 206.168.0.9
> ```

cacheClientHttpRequests.A.B.C.D

> The number of HTTP requests received from this client. For example:
>
> ```
> SQUID-MIB::cacheClientHttpRequests.206.168.0.9 = Counter32: 108281
> ```

cacheClientHttpKb.A.B.C.D

> The amount of traffic, in kilobytes, sent to this client. For example:
>
> ```
> SQUID-MIB::cacheClientHttpKb.206.168.0.9 = Counter32: 921447
> ```

cacheClientHttpHits.A.B.C.D

> The number of cache hits sent to this client. For example:
>
> ```
> SQUID-MIB::cacheClientHttpHits.206.168.0.9 = Counter32: 32365
> ```

cacheClientHTTPHitKb.A.B.C.D

The amount of traffic, in kilobytes, sent to this client for cache hits. For example:

```
SQUID-MIB::cacheClientHTTPHitKb.206.168.0.9 = Counter32: 141638
```

cacheClientIcpRequests.A.B.C.D

The number of ICP (but not HTCP) queries received from this client. For example:

```
SQUID-MIB::cacheClientIcpRequests.206.168.0.9 = Counter32: 79120
```

cacheClientIcpKb.A.B.C.D

The amount of traffic, in kilobytes, received from this client in ICP queries. For example:

```
SQUID-MIB::cacheClientIcpKb.206.168.0.9 = Counter32: 5986
```

cacheClientIcpHits.A.B.C.D

The number of ICP_HIT replies sent to this client. For example:

```
SQUID-MIB::cacheClientIcpHits.206.168.0.9 = Counter32: 21897
```

cacheClientIcpHitKb.A.B.C.D

The amount of traffic, in kilobytes, sent to this client for ICP_HIT messages. A somewhat silly measurement because ICP_HIT and ICP_MISS messages have the same size. However, old versions of Squid used the now-obsolete ICP_HIT_OBJ opcode, which included the object content. For example:

```
SQUID-MIB::cacheClientIcpHitKb.206.168.0.9 = Counter32: 1679
```

Exercises

- Write a shell script that uses squidclient to collect and save the total number of HTTP requests and the five-minute median overall response time.

- Write a shell script to periodically retrieve and archive the running configuration. It should also compare the current and most recent configurations and email you the changes, if any.

- Download, compile, and install the NET-SNMP package. Use snmpwalk to view Squid's entire MIB tree.

- Create and deploy a simple redirector (Chapter 11) that sleeps for 250 milliseconds on each request. Watch the cache manager's redirector page as Squid runs.

CHAPTER 15
Server Accelerator Mode

Throughout most of this book, I've been talking about Squid as a client-side caching proxy. However, with just a few special *squid.conf* settings, Squid is able to function as an origin server accelerator as well. In this mode, it accepts normal HTTP requests and forwards cache misses to the real origin server (or *backend server*). In the parlance of RFC 3040, Squid is operating as a *surrogate*. This configuration is similar to what I talked about in Chapter 9. The primary difference is that, as a surrogate, Squid accepts requests for one, or maybe a few, origin server(s), rather than any and all origins. HTTP interception isn't required for server acceleration.

As the name implies, server acceleration is generally used as a technique to improve the performance of slow, or heavily loaded, backend servers. It works well because origin servers tend to have a relatively small hot set. Most likely, the objects responsible for 90% of origin server traffic can fit entirely in memory. Depending on your particular backend server software and configuration, Squid may be able to serve requests much faster.

Security is another good reason to consider Squid as a surrogate. Think of Squid as a dedicated firewall in front of your origin server. The Squid source code is too large to be trusted as completely secure. However, you may sleep better with Squid protecting your backend server. It is simply a cache, so it doesn't permanently store the source of your data. If the Squid box is attacked or compromised, you won't lose any data. You may find it easier to secure a system running Squid than the system running your backend server application(s).

You might also be interested in server acceleration to implement load balancing. If your origin server runs on expensive boxes, you can save money by deploying Squid on a number of cheaper boxes. By placing Squid at a number of different locations, you can even build your own content delivery network (CDN).

Overview

Assuming that you already have an origin server in place, you need to move it to a different IP address or TCP port. For example, you can (1) install Squid on a separate machine, (2) give the origin server a new IP address, and (3) give Squid the origin server's old IP address. In the interest of security, you can use non-globally routable addresses (i.e., from RFC 1918) on the link between Squid and the backend server. See Figure 15-1.

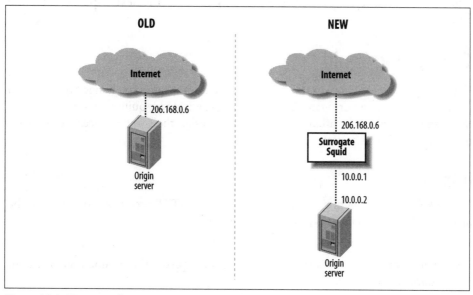

Figure 15-1. How to replace your origin server with Squid

Another option is to configure Squid for HTTP interception, as described in Chapter 9. For example, you can configure the origin server's nearest router or switch to intercept HTTP requests and divert them to Squid.

If you don't have the resources to put Squid on a dedicated system, you can run it alongside the HTTP server. However, both applications can't share the same IP address and port number. You need to make the backend server bind to a different address (e.g., 127.0.0.1) or move it to another port number. It might seem easiest to change the port number, but I recommend changing the IP address instead.

Changing the port number can be problematic. For example, when the backend server generates an error message, it may expose the "wrong" port. Even worse, if the server generates an HTTP redirect, it typically appends the nonstandard port number to the Location URI:

```
HTTP/1.1 301 Moved Permanently
Date: Mon, 29 Sep 2003 03:36:13 GMT
```

```
Server: Apache/1.3.26 (Unix)
Location: http://www.squid-cache.org:81/Doc/
```

If a client receives this response, it makes a connection to the nonstandard port (81), thus bypassing the server accelerator. If you must run Squid on the same host as your backend server, it is better to tell the backend server to listen on the loopback address (127.0.0.1). With Apache, you'd do it like this:

```
BindAddress 127.0.0.1
ServerName www.squid-cache.org
```

Once you've decided how to relocate your origin server, the next step is to configure Squid.

Configuring Squid

Technically, a single configuration file directive is all it takes to change Squid from a caching proxy into a surrogate. Unfortunately, life is never quite that simple. Due to the myriad of ways that different organizations design their web services, Squid has a number of directives to worry about.

http_port

Most likely, Squid is acting as a surrogate for your HTTP server on port 80. Use the *http_port* directive to make Squid listen on that port:

```
http_port 80
```

If you want Squid to act as surrogate and a caching proxy at the same time, list both port numbers:

```
http_port 80
http_port 3128
```

You can configure your clients to send their proxy requests to port 80 as well, but I strongly discourage that. By using separate ports, you'll find it easier to migrate the two services to separate boxes later if it becomes necessary.

https_port

You can configure Squid to terminate encrypted HTTP (SSL and TLS) connections. This feature requires the --enable-ssl option when running ./configure. In this mode, Squid decrypts SSL/TLS connections from clients and forwards unencrypted requests to your backend server. The *https_port* directive has the following format:

```
https_port [host:]port cert=certificate.pem [key=key.pem] [version=1-4]
           [cipher=list] [options=list]
```

The cert and key arguments are pathnames to OpenSSL-compatible certificate and private key files. If you omit the key argument, the OpenSSL library looks for the private key in the certificate file.

The (optional) version argument specifies your requirements for various SSL and TLS protocols to support: 1=automatic, 2=SSLv2 only, 3=SSLv3 only, 4=TLSv1 only.

The (optional) cipher argument is a colon-separated list of ciphers. Squid simply passes it to the SSL_CTX_set_cipher_list() function. For more information, read the ciphers(1) manpage on your system or try running: openssl ciphers.

The (optional) options argument is a colon-separated list of OpenSSL options. Squid simply passes these to the SSL_CTX_set_options() function. For more information, read the SSL_CTX_set_options(3) manpage on your system.

Here are a few example *https_port* lines:

```
https_port 443 cert=/usr/local/etc/certs/squid.cert
https_port 443 cert=/usr/local/etc/certs/squid.cert version=2
https_port 443 cert=/usr/local/etc/certs/squid.cert cipher=SHA1
https_port 443 cert=/usr/local/etc/certs/squid.cert options=MICROSOFT_SESS_ID_BUG
```

httpd_accel_host

This is where you tell Squid the IP address, or hostname, of the backend server. If you use the loopback trick described previously, you write:

```
httpd_accel_host 127.0.0.1
```

Squid then prepends this value to partial URIs that get accelerated. It also changes the value of the Host header.* For example, if the client makes this request:

```
GET /index.html HTTP/1.1
Host: squidbook.org
```

Squid turns it into this request:

```
GET http://127.0.0.1/index.html HTTP/1.1
Host: 127.0.0.1
```

As you can see, the request no longer contains any information that indicates the request is for *squidbook.org*. This shouldn't be a problem as long as the backend server isn't configured for virtual hosting of multiple domains.

If you want Squid to use the origin server's hostname, you can put it in the *httpd_accel_host* directive:

```
httpd_accel_host squidbook.org
```

---

* Technically, the Host header is changed only in requests Squid forwards to the backend server (cache misses).

Then the request is as follows:

```
GET http://squidbook.org/index.html HTTP/1.1
Host: squidbook.org
```

Another option is to enable the *httpd_accel_uses_host_header* directive. Squid then inserts the Host header value into the URI for most requests, and the *httpd_accel_host* value is used only for requests that lack a Host header.

When you use a hostname, Squid goes through the normal steps to look up its IP address. Because you want the hostname to resolve to two different addresses (one for clients connecting to Squid and another for Squid connecting to the backend server), you should also add a static DNS entry to your system's */etc/hosts* file. For example:

```
127.0.0.1          squidbook.org
```

You might want to use a redirector instead. For example, you can write a simple Perl program that changes http://squidbook.org/... to http://127.0.0.1/.... See Chapter 11 for the nuts and bolts of redirecting client requests.

The *httpd_accel_host* directive has a special value. If you set it to virtual, Squid inserts the origin server's IP address into the URI when the Host header is missing. This feature is useful only when using HTTP interception, however.

httpd_accel_port

This directive tells Squid the port number of the backend server. It is 80 by default. You won't need to change this unless the backend server is running on a different port. Here is an example:

```
httpd_accel_port 8080
```

If you are accelerating origin servers on multiple ports, you can use the value 0. In this case, Squid takes the port number from the Host header.

httpd_accel_uses_host_header

This directive controls how Squid determines the hostname it inserts into accelerated URIs. If enabled, the request's Host header value takes precedence over *httpd_accel_host*.

The *httpd_accel_uses_host_header* directive goes hand in hand with virtual domain hosting on the backend server. You can leave it disabled if the backend server is handling only one domain. If, on the other hand, you are accelerating multiple origin server names, turn it on:

```
httpd_accel_uses_host_header on
```

If you enable *httpd_accel_uses_host_header*, be sure to install some access controls as described later in this chapter. To understand why, consider this configuration:

```
httpd_accel_host does.not.exist
httpd_accel_uses_host_header on
```

Because most requests have a Host header, Squid ignores the *httpd_accel_host* setting and rarely inserts the bogus *does.not.exist* name into URIs. This essentially turns your surrogate into a caching proxy for anyone smart enough to fake an HTTP request. If I know that you are using Squid as a surrogate without proper access controls, I can send a request like this:

```
GET /index.html HTTP/1.1
Host: www.mrcranky.com
```

If you've enabled *httpd_accel_uses_host_header* and don't have any destination-based access controls, Squid should forward my request to *www.mrcranky.com*. Read the "Access Controls" section and install access controls to ensure that Squid doesn't talk to foreign origin servers.

httpd_accel_single_host

Whereas the *httpd_accel_uses_host_header* directive determines the hostname Squid puts into a URI, this one determines where Squid forwards its cache misses. By default (i.e., with *httpd_accel_single_host* disabled), Squid forwards surrogate cache misses to the host in the URI. If the URI contains a hostname, Squid performs a DNS lookup to get the backend server's IP address.

When you enable *httpd_accel_single_host*, Squid always forwards surrogate cache misses to the host defined by *httpd_accel_host*. In other words, the contents of the URI and the Host header don't affect the forwarding decision. Perhaps the best reason to enable this directive is to avoid DNS lookups. Simply set *httpd_accel_host* to the backend server's IP address. Another reason to enable it is if you have another device (load balancer, virus scanner, etc.) between Squid and the backend server. You can make Squid forward the request to this other device without changing any aspect of the HTTP request.

Note that enabling both *httpd_accel_single_host* and *httpd_accel_uses_host_header* is a dangerous combination that might allow an attacker to poison your cache. Consider this configuration:

```
httpd_accel_single_host on
httpd_accel_host 172.16.1.1
httpd_accel_uses_host_header on
```

and this HTTP request:

```
GET /index.html HTTP/1.0
Host: www.othersite.com
```

Squid forwards the request to your backend server at 172.16.1.1 but stores the response under the URI *http://www.othersite.com/index.html*. Since 172.16.1.1 isn't actually *www.othersite.com*, Squid now contains a bogus response for that URI. If you enable *httpd_accel_with_proxy* (next section) or your cache participates in a hier-archy or mesh, it may give out the bad response to unsuspecting users. To prevent such abuse, be sure to read the "Access Controls" section.

Server-side persistent connections may not work if you use the *httpd_accel_single_host* directive. This is because Squid saves idle connections under the origin server hostname, but the connection-establishment code looks for an idle connection named by the *httpd_accel_host* value. If the two values are different, Squid fails to locate an appropriate idle connection. The idle connections are closed after the time-out, without being reused. You can avoid this little problem by disabling server-side persistent connections with the *server_persistent_connections* directive (see Appendix A).

httpd_accel_with_proxy

By default, whenever you enable the *httpd_accel_host* directive, Squid goes into strict surrogate mode. That is, it refuses proxy HTTP requests and accepts only surrogate requests, as though it were truly an origin server. Squid also disables the ICP port (although not HTCP, if you have it enabled). If you want Squid to accept both surro-gate and proxy requests, enable this directive:

```
httpd_accel_with_proxy on
```

Gee, That Was Confusing!

Yeah, it was for me too. Let's look at it another way. The settings that you need to use depend on how many backend boxes you have and how many origin server names you are accelerating. Let's consider the four separate cases in the following sections.

One Box, One Server Name

This is the simplest sort of configuration. Because you have only one box and one hostname, the Host header values don't matter much. You should probably use:

```
httpd_accel_host www.example.com
httpd_accel_single_host on
httpd_accel_uses_host_header off
```

If you like, you can use an IP address for *httpd_accel_host*, although it will appear in URIs in your *access.log*.

One Box, Many Server Names

Because you have many origin server names being virtually hosted on a single box, the Host header becomes important. We want Squid to insert it into the URIs it generates from partial requests. Your configuration should be:

```
httpd_accel_host www.example.com
httpd_accel_single_host on
httpd_accel_uses_host_header on
```

In this case, Squid generates the URI based on the Host header. If absent, Squid inserts *www.example.com*. You can disable *httpd_accel_single_host* if you prefer. As before, you can use an IP address in *httpd_accel_host* to avoid DNS lookups.

Many Boxes, One Server Name

This sounds like a load-balancing configuration. One way to accomplish it is to create a DNS name for the backend servers with multiple IP addresses. Squid iterates between all addresses (a.k.a. round-robin) for each cache miss. In this situation, the configuration is the same as for the one box/one name case:

```
httpd_accel_host roundrobin.example.com
httpd_accel_single_host on
httpd_accel_uses_host_header off
```

The only difference is that the *httpd_accel_host* name resolves to multiple addresses. It might look like this in a Berkeley Internet Name Daemon (BIND) zone file:

```
$ORIGIN example.com.
roundrobin    IN    A    192.168.1.2
              IN    A    192.168.1.3
              IN    A    192.168.1.4
```

With this DNS configuration, Squid uses the next address in the list each time it opens a new connection to *roundrobin.example.com*. When it gets to the end of the list, it starts over at the top. Note that Squid caches these DNS answers internally according to their TTLs. You aren't relying on the name server to return the address list in a different order for each DNS query.

Another option is to use a redirector (see Chapter 11) to select the backend server. You can write a simple script to replace the URI hostname (e.g., *roundrobin.example. com*) with a different hostname or an IP address. You might even make the redirector smart enough to make its selection based on the current state of the backend servers. Use the following configuration with this approach:

```
httpd_accel_host roundrobin.example.com
httpd_accel_single_host off
httpd_accel_uses_host_header off
```

Many Boxes, Many Server Names

In this case, you want to use the Host header. You also want Squid to select the back-end server based on the origin server's name (i.e., a DNS lookup). The configuration is as follows:

```
httpd_accel_host www.example.com
httpd_accel_single_host off
httpd_accel_uses_host_header on
```

You might be tempted to set *httpd_accel_host* to virtual. However, that would be a mistake unless you are using HTTP interception.

Access Controls

A typically configured surrogate accepts HTTP requests from the whole Internet. This doesn't mean, however, that you can forget about access controls. In particular, you'll want to make sure Squid doesn't accept requests belonging to foreign origin servers. The exception is when you have *httpd_accel_with_proxy* enabled.

For a surrogate-only configuration, use one of the destination-based access controls. For example, the *dst* type accomplishes the task:

```
acl All src 0/0
acl TheOriginServer dst 192.168.3.2
http_access allow TheOriginServer
http_access deny All
```

Alternatively, you can use a *dstdomain* ACL if you prefer:

```
acl All src 0/0
acl TheOriginServer dstdomain www.squidbook.org
http_access allow TheOriginServer
http_access deny All
```

Note that enabling *httpd_accel_single_host* somewhat bypasses the access control rules. This is because the origin server location (i.e., the *httpd_accel_host* value) is then set after Squid performs the access control checks.

Access controls become really tricky when you combine surrogate and proxy modes in a single instance of Squid. You can no longer simply deny all requests to foreign origin servers. You can, however, make sure that outsiders aren't allowed to make proxy requests to random origin servers. For example:

```
acl All src 0/0
acl ProxyUsers src 10.2.0.0/16
acl TheOriginServer dst 192.168.3.2
http_access allow ProxyUsers
http_access allow TheOriginServer
http_access deny All
```

You can also use the local port number in your access control rules. It doesn't really protect you from malicious activity, but does ensure, for example, that user-agents send their proxy requests to the appropriate port. This also makes it easier for you to split the service into separate proxy- and surrogate-only systems later. Assuming you configure Squid to listen on ports 80 and 3128, you might use:

```
acl All src 0/0
acl ProxyPort myport 3128
acl ProxyUsers src 10.2.0.0/16
acl SurrogatePort myport 80
acl TheOriginServer dst 192.168.3.2
http_access allow ProxyUsers ProxyPort
http_access allow TheOriginServer SurrogatePort
http_access deny All
```

Unfortunately, these access control rules don't prevent attempts to poison your cache when you enable *httpd_accel_single_host*, *httpd_accel_uses_host_header*, and *httpd_accel_with_proxy* simultaneously. This is because the valid proxy request:

```
GET http://www.bad.site/ HTTP/1.1
Host: www.bad.site
```

and the bogus surrogate request:

```
GET / HTTP/1.1
Host: www.bad.site
```

have the same access control result but are forwarded to different servers. They have the same access control result because, after Squid rewrites the surrogate request, it has the same URI as the proxy request. However, they don't get sent to the same place. The surrogate request goes to the server defined by *httpd_accel_host* because *httpd_accel_single_host* is enabled.

You can take steps towards solving this problem. Make sure your backend server generates an error for unknown server names (e.g., when the Host header refers to a nonlocal server). Better yet, don't run Squid as a surrogate and proxy at the same time.

Content Negotiation

Recent versions of Squid support the HTTP/1.1 Vary header. This is good news if your backend server uses content negotiation. It might, for example, send different responses depending on which web browser makes the request (e.g., the User-Agent header), or based on the user's language preferences (e.g., the Accept-Language header).

When the response for a URI varies on some aspect of the request, the origin (backend) server includes a Vary header. This header contains the list of request headers used to select the variant. These are the *selecting* headers. When Squid receives a response with a Vary header, it includes the selecting header values when it generates the internal cache key. Thus, a subsequent request with the same values for the selecting headers may generate a cache hit.

If you use the --enable-x-accelerator-vary option when running ./configure, Squid looks for a response header named X-Accelerator-Vary. Squid treats this header exactly like the Vary header. Because this is an extension header, however, it is ignored by downstream agents. It essentially provides a means for private content negotiation between Squid and your backend server. In order to use it you must also modify your server application to send the header in its responses. I don't know of any situation in which this header would be useful. If you serve negotiated responses, you probably want to use the standard Vary header so that all agents know what's going on.

Gotchas

Using Squid as a surrogate may improve your origin server's security and performance. However, there are some potentially negative side effects as well. Here are a few things to keep in mind.

Logging

When using a surrogate, the origin server's access log contains only the cache misses from Squid. Furthermore, those log-file entries have Squid's IP address, rather than the client's. In other words, Squid's *access.log* is where all the good information is now stored.

Recall that, by default, Squid doesn't use the common log-file format. You should use the *emulate_httpd_log* directive to make Squid's *access.log* look just like Apache's default log-file format.

Ignoring Reloads

The *Reload* button found on most browsers generates HTTP requests with the Cache-Control: no-cache directive set. While this is usually desirable for client-side caching proxies, it may ruin the performance of a surrogate. This is especially true if the backend server is heavily loaded. A reload request forces Squid to purge the currently cached response while retrieving the new response from the origin server. If those origin server responses arrive slowly, Squid consumes a larger than normal number of file descriptors and network resources.

To help in this situation, you may want to use one of the *refresh_pattern* options. When the ignore-reload option is set, Squid pretends that the request doesn't contain the no-cache directive. The ignore-reload option is generally safe for surrogates, although it does, technically, violate the HTTP protocol.

To make Squid ignore reloads for all requests, use a line like this in *squid.conf*:

```
refresh_pattern . 0 20% 4320 ignore-reload
```

For a somewhat safer alternative, you can use the `reload-into-ims` option. It causes Squid to validate its cached response when the request contains `no-cache`. Note, however, that this works only for responses that have cache validators (such as `Last-Modified` timestamps).

Uncachable Content

As a surrogate, Squid obeys the standard HTTP headers for caching responses from your backend server. This means, for example, that certain dynamic responses might not be cached. You might want to use the *refresh_pattern* directive to force caching of these objects. For example:

```
refresh_pattern \.dhtml$ 60 80% 180
```

This trick only works for certain types of responses, namely, those without a `Last-Modified` or `Expires` header. By default, Squid doesn't cache such responses. However, using a nonzero minimum time in a *refresh_pattern* rule instructs Squid to cache the response, and serve it as a cache hit for that amount of time anyway. See Chapter 7 for the details.

If your backend server generates other types of uncachable responses, you may not be able to trick Squid into storing them.

Errors

With Squid as a surrogate in front of your origin server, you should be aware that visitors to your site may see an error message from Squid, rather than the origin server itself. In other words, your use of Squid may be "exposed" through certain error messages. For example, Squid returns its own error message when it fails to parse the client's HTTP request, which could happen if the request is incomplete or is malformed in some way. Squid also returns an error message if it can't connect to the backend server for some reason.

If your site is consistent and functioning properly, you probably don't need to worry about Squid's error messages. Nonetheless, you may want to take a close look at the *access.log* from time to time and see what sort of errors, if any, your users might be seeing.

Purging Objects

You may find the PURGE method particularly useful when operating a surrogate. Because you have a good understanding of the content being served, you are more likely to know when a cached object must be purged. The technique for purging an object is the same as I mentioned previously. See Chapter 7 for a refresher.

Neighbors

Although I don't recommend it, you can configure Squid as a surrogate and as part of a mesh or hierarchy. If you choose to take on such an arrangement, note that, by default, Squid forwards cache misses to parents (rather than the backend server). Assuming that isn't what you really want, be sure to use the *cache_peer_access* directives so that requests for your backend server don't go to your neighbors instead.

Exercises

- Install and configure Squid as a surrogate on the same system where you run an HTTP server.
- Make a few test requests with squidclient. Pay particular attention to the reply headers and notice how the requests appear in both access logs.
- Try to poison your own surrogate with fake HTTP requests. It is probably easier with *httpd_accel_single_host* enabled.
- Estimate the size of your origin server's document set. What percentage of the data can fit into 1 GB of memory or disk space?

## CHAPTER 16

Debugging and Troubleshooting

No matter how hard the Squid developers try to be perfect, you may encounter some problems with Squid. These problems range from misbehaving clients and servers to fatal bugs in the Squid code. In this chapter, I'll talk about various ways you can debug these problems.

Some Squid problems may require you to turn on debugging. In most cases, you'll want to increase the debugging levels for specific parts of the code. I'll describe how to find out what those debugging sections are and how to change the settings. Also, I'll talk about the importance of providing detailed debugging when reporting bugs.

Finally, you may experience fatal bugs in the Squid code. These can result in segmentation violations, aborts, assertions, and core dumps. The core dump is a useful debugging aid. With a debugger, such as gdb, you can generate a process stack trace and send it to the developers for assistance.

If you suspect you have a Squid bug, but aren't sure, check with the *squid-users* mailing list or one of the other resources described in Chapter 1.

Some Common Problems

Before discussing debugging in general, I'll mention a few specific problems that commonly arise.

"Failed to make swap directory"

```
Failed to make swap directory /var/spool/cache: (13) Permission denied
```

This happens when you run squid -z, and the Squid user ID doesn't have write permission to the */var/spool* directory. Remember that if you start Squid as *root* and don't add a *cache_effective_user* line, Squid runs as the user *nobody* by default. Thus, your solution may be to simply run:

```
# chown nobody:nobody /var/spool
```

"Address already in use"

```
commBind: Cannot bind socket FD 10 to *:3128: Address already in use
```

This message appears when the bind( ) system call fails because the requested port is already opened by another application. Usually, this happens when you try to start a second instance of Squid when the first one is still running. If you see this error message, use ps to see if Squid is already running.

Squid uses the SO_REUSEADDR socket option, so that the bind( ) call should succeed even if there are some leftover sockets in the TIME_WAIT state. If you get the message, even though Squid isn't already running, your operating system may be buggy or especially finicky. Rebooting your system is one way to get around this problem.

Another possibility to consider is that the port (e.g., 3128) is currently being used by a different application. If you suspect this, you can use the lsof program (*ftp://lsof. itap.purdue.edu/pub/tools/unix/lsof*) to find which application is listening on the port. FreeBSD users can use sockstat instead.

"Could not determine fully qualified hostname"

```
FATAL: Could not determine fully qualified hostname.  Please set 'visible_hostname'
```

You'll see this if Squid can't figure out its own fully qualified domain name. Here is the algorithm Squid uses:

- If you told Squid to bind the HTTP port to a specific interface address, Squid attempts a reverse DNS lookup of that address. If successful, the answer is used.

- Squid calls the gethostname( ) function, and then attempts to resolve its IP address with gethostbyname( ). If successful, Squid uses the official hostname string returned by the latter function.

If neither technique works, Squid exits with the fatal message shown earlier. In this case, you must tell Squid its hostname with the *visible_hostname* directive. For example:

```
visible_hostname my.host.name
```

"DNS name lookup tests failed"

By default, Squid makes a few DNS queries before starting. This ensures that your DNS servers are reachable and functioning properly. If these tests fail, you'll see the following message in *cache.log* and/or syslog:

```
FATAL: ipcache_init: DNS name lookup tests failed
```

If you use Squid on an intranet, Squid may be unable to query its standard list of hostnames. You can specify your own hostnames with the *dns_testnames* directive. Squid considers the DNS test successful as soon as it receives any reply.

If you want to skip the DNS tests altogether, simply use the -D command-line option when starting Squid:

```
% squid -D ...
```

"Illegal character in hostname"

```
urlParse: Illegal character in hostname 'super_bikes.tripod.com'
```

By default, Squid checks the characters in the hostname part of URLs and complains if it finds nonstandard characters. According to RFCs 1034 and 1035, names must consist of the letters A–Z, the digits 0–9, and a hyphen (-). The underscore (_) is one of the most problematic characters.

Squid validates hostnames because, in some cases, DNS resolvers behave differently with respect to illegal characters. For example:

```
% host super_bikes.tripod.com
super_bikes.tripod.com has address 209.202.196.70

% ping super_bikes.tripod.com
ping: cannot resolve super_bikes.tripod.com: Unknown server error
```

Rather than return the Unknown server error message, Squid checks the hostname first. It can then tell the user when the hostname contains illegal characters.

Some DNS resolvers do work with underscores and other nonstandard characters. If you'd prefer that Squid not check hostnames, use the --disable-hostname-checks option when running ./configure. If you want to allow underscores as the only exception, use the --enable-underscores option.

"Running out of filedescriptors"

```
WARNING! Your cache is running out of filedescriptors
```

The above message appears when Squid uses up all available file descriptors. If this happens under normal conditions, you need to increase the kernel's file-descriptor limits and recompile Squid. See Chapter 3.

You might also see this message if Squid is the target of a denial-of-service attack. Someone may be intentionally, or unintentionally, sending Squid hundreds or thousands of requests at once. If this is the case, you can probably add a packet-filtering rule to block incoming TCP connections from the offending address(es). If the attack is distributed or using a spoofed source address, you'll have a harder time stopping it.

Forwarding loops (see Chapter 10) might also consume all of Squid's file descriptors, but only if Squid can't detect the loop. The Via header contains the hostname of all proxies that have seen a particular request. Squid looks for its own hostname in the header, and, if found, reports the loop. If, for some reason, the Via header is filtered from outgoing or incoming HTTP requests, Squid can't detect the loop. In this case, all file descriptors are quickly consumed by the same request going through Squid over and over.

"icmpRecv: Connection refused"

You'll see the following message if the `pinger` program isn't correctly installed:

```
icmpRecv: recv: (61) Connection refused
```

Most likely, the `pinger` program exits immediately because it doesn't have permission to open a raw ICMP socket. Because the process isn't running, Squid receives an I/O error when trying to talk to it. To alleviate the problem, go to the source directory and, as *root*, type:

```
# make install-pinger
```

If successful, you should find that the `pinger` program has the following file ownership and permission settings:

```
# ls -l /usr/local/squid/libexec/pinger
-rws--x--x  1 root  squid  140728 Sep 16 19:58 /usr/local/squid/libexec/pinger
```

Squid Becomes Slow After Running for Some Time

Most likely, Squid is competing with other processes, or with itself, for memory on your system. When the Squid process no longer fits entirely in memory, the operating system is forced to read and write areas of memory to and from the swap space. This has a drastic effect on Squid's performance.

To validate this theory, check the Squid process size with utilities such as top and ps. Also check Squid's own page fault counter, as described in Chapter 14. Once you've identified memory consumption as the problem, try the following steps to reduce Squid's memory usage:

1. Reduce the value of *cache_mem* and read Appendix B.
2. Turn off memory pooling with this option:

   ```
   memory_pools off
   ```
3. Reduce the size of the disk cache by lowering the size of one or more cache directories. See Chapter 7.

Debugging Access Controls

If you're having no luck getting your access controls to work properly, here's a little tip that might help. Edit your *squid.conf* file and set the *debug_options* line to this:

```
debug_options ALL,1 33,2
```

Then, reconfigure Squid:

```
% squid -k reconfigure
```

Now, Squid writes a message to *cache.log* for each client request and another for each reply. The messages contain the request method, URI, whether the request/ reply is allowed or denied, and the name of the last ACL that matched it. For example:

```
2003/09/29 20:22:05| The request
    GET http://images.slashdot.org:80/topics/topicprivacy.gif is ALLOWED,
    because it matched 'localhost'
2003/09/29 20:22:05| The reply for
    GET http://images.slashdot.org/topics/topicprivacy.gif is ALLOWED,
    because it matched 'all'
```

Knowing the name of the ACL doesn't always tell you the corresponding *http_access* line, but it gets you pretty close. If necessary, you can replicate your *acl* lines and give them unique names so that a given ACL name appears on only one *http_access* rule.

Debugging via cache.log

You already know from Chapter 13 that *cache.log* contains various operational messages Squid thinks are important enough to tell you about. We also refer to these as debugging messages. You can use the *debug_options* directive to control the verbosity of messages that appear in *cache.log*. By increasing the debugging levels, you'll see more detailed messages that may help you understand what Squid is doing. For example:

```
debug_options ALL,1 11,3 20,3
```

Every debugging message in the Squid source code has two numeric attributes: a *section* and a *level*. Sections range from 0 to 100, and levels range from 0 to 10. In general, section numbers correspond to particular components of the source code. In other words, all the messages within a single source file have the same section number. In some cases, multiple files use the same debugging section. This tends to happen when a source file becomes too large and is split into smaller chunks.

The top of each source file has line that mentions the debugging section. It looks like this:

```
* DEBUG: section 9     File Transfer Protocol (FTP)
```

I don't expect you to look at the source files to find the section numbers. The same information appears here in Table 16-1.

Table 16-1. Debugging section numbers for the debug_options directive

Number	Description	Source file(s)
0	Client Database	*client_db.c*
1	Startup and Main Loop	*main.c*
2	Unlink Daemon	*unlinkd.c*
3	Configuration File Parsing	*cache_cf.c*

Table 16-1. Debugging section numbers for the debug_options directive (continued)

Number	Description	Source file(s)
4	Error Generation	*errorpage.c*
5	Socket Functions	*comm.c*
5	Socket Functions	*comm_select.c*
6	Disk I/O Routines	*disk.c*
7	Multicast	*multicast.c*
8	Swap File Bitmap	*filemap.c*
9	File Transfer Protocol (FTP)	*ftp.c*
10	Gopher	*gopher.c*
11	Hypertext Transfer Protocol (HTTP)	*http.c*
12	Internet Cache Protocol	*icp_v2.c*
12	Internet Cache Protocol	*icp_v3.c*
13	High Level Memory Pool Management	*mem.c*
14	IP Cache	*ipcache.c*
15	Neighbor Routines	*neighbors.c*
16	Cache Manager Objects	*cache_manager.c*
17	Request Forwarding	*forward.c*
18	Cache Manager Statistics	*stat.c*
19	Store Memory Primitives	*stmem.c*
20	Storage Manager	*store.c*
20	Storage Manager Client-Side Interface	*store_client.c*
20	Storage Manager Heap-Based Replacement	*repl/heap/store_heap_replacement.c*
20	Storage Manager Logging Functions	*store_log.c*
20	Storage Manager MD5 Cache Keys	*store_key_md5.c*
20	Storage Manager Swapfile Metadata	*store_swapmeta.c*
20	Storage Manager Swapin Functions	*store_swapin.c*
20	Storage Manager Swapout Functions	*store_swapout.c*
20	Store Rebuild Routines	*store_rebuild.c*
21	Misc Functions	*tools.c*
22	Refresh Calculation	*refresh.c*
23	URL Parsing	*url.c*
24	WAIS Relay	*wais.c*
25	MIME Parsing	*mime.c*
26	Secure Sockets Layer Proxy	*ssl.c*
27	Cache Announcer	*send-announce.c*
28	Access Control	*acl.c*
29	Authenticator	*auth/basic/auth_basic.c*

Number	Description	Source file(s)
29	Authenticator	*auth/digest/auth_digest.c*
29	Authenticator	*authenticate.c*
29	NTLM Authenticator	*auth/ntlm/auth_ntlm.c*
30	Ident (RFC 1413)	*ident.c*
31	Hypertext Caching Protocol	*htcp.c*
32	Asynchronous Disk I/O	*fs/aufs/async_io.c*
33	Client-Side Routines	*client_side.c*
34	Dnsserver Interface	*dns.c*
35	FQDN Cache	*fqdncache.c*
37	ICMP Routines	*icmp.c*
38	Network Measurement Database	*net_db.c*
39	Cache Array Routing Protocol	*carp.c*
40	Referer Logging	*referer.c*
40	User-Agent Logging	*useragent.c*
41	Event Processing	*event.c*
42	ICMP Pinger Program	*pinger.c*
43	AIOPS	*fs/aufs/aiops.c*
44	Peer Selection Algorithm	*peer_select.c*
45	Callback Data Registry	*cbdata.c*
45	Callback Data Registry	*leakfinder.c*
46	Access Log	*access_log.c*
47	Store COSS Directory Routines	*fs/coss/store_dir_coss.c*
47	Store Directory Routines	*fs/aufs/store_dir_aufs.c*
47	Store Directory Routines	*fs/diskd/store_dir_diskd.c*
47	Store Directory Routines	*fs/null/store_null.c*
47	Store Directory Routines	*fs/ufs/store_dir_ufs.c*
47	Store Directory Routines	*store_dir.c*
48	Persistent Connections	*pconn.c*
49	SNMP Interface	*snmp_agent.c*
49	SNMP Support	*snmp_core.c*
50	Log File Handling	*logfile.c*
51	File Descriptor Functions	*fd.c*
52	URN Parsing	*urn.c*
53	AS Number Handling	*asn.c*
54	Interprocess Communication	*ipc.c*
55	HTTP Header	*HttpHeader.c*

Table 16-1. Debugging section numbers for the debug_options directive (continued)

Number	Description	Source file(s)
56	HTTP Message Body	*HttpBody.c*
57	HTTP Status-Line	*HttpStatusLine.c*
58	HTTP Reply (Response)	*HttpReply.c*
59	Auto-Growing Memory Buffer with printf	*MemBuf.c*
60	Packer: A Uniform Interface to Store Like Modules	*Packer.c*
61	Redirector	*redirect.c*
62	Generic Histogram	*StatHist.c*
63	Low Level Memory Pool Management	*MemPool.c*
64	HTTP Range Header	*HttpHdrRange.c*
65	HTTP Cache Control Header	*HttpHdrCc.c*
66	HTTP Header Tools	*HttpHeaderTools.c*
67	String	*String.c*
68	HTTP Content-Range Header	*HttpHdrContRange.c*
69	HTTP Header: Extension Field	*HttpHdrExtField.c*
70	Cache Digest	*CacheDigest.c*
71	Store Digest Manager	*store_digest.c*
72	Peer Digest Routines	*peer_digest.c*
73	HTTP Request	*HttpRequest.c*
74	HTTP Message	*HttpMsg.c*
75	WHOIS Protocol	*whois.c*
76	Internal Squid Object handling	*internal.c*
77	Delay Pools	*delay_pools.c*
78	DNS Lookups; interacts with lib/rfc1035.c	*dns_internal.c*
79	Squid-Side DISKD I/O Functions	*fs/diskd/store_io_diskd.c*
79	Storage Manager COSS Interface	*fs/coss/store_io_coss.c*
79	Storage Manager UFS Interface	*fs/ufs/store_io_ufs.c*
80	WCCP Support	*wccp.c*
82	External ACL	*external_acl.c*
83	SSL Accelerator Support	*ssl_support.c*
84	Helper Process Maintenance	*helper.c*

Debugging levels are assigned such that more important messages have smaller values and less important messages have higher values. Level 0 is for very important messages, while level 10 is for those that are relatively unimportant. Other than that, there are no strict guidelines or requirements. Developers are generally free to choose which debugging levels are appropriate.

The *debug_options* directive determines which messages appear in *cache.log*. Its syntax is:

```
debug_options section,level section,level ...
```

The default setting is ALL,1 such that Squid prints any debugging message with level 0 or 1. If you want to make even less output appear in *cache.log*, you can set *debug_options* to ALL,0.

If you want to see additional debugging for a particular component, simply add the appropriate section and level to the end of the *debug_options* list. For example, this line adds level 5 debugging for the FTP server-side code:

```
debug_options ALL,1 9,5
```

As with other configuration directives, you can change *debug_options*, then send Squid the reconfigure signal:

```
% squid -k reconfigure
```

Note that the *debug_options* parameters are processed sequentially, and a later value can override an earlier one. This is of particular concern if you use the ALL keyword. Consider this example:

```
debug_options 9,5 20,9 4,2 ALL,1
```

In this case, the final value overwrites all of the preceding settings because ALL,1 sets the debugging level to 1 for all sections.

Selecting appropriate debugging sections and levels is sometimes quite difficult, especially for novice Squid users. Many of the more detailed debugging messages are meaningful only to developers and those familiar with the source code. Inexperienced Squid users are likely to find many of the debugging messages meaningless and overwhelming. Furthermore, you may have difficulty isolating the debugging for a particular request or event if Squid is relatively busy. The higher debugging levels are often more useful if you can test Squid with one request at a time.

You must also be particularly careful about running Squid with high debugging levels for a long amount of time. If Squid is busy, the *cache.log* file grows very quickly and may eventually consume all free space on its partition. If this happens, Squid exits with a fatal message. Another concern is that performance may degrade significantly. Due to the high number of debugging messages, Squid devotes a lot of CPU resources to formatting and printing strings. It also consumes a lot of disk bandwidth writing them all to *cache.log*.

Core Dumps, Assertions, and Stack Traces

If you are unlucky, Squid may experience a fatal error while running. These sorts of errors come in three flavors: assertions, bus errors, and segmentation violations.

An *assertion* is a sanity check in the source code. It is a tool, used by developers, to make sure that some condition is always true before proceeding. If the condition is false, the program exits and creates a core file so that the developer can analyze the situation. Here is a typical example:

```
int some_array[100];

void
some_func(int idx)
{
        ...
        assert(idx < 100);
        some_array[idx]++;
        ...
}
```

Here, the assertion makes sure that the value of the array index is within the bounds of the array. It would be an error to access array elements greater than (or equal to) 100. If, somehow, the value of *idx* isn't less than 100, the program prints a message like this when it runs:

```
assertion failed: filename.c:123: "idx < 100"
```

If this happens with Squid, you'll see an "assertion failed" message in *cache.log*. In addition, your operating system should create a *core* file, which is helpful in the post-mortem analysis. I'll explain what to do with a *core* file at the end of this section.

A *bus error* is "a fatal failure in the execution of a machine language instruction resulting from the processor detecting an anomalous condition on its bus."* They typically occur when the processor attempts an operation on a nonaligned memory address. You are, perhaps, more likely to see a bus error on a 64-bit processor system, such as the Alpha and some SPARC CPUs. Fortunately, they are easy to fix.

Segmentation violation errors are, unfortunately, more common and sometimes harder to fix. A "SEGV" usually occurs when the process tries to access an invalid memory area. It might be a NULL pointer or a memory address outside the scope of the process. They are particularly difficult to track down when the cause (the bug) and effect (the SEGV) are separated in time.

By default, Squid traps bus errors and segmentation violations, and attempts a clean shutdown when they occur. You'll see something like this in *cache.log*:

```
FATAL: Received Bus Error...dying.
2003/09/29 23:18:01| storeDirWriteCleanLogs: Starting...
```

In most cases, Squid is able to write clean versions of the *swap.state* files. Just before exiting, Squid calls abort( ) to create a *core* file. The *core* file may help you, or other developers, track down and fix the bug.

---

* From the Free On-line Dictionary of Computing (FOLDOC), *http://wombat.doc.ic.ac.uk/foldoc/*.

A *core* file is generally more useful when it is created immediately following the error, rather than calling the clean shutdown procedure first. You can tell Squid not to trap bus errors and segmentation violations with the -C command line option:

```
% squid -C ...
```

Note that some operating systems use the filename *core*, while others prepend the process name (i.e., *squid.core*). Once you have the *core* file, use a debugger to get a stack trace. gdb is the GNU debugger—a companion to the GNU C compiler. If you don't have gdb, try running dbx or adb instead. Here's how you can use gdb to get a stack trace:

```
% gdb /usr/local/squid/sbin/squid /path/to/squid.core
...
Core was generated by 'squid'.
Program terminated with signal 6, Abort trap.
...
```

Then, type **where** to print the stack trace:

```
(gdb) where
#0  0x28168b54 in kill () from /usr/lib/libc.so.4
#1  0x281aa0ce in abort () from /usr/lib/libc.so.4
#2  0x80a2316 in death (sig=10) at tools.c:301
#3  0xbfbfffac in ?? ()
#4  0x80abe0a in storeDiskdSend (mtype=4, sd=0x82101e0, id=1214000,
       sio=0x9e90a10, size=4096, offset=-1, shm_offset=0)
       at diskd/store_io_diskd.c:485
#5  0x80ab726 in storeDiskdWrite (SD=0x82101e0, sio=0x9e90a10,
       buf=0x13e94000 "...", size=4096, offset=-1, free_func=0)
       at diskd/store_io_diskd.c:251
#6  0x809d2fb in storeWrite (sio=0x9e90a10, buf=0x13e94000 "...",
       size=4096, offset=-1, free_func=0) at store_io.c:89
#7  0x80a1c2d in storeSwapOut (e=0xc5a7800) at store_swapout.c:259
#8  0x809b667 in storeAppend (e=0xc5a7800, buf=0x810f9a0 "...", len=57344)
       at store.c:533
#9  0x807873b in httpReadReply (fd=134, data=0xc343590) at http.c:642
#10 0x806492f in comm_poll (msec=10) at comm_select.c:445
#11 0x8084404 in main (argc=2, argv=0xbfbffa8c) at main.c:742
#12 0x804a465 in _start ()
```

As you can see, the stack trace prints the name of each function, its arguments, and the source code filenames and line numbers. This information is extremely useful when tracking down bugs. In some cases, however, it isn't sufficient. You might be asked to execute additional commands in the debugger, such as printing the value of a variable from within a certain function:

```
(gdb) frame 4
#4  0x80abe0a in storeDiskdSend (mtype=4, sd=0x82101e0, id=1214000,
       sio=0x9e90a10, size=4096, offset=-1, shm_offset=0)
       at diskd/store_io_diskd.c:485
485            x = msgsnd(diskdinfo->smsgid, &M, msg_snd_rcv_sz, IPC_NOWAIT);
(gdb) set print pretty
(gdb) print M
```

```
$2 = {
  mtype = 4,
  id = 1214000,
  seq_no = 7203103,
  callback_data = 0x9e90a10,
  size = 4096,
  offset = -1,
  status = -1,
  shm_offset = 0
}
```

After you've reported a bug, try to keep the *core* file around for a few days, in case you need additional information from it.

Can't Find the Core File?

core files are written in the process' current directory. By default, Squid doesn't change its current directory at startup. Thus, your *core* file, if any, should be written in the directory in which Squid was started. You won't find a *core* file if the filesystem doesn't have enough free space or if the process owner doesn't have write permission in the directory. You can use the *coredump_dir* directive to make Squid use a specific location—somewhere with plenty of space and sufficient permissions.

Process resource limits may also prevent the creation of a *core* file. One of the process limit parameters is the size of the core dump file. Usually, most systems set this to "unlimited" by default. You can check the current limit from your shell with the limits or ulimit commands. Note, however, that your shell's limit might be different than the Squid process limit, especially when Squid is started automatically at boot time. If you suspect process limits prevent generation of a *core* file, try this:

```
csh% limit coredumpsize unlimited
csh% squid -NCd1
```

On FreeBSD, a sysctl parameter controls whether or not the operating system generates a *core* file for processes that call setuid( ) and/or setgid( ). Squid uses those functions if you start it as *root*. To get a core dump, then, you must tell the kernel to create the *core* file with this command:

```
# sysctl kern.sugid_coredump=1
```

See the *sysctl.conf* manpage for information on how to set the variable automatically when your system boots.

Replicating Problems

Occasionally you may encounter a certain request or origin server that seems not to work with Squid. You can use the following technique to determine if the problem lies with Squid, the client, or the origin server. The trick is to capture the HTTP request, then replay it in different ways until you identify the problem.

Capturing the HTTP request means getting more than just the URL. You also need the request method, HTTP version number, and all of the request headers. One way to capture the request is by enabling full debugging in Squid for a short time. On the Squid box, type:

```
% squid -kdebug
```

Then, go to the web browser and issue the request. Squid should receive the request almost immediately. After a few seconds, go back to the Squid box and issue the same command:

```
% squid -kdebug
```

Now your *cache.log* file should contain the client's request. If your Squid is busy, the *cache.log* will contain a lot of requests, so you'll have to search for it. It looks something like this:

```
2003/09/29 10:37:40| parseHttpRequest: Method is 'GET'
2003/09/29 10:37:40| parseHttpRequest: URI is 'http://squidbook.org/'
2003/09/29 10:37:40| parseHttpRequest: Client HTTP version 1.1.
2003/09/29 10:37:40| parseHttpRequest: req_hdr = {
User-Agent: Mozilla/5.0 (compatible; Konqueror/3)
Pragma: no-cache
Cache-control: no-cache
Accept: text/*, image/jpeg, image/png, image/*, */*
Accept-Encoding: x-gzip, gzip, identity
Accept-Charset: iso-8859-1, utf-8;q=0.5, *;q=0.5
Accept-Language: en
Host: squidbook.org
```

Note that Squid prints the components of the first line separately. You'll have to manually reassemble them like this:

```
GET http://squidbook.org/ HTTP/1.1
```

Another way to capture the full request is with a utility such as netcat or socket (*http://www.jnickelsen.de/socket/*). Start the socket program listening on some port, then configure the browser to use that port as the proxy address. When you make the request again, socket prints the HTTP request:

```
% socket -s 8080
GET http://squidbook.org/ HTTP/1.1
User-Agent: Mozilla/5.0 (compatible; Konqueror/3)
Pragma: no-cache
Cache-control: no-cache
Accept: text/*, image/jpeg, image/png, image/*, */*
Accept-Encoding: x-gzip, gzip, identity
Accept-Charset: iso-8859-1, utf-8;q=0.5, *;q=0.5
Accept-Language: en
Host: squidbook.org
```

Finally, you can also use a network packet capture utility, such as `tcpdump` or `ethereal`. After capturing a few packets with `tcpdump`, you can then use `tcpshow` to view them:

```
# tcpdump -w tcpdump.log -c 10 -s 1500 port 80
# tcpshow -noHostNames -noPortNames < tcpdump.log | less
...
Packet 4
TIME:   08:39:29.593051 (0.000627)
LINK:   00:90:27:16:AA:75 -> 00:00:24:C0:0D:25 type=IP
  IP:   10.0.0.21 -> 206.168.0.6 hlen=20 TOS=00 dgramlen=304 id=4B29
        MF/DF=0/1 frag=0 TTL=64 proto=TCP cksum=15DC
 TCP:   port 2074 -> 80 seq=0481728885 ack=4107144217
        hlen=32 (data=252) UAPRSF=011000 wnd=57920 cksum=EB38 urg=0
DATA:   GET / HTTP/1.0.
        Host: www.ircache.net.
        Accept: text/html, text/plain, application/pdf, application/
        postscript, text/sgml, */*;q=0.01.
        Accept-Encoding: gzip, compress.
        Accept-Language: en.
        Negotiate: trans.
        User-Agent: Lynx/2.8.1rel.2 libwww-FM/2.14.
        .
```

Note that `tcpshow` prints a period where the data contains a newline character.

Once you've captured a request, save it to a file. Then you can replay it through Squid with `netcat` or `socket`:

```
% socket squidhost 3128 < request | less
```

If the response looks normal, the problem might be with the user-agent. Otherwise, you can change various things to isolate the problem. For example, if you see some funny-looking HTTP headers, delete them from the request and try it again. You may also find it useful to try the request directly with the origin server, instead of going through Squid. To do that, remove the `http://host.name/` from the request and send it to the origin server:

```
% cat request
GET / HTTP/1.1
User-Agent: Mozilla/5.0 (compatible; Konqueror/3)
Pragma: no-cache
Cache-control: no-cache
Accept: text/*, image/jpeg, image/png, image/*, */*
Accept-Encoding: x-gzip, gzip, identity
Accept-Charset: iso-8859-1, utf-8;q=0.5, *;q=0.5
Accept-Language: en
Host: squidbook.org

% socket squidbook.org 80 < request | less
```

When working with HTTP in this manner, you might find it useful to refer to RFC 2616 and O'Reilly's *HTTP: The Definitive Guide*.

Reporting a Bug

If your Squid version is more than a few months old, you should probably update it before reporting any bugs. Chances are that others noticed the same bug, and it may already be fixed.

If you discover a legitimate bug in Squid, please enter it into the Squid bug tracking database: *http://www.squid-cache.org/bugs/*. This is currently a "bugzilla" database, which requires you to create an account. You will receive updates as the bug is processed by Squid developers.

If you are new at reporting bugs, please take the time to read "How to Report Bugs Effectively," by Simon Tatham (*http://www.chiark.greenend.org.uk/ ~sgtatham/bugs.html*).

When reporting a bug, be sure to include the following information:

- Squid version number. If the bug happens with more than one version, include the other versions as well.
- Your operating system name and version.
- Whether the bug happens every time or occasionally.
- A good description of exactly what happens. Phrases such as "it doesn't work," and "the request fails" are essentially useless to bug fixers. Be very specific.
- A stack trace in the case of an assertion, bus error, or segmentation violation.

Remember that Squid developers are generally unpaid volunteers, so be patient. Critical bugs have more priority over minor annoyances.

Exercises

- Use `tcpdump` or `ethereal` to capture some real HTTP requests. Save them to a file and replay the requests through Squid. Feel free to modify or delete some of the HTTP headers.
- Try to make Squid run out of file descriptors.
- Run **`tail -f cache.log`** and start Squid with *debug_options* set to ALL,3. If that is too overwhelming, try ALL,2.
- Force Squid to generate a *core* file by sending each of the following signals: SIGBUS, SIGSEGV, and SIGABRT. Find the *core* file and use gdb or another debugger to get a stack trace.

Config File Reference

This appendix contains descriptions and examples for every *squid.conf* directive. I present them here in the same order they appear in the default *squid.conf*. That means certain related directives are grouped together, and some recently added directives are at the end. You may want to use the book's index to locate a particular directive by name.

In the following sections, the descriptive text is followed by a table that contains the directive's syntax, a default value, an example, and related directives.

http_port

This is the port, or ports, Squid uses to listen for HTTP requests from cache clients. If your system has more than one network interface, you can use the optional hostname prefix to make Squid bind the socket to a specific IP address. The hostname must correspond to one of your interface addresses. I recommend using an IP address here, instead of a hostname, to avoid DNS lookup delays at startup.

If you run Squid as a surrogate (accelerator), you probably want to accept HTTP connections on port 80. Binding to privileged ports requires root permissions.

Syntax	http_port [hostname:]port [[hostname:]port] ...
Default	http_port 3128
Example	http_port 8080 http_port 3128 3129 3130 3131 http_port 192.168.1.1:3128
Related	*https_port, icp_port, htcp_port, snmp_port, httpd_accel_port, http_access*

https_port

This directive allows Squid to accept encrypted (SSL or TLS) connections. It is available only when you use the /configure --enable-ssl option.

The mandatory cert= argument specifies the pathname to an SSL certificate file in PEM format. This is the format commonly used by OpenSSL and other security software for portable representation of encryption keys.

The optional key= argument is the path to a private key file. If you omit this option, Squid assumes the former key file also contains a private key.

You can use the version= argument to tell Squid which protocol versions are allowed: 1=automatic, 2=SSLv2 only, 3=SSLv3 only, 4=TLSv1 only.

The cipher= argument is an optional colon-separated list of allowed ciphers. Squid simply passes this list to the SSL_CTX_set_cipher_list( ) function.

Lastly, the options= argument allows you to pass additional configuration parameters to the OpenSSL library. For example, NO_SSLv2, NO_SSLv3, and NO_TLSv1 disable the use of those particular protocols. Additional option keywords are defined in Squid's *src/ssl_support.c* file.

Syntax	https_port [*hostname:*]*port* cert=*certificate.pem* [key=*key.pem*] [version=*N*] [cipher=*list*] [options=*SSL_Options*]
Default	No default
Example	https_port 443 cert=/etc/squid-cert.pem key=/etc/squid-privkey.pem
Related	*http_port, http_access*

ssl_unclean_shutdown

This a hack borrowed from mod_ssl for Apache. Certain user-agents, notably Microsoft Internet Explorer, may not execute the SSL shutdown procedure correctly, especially when persistent connections are involved. Enabling this directive violates the SSL/TLS standard but may eliminate error messages from broken clients.

Syntax	ssl_unclean_shutdown on|off
Default	ssl_unclean_shutdown off
Example	ssl_unclean_shutdown on
Related	*https_port*

icp_port

This is the UDP port Squid uses for ICP messages. In particular, it is used both for sending and receiving queries and replies. Your Squid receives ICP queries from other caches on this port. It also receives ICP replies from other caches, in response to its own queries, on this port.

Unlike *http_port*, you can't specify a list of ICP port numbers. Furthermore, you must use the *udp_incoming_address* and *udp_outgoing_address* directives if you want to restrict ICP traffic to a specific interface address.

Setting *icp_port* to 0 disables ICP.

Syntax	icp_port *port*
Default	icp_port 3130
Example	icp_port 4130
Related	*icp_query_timeout, icp_access, log_icp_queries, icp_hit_stale, udp_incoming_address, htcp_port, http_port, cache_peer*

htcp_port

The Hypertext Caching Protocol is an alternative to ICP. It provides better security and better cache hit predictions. However, HTCP messages are larger and more complicated. HTCP must be enabled at compile-time with the --enable-htcp option.

This directive specifies the UDP port Squid uses to send and receive HTCP queries and replies. You may only specify one HTCP port number. As with ICP, the *udp_incoming_address* and *udp_outgoing_address* directives also control HTCP packets.

You may configure Squid to receive both ICP and HTCP queries at the same time. Setting *htcp_port* to 0 disables HTCP.

Syntax	htcp_port *port*
Default	htcp_port 4827
Example	htcp_port 9999
Related	*icp_port, http_port, udp_incoming_address, udp_outgoing_address, cache_peer*

mcast_groups

As discussed in Chapter 10, Squid supports receiving ICP queries via multicast. This option specifies a list of multicast addresses Squid should join to receive these ICP queries.

IP multicast is a very tricky and often fragile feature of the Internet. I strongly recommend you avoid using multicast for ICP unless you are already familiar with it. Don't try to guess appropriate values for these directives, and don't expect it to work the first time.

Syntax	mcast_groups *multicast-address* [*multicast-address*] ...
Default	No default
Example	mcast_groups 239.128.16.128
Related	*cache_peer, mcast_icp_query_timeout*

udp_incoming_address

This directive causes Squid to bind all UDP sockets to a specific interface address. The IP address must correspond to one of the system's network interfaces. This directive affects the DNS (when using the internal implementation), ICP, HTCP, and SNMP sockets.

If your system has just one IP address, you probably shouldn't use this directive.

If you set *udp_outgoing_address* to one of your other network interface addresses, Squid can receive UDP datagrams on that interface as well.

Syntax	udp_incoming_address *ip-address*
Default	udp_incoming_address 0.0.0.0
Example	udp_incoming_address 192.168.4.5
Related	*udp_outgoing_address, icp_port, htcp_port, snmp_port*

udp_outgoing_address

This directive specifies the source address for UDP messages that Squid sends. It affects DNS (when using the internal implementation), ICP, HTCP, and SNMP messages. The specified address must correspond to one of the system's network interfaces. You should use this directive only if your system has multiple IP addresses.

The default value of 255.255.255.255 causes Squid to use the incoming address for sending, as well as receiving. In other words, rather than creating a separate UDP socket for sending, Squid sends and receives messages through a single socket.

If you use this directive, it must have a different value than *udp_incoming_address*. Squid can't create two UDP sockets bound to the same IP address and port number.

Syntax	udp_outgoing_address *ip-address*
Default	udp_outgoing_address 255.255.255.255
Example	udp_outgoing_address 192.168.5.6
Related	*udp_outgoing_address, icp_port, htcp_port, snmp_port*

cache_peer

Okay, this one's long, so hang on...

This directive defines your neighbor caches and tells Squid how to communicate with them. See Chapter 10 for the lowdown on neighbor caches.

The first argument is the neighbor cache's hostname, or IP address. You can safely use hostnames here because Squid doesn't block while resolving them. In fact, Squid periodically re-resolves the hostname so that if the address changes, you won't need to restart. Neighbor hostnames must be unique; you can't have two neighbors with the same name, even if they have different ports.

The second argument specifies the type of neighbor cache. The choices are parent, sibling, or multicast. Recall from Chapter 10 that for a multicast neighbor, Squid sends ICP queries only to the neighbor's IP address, which must be a valid multicast address. Squid makes HTTP requests to parents and siblings but never to a multicast neighbor.

The third and fourth arguments are HTTP and ICP/HTCP port numbers. The HTTP port number corresponds to the neighbor cache's *http_port* (or equivalent) setting. A value of 0 for the ICP/HTCP port disables those protocols for the neighbor. If you add the htcp option (described in the subsequent paragraphs), Squid sends HTCP queries to the neighbor. Otherwise, Squid sends ICP queries. If you choose not to use ICP or HTCP, you must specify the neighbor as a parent cache.

This brings us to the options field. The *cache_peer* directive has numerous options, which can be very confusing:

proxy-only

Instructs Squid to not store any responses received from the neighbor. This is often useful when you have a cluster and don't want a resource to be stored on more than one cache.

weight=*n*

> Allows you to weight parent caches artificially when using ICP/HTCP and all parents report a cache miss. Normally Squid selects the parent whose reply arrived first. In fact, it remembers which parent has the best round-trip time for the query. Squid actually divides the RTT by the weight, so that a parent with weight=2 has lower (better) round-trip times and should be selected more often.

ttl=*n*

> An option for multicast neighbors only. It is the multicast TTL value to use for ICP queries and it controls how far away the ICP queries can travel. The valid range is 0–128. A larger value allows the multicast queries to travel farther and possibly be intercepted by outsiders. Use a lower number to keep the queries close to the source and within your network.

no-query

> Disables ICP/HTCP for the neighbor. That is, your cache won't send any queries to the neighbor for cache misses. It is often used with the default option.

default

> Specifies the neighbor as a suitable choice in the absence of other hints. Squid would prefer to forward a cache miss to a parent that is likely to have a cached copy of the particular resource. Sometimes Squid won't have any clues (e.g., if you disable ICP/HTCP with no-query). In these cases, Squid looks for a parent that has been marked as a default choice.

round-robin

> A simple load-sharing technique. It only makes sense when you mark two or more parent caches as round-robin. Squid keeps a counter for each parent. When it needs to forward a cache miss, Squid selects the parent with the lowest counter.

multicast-responder

> Tells Squid to expect ICP replies from the neighbor in response to multicast queries.

closest-only

> Refers to Squid's *netdb* features. When your neighbor has enabled the network database, it may return ICMP RTT measurements in ICP miss replies. This option instructs Squid to select a parent based on the RTT between the parent and the origin server, rather than the RTT between your cache and the parent.

no-digest

> Tells Squid not to request a Cache Digest from the neighbor. See Chapter 10.

no-netdb-exchange

> Tells Squid not to request the neighbor's *netdb* database. Note, this refers to the bulk transfer of the RTT measurements, not the inclusion of these measurements in ICP miss replies.

no-delay

> Tells Squid to ignore any delay pools settings for requests to the neighbor. See Appendix C.

login=*credentials*

> Instructs Squid to send authentication credentials to the neighbor. This option has three different formats, which I've fully described in Chapter 10.

connect-timeout=n

> Specifies how long Squid should wait when establishing a TCP connection to the neighbor. Without this option, the timeout is taken from the global *connect_timeout* directive. By using a lower timeout, Squid gives up on the neighbor quickly and tries forwarding the request elsewhere.

digest-url=url

> Specifies the URL for the neighbor's Cache Digest. Without this option, Squid assumes the digest URL is *http://neighbor.host.name:port/squid-internal-periodic/store_digest*.

allow-miss

> Instructs Squid to omit the Cache-control: only-if-cached directive for requests sent to a sibling. You should use this only if the neighbor is using the *icp_hit_stale* and isn't using a *miss_access* list.

max-conn

> Places a limit on the number of simultaneous connections that Squid can open to the neighbor. When this limit is reached, Squid excludes the neighbor from its selection algorithm.

htcp

> Tells Squid to send HTCP, instead of ICP, queries to this neighbor. If you add this option, don't forget to also change the port number. Squid uses 4827 as the default HTCP port. See Chapter 10.

carp-load-factor=f

> Tells Squid that this neighbor is a member of a CARP array. The load factor value specifies the fraction of requests that this neighbor will receive. The load factor values for all neighbors must add up to 1.0. See Chapter 10.

Syntax	cache_peer *hostname type http-port icp-port* [*options*]
Default	No default
Example	cache_peer bigcache.isp.net parent 3128 3130 cache_peer medcache.isp.net sibling 3128 4827 htcp cache_peer 172.16.45.111 parent 3128 0 no-query default
Related	*cache_peer_access, http_port, icp_port, htcp_port, icp_query_timeout, dead_peer_timeout, peer_connect_timeout, cache_peer_domain, neighbor_type_domain*

---

cache_peer_domain

This directive allows you to restrict forwarded requests by their domain names. For example, you can make sure that URIs in a certain domain never go to your parent cache. Similarly, you can make sure that requests for only a few specific domain names are sent to a neighbor. The *cache_peer_domain* directive has been largely superseded by *cache_peer_access*, which is much more flexible.

Following the neighbor's hostname, you can specify a list of domain names. These are searched in order, until Squid finds a match. A match means that the request can be sent to the neighbor, unless you prefix the domain name with ! ("not"). For example, .foo.com means "allow .foo.com," while !.bar.net means "disallow .bar.net." If none of the listed domains match the URL, the default action (allow or deny) is the opposite of the last one in the list.

Note, the domain name matching algorithm is somewhat tricky. See the description in Chapter 6.

Syntax	cache_peer_domain *hostname domain* ...
Default	No default
Example	cache_peer_domain bigcache.isp.net .net .org cache_peer_domain aol.web-cache.net !.ads.aol.com .aol.com
Related	*cache_peer, cache_peer_access, neighbor_type_domain*

---

neighbor_type_domain

You can use this directive to modify the relationship for a neighbor cache selectively. For example, you may have a sibling neighbor that allows you to fetch misses for certain, nearby domains. The *neighbor_type_domain* option overrides the type given in the *cache_peer* line for requests that match the listed domains.

The syntax and algorithms for matching domain names are identical to the *cache_peer_domain* directive.

Syntax	neighbor_type_domain parent|sibling *hostname domain* ...
Default	No default
Example	neighbor_type_domain bigcache.isp.net parent .customer.isp.net
Related	*cache_peer, cache_peer_domain*

---

icp_query_timeout

When Squid sends an ICP/HTCP query to one or more neighbors, it waits some amount of time for the replies to arrive. Because the messages are unreliable UDP datagrams, the queries and/or replies may never arrive. Squid automatically figures out how long to wait for ICP/HTCP replies. For a particular query, the timeout is twice the mean of how long it took for recent replies to arrive. In other words, Squid averages the query RTT values from previous requests, doubles it, and waits that amount of time. This algorithm works best when all your neighbors have about the same RTT, and when network conditions are consistent.

You can override this algorithm with the *icp_query_timeout* directive. Instead of dynamically calculating the timeout, Squid waits a fixed amount of time for every ICP/HTCP query.

Syntax	icp_query_timeout *milliseconds*
Default	No default
Example	icp_query_timeout 1500
Related	*icp_port, htcp_port, maximum_icp_query_timeout, mcast_icp_query_timeout, dead_peer_timeout*

maximum_icp_query_timeout

I described Squid's dynamic ICP/HTCP timeout algorithm under *icp_query_timeout*. If you'd like to use that algorithm, but wish to place an upper limit on the timeout, use the *maximum_icp_query_timeout* directive instead. Rather than a fixed timeout, Squid uses the dynamic timeout but makes sure it doesn't exceed the limit that you specify.

Syntax	maximum_icp_query_timeout *milliseconds*
Default	No default
Example	maximum_icp_query_timeout 3000
Related	*icp_port, htcp_port, icp_query_timeout*

mcast_icp_query_timeout

When you use multicast ICP, Squid doesn't know in advance how many multicast-capable neighbors are listening for its messages. Squid determines this by sending periodic probes to the multicast group and counting the number of replies. Squid uses this count when waiting for replies to real multicast queries.

The *mcast_icp_query_timeout* directive specifies how long Squid should wait when counting replies to its fake probe queries. Why not just use this timeout when sending real multicast ICP queries? The reason is that Squid might be sending queries to both multicast and unicast neighbors.

The *mcast_icp_query_timeout* directive essentially controls how long Squid waits for replies to real multicast queries. Let's say you have an ICP multicast group with 10 neighbor caches, and that it typically takes 3000 msec for all 10 replies to arrive but only takes 1000 msec to receive 5 replies. If you set *mcast_icp_query_timeout* to 1000 msec, Squid's periodic probes will count 5 neighbors. Then, for a real multicast ICP query, Squid waits for only 5 replies from multicast responders. On average, this should take only 1000 milliseconds.

Another nice feature of this algorithm is that Squid does the right thing if, for some reason, all your multicast neighbors stop responding. In that case, Squid counts zero neighbors and doesn't wait for any replies from multicast responders.

 Squid doesn't send multicast HTCP queries.

Syntax	mcast_icp_query_timeout *milliseconds*
Default	mcast_icp_query_timeout 2000
Example	mcast_icp_query_timeout 750
Related	*icp_port, icp_query_timeout*

dead_peer_timeout

This is another directive that controls the way Squid waits for ICP/HTCP replies. Squid marks each of its peers as either dead (down) or alive (up). Squid uses ICP/HTCP replies (and other techniques) to determine a peer's state. If Squid doesn't receive any replies for the time specified by *dead_peer_timeout*, the peer is declared dead.

When a peer is declared dead, Squid continues to send it ICP/HTCP queries. However, it doesn't expect to receive replies. That is, a dead peer isn't included in the algorithm that decides when all ICP replies have been received. As soon as Squid receives an ICP/HTCP reply from a dead peer, its state is changed to alive.

Squid tends to be paranoid about the state of its peers. Additionally, Squid doesn't proactively monitor the peers when there are no client requests. When Squid has no occasion to send ICP/HTCP queries, the state of the peer is unknown. If Squid doesn't send any ICP/HTCP queries for an amount of time longer than *dead_peer_timeout*, Squid treats the peer as dead.

Syntax	dead_peer_timeout *time-specification*
Default	dead_peer_timeout 10 seconds
Example	dead_peer_timeout 30 seconds
Related	*icp_port, htcp_port, icp_query_timeout*

hierarchy_stoplist

Every HTTP request that Squid receives is marked as either hierarchical or nonhierarchical. This terminology is somewhat confusing. A request is hierarchical when there is a possibility it could be a cache hit in one of the neighbors. In other words, if the information in the request indicates that the response may be cachable, the request is hierarchical. A request is marked nonhierarchical when Squid thinks there is no chance of getting a hit from a neighbor.

Squid uses the hierarchical flag to decide whether or not it should query neighbors for the request. If the request is hierarchical, Squid may perform ICP/HTCP queries, or use Cache Digests, to locate cache hits in neighbors. Otherwise, Squid may forward the request directly to the origin server or select a parent based on some other technique.

Squid has a few hardcoded rules that determine if a request is hierarchical. For example, only GET requests are hierarchical. Squid never expects cache hits on non-GET requests. Another rule is that requests including authentication information are nonhierarchical. The *hierarchy_stoplist* directive allows you to customize the algorithm further. The stoplist is simply a list of strings. Squid searches the requested URL for these strings. The string comparison is case-sensitive. In the case of a match, the request becomes nonhierarchical. The default configuration is to search for cgi-bin and ? so that queries and other CGI responses aren't hierarchical.

Note that the hierarchical flag determines only whether or not Squid queries its neighbor caches. It doesn't determine which requests must, or must not, be sent to parent caches. The *always_direct* and *never_direct* access lists have that responsibility.

no_cache

Syntax	`hierarchy_stoplist string ...`
Default	`hierarchy_stoplist cgi-bin ?`
Example	`hierarchy_stoplist .cgi` `hierarchy_stoplist http://www.mysite.org`
Related	*always_direct, never_direct*

no_cache

no_cache is a sequence of access control rules (see Chapter 6) that specify responses that must not be cached by Squid. Of course, Squid has some hardcoded rules for responses that must not be cached according to the HTTP RFC. The *no_cache* rules are in addition to those.

The *no_cache* syntax is a little tricky. You must use deny for rules where the response must not be cached. Consider this example:

```
acl GoodStuff url_regex /foo/bar/
acl BadStuff url_regex /bar/
no_cache allow GoodStuff
no_cache deny BadStuff
```

Here, a URL containing /foo/bar/ may be cached, but any other URL containing only /bar/ isn't cached. The meaning of the allow and deny might be the opposite of what you expect. Just remember that deny carries the same negative connotation as "not caching" something.

Syntax	`no_cache allow|deny [!]ACLname ...`
Default	No default
Example	`acl LocalServers dst 192.168.8.0/24` `no_cache deny LocalServers`
Related	*always_direct, never_direct, http_access*

cache_access_log

This is the location of Squid's *access.log*, which contains one entry for each client request. See Chapter 13 for the details. If you want to disable the access log, set this to */dev/null*.

Syntax	`cache_access_log pathname`
Default	`cache_access_log $prefix/var/logs/access.log`
Example	`cache_access_log /var/log/squid-access.log`
Related	*emulate_httpd_log, cache_log, cache_store_log, log_ip_on_direct, logfile_rotate*

cache_log

This log file contains various operational and debugging messages from Squid. See Chapter 13 for more information. If you want to disable *cache.log*, set this directive to */dev/null*.

Syntax	cache_log *pathname*
Default	cache_log *$prefix*/var/logs/cache.log
Example	cache_log /var/log/squid.log
Related	*debug_options, cache_access_log, cache_store_log, logfile_rotate*

cache_store_log

The *store.log* contains details about Squid's interaction with the disk cache. You'll see entries as objects are stored to disk, read from disk, and removed from the cache. See Chapter 13 for the details. You can disable this log by setting it to *none*.

Syntax	cache_store_log *pathname*
Default	cache_store_log *$prefix*/var/logs/store.log
Example	cache_store_log /var/log/squid-store.log
Related	*cache_access_log, cache_log, logfile_rotate*

cache_swap_log

Each cache directory has its own swap log file. These are binary-format journal files Squid uses to rebuild the in-memory indexes when in starts up. Each swap log file is located in the corresponding cache directory by default. If you use this option, Squid puts all swap log files in one directory. See Chapter 13 for more information.

Syntax	cache_swap_log *pathname*
Default	swap.state in each *cache_dir*
Example	cache_swap_log /var/log/squid-swap-state
Related	*cache_store_log, logfile_rotate, cache_dir*

emulate_httpd_log

Squid uses its own native format for the *access.log* by default. If you enable this directive, the access log is written in the HTTPD common log file format. Often useful when Squid is accelerating an origin server site.

Syntax	emulate_httpd_log on|off
Default	emulate_httpd_log off
Example	emulate_httpd_log on
Related	*cache_access_log, httpd_accel_host*

log_ip_on_direct

By default, Squid puts origin server IP addresses into the ninth field of the *access.log*. If you enable this directive, Squid puts the origin server hostname there instead.

cache_dir

Syntax	log_ip_on_direct on|off
Default	log_ip_on_direct on
Example	log_ip_on_direct off
Related	*cache_access_log*

cache_dir

This directive instructs Squid where, and how, to store cached objects on disk. See Chapter 7 for the details on cache directories.

The second parameter selects the storage scheme. Your choices are ufs, aufs, diskd, coss, and null. To use any scheme other than ufs, you must use the --enable-storeio option with ./configure. See Chapter 3.

The third parameter is the amount of disk space to use for the cache. The units are in megabytes.

The fourth and fifth parameters are the number of L1 and L2 directories. Don't change these values for directories that already contain cached objects.

Some *cache_dir* schemes have additional, optional parameters. Refer to the scheme-specific sections in Chapter 8.

Syntax	cache_dir *scheme directory size-MB L1 L2* [*options...*]
Default	cache_dir ufs *$prefix*/var/cache 100 16 256
Example	cache_dir ufs /cache0 3072 16 128
Related	*cache_replacement_policy, cache_mem*

cache_mem

Squid uses memory to store recently received objects and to buffer active responses. This directive specifies the amount of memory to use for storing these objects.

 This directive doesn't entirely control the size of the Squid process. See Appendix B for additional information.

Syntax	cache_mem *bytes-specification*
Default	cache_mem 8 MB
Example	cache_mem 16 MB
Related	*cache_dir, maximum_object_size_in_memory, memory_replacement_policy*

cache_swap_low

This directive, along with *cache_swap_high* controls the replacement of objects stored on disk. It is a percentage of the maximum cache size, which comes from the sum of all *cache_dir* sizes. See Chapter 7 for additional information.

Syntax	cache_swap_low *percent*
Default	cache_swap_low 90
Example	cache_swap_low 85
Related	*cache_swap_high, cache_dir*

cache_swap_high

See the description for *cache_swap_low*. Note that changing *cache_swap_high* probably won't have a big impact on Squid's disk usage. See Chapter 7 for additional information.

Syntax	cache_swap_high *percent*
Default	cache_swap_high 95
Example	cache_swap_high 99
Related	*cache_swap_low, cache_dir*

maximum_object_size

This directive places a limit on the largest object that Squid can store on disk. Responses larger than this size aren't cached. See Chapter 7 for additional information.

Syntax	maximum_object_size *bytes-specification*
Default	maximum_object_size 4096 MB
Example	maximum_object_size 250 MB
Related	*minimum_object_size, maximum_object_size_in_memory, reply_body_max_size*

minimum_object_size

With this directive, you can also place lower limits on the size of cached objects. Responses smaller than this size aren't stored on disk or in memory. See Chapter 7 for additional information.

Syntax	minimum_object_size *bytes-specification*
Default	minimum_object_size 0 bytes
Example	minimum_object_size 300 bytes
Related	*maximum_object_size*

maximum_object_size_in_memory

This directive allows you to control the size of objects stored in memory. Objects that are larger than this value aren't kept in memory. See Chapter 7 for additional information.

Syntax	maximum_object_size_in_memory *bytes-specification*
Default	maximum_object_size_in_memory 8 KB
Example	maximum_object_size_in_memory 12 KB
Related	*cache_mem, maximum_object_size*

cache_replacement_policy

This directive controls the replacement policy for Squid's disk cache. Version 2.5 offers three different replacement policies: least recently used (LRU), greedy dual-size frequency (GDSF), and least frequently used with dynamic aging (LFUDA). Note that the keywords (lru, GDSF, etc.) are case-sensitive! See Chapter 7 for additional information.

Syntax   cache_replacement_policy lru
                cache_replacement_policy heap GDSF|LFUDA|LRU
Default   cache_replacement_policy lru
Example   cache_replacement_policy heap GDSF
Related   *memory_replacement_policy, cache_dir*

memory_replacement_policy

This directive controls the replacement policy for objects cached in memory. See Chapter 7 for additional information.

Syntax   memory_replacement_policy lru
                memory_replacement_policy heap GDSF|LFUDA|LRU
Default   memory_replacement_policy lru
Example   memory_replacement_policy heap LFUDA
Related   *cache_replacement_policy, cache_mem*

store_dir_select_algorithm

This directive controls the algorithm Squid uses when selecting a *cache_dir* for a new cache file. The possible choices are: least-load and round-robin. See Chapter 7 for additional information.

Syntax   store_dir_select_algorithm round-robin|least-load
Default   store_dir_select_algorithm least-load
Example   store_dir_select_algorithm round-robin
Related   *cache_dir*

mime_table

Squid uses the information in this file for FTP and Gopher requests. Unlike HTTP, these protocols don't inform clients about the type of data they transfer. When Squid gateways the response from an FTP server to an HTTP client, it must insert Content-Type and other headers. Squid uses the MIME table file to convert filename extensions into:

- Values for the Content-Type header
- Icons that are displayed for directory listings

- Content-Encoding header values for compressed data
- Transfer type options for FTP servers, either *image* or *ascii*; this corresponds to the TYPE command in the FTP protocol

Please refer to the sample *mime.conf* for an explanation of the format of this file.

Syntax	mime_table *pathname*
Default	mime_table *$prefix*/etc/mime.conf
Example	mime_table /usr/local/squid/etc/my-mime-types.txt

ipcache_size

Squid's IP cache holds recent DNS name-to-address lookups. This directive limits the number of names in the cache. Each IP cache entry uses a relatively small amount of memory, so you can safely increase this limit to 10,000 or more.

Syntax	ipcache_size *count*
Default	ipcache_size 1024
Example	ipcache_size 5000
Related	*ipcache_low, ipcache_high, fqdncache_size*

ipcache_low

This directive controls the IP cache LRU replacement algorithm. The replacement function runs periodically and removes the least recently used IP cache entries until reaching this low watermark. You should have almost no reason to change this value. You'd be better off changing *ipcache_size* instead.

Syntax	ipcache_low *percent*
Default	ipcache_low 90
Example	ipcache_low 95
Related	*ipcache_size, ipcache_high*

ipcache_high

This directive is essentially unused in current versions of Squid. The LRU replacement routine uses only *ipcache_low*. The only time that Squid uses *ipcache_high* is when calculating the hash table size for the IP cache at startup.

Syntax	ipcache_high *percent*
Default	ipcache_high 95
Example	ipcache_high 99
Related	*ipcache_size, ipcache_low*

fqdncache_size

Squid's FQDN cache holds recent DNS address-to-name lookups. However, Squid makes these reverse DNS lookups only when you enable the *log_fqdn* directive or use a *dstdomain* ACL. This directive limits the number of names in the cache. Each FQDN cache entry uses a relatively small amount of memory, so you can safely increase this limit to 10,000 or more.

Syntax	fqdncache_size *count*
Default	fqdncache_size 1024
Example	fqdncache_size 6000
Related	*ipcache_size, log_fqdn*

log_mime_hdrs

When you enable this directive, Squid writes the HTTP request and response headers to the *access.log* file. The headers appear as two additional fields on each line. All whitespace and other special characters are encoded with URL-style escape codes. Enabling this option may assist in tracking down certain problems. Note that HTTP headers are relatively large (a few hundred bytes each). Logging them dramatically increases the size of your *access.log* file.

Syntax	log_mime_hdrs on|off
Default	log_mime_hdrs off
Example	log_mime_hdrs on
Related	*cache_access_log*

useragent_log

This directive causes Squid to create a log file of User-Agent strings. The file contains three fields: client identifier, timestamp, and user-agent string. The client identifier is an IP address, unless you enable the *log_fqdn* directive, in which case it is a hostname if one is available. Squid writes an entry for every HTTP request that has a User-Agent header. Unlike *access.log*, entries are written to this file when the request is received.

Syntax	useragent_log *pathname*
Default	No default
Example	useragent_log /usr/local/squid/var/logs/useragent.log
Related	*log_fqdn, cache_access_log, referer_log*

referer_log

This directive causes Squid to create a log file of Referer values from client requests. The file contains four fields: time, client identifier, Referer value, and the URI request. For example, when a client requests the image *foo.png* embedded in an *index.html*, the referer log contains:

```
1068047502.377 192.168.1.2 /index.html /foo.png
```

Squid writes an entry for every HTTP request that has a Referer header. Unlike *access.log*, entries are written to this file when the request is received.

Syntax	`referer_log` *pathname*
Default	No default
Example	`referer_log /usr/local/squid/var/logs/referer.log`
Related	*log_fqdn, cache_access_log, useragent_log*

pid_filename

This is the file in which Squid writes its process ID (PID) number. Squid uses the PID file in a couple of ways. First, it looks for and reads this file when starting. If the file exists and contains a valid PID, Squid reports it is already running under that PID so that you don't accidentally start Squid twice. The PID file is also read when you use one of the -k commands such as `squid -k rotate`.

You probably don't need to worry about this directive unless you actually do want to run two (or more) Squid processes on the same machine. Each instance of Squid requires a unique PID filename.

Syntax	`pid_filename` *pathname*
Default	`pid_filename` *$prefix*`/var/logs/squid.pid`
Example	`pid_filename /var/run/squid.pid`

debug_options

This directive controls the amount of debugging information written to *cache.log*. Each source code module has a section number. Individual debugging statements in the code have a level. Higher debugging levels correspond to more verbose debugging. For a list of section numbers, refer to Chapter 16 or the *doc/debug-sections.txt* file in the source distribution.

Syntax	`debug_options` *section,level* ...
Default	`debug_options ALL,1`
Example	`debug_options ALL,1 42,5`
Related	*cache_log*

log_fqdn

This directive controls whether or not Squid places client IP addresses or hostnames in the log files. By default Squid writes the IP address. If you enable this feature, Squid queries the DNS for client hostnames or fully qualified domain names (FQDN). These address-to-name lookups sometimes take a long time. Squid never postpones logging to wait for an answer. If the FQDN isn't available when Squid is ready to write the log entry, it uses the IP address.

Syntax	`log_fqdn on|off`
Default	`log_fqdn off`
Example	`log_fqdn on`
Related	*cache_access_log, useragent_log, referer_log, fqdncache_size, client_netmask*

client_netmask

This directive is available to provide privacy for users. When Squid writes *access.log* and other log files, it applies this mask to the client's IP address. For example, if you set the netmask to 255.255.255.0, Squid logs a request from 1.2.3.0 instead of 1.2.3.4. Thus, if someone manages to read the log file, they know only approximately, not exactly, which host (or user) made each request.

If you use *log_fqdn*, Squid applies the *client_netmask* before issuing the DNS lookup. For example, Squid will try to find a hostname record for 1.2.3.0 instead of 1.2.3.4.

Syntax	`client_netmask IPv4-netmask`
Default	`client_netmask 255.255.255.255`
Example	`client_netmask 255.255.255.0`
Related	*cache_access_log, useragent_log, referer_log, log_fqdn*

ftp_user

This directive contains the password Squid sends when logging in to anonymous FTP servers. Convention dictates that anonymous FTP clients send the user's email address as the login password. Most anonymous FTP servers accept an abbreviated form with only a username followed by @ (e.g., joe_blow@). You probably won't need to change this directive unless you encounter a very picky FTP server.

Syntax	`ftp_user email-address`
Default	`ftp_user Squid@`
Example	`ftp_user joe_blow@company.com`
Related	*ftp_list_width, ftp_passive*

ftp_list_width

This directive controls the width of the filename column in FTP directory listings that Squid generates. The default value is chosen so that the listings fit inside a typical browser window. This also means that long filenames may be truncated. If you'd like to see more characters in long filenames, increase this value.

Syntax	`ftp_list_width character-count`
Default	`ftp_list_width 32`

Example	ftp_list_width 64
Related	*ftp_user*

ftp_passive

Squid normally uses FTP's so-called passive mode for file transfers. This means that the FTP server creates a TCP socket for data transfer and waits for the client to connect. Passive mode works much better through most Internet firewalls. The alternative is to have the FTP client (Squid in this case) create a TCP socket and wait for a connection from the server. Most likely, you'll never have problems with FTP passive mode. However, you can force nonpassive operation by turning off this directive.

Syntax	ftp_passive on|off
Default	ftp_passive on
Example	ftp_passive off
Related	*ftp_user, ftp_list_width, ftp_sanitycheck*

ftp_sanitycheck

When using FTP passive mode (the default), the FTP server tells Squid the IP address and port number for each data connection. Squid normally checks the given values to make sure they match the server's IP address. In other words, an FTP server should always use its own IP address in the PASV reply message. If it doesn't, Squid complains to *cache.log* and attempts a data connection with the PORT command. Disable the *ftp_sanitycheck* directive if you want Squid to skip the IP address sanity check.

Syntax	ftp_sanitycheck on|off
Default	ftp_sanitycheck on
Example	ftp_sanitycheck off
Related	*ftp_passive*

cache_dns_program

Recall that, by default, Squid uses an internal DNS client implementation. However, you also have the choice of using an external helper program to perform DNS lookups. This choice must be made when you run ./configure, with the --disable-internal-dns option.

If you elect to use the external DNS, this directive specifies the pathname to the dnsserver program. This is a misleading name in that the program isn't really a DNS server. It is more like a DNS proxy. The program reads hostnames (or IP addresses) from Squid, executes the necessary lookup, and writes IP addresses (or hostnames) back.

You probably won't need to use this directive, unless you move the Squid binaries after running make install or you're inclined to experiment with the external DNS program.

Syntax	cache_dns_program *pathname*
Default	cache_dns_program *$prefix*/libexec/dnsserver

Example	`cache_dns_program /usr/local/squid/libexec/better_dnsserver`
Related	*dns_children*

dns_children

This directive is meaningful only with the `--disable-internal-dns` option.

The interface between Squid and the external DNS program is built around the `gethostbyname( )` function. Squid writes a request to a `dnsserver` process, which performs the query. The `gethostbyname( )` call blocks the process until the reply arrives. This is why Squid can't use the function internally.

Each `dnsserver` handles only one request at a time, so you need enough of them to handle the load from your cache. Unfortunately, you may need to experiment with different values to discover the appropriate setting for your particular situation. In theory, you can calculate the number of child processes if you know the rate of DNS lookups and how long lookups take on average. Unfortunately, both values can vary significantly over time.

Squid writes a warning into *cache.log* if you have too few `dnsserver` child processes. If all helper processes are busy, Squid queues up new lookups. If the queue grows too large, Squid emits an error message and exits. Thus, too many child processes are better than too few.

You can use the *dns* entry in the cache manager menu to see `dnsserver` utilization information. Requests are always sent to the first idle process, so you can see if some processes never receive any DNS lookup requests. In that case you may want to lower the *dns_children* value.

Why doesn't Squid just create and destroy child processes as necessary? The primary reason is that the creation of a child process, via `fork( )`, is a relatively "heavy" operation. It may introduce significant delays for active HTTP requests. A Squid process typically consumes a lot of memory. In some cases, `fork( )` may fail due to lack of available memory or swap space. Rather than try to fix all these issues with the external DNS implementation, Squid can read and write DNS messages internally.

Syntax	`dns_children number`
Default	`dns_children 5`
Example	`dns_children 16`
Related	*cache_dns_program*

dns_retransmit_interval

This directive is meaningful only when you use the internal DNS implementation (the default).

This directive is the initial retransmission interval for unacknowledged DNS queries. Each time Squid retransmits a DNS query, it's sent to the next DNS server in the list. If none of the servers answer, Squid starts at the top of the list again and doubles the retransmit interval.

Syntax	dns_retransmit_interval *time-specification*
Default	dns_retransmit_interval 5 seconds
Example	dns_retransmit_interval 10 seconds
Related	*dns_timeout*

dns_timeout

This directive is meaningful only when you use the internal DNS implementation (the default).

This directive is the total amount of time that Squid waits for a DNS answer. If the timeout occurs, Squid returns an error message to the user.

Syntax	dns_timeout *time-specification*
Default	dns_timeout 5 minutes
Example	dns_timeout 2 minutes
Related	*dns_retransmit_interval*

dns_defnames

This directive is meaningful only with the --disable-internal-dns option.

By default, Squid's dnsserver program doesn't attempt to expand single-word hostnames (such as *www*) into fully qualified domain names. If your users are accustomed to using single-word hostnames, you may want to enable this directive.

Syntax	dns_defnames on|off
Default	dns_defnames off
Example	dns_defnames on
Related	*append_domain*

dns_nameservers

By default, Squid sends DNS queries to the name servers listed in the */etc/resolv.conf* file. If you want Squid to use a different set of name servers, you can specify them with this directive. Of course, you can also just change your *resolv.conf* file.

Syntax	dns_nameservers *ip-address* ...
Default	No default
Example	dns_nameservers 127.0.0.1 192.168.0.1

hosts_file

When you use the internal DNS implementation (the default), Squid always uses the DNS name servers to resolve names and addresses. The external dnsserver program, on the other hand, may check a local database—the *hosts file*—before querying the DNS. With this directive, you can make Squid preload the contents of a *hosts* file into its IP and FQDN caches.

Squid rereads the *hosts* file when you send it the reconfigure signal (squid -k reconfigure).

If you configure the *append_domain* directive, it's appended to any single-component names in the *hosts* file.

Syntax	hosts_file *pathname*
Default	No default
Example	hosts_file /usr/local/squid/etc/hosts
Related	*dns_defnames, append_domain*

diskd_program

This is the pathname to the diskd helper program. It gets executed for each *cache_dir* of type *diskd*.

Syntax	diskd_program *pathname*
Default	diskd_program *$prefix*/libexec/diskd
Example	diskd_program /usr/local/squid-2.4/libexec/squid/diskd
Related	*cache_dir*

unlinkd_program

This is the pathname to the unlinkd program. By executing the unlink operations in this external process, Squid's performance improves significantly. You can disable the external unlinker with the --disable-unlinkd option to ./configure.

Syntax	unlinkd_program *pathname*
Default	unlinkd_program *$prefix*/libexec/unlinkd
Example	unlinkd_program /usr/local/squid-2.4/libexec/unlinkd

pinger_program

Squid uses the pinger program to send ICMP pings to origin server sites. Squid uses these ICMP measurements to estimate network proximity. Note that the pinger program must be installed as setuid root because it opens a raw ICMP socket. To enable the ICMP measurement features, use the ./configure --enable-icmp option.

Syntax	pinger_program *pathname*
Default	pinger_program *$prefix*/libexec/pinger
Example	pinger_program /usr/local/squid-2.4/libexec/pinger
Related	*netdb_low, netdb_high, netdb_ping_period*

redirect_program

This directive specifies the pathname of a redirector program. It must be executable by the Squid user ID. See Chapter 11.

Syntax   `redirect_program pathname`
Default   No default
Example   `redirect_program /usr/local/squid/libexec/my_redirector`
Related   *redirect_children, redirect_rewrites_host_header, redirector_access, redirector_bypass*

redirect_children

This directive specifies how many redirector processes Squid should start. Client requests are written to the first idle redirector process. Squid warns you (via *cache.log*) when all processes are simultaneously busy. If you see this warning, you should increase the number of child processes and restart Squid.

Syntax   `redirect_children number`
Default   `redirect_children 5`
Example   `redirect_children 20`
Related   *redirect_program, sleep_after_fork, redirector_bypass*

redirect_rewrites_host_header

Squid normally updates a request's Host header when using a redirector. If you use Squid as a surrogate (HTTP accelerator), you might want to disable this behavior by setting this directive to off.

Syntax   `redirect_rewrites_host_header on|off`
Default   `redirect_rewrites_host_header on`
Example   `redirect_rewrites_host_header off`
Related   *httpd_accel_single_host*

redirector_access

If you use this directive, only the requests that match the access list rules are sent to the redirector processes. Without any *redirector_access* rules, all requests are sent to the redirector processes.

Syntax   `redirector_access allow|deny [!]ACLname ...`
Default   No default
Example
```
acl Foo src 192.168.1.0/24
acl All src 0/0
redirector_access deny Foo
redirector_access allow All
```
Related   *acl, http_access*

redirector_bypass

Squid uses a pool of redirectors to service client requests. This directive determines Squid's behavior when all redirectors in the pool are busy. Normally, Squid queues subsequent requests, waiting for one of the redirectors to become free. If the queue becomes too large, Squid exits with a fatal message. If you enable this directive, however, Squid simply skips the redirection step if all redirectors are busy.

Syntax	`redirector_bypass on|off`
Default	`redirector_bypass off`
Example	`redirector_bypass on`
Related	*redirect_program, redirector_access*

auth_param

The *auth_param* directive controls almost every aspect of Squid's external user authentication interface. Squid currently supports three authentication schemes: Basic, Digest, and NTLM. Basic authentication support is compiled by default. For the others, you must use the --enable-auth option with ./configure.

Since the *auth_param* directive is very complex, I'm presenting it here as a separate directive for each combination of parameters.

Syntax	See the following subsections
Default	See the following subsections
Example	See the following subsections
Related	*authenticate_cache_garbage_interval, authenticate_ttl, authenticate_ip_ttl*

auth_param basic program

The command for the HTTP Basic authentication helper. You need to specify the full pathname to the program, plus any command-line options.

Syntax	`auth_param basic program command ...`
Default	No default
Example	`auth_param basic program /usr/local/squid/libexec/ncsa_auth /usr/local/squid/etc/ncsa_passwd`
Related	*auth_param basic children, auth_param basic realm, auth_param basic credentialsttl*

auth_param basic children

This is the number of Basic authentication helper processes Squid uses.

Syntax	`auth_param basic children count`
Default	`auth_param basic children 5`
Example	`auth_param basic children 10`
Related	*auth_param basic program, auth_param basic realm, auth_param basic credentialsttl*

auth_param basic realm

This is the Basic authentication realm Squid sends in 407 (Proxy Authentication Required) responses. User agents typically display the realm string to the user when requesting a user-name and password. Refer to RFC 2617, Section 2.

Syntax	auth_param basic realm *string*
Default	No default
Example	auth_param basic realm Squid proxy-caching web server
Related	*auth_param basic program, auth_param basic children, auth_param basic credentialsttl*

auth_param basic credentialsttl

To reduce load on the external authentication processes, Squid caches successful answers for this amount of time. In other words, once a user is authenticated, Squid doesn't query the helper program again until this TTL expires. If you change the external database (e.g., password file), Squid may not notice the change until the cached credentials time out.

Syntax	auth_param basic credentialsttl *time-specification*
Default	auth_param basic credentialsttl 5 minutes
Example	auth_param basic credentialsttl 15 minutes
Related	*auth_param basic program, auth_param basic children, auth_param basic realm*

auth_param digest program

As with Basic authentication, this specifies the command to execute for the external Digest authentication program.

Syntax	auth_param digest program *command* ...
Default	No default
Example	auth_param digest program /usr/local/squid/libexec/digest_auth /usr/local/squid/etc/digest_passwd
Related	*auth_param digest children, auth_param digest realm, auth_param digest nonce_garbage_interval, auth_param digest nonce_max_duration, auth_param digest nonce_max_count*

auth_param digest children

This is the number of Digest authentication helper processes that Squid uses.

Syntax	auth_param digest children *count*
Default	auth_param digest children 5
Example	auth_param digest children 11
Related	*auth_param digest program, auth_param digest realm, auth_param digest nonce_garbage_interval, auth_param digest nonce_max_duration, auth_param digest nonce_max_count*

auth_param digest realm

This is the Digest authentication realm that Squid sends in 407 (Proxy Authentication Required) responses. User agents typically display the realm string to the user when requesting a username and password. Refer to RFC 2617, Section 3.2.1.

auth_param

Syntax	`auth_param digest realm string`
Default	No default
Example	`auth_param digest realm Squid proxy-caching web server`
Related	*auth_param digest program, auth_param digest children, auth_param digest nonce_garbage_interval, auth_param digest nonce_max_duration, auth_param digest nonce_max_count*

auth_param digest nonce_garbage_interval

As I explained in Chapter 12, a nonce is a special string of data that changes from time to time. Its purpose is to prevent replay attacks with captured digest authentication data.

Squid maintains a cache of nonce values it has sent to clients requiring authentication. This cache must be pruned occasionally because nonce strings expire. This directive specifies how often Squid executes the garbage collection procedure for the nonce cache.

If Squid is very busy, you may want to clean the nonce cache more frequently to reduce the amount of time spent in the garbage collection function each time it runs.

Syntax	`auth_param digest nonce_garbage_interval time-specification`
Default	`auth_param digest nonce_garbage_interval 5 minutes`
Example	`auth_param digest nonce_garbage_interval 5 minutes`
Related	*auth_param digest program, auth_param digest children, auth_param digest realm, auth_param digest nonce_max_duration, auth_param digest nonce_max_count*

auth_param digest nonce_max_duration

This directive specifies how long a Digest nonce value remains valid. It is similar to the *credentialsttl* directive for Basic authentication.

If an attacker captures the client's digest authentication headers from an HTTP request, a simple replay attack provides authenticated access to Squid until the nonce value times out or until the maximum usage count is reached. Decrease this value to reduce that risk.

Syntax	`auth_param digest nonce_max_duration time-specification`
Default	`auth_param digest nonce_max_duration 5 minutes`
Example	`auth_param digest nonce_max_duration 30 minutes`
Related	*auth_param digest program, auth_param digest children, auth_param digest realm, auth_param digest nonce_garbage_interval, auth_param digest nonce_max_count, auth_param basic credentialsttl*

auth_param digest nonce_max_count

This directive specifies a limit on the number of requests for a Digest nonce value. If a client issues this many requests with the same nonce value, Squid invalidates it and causes a new one to be generated. See Section 4.3 of RFC 2617.

Syntax	`auth_param digest nonce_max_count count`
Default	`auth_param digest nonce_max_count 50`
Example	`auth_param digest nonce_max_count 50`
Related	*auth_param digest program, auth_param digest children, auth_param digest realm, auth_param digest nonce_garbage_interval, auth_param digest nonce_max_duration*

auth_param ntlm program

This directive specifies the command, including options, to execute for the external NTLM authentication program.

Syntax	`auth_param ntlm program` *`command`*
Default	No default
Example	`auth_param ntlm program /usr/local/squid/libexec/ntlm_auth /usr/local/` `squid/etc/ntlm_db`
Related	*auth_param ntlm children, auth_param ntlm max_challenge_reuses, auth_param ntlm max_challenge_lifetime*

auth_param ntlm children

Specifies the number of NTLM authentication helper process that Squid uses.

Syntax	`auth_param ntlm children` *`count`*
Default	`auth_param ntlm children 5`
Example	`auth_param ntlm children 14`
Related	*auth_param ntlm program, auth_param ntlm max_challenge_reuses, auth_param ntlm max_challenge_lifetime*

auth_param ntlm max_challenge_reuses

In Squid's NTLM implementation, the NTLM challenge token comes from the external helper process, rather than Squid itself. Each helper process generates its own challenge token. This directive specifies how many times each token may be reused. By default, the tokens are never reused. Challenge reuse is also subject to the *max_challenge_lifetime* restriction.

Syntax	`auth_param ntlm max_challenge_reuses` *`count`*
Default	`auth_param ntlm max_challenge_reuses 0`
Example	`auth_param ntlm max_challenge_reuses 5`
Related	*auth_param ntlm program, auth_param ntlm children, auth_param ntlm max_challenge_lifetime*

auth_param ntlm max_challenge_lifetime

This directive also controls whether the external NTML helper processes can reuse their challenge tokens. It specifies the maximum amount of time a single challenge can be used.

Syntax	`auth_param ntlm max_challenge_lifetime` *`time-specification`*
Default	`auth_param ntlm max_challenge_lifetime 1 minute`
Example	`auth_param ntlm max_challenge_lifetime 2 minutes`
Related	*auth_param ntlm program, auth_param ntlm children, auth_param ntlm max_challenge_reuses*

authenticate_ttl

Squid maintains a cache of proxy authentication usernames and credentials. Squid periodically removes unused entries to keep memory usage down. This directive specifies how long Squid keeps entries in the proxy authentication username cache. A user's TTL is extended each time Squid receives a request from that user.

 This directive doesn't determine how long credentials remain valid. It only affects whether or not an entry is removed from the username cache. Squid may decide to revalidate the credentials of a user that is in the cache. Each authentication scheme has its own way of determining when to revalidate credentials with the external helper.

Syntax	authenticate_ttl *time-specification*
Default	authenticate_ttl 1 hour
Example	authenticate_ttl 30 minutes
Related	*authenticate_cache_garbage_interval, auth_param*

authenticate_cache_garbage_interval

This directive specifies how often Squid executes the function to clean up the proxy authentication username cache. During this process, usernames that have been inactive for some amount of time (defined by *authenticate_ttl*) are purged.

Syntax	authenticate_cache_garbage_interval *time-specification*
Default	authenticate_cache_garbage_interval 1 hour
Example	authenticate_cache_garbage_interval 8 hours
Related	*authenticate_ttl, auth_param*

authenticate_ip_ttl

This directive causes Squid to deny requests if the same proxy authentication username comes from more than one IP address within a given amount of time. It's designed to discourage users from sharing their username and password with others. When Squid detects the same username from multiple IP addresses, it forces the user to reauthenticate by denying the request.

This feature is disabled by default (0 seconds). If your users normally have the same IP address (e.g., static addressing or DHCP with long leases), you can set *authenticate_ip_ttl* to a large value such as 1 hour. However, if your users are on dial-up connections, they may be more likely to change IP addresses within a short period of time. To make their lives easier, use a small *authenticate_ip_ttl* value, such as 1 minute.

Syntax	authenticate_ip_ttl *time-specification*
Default	authenticate_ip_ttl 0 seconds
Example	authenticate_ip_ttl 1 minute
Related	*auth_param*

external_acl_type

This directive defines new ACL types implemented as external programs. See Chapter 6.

Syntax	external_acl_type *type-name* [*options*] *format helper-command*
Default	No default
Example	external_acl_type MyAcltype %LOGIN /usr/local/squid/libexec/my-acl-prog.pl
Related	*acl, http_access*

wais_relay_host

The Wide Area Information Service (WAIS) is an obsolete protocol that predates the Web. This directive is largely historical. Its purpose is to make Squid forward all WAIS requests to another proxy, perhaps a dedicated WAIS gateway. You can accomplish the same effect with ACLs and *cache_peer_access*.

Syntax	wais_relay_host *hostname*
Default	No default
Example	wais_relay_host some.host.name
Related	*wais_relay_port*

wais_relay_port

If, for some reason, you use *wais_relay_host*, you must set the WAIS relay port number with this directive. Arguably you should be able to specify both with a single directive. However, they were split some time ago to simplify Squid's parsing code.

Syntax	wais_relay_port *port-number*
Default	No default
Example	wais_relay_port 8001
Related	*wais_relay_host*

request_header_max_size

This directive places an upper limit on the size of headers in an HTTP request. When Squid receives an HTTP request with headers that exceed this value, it returns a 413 (Request Entity Too Large) error response. In most cases, request headers are smaller than 512 bytes. This directive exists to catch certain abnormal conditions, such as persistent connection bugs, buffer overflow attempts, and denial-of-service attacks.

Syntax	request_header_max_size *size-specification*
Default	request_header_max_size 10 KB
Example	request_header_max_size 35 KB
Related	*request_body_max_size, reply_body_max_size*

request_body_max_size

This directive, if nonzero, places an upper limit on the size of a client's HTTP request body. Most requests (i.e., GET requests) don't have request bodies. This directive applies to PUT and POST requests. A request that exceeds this limit generates a 413 (Request Entity Too Large) error response.

Syntax	request_body_max_size *size-specification*
Default	No limit
Example	request_body_max_size 100 KB
Related	*request_header_max_size, reply_body_max_size*

refresh_pattern

This directive provides a way to customize Squid's algorithm for validating cached responses. HTTP has a relatively complex procedure for determining whether or not a cached response is fresh or stale. In some cases, origin servers provide an explicit expiration time. However, the majority of responses don't have this information. For these, Squid applies some heuristics to the response. See Chapter 7 for more information.

Syntax	refresh_pattern *regex mintime percent maxtime* [options]
Default	refresh_pattern . 0 20% 4320
Example	refresh_pattern \.jpg$ 0 75 7200

quick_abort_min

This directive controls Squid's behavior for requests aborted by the user. In some cases, Squid continues reading data from the origin server so that future requests may be satisfied as cache hits. If Squid knows that the transfer (between itself and the origin server) has no more than this many bytes remaining, it continues receiving the object. Otherwise, Squid checks the *quick_abort_max* setting next.

Syntax	quick_abort_min *size-specification*
Default	quick_abort_min 16 KB
Example	quick_abort_min 50 KB
Related	*quick_abort_max, quick_abort_pct*

quick_abort_max

After checking *quick_abort_min*, Squid checks the value of this directive. If an aborted request has more than this many bytes remaining in the transfer, Squid terminates the connection to the origin server. Otherwise, it checks the *quick_abort_pct* setting.

Syntax	quick_abort_max *size-specification*
Default	quick_abort_max 16 KB

Example	quick_abort_max 1 MB
Related	*quick_abort_min, quick_abort_pct*

quick_abort_pct

Squid checks this value last, after checking *quick_abort_max,* for a transfer aborted by the user. If Squid has already received at least this percentage of the response, it continues reading the data from the origin server so the entire response is cached.

Syntax	quick_abort_pct *percentage*
Default	quick_abort_pct 95%
Example	quick_abort_pct 75%
Related	*quick_abort_min, quick_abort_max*

negative_ttl

Squid takes the liberty of caching certain error responses, such as "connection refused" and 404 (Not Found) messages. In most cases, repeating the request again immediately is likely to result in the same error. This directive specifies how long Squid caches these errors. Cache hits for negatively cached responses are logged with TCP_NEGATIVE_HIT in *access.log*.

Syntax	negative_ttl *time-specification*
Default	negative_ttl 5 min
Example	negative_ttl_1 minute
Related	*refresh_pattern*

positive_dns_ttl

Each and every DNS resource record carries an explicit TTL that specifies how long the information may be cached. In most situations, Squid has access to the TTL values and doesn't store DNS answers longer than allowed. This is certainly true when you use Squid's internal DNS implementation, which is enabled by default.

However, if you elect to use the (external) dnsserver processes, Squid may not receive TTL values for DNS answers. In this case, successful DNS answers are cached for the amount of time specified by this directive.

Syntax	positive_dns_ttl *time-specification*
Default	positive_dns_ttl 6 hours
Example	positive_dns_ttl 1 hour
Related	*negative_dns_ttl*

negative_dns_ttl

This is similar to *positive_dns_ttl*, except that it applies only to failed DNS queries. That is, when Squid receives an error for a DNS lookup, it negatively caches the error for this amount of time. It doesn't retry the query until the negative TTL expires. This applies to both internal and external DNS implementation choices.

Syntax	`negative_dns_ttl` *time-specification*
Default	`negative_dns_ttl 5 minutes`
Example	`negative_dns_ttl 1 minute`
Related	*positive_dns_ttl*

range_offset_limit

A *range request* comes from a client that wants only some subset of an HTTP response. They are sometimes used to resume a failed transfer of a large file. Squid isn't yet able to cache partial responses and thus must make a decision when forwarding a range request: either remove the Range header or leave it in.

If Squid leaves the Range header in, the origin server sends only the subset that the client wants, and the client receives the response immediately. However, this partial response isn't cached.

On the other hand, if Squid removes the header before forwarding, it receives the entire response, which may be cached. Squid is then responsible for ensuring that the client receives only the subset it needs. The origin server may send a lot of data the client doesn't want. Depending on the speed of your connection, the client may be forced to wait a long time until its range is available.

If the beginning of the requested range is larger than the *range_offset_limit* value, Squid forwards the Range header and doesn't cache the response. Setting *range_offset_limit* to 0 causes Squid to always forward the Range header (the default). Setting it to -1 causes Squid to never forward the header.

Syntax	`range_offset_limit` *size-specification*
Default	`range_offset_limit 0 KB`
Example	`range_offset_limit 100 KB`

connect_timeout

This directive tells Squid how long to wait when trying to connect to an origin server. After this amount of time, Squid gives up and tries another location or returns an error to the user. Your operating system's TCP implementation has its own connection timeout. If the TCP timeout occurs before *connect_timeout*, Squid creates a new TCP connection and tries again.

Syntax	`connect_timeout` *time-specification*
Default	`connect_timeout 2 minutes`

Example	connect_timeout 30 seconds
Related	*peer_connect_timeout, read_timeout, write_timeout, request_timeout, pconn_timeout, minimum_retry_timeout*

peer_connect_timeout

This is similar to *connect_timeout*, except that it applies to connections to your neighbors. Most likely, you'll want a smaller timeout for neighbor connections because they should be closer to you than most origin servers. If a neighbor is down, you want the connection to time out quickly so that you can try another source. Note that you can also specify individual neighbor timeouts with the connect-timeout option of the *cache_peer* directive.

Syntax	peer_connect_timeout *time-specification*
Default	peer_connect_timeout 30 seconds
Example	peer_connect_timeout 15 seconds
Related	*connect_timeout*

read_timeout

This timeout applies to server connections (between Squid and origin servers or neighbor caches). If Squid doesn't receive any data for this amount of time, it closes the connection. If the user hasn't yet received any part of the response, Squid generates a "read timeout" error message.

Syntax	read_timeout *time-specification*
Default	read_timeout 15 minutes
Example	read_timeout 1 hour
Related	*connect_timeout, write_timeout, request_timeout, client_lifetime*

request_timeout

This timeout applies to client connections. Once a client establishes a connection, Squid waits this long to receive the client's HTTP request. If the client fails to send a complete request, Squid simply closes the connection without sending any error message.

Syntax	request_timeout *time-specification*
Default	request_timeout 5 minutes
Example	request_timeout 30 seconds
Related	*read_timeout, connect_timeout*

persistent_request_timeout

This timeout is similar to *request_timeout*, except that it applies only to idle, persistent connections.

Syntax	persistent_request_timeout *time-specification*
Default	persistent_request_timeout 1 minute
Example	persistent_request_timeout 30 seconds
Related	*request_timeout*

client_lifetime

This timeout specifies the maximum amount of time for a client connection. In most cases, client connections should never last longer than a few hours. Long-lived client connections may be the result of a network outage, user-agent bugs, or mischievous activity.

Syntax	client_lifetime *time-specification*
Default	client_lifetime 1 day
Example	client_lifetime 3 hours
Related	*read_timeout*

half_closed_clients

TCP allows applications to close connections in one direction. That is, a client may close its connection for writing but keep it open for reading. These half-closed connections are confusing because Squid can't easily tell the difference between a client that intentionally closed half the connection and a client that simply aborted the entire connection. The only way Squid knows for sure is when its attempt to write some data returns an error. Most user-agents don't use the TCP half-close, but some may.

When the *half_closed_clients* directive is enabled (the default), Squid keeps these connections open until a write error (or some other error) occurs. When disabled, Squid fully closes the connection. Thus, if you disable this directive and have clients that use the TCP half-close, they can't receive any data from Squid.

Syntax	half_closed_clients on|off
Default	half_closed_clients on
Example	half_closed_clients off
Related	*client_lifetime, read_timeout*

pconn_timeout

This timeout applies to idle server persistent connections (i.e., connections between Squid and origin servers or neighbors). If the idle connection isn't reused within this amount of time, Squid closes it to conserve resources.

Syntax	pconn_timeout *time-specification*
Default	pconn_timeout 2 minutes
Example	pconn_timeout 45 seconds
Related	*persistent_request_timeout, connect_timeout, read_timeout*

ident_timeout

This timeout applies to ident (RFC 1413) requests made to client hosts. Squid makes ident lookups for one of two reasons: to satisfy an ACL check or for logging in *access.log*. In the ACL case, Squid blocks the request until the ident lookup returns, or this timeout occurs. When only logging, Squid doesn't block on the ident lookup.

Syntax	ident_timeout *time-specification*
Default	ident_timeout 10 seconds
Example	ident_timeout 1 minute
Related	*ident_lookup_access, acl ident*

shutdown_lifetime

When you shut down the Squid process, some user requests will still be active. This directive specifies how long to wait until all client requests are complete. Squid finally exits when all client connections have been closed or when this timeout occurs.

Syntax	shutdown_lifetime *time-specification*
Default	shutdown_lifetime 30 seconds
Example	shutdown_lifetime 60 seconds

acl

The *acl* directive defines an access control element, such as a client IP address, origin server hostname, or server port number. The syntax depends on the particular ACL type you wish to define. See Chapter 6 for the full-blown explanation.

Syntax	acl *name type data...*
Default	No default
Example	acl MyClients src 172.16.1.0/24
Related	*http_access, icp_access, miss_access, no_cache, redirector_access, http_reply_access, ident_lookup_access, always_direct, never_direct, snmp_access, broken_posts*

http_access

The *http_access* directive is one of the most important aspects of your configuration. It determines whether or not Squid allows or denies a client's request. If you don't get your access-control rules just right, savvy Internet users can abuse your resources (e.g., bandwidth, disk storage, address space). Some people find the access control rule syntax confusing. Be sure to read Chapter 6 closely.

Syntax	http_access allow|deny [!]*ACLname* ...
Default	http_access deny all

Example	`http_access allow MyClients`
Related	*acl, http_reply_access, miss_access, icp_access*

http_reply_access

The *http_reply_access* rules are similar to *http_access*, except that they are checked after Squid receives the HTTP response headers for a cache miss. You might want to use this access list to deny requests based on some characteristic of the response, such as the content type.

Syntax	`http_reply_access allow|deny [!]ACLname ...`
Default	`http_reply_access allow all`
Example	`http_reply_access deny MP3Files`
Related	*acl, http_access*

icp_access

This access list applies to ICP queries. If a particular ICP query is denied by the *icp_access* rules, Squid returns an ICP_DENIED message to the neighbor.

Syntax	`icp_access allow|deny [!]ACLname ...`
Default	`icp_access deny all`
Example	`icp_access allow Neighbor1`
Related	*acl, http_access*

miss_access

The *miss_access* rules are similar to *http_access*. However, they are applied to cache misses only. This allows you to enforce sibling relationships with your neighbor caches. See Chapter 6.

Syntax	`miss_access allow|deny [!]ACLname ...`
Default	`miss_access allow all`
Example	`miss_access deny MySiblings`
Related	*acl, http_access*

cache_peer_access

The *cache_peer_access* rules determine which requests Squid will forward to a particular neighbor. If a particular request is denied by a *cache_peer_access* list, Squid doesn't forward the request to that neighbor. See Chapter 10.

Syntax	`cache_peer_access peername allow|deny [!]ACLname ...`
Default	No default

Example	`cache_peer_access neighbor.host.name allow SomeOriginDomains`
Related	*acl, cache_peer, cache_peer_domain, http_access*

ident_lookup_access

The *ident_lookup_access* rules determine whether or not Squid performs an RFC 1413 user-name lookup for a client's TCP connection. These rules are checked before Squid reads any part of the HTTP request. Thus, only TCP/IP-based ACL elements (e.g., client address, port number) should be used in these rules.

Syntax	`ident_lookup_access allow|deny [!]ACLname ...`
Default	`ident_lookup_access deny all`
Example	`ident_lookup_access allow TheseClients`
Related	*acl, ident_timeout*

tcp_outgoing_tos

This directive allows you to set specific DSCP (differential services code point) values for outgoing TCP connections—those made to origin servers and neighbors. The differential services protocol is quite complex. Simply using the example in the following table will get you nowhere. Make sure that you understand what you are doing before using this directive. See RFCs 2474, 2475, and 3140 for additional information on differential services.

Syntax	`tcp_outgoing_tos byte-value [!]ACLname ...`
Default	No default

Example	`acl NormalService src 10.0.0.0/255.255.255.0`
	`acl BetterService src 10.0.1.0/255.255.255.0`
	`tcp_outgoing_tos 0x00 NormalService`
	`tcp_outgoing_tos 0x20 BetterService`

tcp_outgoing_address

You can use this access list-based directive to bind outgoing TCP connections to specific local addresses. It might be useful if your system has multiple network interfaces, and you want to make sure all of Squid's traffic leaves through one and not the other. Another possibility is that you have two or more interfaces with different costs or characteristics. You may want to send privileged user's traffic through the expensive, uncongested link, while other users go out the cheap, low-quality connection. Don't use this directive if your system has only one network interface.

If you have an *tcp_outgoing_address* rule with no ACLs, that address is used for requests that don't match any of the other rules.

Syntax	`tcp_outgoing_address ipaddr [[!]ACLname] ...`
Default	No default

Example	`acl SomeUsers src 10.0.0.0/24`
	`acl OtherUsers src 10.0.1.0/24`
	`tcp_outgoing_address 172.16.0.1 SomeUsers`
	`tcp_outgoing_address 192.168.0.1 OtherUsers`
	`tcp_outgoing_address 172.16.5.1`

Related	*udp_incoming_address, udp_outgoing_address*

reply_body_max_size

This directive allows you to limit the size of HTTP reply bodies based on ACL elements. When a request matches one of the *reply_body_max_size* rules, Squid places a limit on the size of the HTTP response. A value of 0 indicates no limit. Squid checks the reply size first when all HTTP headers have been received. If the headers contain a `Content-Length` value that exceeds the specified limit, the user receives a message that states "the request or reply is too large." If the content length is unavailable, Squid continues checking the limit as data comes in from the server. If the reply size exceeds the limit, Squid closes the client's connection, which causes the client to receive a partial reply.

Downstream caches often can't detect partial replies. Because the headers lack a content length value, the downstream cache (or user-agent) doesn't know that additional data is missing. Thus, you shouldn't use *reply_body_max_size* if you have child or sibling caches.

The code that checks the *reply_body_max_size* list ignores deny rules. In other words, it is pointless to include `deny` rules in this list.

Make sure that the maximum reply size is large enough for a Squid error message (typically 1K–2K bytes). An error message that is larger than the maximum reply body size causes Squid to crash.

Syntax	`reply_body_max_size` *bytes* `allow [!]`*ACLname* `...`
Default	`reply_body_max_size 0 allow all`
Example	`acl WorkingHours time 08:00-17:00` `reply_body_max_size 10485760 allow WorkingHours`
Related	*maximum_object_size, request_body_max_size, request_header_max_size*

cache_mgr

This email address is printed in error messages generated by Squid. Set this as an address to which your users should send support messages and problem reports. This address also receives a notification message if Squid dies unexpectedly.

Syntax	`cache_mgr` *email@address*
Default	`cache-mgr webmaster`
Example	`cache_mgr support@example.com`

cache_effective_user

In the interest of security, Squid doesn't allow itself to run as *root*. If you start the process as *root*, Squid changes its *effective userid* to a nonprivileged user. This user ID must have write permission to the cache directories and log file directory.

You need to set this directive only if you're starting Squid as *root*. If you start Squid as a non-*root* user, this directive is ignored.

Syntax	cache_effective_user *username*
Default	cache_effective_user nobody
Example	cache_effective_user squid
Related	*cache_effective_group*

cache_effective_group

If you start Squid as *root*, it changes the process' user ID to the username specified by *cache_effective_user*. By default, Squid sets the process' group ID to the group associated with the *cache_effective_user*. You can set the *cache_effective_group* directive if you want Squid to use some other group ID.

You only need to set this directive if you're starting Squid as *root*. If you start Squid as a non-*root* user, this directive is ignored.

Syntax	cache_effective_group *groupname*
Default	No default
Example	cache_effective_group squid
Related	*cache_effective_user*

visible_hostname

Use this directive when Squid can't determine the fully qualified domain name on its own or if you want to present a special, external name to the world. Squid uses this name in error messages, FTP directory listings, X-Cache header values, cache announcements, and for internal URLs.

Squid also puts the visible hostname into HTTP Via headers, unless you also define the *unique_hostname* directive. Note that you must use *unique_hostname* if you have a cluster of caches that have the same visible hostname.

Syntax	visible_hostname *hostname*
Default	No default
Example	visible_hostname my.host.name
Related	*unique_hostname, hostname_aliases, announce_period*

unique_hostname

If you have a cluster of caches talking to each other and sharing a single *visible_hostname* value, you must use this directive to give each a unique name. Squid uses the unique name in HTTP Via headers to detect forwarding loops (see Chapter 10).

Syntax	unique_hostname *hostname*
Default	No default
Example	unique_hostname cache1.host.name
Related	*visible_hostname, hostname_aliases*

hostname_aliases

You may find yourself in a situation where more than one hostname resolves to Squid's IP address. For example, both *sv.us.ircache.net* and *sv.cache.nlanr.net* resolve to 192.203.230. 19. If you have neighbors, they may send requests for certain Squid-specific internal URLs, as in the case of Cache Digests. These URLs might contain either hostname. You must use this directive to tell Squid that it is known by names other than its *visible_hostname*.

Syntax	hostname_aliases *hostname* ...
Default	No default
Example	hostname_aliases this.host.name that.host.name
Related	*visible_hostname, unique_hostname*

announce_period

Squid's announcement feature allows Squid administrators to find nearby caches that might be interested in joining a cache hierarchy. When you enable this directive, Squid periodically sends a small announcement message to a central server. By default, the announcement message contains five fields:

- The IP address and hostname that sent the announcement
- The Squid version
- The hostname Squid uses internally—either your hostname if Squid can figure it out or the value of the *visible_hostname* directive
- The value of the *cache_mgr* directive
- The date and time of the announcement

Setting *announce_period* to 0 disables the announcement feature.

Syntax	announce_period *time-specification*
Default	announce_period 0
Example	announce_period 4 hours
Related	*announce_host, announce_file, announce_port*

announce_host

This is the host setup to receive Squid's announcement messages. The default value, *tracker.ircache.net* is the only server I know about. You can search the *tracker.ircache.net* database by visiting *http://www.ircache.net/Tracker/*.

Note that if you set *cache_mgr*, your email address may be available to random people. On more than one occasion I have seen commercial caching vendors target Squid users by collecting their email addresses from this database.

Syntax	announce_host *hostname*
Default	announce_host tracker.ircache.net
Example	announce_host some.host.name
Related	*announce_period, announce_file, announce_port*

announce_file

You can customize your cache announcement message by setting this directive to a file containing additional information. For example, you can include information about your upstream service provider, telephone number, other caches that you peer with, etc.

Announcement messages are sent via UDP, so this file shouldn't be too large. Some systems can't send or receive UDP messages larger than 9 KB. Furthermore, larger messages are more likely to be dropped before reaching their destination.

Syntax	announce_file *pathname*
Default	No default
Example	announce_file /usr/local/squid/etc/announce.txt
Related	*announce_period, announce_host, announce_port*

announce_port

This is the UDP port number to which the announcement messages are sent.

Syntax	announce_port *port-number*
Default	announce_port 3131
Example	announce_port 1234
Related	*announce_period, announce_host, announce_file*

httpd_accel_host

This directive enables HTTP server acceleration (see Chapter 15) and HTTP interception (see Chapter 9). When Squid is configured for server acceleration, this directive specifies the hostname or IP address of the backend server. When used in an interception configuration, you should probably use the keyword virtual here.

When this directive is set, Squid disables ICP and rejects proxy-HTTP requests unless you also enable *httpd_accel_with_proxy*.

Syntax	httpd_accel_host *hostname*|virtual
Default	No default
Example	httpd_accel_host virtual
Related	*httpd_accel_port, httpd_accel_single_host, httpd_accel_with_proxy, httpd_accel_uses_host_header, emulate_httpd_log*

httpd_accel_port

This is the TCP port number to which accelerated/intercepted requests are sent. In most cases, you should leave it set to port 80. If you are accelerating/intercepting more than one port, set it to 0. That is similar to the virtual setting for *httpd_accel_host*.

Syntax	httpd_accel_port *port-number*
Default	httpd_accel_port 80
Example	httpd_accel_port 0
Related	*httpd_accel_host, httpd_accel_single_host, httpd_accel_with_proxy, httpd_accel_uses_host_header*

httpd_accel_single_host

When enabled, this directive makes Squid forward all accelerated/intercepted requests to the *httpd_accel_host* address. See Chapter 15.

 If you enable this directive and *httpd_accel_with_proxy*, Squid may become susceptible to cache poisoning. Please read Chapter 15 thoroughly before running such a configuration.

Syntax	httpd_accel_single_host on|off
Default	httpd_accel_single_host off
Example	httpd_accel_single_host on
Related	*httpd_accel_host, httpd_accel_port, httpd_accel_with_proxy, httpd_accel_uses_host_header*

httpd_accel_with_proxy

Enabling HTTP acceleration/interception normally disables proxy-HTTP caching. That is, Squid refuses to handle proxy requests (with a full URI) when in HTTP server accelerator mode. Although I don't recommend it, you can force Squid to accept both types of requests by enabling this directive.

Syntax	httpd_accel_with_proxy on|off
Default	httpd_accel_with_proxy off
Example	httpd_accel_with_proxy on
Related	*httpd_accel_host, httpd_accel_port, httpd_accel_single_host, httpd_accel_uses_host_header*

httpd_accel_uses_host_header

When this directive is enabled, Squid uses a request's Host header when rewriting accelerated/intercepted requests. When disabled, Squid uses either the origin server's IP address or the *httpd_accel_host* value.

You should probably enable *httpd_accel_uses_host_header* when running Squid as an HTTP-intercepting proxy. If Squid is a surrogate (accelerator), you only need to enable this directive if the backend server is configured for virtual hosting.

Syntax	httpd_accel_uses_host_header on|off
Default	httpd_accel_uses_host_header off
Example	httpd_accel_uses_host_header on
Related	*httpd_accel_host, httpd_accel_port, httpd_accel_single_host, httpd_accel_with_proxy*

dns_testnames

Squid uses these hostnames to test the DNS before starting. If Squid can't resolve any of these names, it prints an error and refuses to run. If the default list doesn't seem to work on your network, try listing some local hostnames instead.

Syntax	dns_testnames *hostname* ...
Default	dns_testnames netscape.com internic.net nlanr.net microsoft.com
Example	dns_testnames yahoo.com example.com squid-cache.org

logfile_rotate

You must periodically signal Squid to rotate its log files. If you don't, they will increase in size and eventually fill up the disk partition. This directive specifies how many old copies of each log file to keep around. See Chapter 13 for more information.

Syntax	logfile_rotate *N*
Default	logfile_rotate 10
Example	logfile_rotate 5
Related	*cache_access_log, cache_log, cache_store_log, cache_swap_log, useragent_log, referer_log*

append_domain

This directive helps Squid turn single-component hostnames into fully qualified domain names. For example, *http://www/* becomes *www.example.com/*. This is especially important if you are participating in a cache hierarchy.

Syntax	append_domain .*domain.name*
Default	No default
Example	append_domain .example.com
Related	*dns_defnames, hosts_file*

tcp_recv_bufsize

If you use this directive, Squid sets the receive buffer size for each TCP socket that it creates. This value refers to the amount of data that the TCP/IP stack will buffer on behalf of the application. You can see how much data is being buffered at any given time by looking at the Recv-Q column of netstat -n output. Larger TCP buffers lead to increased memory usage and better performance.

In general, you shouldn't need to use this directive. Most operating systems in use today have default TCP buffer sizes greater than 32 KB. Empirical evidence suggests that fewer than 5% of typical web objects are larger than 32 KB.

When *tcp_recv_bufsize* is set to 0, Squid doesn't change the TCP buffer size from its default value.

Syntax   tcp_recv_bufsize *size-specification*
Default   tcp_recv_bufsize 0
Example   tcp_recv_bufsize 8 kb

err_html_text

This directive is one way to customize Squid's error messages. The error message files contain printf-like tokens. Squid dynamically replaces the tokens with appropriate values for each error. If Squid encounters the token %L, it inserts the contents of this directive. Note that none of the default error messages contain a %L. Thus, to use this feature, you must modify the default error files.

Syntax   err_html_text *character string*
Default   No default
Example   err_html_text Call 555-1234 to report problems with Squid.
Related   *error_directory*

deny_info

This directive allows you to show specific error messages to users when a request matches certain ACL elements. This is more informative than sending a generic "access denied" error message, as happens by default.

When Squid checks its access control rules to see whether or not a particular request is allowed or denied, it remembers the ACL element that causes the search to terminate. You can use these ACL element names in a *deny_info* line to correlate error messages with a specific request characteristic. Consider, for example, this configuration:

```
acl Unsafe_Ports 7 9 19 22 23 25 53 109 110 119
...
http_access deny Unsafe_Ports
...
deny_info ERR_PORT_IS_UNSAFE Unsafe_Ports
```

When a user makes a request to an origin server on one of the ports listed in the *Unsafe_Ports* ACL, Squid denies the request. Furthermore, Squid generates an error message from the *ERR_PORT_IS_UNSAFE* file, found in the *error_directory* directory.

Alternatively, you can specify a URI instead of an error message template. In this case, Squid sends an HTTP 302 (Moved Temporarily) redirect to the given URI.

Finally, if you specify TCP_RESET as the error message template, Squid closes the client's connection in a way that generates a TCP reset.

Syntax	`deny_info error-page-name|URI acl-name`
Default	No default
Example	`deny_info ERR_PORT_IS_UNSAFE Unsafe_Ports`
Related	*error_directory, acl*

memory_pools

Squid's memory pools are an attempt to optimize the way Squid allocates and frees memory. Certain data structures inside Squid are *pooled*. This means that rather than freeing unused memory, Squid holds onto it for future use. It also means that a particular chunk of memory is normally used for the same type of data structure. Memory pools may improve Squid's performance by avoiding frequent calls to `malloc()` and `free()`. The downside, however, is that the overall memory usage may be higher. If memory is a precious resource on your system, you might want to disable memory pools.

Syntax	`memory_pools on|off`
Default	`memory_pools on`
Example	`memory_pools off`
Related	*cache_mem, memory_pools_limit*

memory_pools_limit

This directive specifies an upper limit on the amount of unused memory to hold onto. If the total size of all unused, pooled memory exceeds this value, Squid begins returning unused memory to the *malloc* library by calling `free()`.

If set to 0 (the default), Squid doesn't place any limit on the amount of unused memory to keep in the pools.

Syntax	`memory_pools_limit size-specification`
Default	`memory_pools_limit 0`
Example	`memory_pools_limit 100 MB`
Related	*memory_pools*

forwarded_for

Squid appends an item to the X-Forwarded-For header in requests sent to origin servers and neighbors. When this directive is enabled, Squid places the client's IP address there. When it is disabled, Squid prints the word unknown instead. Thus, disabling *forwarded_for* increases your user's privacy.

Syntax	forwarded_for on|off
Default	forwarded_for on
Example	forwarded_for off

log_icp_queries

By default, ICP queries appear in Squid's *access.log*. If Squid receives a large amount of ICP queries from neighbors, your *access.log* file may become too large to effectively manage. If you disable this directive, ICP queries are never logged.

Syntax	log_icp_queries on|off
Default	log_icp_queries on
Example	log_icp_queries off
Related	*access_log, icp_port*

icp_hit_stale

Squid normally returns ICP_MISS for queries to stale objects. This causes an annoying problem described in Chapter 10. If you enable this directive, Squid returns ICP_HIT messages instead.

Syntax	icp_hit_stale on|off
Default	icp_hit_stale off
Example	icp_hit_stale on
Related	*cache_peer, miss_access*

minimum_direct_hops

If you're using *netdb* (see Chapter 10), and a cache hierarchy, Squid forwards requests directly to origin servers that are within this many router hops. Such requests are marked with CLOSEST_DIRECT in *access.log*.

Syntax	minimum_direct_hops *N*
Default	minimum_direct_hops 4
Example	minimum_direct_hops 6
Related	*minimum_direct_rtt, always_direct*

minimum_direct_rtt

Similar to *minimum_direct_hops*. If Squid is within *minimum_direct_rtt* milliseconds (as measured by ICMP pings) to the origin server, the request is sent there directly. These requests are marked with CLOSEST_DIRECT in *access.log*.

Syntax	minimum_direct_rtt *milliseconds*
Default	minimum_direct_rtt 400
Example	minimum_direct_rtt 100
Related	*minimum_direct_hops, always_direct*

cachemgr_passwd

This directive allows you to protect cache manager pages with a password. Unfortunately, this is an extremely weak authorization scheme, because passwords are sent as cleartext in the cache manager HTTP request. See Chapter 14 for a discussion of cache manager passwords.

Syntax	cachemgr_passwd *password cachemgr-page* ...
Default	No default
Example	cachemgr_passwd SekrIt config objects vm_objects
Related	*http_access*

store_avg_object_size

Squid uses this value as a hint for estimating the size of certain data structures. In particular, Squid calculates an estimate for the total number of objects in the cache, based on this value and the sum of all *cache_dir* sizes. This estimate is, in turn, used to calculate the number of hash buckets for the primary index to cached objects. Additionally, it can estimate the cache digest size, if that feature is enabled.

In most cases the default should be sufficient. You can find the actual value for your cache by querying the cache manager. Look for "Mean Object Size" on the *info* page (see Chapter 14).

Syntax	store_avg_object_size *size-specification*
Default	store_avg_object_size 13 KB
Example	store_avg_object_size 10 KB
Related	*cache_dir, digest_bits_per_entry, store_objects_per_bucket*

store_objects_per_bucket

This directive allows you to tune the tradeoff between increased memory usage and longer searching times. Squid calculates the number of hash table buckets, depending on this directive, the average object size, and the total cache size. Squid's goal is to have this many objects in each bucket of the hash table.

A larger value here leads to reduced memory usage but longer search times. Conversely, a smaller value leads to faster search times, at the expense of increased memory usage.

Syntax	store_objects_per_bucket *N*
Default	store_objects_per_bucket 20
Example	store_objects_per_bucket 15
Related	*store_avg_object_size*

client_db

Squid keeps a number of statistics for each cache client (IP address). You can view them by visiting the cache manager *client_list* page. The ClientInfo data structure is about 240 bytes on 32-bit systems and 300 bytes on 64-bit systems. If you have thousands of clients, this database can consume a significant amount of memory. You can disable this directive and free up that memory for other uses.

Syntax	client_db on|off
Default	client_db on
Example	client_db off

netdb_low

The *netdb* database contains round-trip time and hop-count measurements derived from ICMP pings. This directive specifies the lower limit for the *netdb* replacement policy. In other words, when Squid is removing *netdb* entries, it stops when the total number reaches *netdb_low*.

Syntax	netdb_low *N*
Default	netdb_low 900
Example	netdb_low 9900
Related	*netdb_high, query_icmp*

netdb_high

The *netdb* database contains round-trip time and hop-count measurements derived from ICMP pings. This directive specifies an upper limit on the number entries in the database. When Squid finds more than *netdb_high* entries, it removes least-recently used networks until the size reaches *netdb_low*.

Syntax	netdb_high *N*
Default	netdb_high 1000
Example	netdb_high 10000
Related	*netdb_low, query_icmp*

netdb_ping_period

This directive specifies how long Squid must wait between sending consecutive ICMP pings to the same /24 network. The interval is relatively long so that Squid's ICMP traffic doesn't upset server administrators.

Syntax	netdb_ping_period *time-specification*
Default	netdb_ping_period 5 min
Example	netdb_ping_period 3 min
Related	*pinger_program, query_icmp*

query_icmp

Enabling this directive instructs Squid to ask its neighbors for their ICMP measurements, which are included in ICP/HTCP replies. This, essentially, populates your *netdb* database with your neighbors' ICMP measurements. The bulk "netdb exchange" is another way to receive those measurements (see Chapter 10).

Squid uses the neighbors' *netdb* measurements when making forwarding decisions. If one of the parents is closer to the origin server, Squid forwards the request there and marks it with CLOSEST_PARENT_MISS in *access.log*.

Syntax	query_icmp on|off
Default	query_icmp off
Example	query_icmp on
Related	*pinger_program, netdb_ping_period*

test_reachability

When you enable this directive, Squid looks at its *netdb* database while processing ICP queries. If Squid normally returns ICP_MISS, but the origin server isn't in the database or doesn't respond to ICMP pings, it returns ICP_MISS_NOFETCH instead. The ICP_MISS_NOFETCH reply signals the neighbor cache that Squid might not be able to communicate with the origin server.

Syntax	test_reachability on|off
Default	test_reachability off
Example	test_reachability on
Related	*pinger_program, query_icmp, netdb_ping_period*

buffered_logs

While this directive used to affect multiple log files, it now only applies to *cache.log*. Squid uses the *stdio* library for *cache.log*. If this directive is enabled, Squid calls fflush( ) after every write. This allows you to see log file entries as they are written. You might want to disable *buffered_logs* if you are debugging Squid in a way that creates a large number of *cache.log* entries.

Syntax	`buffered_logs on|off`
Default	`buffered_logs off`
Example	`buffered_logs on`
Related	*cache_log*

reload_into_ims

If you enable this directive, Squid adds an `If-Modified-Since` header to requests that contain a no-cache directive. This is a global version of the `reload-into-ims` option for the *refresh_pattern* directive (see Chapter 7).

 Altering the client's request in this manner is a violation of HTTP.

Syntax	`reload_into_ims on|off`
Default	`reload_into_ims off`
Example	`reload_into_ims on`
Related	*refresh_pattern*

always_direct

The *always_direct* access rules define a class of requests that must always be forwarded directly to the origin server. For these, Squid doesn't query or otherwise consider any neighbor caches. See Chapter 10.

Syntax	`always_direct allow|deny [!]ACLname ...`
Default	No default
Example	`acl LocalServers dst 172.17.0.0/24` `always_direct allow LocalServers`
Related	*acl, never_direct, prefer_direct, nonhierarchical_direct, minimum_direct_hops, minimum_direct_rtt, cache_peer_access*

never_direct

The *never_direct* access rules define a class of requests that must never be forwarded to the origin server. For these, Squid must select an appropriate neighbor cache to handle the request. See Chapter 10.

Syntax	`never_direct allow|deny [!]ACLname ...`
Default	No default

Example   `acl SpecialServers dstdomain .example.com`
              `never_direct allow SpecialServers`

Related   *acl, always_direct, prefer_direct, nonhierarchical_direct, minimum_direct_hops, minimum_direct_rtt,*
              cache_peer_access

header_access

This directive defines a set of access rules for filtering HTTP headers from both requests and responses. You can use it to remove headers that may violate your privacy, or that cause interoperation issues. For example, this configuration removes Cookie headers sent to a well-known web advertising company:

```
acl DC dstdomain .doubleclick.net
header_access Cookie deny DC
```

The *header-name* field must be one of the HTTP headers Squid knows about or one of the keywords Other or All. Squid currently knows the following HTTP headers:

Accept	Accept-Charset	Accept-Encoding
Accept-Language	Accept-Ranges	Age
Allow	Authentication-Info	Authorization
Cache-Control	Connection	Content-Base
Content-Encoding	Content-Language	Content-Length
Content-Location	Content-MD5	Content-Range
Content-Type	Cookie	Date
ETag	Expires	From
Host	If-Match	If-Modified-Since
If-None-Match	If-Range	Last-Modified
Link	Location	Max-Forwards
Mime-Version	Negotiate	Pragma
Proxy-Authenticate	Proxy-Authentication-Info	Proxy-Authorization
Proxy-Connection	Public	Range
Referer	Request-Range	Retry-After
Server	Set-Cookie	Title
Transfer-Encoding	Upgrade	User-Agent
Vary	Via	WWW-Authenticate
Warning	X-Accelerator-Vary	X-Cache
X-Cache-Lookup	X-Forwarded-For	X-Request-URI
X-Squid-Error		

Unfortunately, you can't refer to an unknown header individually. The best you can do is use the keyword Other to refer to all unknown HTTP headers. The keyword All refers to all (known and unknown) HTTP headers.

Note that if you deny the Via header, Squid can't detect forwarding loops (see Chapter 10).

 Removing headers from requests and responses is a violation of HTTP.

header_replace

Syntax	header_access *header-name* allow|deny [!]*ACLname* ...
Default	No default
Example	header_access From deny All
Related	*acl, header_replace*

header_replace

This directive works in conjunction with *header_access*. If you use *header_replace*, Squid replaces HTTP headers that are denied (removed) by an *header_access* rule. In other words, an HTTP header must be filtered out by *header_access* before it can be replaced by *header_replace*.

header_replace isn't especially flexible. You can only define one replacement value for each header. You can't, for example, use one value for some requests and a different value for others.

 Changing HTTP request and response headers is a violation of HTTP.

Syntax	header_replace *header-name* *string*
Default	No default
Example	header_replace User-Agent Nutscrape/1.0 (CP/M; 8-bit)
Related	*header_access*

icon_directory

This directive specifies the location of the icons Squid uses in FTP and Gopher directory listings. The icon filenames are defined in *mime.conf* (see the "mime_table" section). If you don't like Squid's icons, you can use your own, as long as the filenames found in *mime.conf* exist in the *icon_directory* directory.

Syntax	icon_directory *directory*
Default	icon_directory *$prefix*/share/icons
Example	icon_directory /usr/local/squid/share/myicons
Related	*error_directory, mime_table*

error_directory

This directive specifies the location of Squid's error message files. If you want to customize the error messages, you should put them into a nondefault directory. Otherwise, they may be overwritten if you run make install in the future.

Syntax	error_directory *directory*
Default	error_directory *$prefix*/share/errors/$language

Example   error_directory /usr/local/squid/share/my_errors
Related   *icon_directory, err_html_text, deny_info*

---

maximum_single_addr_tries

This directive places a limit on the number of times Squid attempts to connect to a single IP address when forwarding a request. It can't be set higher than 10.

Syntax   maximum_single_addr_tries *N*
Default   maximum_single_addr_tries 3
Example   maximum_single_addr_tries 5
Related   *connect_timeout*

---

snmp_port

This is the UDP port to which Squid listens for SNMP queries. SNMP support requires the `--enable-snmp` option to `./configure`. Set the SNMP port to 0 if Squid shouldn't accept any SNMP messages.

Syntax   snmp_port *port-number*
Default   snmp_port 3401
Example   snmp_port 3161
Related   *snmp_access, snmp_incoming_address, snmp_outgoing_address*

---

snmp_access

The *snmp_access* rules apply to SNMP queries. Although this is a standard Squid access list rule, many ACL elements are undefined for SNMP. In fact, you can only use *src* and *snmp_community* ACLs.

Syntax   snmp_access allow|deny [!]*ACLname* ...
Default   No default (all queries denied by default)
Example   acl SNMPPasswd snmp_community sekrit
           acl SNMPClients src 172.16.1.2 10.0.5.1
           acl All src 0/0
           snmp_access allow SNMPClients SNMPPasswd
           snmp_access deny All
Related   *acl, snmp_port*

---

snmp_incoming_address

By default, Squid opens the SNMP socket to receive packets on all local interfaces. You can use this directive to bind the SNMP socket to a particular interface.

Syntax   snmp_incoming_address *ip-address*
Default   snmp_incoming_address 0.0.0.0

Example	snmp_incoming_address 172.16.0.1
Related	*snmp_port, snmp_access, udp_incoming_address*

snmp_outgoing_address

Squid uses a single SNMP socket by default. If you set this directive, however, Squid opens a separate socket for SNMP replies only. In most cases, you shouldn't use this directive because SNMP queries should come from the same address to which the queries are sent.

Syntax	snmp_outgoing_address *ip-address*
Default	No default
Example	snmp_outgoing_address 192.168.5.5
Related	*snmp_port, snmp_access, udp_outgoing_address*

as_whois_server

This is the hostname of the *whois* server Squid uses to resolve Autonomous System numbers into IP networks. You only need to worry about this if you use AS-based ACLs (*src_as, dst_as*).

The default server, *whois.ra.net*, seems to work relatively well. It may be too far away (and unreliable) for non-U.S. users. If you know of a local *whois* server that returns AS queries, feel free to use it instead.

Syntax	as_whois_server *hostname*
Default	as_whois_server whois.ra.net
Example	as_whois_server whois.host.name
Related	*acl*

wccp_router

This directive defines Squid's home router for WCCP. When you enter an IP address (or hostname) here, Squid sends WCCP "Here I Am" messages to the router. See Chapter 9 for more information.

Routers, by definition, have multiple network interfaces. You should probably use the address of the interface that is connected, or has the route, to Squid. Squid ignores WCCP messages that don't have the *wccp_router* value as their source address.

Syntax	wccp_router *ip-address*
Default	No default
Example	wccp_router 172.16.5.1
Related	*wccp_version, wccp_incoming_address, wccp_outgoing_address*

wccp_version

This particular version number refers to second field of the WCCP "Here I Am" message. It isn't the same as WCCPv1 versus WCCPv2. Some users report that older installations of Cisco IOS only work when this directive is set to 3.

Syntax	wccp_version N
Default	wccp_version 4
Example	wccp_version 3
Related	*wccp_router*

wccp_incoming_address

Squid listens for WCCP messages on all local interfaces by default. If you set this directive, Squid listens on only the specified address.

Syntax	wccp_incoming_address ip-address
Default	wccp_incoming_address 0.0.0.0
Example	wccp_incoming_address 10.1.2.3
Related	*wccp_router, wccp_outgoing_address, udp_incoming_address*

wccp_outgoing_address

If, for some reason, you want Squid to send and receive WCCP messages on different interfaces, set this directive to the address of the outgoing interface. If this directive isn't set, as is the default, Squid uses the same socket for incoming and outgoing messages.

Syntax	wccp_outgoing_address ip-address
Default	No default
Example	wccp_outgoing_address 172.16.1.1
Related	*wccp_router, wccp_incoming_address, udp_outgoing_address*

delay_pools

This directive specifies the number of delay pools that you will later define with the *delay_class* and *delay_parameters* directives. It tells Squid the size of certain arrays used in the delay pools implementation. It must appear in the configuration file before the other delay pools directives.

Note that in order to use delay pools, you must give the --enable-delay-pools option to ./configure.

Syntax	delay_pools N
Default	delay_pools 0
Example	delay_pools 4
Related	*delay_class, delay_access, delay_parameters, delay_initial_bucket_level*

delay_class

This directive defines the class of each delay pool. The first argument is the delay pool index. Index values start at 1 and must be less than or equal to the *delay_pools* value. The second argument is the delay class, which has three possible values:

- A class 1 pool uses a single, aggregate bucket for all traffic that applies to the pool.
- A class 2 pool uses a single, aggregate bucket, as well as 256 individual buckets. The individual bucket is chosen by the last octet of the client's IPv4 address.
- A class 3 bucket uses a single, aggregate bucket, 256 network buckets, and 65,536 individual buckets. The network bucket is chosen based on the third octet of the client's IPv4 address. The individual bucket is chosen by the third and fourth octets.

Note that the class 2 and class 3 pools have multiple types of buckets (aggregate, network, individual). A client receives a traffic allocation from all relevant buckets, not just one of them. In other words, if any of the relevant buckets are empty, the client doesn't receive any traffic allocation.

Syntax	`delay_class pool-number class`
Default	No default
Example	`delay_class 1 2` `delay_class 2 3`
Related	*delay_pools, delay_access, delay_parameters, delay_initial_bucket_level*

delay_access

This directive maps a client request to a particular delay pool. A client's cache miss is delayed only if it is "allowed" by one of the *delay_access* rules. Squid checks the access rules for all pools in order. If a particular request is denied by all *delay_access* rules, it isn't delayed. You must define at least one rule to use delay pools.

Syntax	`delay_access pool-number allow|deny [!]ACLname ...`
Default	No default
Example	`acl Dorms src 172.17.0.0/16` `delay_access 1 allow Dorms`
Related	*delay_pools, delay_class, delay_parameters, delay_initial_bucket_level*

delay_parameters

The *delay_parameters* directive determines the fill rate and capacity for each delay pools bucket. Following the pool number, you must write one, two, or three pairs of numbers. The number of pairs is the same as the pool's class. A class 1 pool takes one pair, a class 2 pool takes two pairs, and a class 3 pool takes three pairs.

Each pair of numbers specifies the fill rate and maximum bucket size. The fill rate should not be larger than the maximum size. The units are number of bytes. Thus, if you are thinking in terms of bits per second, you must divide by 8 to get bytes per second. For example, if you want to define a bucket that refills at a rate of 100 Kbits/sec, and holds no more than 300 Kbits (3 seconds) of traffic, you would write 12500/37500.

Syntax	delay_parameters *pool-number aggr-rate/aggr-max* [*ind-rate/ind-max* [*net-rate/net-max*]]
Default	No default
Example	delay_parameters 2 16000/32000 4000/8000
Related	*delay_pools, delay_class, delay_access, delay_initial_bucket_level*

delay_initial_bucket_level

This directive determines the amount of traffic that Squid puts into newly created buckets. A bucket is created when Squid starts up or is reconfigured. For class 2 and 3 pools, individual and network buckets are created upon the first client request that uses the bucket. The *delay_initial_bucket_level* value is a percentage of the bucket's maximum size.

Syntax	delay_initial_bucket_level *percent*
Default	delay_initial_bucket_level 50
Example	delay_initial_bucket_level 100
Related	*delay_pools, delay_class, delay_access, delay_parameters*

incoming_icp_average

This directive controls the low-level routines that periodically check the ICP socket for incoming queries and replies. The algorithm is relatively complex to fully describe here. The idea is to make sure Squid checks the ICP socket frequently enough to handle the ICP load but not so often that it is a waste of time. This directive specifies the number of normal I/O events that should occur between checks to the ICP socket. A normal I/O event refers to reading from, and writing to, client- and server-side TCP sockets.

Unless you have a thorough understanding of the polling algorithms in the source code, I strongly recommend that you leave this directive set to its default value.

Syntax	incoming_icp_average *number*
Default	incoming_icp_average 6
Example	incoming_icp_average 20
Related	*incoming_http_average, incoming_dns_average*

incoming_http_average

This directive is similar to *incoming_icp_average*, except that it refers to the HTTP socket with which Squid accepts new client requests. Unless you have a thorough understanding of the polling algorithms in the source code, I strongly recommend that you leave this directive set to its default value.

Syntax	incoming_http_average *number*
Default	incoming_http_average 4

Example	incoming_http_average 15
Related	*incoming_icp_average, incoming_dns_average*

incoming_dns_average

This directive is similar to *incoming_icp_average*, except that it refers to the UDP socket with which Squid receives DNS responses. Unless you have a thorough understanding of the polling algorithms in the source code, I strongly recommend that you leave this directive set to its default value.

Syntax	incoming_dns_average *number*
Default	incoming_dns_average 4
Example	incoming_dns_average 8
Related	*incoming_icp_average, incoming_http_average*

min_icp_poll_cnt

This directive controls the low-level routines that periodically check the ICP socket for incoming queries and replies. It specifies a lower limit on the number of normal I/O events that must occur between checks to the ICP socket. Unless you have a thorough understanding of the polling algorithms in the source code, I strongly recommend that you leave this directive set to its default value.

Syntax	min_icp_poll_cnt *number*
Default	min_icp_poll_cnt 8
Example	min_icp_poll_cnt 10
Related	*incoming_icp_average*

min_dns_poll_cnt

This directive is similar to *min_icp_poll_cnt*, except that it applies to the UDP socket with which Squid receives DNS replies. Unless you have a thorough understanding of the polling algorithms in the source code, I strongly recommend that you leave this directive set to its default value.

Syntax	min_dns_poll_cnt *number*
Default	min_dns_poll_cnt 8
Example	min_dns_poll_cnt 10
Related	*incoming_dns_average*

min_http_poll_cnt

This directive is similar to *min_icp_poll_cnt*, except that it applies to the TCP socket with which Squid accepts new client requests. Unless you have a thorough understanding of the polling algorithms in the source code, I strongly recommend that you leave this directive set to its default value.

Syntax   min_http_poll_cnt *number*
Default   min_http_poll_cnt 8
Example   min_http_poll_cnt 12
Related   *incoming_http_average*

max_open_disk_fds

This directive defines an upper limit on the number of file descriptors that Squid should open for reading and writing cache files on disk. It is relevant for only the *ufs* and *aufs* storage schemes. It is a relatively simple hack for measuring the level of Squid's disk activity. Experience shows that performance degrades significantly when Squid hits a file-system bottleneck.

If Squid reaches this limit, it doesn't attempt to store subsequent cachable responses. Each time that happens, Squid increments the no.too_many_open_files counter (see Chapter 14). Note that hitting this limit has a negative impact on your hit ratio. You can monitor the number of open disk files by requesting the *info* page from the cache manager (see Chapter 14).

If you set this directive to 0, Squid doesn't place any limits on the number of open disk file descriptors.

Syntax   max_open_disk_fds *N*
Default   max_open_disk_fds 0
Example   max_open_disk_fds 100

offline_mode

When you enable *offline_mode*, Squid returns every cached response as an unvalidated cache hit. These are tagged with TCP_OFFLINE_HIT in *access.log*. When in this mode, Squid still attempts to forward cache misses. If your system truly is offline, some requests may hang while waiting for the DNS or HTTP transaction to timeout.

Syntax   offline_mode on|off
Default   offline_mode off
Example   offline_mode on

uri_whitespace

This directive tells Squid what to do about URIs that contain whitespace characters (i.e., space and tab). The default action is to strip out the whitespace and shift the valid characters down as necessary. This is the behavior recommended by RFC 2396.

If you set this directive to allow, Squid doesn't change the URI. It is passed through to the origin server as is. This setting may cause some problems with redirectors and log file parsers. Both use whitespace as a field delimiter, and a URI with whitespace adds an additional field (or fields) to the redirector input line and the *access.log* entry.

The deny setting instructs Squid to deny such a request, as though it were blocked by the access control rules. Note, however, that the URI is still written to *access.log* with the whitespace characters.

With the encode setting, Squid changes whitespace characters into their RFC 1738 equivalents. When some origin servers generate URIs that contain whitespace, this is what they should be doing in the first place.

Finally, the chop setting instructs Squid to simply cut off the URI at the first whitespace character.

Syntax   uri_whitespace allow|deny|strip|encode|chop
Default   uri_whitespace strip
Example   uri_whitespace deny
Related   *access_log, redirector_program*

broken_posts

Certain buggy HTTP servers expect two extra bytes, CR and LF characters, following an HTTP POST message body. It seems unlikely that such uncompliant servers are still in use today. Nonetheless, this access rule list exists to accommodate them. When a request matches a *broken_posts* rule, Squid appends the extra CRLF characters.

Syntax   broken_posts allow|deny [!]ACLname ...
Default   No default
Example   acl NeedsExtraCRLF dstdomain broken.server.com
              broken_posts allow NeedsExtraCRLF
Related   *http_access, acl*

mcast_miss_addr

The *multicast miss stream* is a largely undocumented and unsupported Squid feature. The basic idea is to send a multicast message, containing a URI, for each cache miss. The messages are encrypted with a modest algorithm to prevent casual eavesdropping.

To use this feature, you must manually define the MULTICAST_MISS_STREAM preprocessor symbol before compiling Squid. To learn more about this feature, read the source code surrounded by #if MULTICAST_MISS_STREAM in *src/access_log.c*.

Syntax   mcast_miss_addr *multicast-address*
Default   No default
Example   mcast_miss_addr 224.0.1.1
Related   *mcast_miss_ttl, mcast_miss_port, mcast_miss_encode_key*

mcast_miss_ttl

This is the multicast TTL assigned to outgoing miss stream messages. See the discussion of multicast TTLs in Chapter 10.

Syntax	mcast_miss_ttl *N*
Default	mcast_miss_ttl 16
Example	mcast_miss_ttl 32
Related	*mcast_miss_addr, mcast_miss_port, mcast_miss_encode_key*

mcast_miss_port

This is the UDP port number to which multicast miss stream messages are sent.

Syntax	mcast_miss_port *port-number*
Default	mcast_miss_port 3135
Example	mcast_miss_port 999
Related	*mcast_miss_addr, mcast_miss_ttl, mcast_miss_encode_key*

mcast_miss_encode_key

Squid uses the Tiny Encryption Algorithm (TEA) to encrypt multicast miss messages. This directive specifies the encryption key, which should be 128 bits long.

Syntax	mcast_miss_encode_key *string*
Default	mcast_miss_encode_key XXXXXXXXXXXXXXXX
Example	mcast_miss_encode_key MySekRitPassWord
Related	*mcast_miss_addr, mcast_miss_ttl, mcast_miss_port*

nonhierarchical_direct

A hierarchical request is one that looks like it might result in a cachable response, and therefore might be cached by one of Squid's neighbors. If your Squid doesn't have any neighbors, you don't need to worry about this directive.

By default, Squid prefers to skip the neighbor selection step for nonhierarchical requests (uncachable responses) because the request probably won't result in a cache hit. You can reverse this behavior by disabling the *nonhierarchical_direct* directive. See Chapter 10.

Syntax	nonhierarchical_direct on|off
Default	nonhierarchical_direct on
Example	nonhierarchical_direct off
Related	*prefer_direct, never_direct, always_direct*

prefer_direct

This directive affects Squid's neighbor selection algorithm for hierarchical requests (cachable responses). It is only relevant if you have one or more neighbor caches. When Squid builds a list of next-hop locations for cache misses, it puts neighbor caches before the origin server by default. If you would rather have Squid put the origin server before neighbors, enable the *prefer_direct* directive. See Chapter 10.

Syntax	`prefer_direct on|off`
Default	`prefer_direct off`
Example	`prefer_direct on`
Related	*nonhierarchical_direct, never_direct, always_direct*

strip_query_terms

When this directive is enabled, Squid doesn't log URI query terms in *access.log*. This feature is intended to give your users some privacy. It is enabled by default.

Syntax	`strip_query_terms on|off`
Default	`strip_query_terms on`
Example	`strip_query_terms off`
Related	*access_log, client_netmask*

coredump_dir

Normally Squid doesn't change its current directory at startup. While this isn't usually a problem, it can be if Squid wants to leave a core-dump file. If the *core* file is very large, it might fill up a disk partition. Additionally, the *core* won't be created at all if Squid doesn't have permission to write in the current directory.

This directive changes Squid's current directory. You should set it to a location that has sufficient space, and appropriate permissions, for a large *core* file.

Note that the *coredump_dir* directive is used only when Squid starts up. If you change the value while Squid is running and then reconfigure, Squid doesn't change the current directory.

Syntax	`coredump_dir pathname`
Default	No default
Example	`coredump_dir /squid/var`

ignore_unknown_nameservers

Squid normally checks that DNS replies come from the same IP address to which the query was sent. If the addresses don't match, Squid writes a warning to *cache.log* and ignores the reply. Some installations use an */etc/resolv.conf* trick to query any local name server. If the name server IP address is `0.0.0.0`, DNS queries are broadcast on the local area network.

The replies, however, come from specific addresses. If you want to use this trick, you must disable the *ignore_unknown_nameservers* directive.

Syntax	`ignore_unknown_nameservers on|off`
Default	`ignore_unknown_nameservers on`
Example	`ignore_unknown_nameservers off`
Related	*dns_nameservers*

digest_generation

This directive controls whether or not Squid generates a Cache Digest for its own contents. It is enabled by default, when you give the `--enable-cache-digests` option to `./configure`. You may want to disable it if you know that you don't have any neighbors who request your digest.

Syntax	`digest_generation on|off`
Default	`digest_generation on`
Example	`digest_generation off`
Related	*cache_peer, digest_bits_per_entry, digest_rebuild_period, digest_rewrite_period, digest_swapout_chunk_size, digest_rebuild_chunk_percentage*

digest_bits_per_entry

This directive affects the size of Squid's Cache Digest, based on the estimate for the total number of cache entries. Reducing the size of the digest results in lower memory usage but a higher false hit probability.

Syntax	`digest_bits_per_entry number`
Default	`digest_bits_per_entry 5`
Example	`digest_bits_per_entry 4`
Related	*digest_generation, store_avg_object_size, cache_dir*

digest_rebuild_period

The digest rebuild period is how often Squid generates the digest of its own cache. This is a fairly CPU-intensive procedure, so you don't want to run it too often. On the other hand, the digest becomes less representative of Squid's contents as more time passes.

Syntax	`digest_rebuild_period time-specification`
Default	`digest_rebuild_period 1 hour`
Example	`digest_rebuild_period 4 hours`
Related	*digest_generation, digest_rewrite_period, digest_swapout_chunk_size, digest_rebuild_chunk_percentage*

digest_rewrite_period

The digest rewrite period is how often Squid generates an on-disk cached HTTP response for its Cache Digest. This is the response sent to neighbors that request Squid's digest. In most cases *digest_rewrite_period* should be the same as *digest_rebuild_period*.

Syntax   `digest_rewrite_period` *time-specification*

Default   `digest_rewrite_period 1 hour`

Example   `digest_rewrite_period 4 hours`

Related   *digest_generation, digest_rebuild_period, digest_swapout_chunk_size, digest_rebuild_chunk_percentage*

digest_swapout_chunk_size

This directive controls the amount of data written to disk for each call to the digest swapout function. Squid services normal cache traffic (client requests, server responses, etc.) in between digest swapout calls. If the value is too large, Squid blocks on the disk I/O and delays normal cache traffic.

Syntax   `digest_swapout_chunk_size` *size-specification*

Default   `digest_swapout_chunk_size 4 KB`

Example   `digest_swapout_chunk_size 16 KB`

Related   *digest_generation, digest_rewrite_period, digest_rebuild_chunk_percentage*

digest_rebuild_chunk_percentage

This directive specifies the percentage of hash-table buckets Squid scans during each call to the digest rebuild procedure. Squid services normal cache traffic in between these calls. Since this scanning is CPU-intensive, user requests may be delayed for a small, but noticeable amount of time. If you suspect a performance problem during the rebuild phase, decrease the *digest_rebuild_chunk_percentage* value.

Syntax   `digest_rebuild_chunk_percentage` *percentage*

Default   `digest_rebuild_chunk_percentage 10`

Example   `digest_rebuild_chunk_percentage 3`

Related   *digest_generation, digest_rebuild_period, store_objects_per_bucket*

chroot

When you specify a value for this directive, Squid passes it to the chroot( ) system call. This provides an extra level of security by isolating the Squid process(es) from the rest of your filesystem. See Chapter 5 for more information.

Syntax   `chroot` *pathname*

Default   No default

Example   `chroot /squid`

client_persistent_connections

This directive controls whether or not Squid uses persistent HTTP connections to cache clients. When disabled, Squid sends `Connection: close` headers in its responses to clients. If you suspect problems caused by client-side persistent connections, disable this directive.

Syntax	`client_persistent_connections on|off`
Default	`client_persistent_connections on`
Example	`client_persistent_connections off`
Related	*server_persistent_connections, pipeline_prefetch*

server_persistent_connections

This directive controls whether or not Squid uses persistent HTTP connections to origin servers and neighbors. When disabled, Squid sends `Connection: close` headers in forwarded requests. If you suspect problems caused by server-side persistent connections, disable this directive.

Syntax	`server_persistent_connections on|off`
Default	`server_persistent_connections on`
Example	`server_persistent_connections off`
Related	*client_persistent_connections*

pipeline_prefetch

This directive controls whether or not Squid prefetches pipelined requests. It is disabled by default, so Squid acts only on one request at a time (per connection). If you enable this directive, Squid processes up to two client requests at once.

Note that the order of responses must match the order of requests. Thus, if the prefetched (second) request completes before the first, it is delayed until the first response is sent.

Squid doesn't implement pipelining on the server-side. It always opens a new connection to an origin server (or neighbor) if there are no idle persistent connections.

Syntax	`pipeline_prefetch on|off`
Default	`pipeline_prefetch off`
Example	`pipeline_prefetch on`
Related	*client_persistent_connections*

extension_methods

HTTP (RFC 2616) allows clients and servers to use their own extension methods. If requests with nonstandard HTTP methods go through Squid, the client receives an "Invalid Request" error message. Squid also writes a *cache.log* entry, such as this:

```
2003/09/29 13:40:24| parseHttpRequest: Unsupported method 'XGET'
```

If you want Squid to accept such requests, you must tell it about the nonstandard methods by listing them after the *extension_methods* directive.

Syntax   extension_methods *HTTP-method* ...
Default   No default
Example   extension_methods XGET XPOST

request_entities

This directive determines how Squid handles GET and HEAD requests that have message bodies (entities). Such requests normally don't contain bodies. There is some confusion about whether or not RFC 2616 allows entities in GET/HEAD requests. Squid denies such requests by default. If you would rather have Squid accept them, enable the *request_entities* directive.

Syntax   request_entities on|off
Default   request_entities off
Example   request_entities on

high_response_time_warning

If you provide a non-zero value for this directive, Squid periodically checks the client-side median response time. If it's above this threshold, Squid prints a warning message in *cache.log*. The value is given in milliseconds.

Syntax   high_response_time_warning *milliseconds*
Default   high_response_time_warning 0
Example   high_response_time_warning 2000
Related   *high_page_fault_warning, high_memory_warning*

high_page_fault_warning

If you provide a nonzero value for this directive, Squid periodically checks the process page fault rate. Page faults generally occur when the Squid process doesn't fit entirely in memory. A moderate number of page faults can significantly degrade performance. If the one-minute average rate (page faults per second) exceeds this threshold, Squid prints a warning message in *cache.log*.

Syntax   high_page_fault_warning *number*
Default   high_page_fault_warning 0
Example   high_page_fault_warning 5
Related   *high_response_time_warning, high_memory_warning*

high_memory_warning

If you provide a nonzero value for this directive, Squid periodically checks process size. A large process size can lead to page faults and a significant performance degradation. Squid uses either mstats( ), mallinfo( ), or sbrk( ) to get the process size. If it exceeds the given threshold, Squid prints a warning message in *cache.log*.

Syntax	high_memory_warning *size-specification*
Default	high_memory_warning 0
Example	high_memory_warning 400 MB
Related	*high_response_time_warning, high_page_fault_warning*

ie_refresh

In Chapter 9, I explained that Internet Explorer versions prior to 5.5 SP1 have a bug that make it unable to force a validation of cached responses when using HTTP interception. This directive provides a partial workaround for the bug. When enabled, Squid pretends that the request contains a no-cache directive. Thus, Squid always forwards these requests on to the origin server or a neighbor.

Note this affects only requests that meet the following requirements:

- The User-Agent header indicates Internet Explorer Version 3, 4, 5.0, or 5.01.
- The If-Modified-Since header is present.
- The request contains a partial URI because it was intercepted (see Chapter 9) or Squid is a surrogate (see Chapter 15).

Squid versions prior to 2.5.STABLE3 contain a bug related to this feature. Although Squid behaves as though the client's request contains a no-cache directive, it doesn't add that directive to the outgoing request. This is a problem if you have one or more neighbor caches. Because the request received by the neighbor doesn't contain a no-cache directive, it may decide to return a cache hit, rather than forward it on to the origin server.

Later versions include the no-cache directive so that such requests should always reach the origin server.

Syntax	ie_refresh on|off
Default	ie_refresh off
Example	ie_refresh on

vary_ignore_expire

When certain HTTP/1.1 origin servers receive an HTTP/1.0 request (e.g., from Squid), and the response contains a Vary header, they also add an Expires header set to the current time. This is to prevent HTTP/1.0 caches, which may not understand the Vary header, from incorrectly reusing a cached response.

Squid understands and implements the Vary header but still sends the string "HTTP/1.0" in its requests. You'll need to enable this directive if you want to get cache hits from responses with Vary and with Expires equal to Date. This directive is somewhat dangerous because the origin server may have its own reasons (other than maintaining backward compatibility) for setting the Expires header.

Syntax   vary_ignore_expire on|off
Default   vary_ignore_expire off
Example   vary_ignore_expire on

sleep_after_fork

Squid uses the fork( ) system call to spawn helper processes, such as redirectors, authenticators, and DNS resolvers. On some systems, a rapid sequence of fork( ) calls consumes all available real and virtual memory. Thus, a fork( ) call may fail with an "out of memory" error. Note that this isn't necessarily a fatal error. Squid continues running as long as at least 50% of helper processes are successfully started.

To alleviate this problem, you can instruct Squid to sleep for a small amount of time after each fork( ) call. This gives the recently forked process time to complete its exec( ) call and free up the memory.

Don't set this value too high, especially if you have a large number of helper processes. Squid doesn't service any client requests until all helpers have been started.

Syntax   sleep_after_fork *microseconds*
Default   sleep_after_fork 0
Example   sleep_after_fork 10000

The Memory Cache

Squid stores some of its recently retrieved objects fully in memory. As you might expect, serving objects from memory is generally faster than reading the data from the disk. In some places, Squid calls this the *hot object cache*. The *cache_mem* directive specifies how much memory Squid should use for in-memory objects.

I usually recommend setting *cache_mem* to a small size, such as something between 8 and 32 MB. If you happen to have tons of extra memory, you can set it higher. In most cases, however, your extra memory is better used by increasing your disk cache size (see Chapter 7).

Many people misunderstand the *cache_mem* directive. They expect it to limit the total amount of memory that Squid uses. Unfortunately, for them, this assumption is incorrect. Squid doesn't have a directive that limits total memory consumption. See Chapters 7 and 16.

The current version of Squid (2.5) stores objects in memory only if they come from the network (origin server or neighbor cache). If Squid reads an object from disk, it doesn't also store it in memory. Older versions of Squid had that functionality. However, it was removed during a major rewrite to simplify the source code.

Only objects smaller than a certain size are held in memory. The *maximum_object_size_in_memory* directive controls this setting. Its default value is 8 KB, which is typically large enough to fit more than half of all responses Squid receives. This directive also limits the amount of memory used for each cache miss as the response is being received. If you have a high request rate but are low on memory, you may want to lower this value to 4 KB. Squid allocates memory for object data in 4-KB chunks. Thus, it makes sense to assign this directive a multiple of 4 KB. Other values end up wasting memory.

In-memory objects fall into one of two groups: *in-transit* or *complete*. Squid uses the memory cache for both types. Complete objects are held in memory only if there is some free space. They have lower priority than in-transit objects. If your cache is busy, the memory cache may contain nothing but in-transit objects (or, *maximum_* *object_size_in_memory* chunks of in-transit objects, actually). Furthermore, Squid always allocates memory for in-transit objects, even if it must exceed the *cache_mem* limit. When an in-transit object becomes a complete object, it is kept in memory only if the memory cache size is below the limit.

The *memory_replacement_policy* directive is analogous to *replacement_policy*. It controls the replacement policy for objects cached in memory. Because the memory cache is typically much smaller than the disk cache, your choice of replacement policy may have a bigger impact. See Chapter 7 for a description of available replacement policies.

Delay Pools

Delay pools are Squid's answer to rate limiting and traffic shaping. They work by limiting the rate at which Squid returns data for cache misses. Cache hits are sent as quickly as possible, under the assumption that local bandwidth is plentiful.

Delay pools were written by David Luyer while at the University of Western Australia. The feature was designed for a LAN environment in which different groups of users (for example, students, instructors, and staff) are on different subnets. You'll see some evidence of this in the following descriptions.

Overview

The delay pools are, essentially "bandwidth buckets." A response is delayed until some amount of bandwidth is available from an appropriate bucket. The buckets don't actually store bandwidth (e.g., 100 Kbit/s), but rather some amount of traffic (e.g., 384 KB). Squid adds some amount of traffic to the buckets each second. Cache clients take some amount of traffic out when they receive data from an upstream source (origin server or neighbor).

The size of a bucket determines how much burst bandwidth is available to a client. If a bucket starts out full, a client can take as much traffic as it needs until the bucket becomes empty. The client then receives traffic allotments at the fill rate.

The mapping between Squid clients and actual buckets is a bit complicated. Squid uses three different constructs to do it: access rules, delay pool classes, and types of buckets. First, Squid checks a client request against the *delay_access* list. If the request is a match, it points to a particular delay pool. Each delay pool has a class: 1, 2, or 3. The classes determine which types of buckets are in use. Squid has three types of buckets: aggregate, individual, and network:

- A class 1 pool has a single aggregate bucket.
- A class 2 pool has an aggregate bucket and 256 individual buckets.

- A class 3 pool has an aggregate bucket, 256 network buckets, and 65,536 individual buckets.

As you can probably guess, the individual and network buckets correspond to IP address octets. In a class 2 pool, the individual bucket is determined by the last octet of the client's IPv4 address. In a class 3 pool, the network bucket is determined by the third octet, and the individual bucket by the third and fourth octets.

For the class 2 and 3 delay pools, you can disable buckets you don't want to use. For example, you can define a class 2 pool with only individual buckets by disabling the aggregate bucket.

When a request goes through a pool with more than one bucket type, it takes bandwidth from all buckets. For example, consider a class 3 pool with aggregate, network, and individual buckets. If the individual bucket has 20 KB, the network bucket 30 KB, but the aggregate bucket only 2 KB, the client receives only a 2-KB allotment. Even though some buckets have plenty of traffic, the client is limited by the bucket with the smallest amount.

Configuring Squid

Before you can use delay pools, you must enable the feature when compiling. Use the --enable-delay-pools option when running ./configure. You can then use the following directives to set up the delay pools.

delay_pools

The *delay_pools* directive tells Squid how many pools you want to define. It should go before any other delay pool-configuration directives in *squid.conf*. For example, if you want to have five delay pools:

```
delay_pools 5
```

The next two directives actually define each pool's class and other characteristics.

delay_class

You must use this directive to define the class for each pool. For example, if the first pool is class 3:

```
delay_class 1 3
```

Similarly, if the fourth pool is class 2:

```
delay_class 4 2
```

In theory, you should have one *delay_class* line for each pool. However, if you skip or omit a particular pool, Squid doesn't complain.

delay_parameters

Finally, this is where you define the interesting delay pool parameters. For each pool, you must tell Squid the fill rate and maximum size for each type of bucket. The syntax is:

```
delay_parameters N rate/size [rate/size [rate/size]]
```

The *rate* value is given in bytes per second, and *size* in total bytes. If you think of *rate* in terms of bits per second, you must remember to divide by 8.

Note that if you divide the *size* by the *rate*, you'll know how long it takes (number of seconds) the bucket to go from empty to full when there are no clients using it.

A class 1 pool has just one bucket and might look like this:

```
delay_class 2 1
delay_parameters 2 2000/8000
```

For a class 2 pool, the first bucket is the aggregate, and the second is the group of individual buckets. For example:

```
delay_class 4 2
delay_parameters 4 7000/15000 3000/4000
```

Similarly, for a class 3 pool, the aggregate bucket is first, the network buckets are second, and the individual buckets are third:

```
delay_class 1 3
delay_parameters 1 7000/15000 3000/4000 1000/2000
```

delay_initial_bucket_level

This directive sets the initial level for all buckets when Squid first starts or is reconfigured. It also applies to individual and network buckets, which aren't created until first referenced. The value is a percentage. For example:

```
delay_initial_bucket_level 75%
```

In this case, each newly created bucket is initially filled to 75% of its maximum size.

delay_access

This list of access rules determines which requests go through which delay pools. Requests that are allowed go through the delay pools, while those that are denied aren't delayed at all. If you don't have any *delay_access* rules, Squid doesn't delay any requests.

The syntax for *delay_access* is similar to the other access rule lists (see Chapter 6), except that you must put a pool number before the allow or deny keyword. For example:

```
delay_access 1 allow TheseUsers
delay_access 2 allow OtherUsers
```

Internally, Squid stores a separate access rule list for each delay pool. If a request is allowed by a pool's rules, Squid uses that pool and stops searching. If a request is denied, however, Squid continues examining the rules for remaining pools. In other words, a deny rule causes Squid to stop searching the rules for a single pool but not for all pools.

cache_peer no-delay Option

The *cache_peer* directive has a no-delay option. If set, it makes Squid bypass the delay pools for any requests sent to that neighbor.

Examples

Let's start off with a simple example. Suppose that you have a saturated Internet connection, shared by many users. You can use delay pools to limit the amount of bandwidth that Squid consumes on the link, thus leaving the remaining bandwidth for other applications. Use a class 1 delay pool to limit the bandwidth for all users. For example, this limits everyone to 512 Kbit/s and keeps 1 MB in reserve if Squid is idle:

```
delay_pools 1
delay_class 1 1
delay_parameters 1 65536/1048576
acl All src 0/0
delay_access 1 allow All
```

One of the problems with this simple approach is that some users may receive more than their fair share of the bandwidth. If you want to try something more balanced, use a class 2 delay pool that has individual buckets. Recall that the individual bucket is determined by the fourth octet of the client's IPv4 address. Thus, if you have more than a /24 subnet, you might want to use a class 3 pool instead, which gives you 65536 individual buckets. In this example, I won't use the network buckets. While the overall bandwidth is still 512 Kbit/s, each individual is limited to 128 Kbit/s:

```
delay_pools 1
delay_class 1 3
delay_parameters 1 65536/1048576 -1/-1 16384/262144
acl All src 0/0
delay_access 1 allow All
```

You can also use delay pools to provide different classes of service. For example, you might have important users and unimportant users. In this case, you could use two class 1 delay pools. Give the important users a higher bandwidth limit than everyone else:

```
delay_pools 2
delay_class 1 1
delay_class 2 1
delay_parameters 1 65536/1048576
delay_parameters 2 10000/50000
acl ImportantUsers src 192.168.8.0/22
acl All src 0/0
delay_access 1 allow ImportantUsers
delay_access 2 allow All
```

Issues

Squid's delay pools are often useful, but not perfect. You need to be aware of a few drawbacks and limitations before you use them.

Fairness

One of the most important things to realize about the current delay pools implementation is that it does nothing to guarantee fairness among all users of a single bucket. This is especially important for aggregate buckets (where sharing is high), but less so for individual buckets (where sharing is low).

Squid generally services requests in order of increasing file descriptors. Thus, a request whose server-side TCP connection has a lower file descriptor may receive more bandwidth from a shared bucket than it should.

Application Versus Transport Layer

Bandwidth shaping and rate limiting usually operate at the network transport layer. There, the flow of packets can be controlled very precisely. Delay pools, however, are implemented in the application layer. Because Squid doesn't actually send and receive TCP packets (the kernel does), it has less control over the flow of individual packets. Rather than controlling the transmission and receipt of packets on the wire, Squid controls only how many bytes to read from the kernel.

This means, for example, that incoming response data is queued up in the kernel. The TCP/IP stack can buffer some number of bytes that haven't yet been read by Squid. On most systems, the default TCP receive buffer size is usually between 32 KB and 64 KB. In other words, this much data can arrive over the network very quickly, regardless of anything Squid can do. On the one hand, it seems silly to read this data slowly even though it is already on your system. On the other hand, because the client doesn't receive the whole response right away, it is likely to postpone any future requests until the delayed responses are complete.

If you are concerned that the kernel buffers too much server-side data, you can decrease the TCP receive buffer size with the *tcp_recv_bufsize* directive. Even better, your operating system probably has a way to set this parameter for the whole system. On NetBSD/FreeBSD/OpenBSD, you can use the sysctl variable named *net.inet.tcp.recvspace*. For Linux, read about */proc/sys/net/ipv4/tcp_rmem* in *Documentation/networking/ip-sysctl.txt*.

Fixed Subnetting Scheme

The current delay pools implementation assumes that your LAN uses /24 (class C) subnets, and that all users are in the same /16 (class B) subnet. This might not be so bad, depending on how your network is configured. However, it would be nice if the delay pools subnetting scheme were fully customizable.

If your address space is larger than a /24 and smaller than a 16/, you can always create a class 3 pool and treat it as a class 2 pool (that is one of the examples given earlier).

If you use just one class 2 pool with more than 256 users, some users will share the individual buckets. That might not be so bad, unless you happen to have a bunch of heavy users fighting over one measly bucket.

You might also create multiple class 2 pools and use *delay_access* rules to divide them up among all users. The problem with this approach is that you can't have all users share a single aggregate bucket. Instead, each subgroup has their own aggregate bucket. You can't make a single client go through more than one delay pool.

Monitoring Delay Pools

You can monitor the delay pool levels with the cache manager interface. Request the *delay* page from the CGI interface or with the `squidclient` utility:

```
% squidclient mgr:delay | less
```

See Chapter 14 for a description of the output.

Filesystem Performance Benchmarks

You have a myriad of choices to make when installing and configuring Squid, especially when it comes to the way Squid stores files on disk. Back in Chapter 8, I talked about the various filesystems and storage schemes. Here, I'll provide some hard data on their relative performance.

These tests were done with Web Polygraph, a freely available, high-performance tool for benchmarking HTTP intermediaries (*http://www.web-polygraph.org/*). Over the course of many months, I ran approximately 40 different tests on 5 different operating systems.

The Benchmark Environment

The primary purpose of these benchmarks is to provide a number of measurements that allow you to compare different Squid configurations and features. In order to produce comparable results, I've taken care to minimize any differences between systems being tested.

Hardware for Squid

I used five identical computer systems—one for each of the following operating systems: FreeBSD, Linux, NetBSD, OpenBSD, and Solaris. The boxes are IBM Netfinity servers with one 500-MHz PIII CPU, 1 GB of RAM, an Intel fast-Ethernet NIC, and three 8-GB disk SCSI drives. I realize that these aren't particularly powerful machines by today's standards, but they are good enough for these tests. Anyway, it is more important that they be identical than powerful.

The requirement to use identical hardware means that I can't generate comparable results for other hardware platforms, such as Sun, Digital/Compaq/HP, and others.

Squid Version and Configuration

Except for the *coss* tests, all results are from Squid Version 2.5.STABLE2. The *coss* results are from a patched version of 2.5.STABLE3. Those patches have been committed to the source tree for inclusion into 2.5.STABLE4.

Unless otherwise specified, I used only the --enable-storeio option when running ./configure before compiling Squid. For example:

```
% ./configure --enable-storeio=diskd,ufs,null,coss
```

In all cases, Squid is configured to use 7500 MB of each 8.2-GB disk. This is a total cache size of 21.5 GB. Additionally, *access.log* and *store.log* have been disabled in the configuration file. Here is a sample *squid.conf* file:

```
visible_hostname linux-squid.bench.tst
acl All src 0/0
http_access allow All

cache_dir aufs /cache0 7500 16 256
cache_dir aufs /cache1 7500 16 256
cache_dir aufs /cache2 7500 16 256

cache_effective_user nobody
cache_effective_group nobody
cache_access_log /dev/null
cache_store_log none
logfile_rotate 0
```

Web Polygraph Workload

All the tests in this appendix use the same Polygraph workload file.* Meeting this requirement was, perhaps, the hardest part of running these tests. Normally, the desired throughput is a configuration parameter in a Polygraph workload. However, because the sustainable throughput is different for each configuration, my colleague Alex Rousskov and I developed a workload that can be used for all tests.† We call this the "peak finder" workload because it finds the peak throughput for a device under test.

The name "peak finder" is somewhat misleading because, at least in Squid's case, sustainable throughput decreases over time. The workload is designed to periodically adjust the offered load (throughput) subject to response time requirements. If the measured response time is below a given threshold, Polygraph increases the load. If response time is above the threshold, it decreases the load. Thus, at any point in

---

* Except for the number-of-spindles tests, in which the cache size depends on the number of disks in use.
† You can download this workload at *http://squidbook.org/extras/pf2-pm4.pg.txt*.

time during the test, we know the maximum throughput that still satisfies the response time requirements.

In order to reach a steady-state condition, the test runs until the cache has been filled twice. Polygraph knows the total cache size (21.5 GB) and keeps track of the amount of fill traffic pulled into the cache. These are responses that are cachable but not cache hits. The test duration, then, depends on the sustainable throughput. When the throughput is low, the test takes longer to complete. Some of these tests took more than 10 days to run.

General Comments

I show, for each test, how the sustainable throughput varies over time. The y-axis shows the throughput (responses per second). The x-axis is the ratio of fill-traffic volume to cache size. Because each test takes a different amount of time, this is a nice way to normalize all the results. The test is over when the cache has been filled twice.

In most traces, you'll see that sustainable throughput decreases over time. At the beginning of the test, the throughput is very high. Here, the disks are empty, and Squid doesn't need to replace old objects. The throughput for a full cache is usually worse than for an empty cache. This is a common characteristic of proxy benchmarks and emphasizes the importance of reaching steady-state conditions. Don't be fooled by impressive results from short tests.

The Throughput, Response Time, and Hit Ratio values given in the summary tables are taken from the last 25% of the test. Here, between 1.5 and 2.0 on the x-axis, the throughput is more or less stable and flat. I report the mean of the throughput, response time, and hit ratio values in this range from the trace data.

Throughput is the most interesting metric in these tests. It is given in responses per second. The rows in each summary table are sorted by throughput.

The response time numbers are less interesting because they are all about the same. I decided to report them to show that, indeed, the results stay within the response time window defined by the workload. The target response time is around 1.5 seconds, but the actual response time varies depending on the particular test.

The response hit ratio values are also not particularly interesting. The ideal hit ratio for this workload is about 58%. Due to an as-yet unresolved Polygraph bug, however, the hit ratio decreases slightly as the test progresses.

Keep in mind that these results are meant to demonstrate the relative performance of different options, rather than the absolute values. You'll get different numbers if you repeat the tests on different hardware.

Linux

Linux is obviously a popular choice for Squid. It supports a wide variety of filesystems and storage schemes. These results come from Linux kernel Version 2.4.19 (released August 2, 2002) with SGI's XFS patches Version 1.2.0 (released Feb 11, 2003) and ReiserFS Version 3.6.25.

The kernel's file descriptor limit is set to 8192. I used this command to configure Squid before compiling:

```
% ./configure --enable-storeio=diskd,ufs,aufs,null,coss --with-aufs-threads=32
```

The Linux results are summarized in Table D-1, and Figure D-1 shows the traces. You can see that *coss* is the best performer, with *aufs* coming in second and *diskd* third. As I'm writing this, *coss* is an experimental feature and not necessarily suitable for a production system. In the long run, you'll probably be better off with *aufs*.

Table D-1. Linux benchmarking results

Storage scheme	Filesystem	Mount options	Throughput (xact/sec)	Response time (sec)	Hit ratio (%)
coss			326.3	1.59	53.9
aufs(1)	*ext2fs*	noatime	168.5	1.45	56.3
diskd(1)	*ext2fs*	noatime	149.4	1.53	56.1
aufs(2)	*ext2fs*		110.0	1.46	55.6
ufs(1)	*ext2fs*		54.9	1.52	55.6
ufs(2)	*ext3fs*		48.4	1.49	56.8
ufs(3)	*xfs*		40.7	1.54	55.3
ufs(4)	*reiserfs*	notail, noatime	29.7	1.55	55.0
ufs(5)	*reiserfs*		21.4	1.55	55.1

Note that the noatime option gives a significant boost in performance to *aufs*. The throughput jumps from 110 to 168 transactions per second with the addition of this mount option. Linux also has an async option, but it is enabled by default. I did not run any tests with async disabled.

Of the many filesystem choices, *ext2fs* seems to give the best performance. *ext3fs* (*ext2* plus journaling) is only slightly lower, followed by *xfs*, and *reiserfs*.

FreeBSD

FreeBSD is another popular Squid platform, and my personal favorite. Table D-2 and Figure D-2 summarize the results for FreeBSD. Again, *coss* exhibits the highest throughput, followed by *diskd*. The *aufs* storage scheme doesn't currently run on

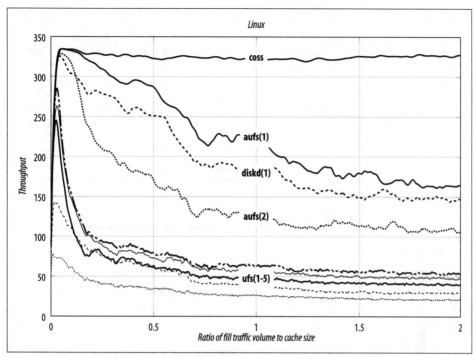

Figure D-1. Linux filesystem benchmarking traces

FreeBSD. These results come from FreeBSD Version 4.8-STABLE (released April 3, 2003). I built a kernel with the following noteworthy options:

```
options         MSGMNB=16384
options         MSGMNI=41
options         MSGSEG=2049
options         MSGSSZ=64
options         MSGTQL=512
options         SHMSEG=16
options         SHMMNI=32
options         SHMMAX=2097152
options         SHMALL=4096
options         MAXFILES=8192
options         NMBCLUSTERS=32768
options         VFS_AIO
```

Table D-2. FreeBSD benchmarking results

Storage scheme	Filesystem	Mount options	Throughput	Response time	Hit ratio
coss			330.7	1.58	54.5
diskd(1)	UFS	async, noatime, softupdate	129.0	1.58	54.1
diskd(2)	UFS		77.4	1.47	56.2
ufs(1)	UFS	async, noatime, softupdate	38.0	1.49	56.8

Table D-2. FreeBSD benchmarking results (continued)

Storage scheme	Filesystem	Mount options	Throughput	Response time	Hit ratio
ufs(2)	UFS	noatime	31.1	1.54	55.0
ufs(3)	UFS	async	30.2	1.51	55.9
ufs(4)	UFS	softupdate	29.9	1.51	55.7
ufs(5)	UFS		24.4	1.50	56.4

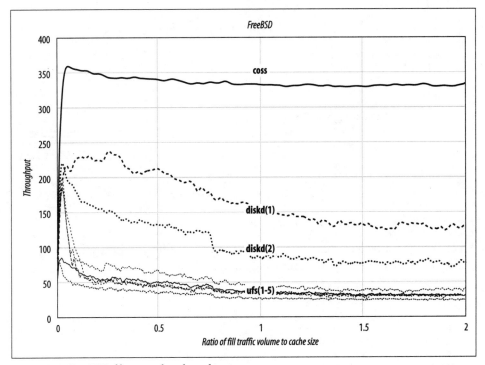

Figure D-2. FreeBSD filesystem benchmarking traces

Enabling the async, noatime, and softupdate* options boosts the standard *ufs* performance from 24 to 38 transactions per second. However, using one of the other storage schemes increases the sustainable throughput even more.

FreeBSD's *diskd* performance (129/sec) isn't quite as good as on Linux (169/sec), perhaps because the underlying filesystem (*ext2fs*) is better.

Note that the trace for *coss* is relatively flat. Its performance doesn't change much over time. Furthermore, both FreeBSD and Linux report similar throughput numbers: 326/sec and 331/sec. This leads me to believe that the disk system isn't a bottle-

---

* On FreeBSD, softupdates aren't a mount option, but must be set with the tunefs command.

neck in these tests. In fact, the test with no disk cache (see the section "Number of Disk Spindles") achieves essentially the same throughput (332/sec).

OpenBSD

The results in this section are from OpenBSD Version 3.3 (released May 1, 2003). I built a kernel with the following notable configuration options:

```
option      MSGMNB=8192
option      MSGMNI=40
option      MSGSEG=512
option      MSGSSZ=64
option      MSGTQL=2048
option      SHMSEG=16
option      SHMMNI=32
option      SHMMAX=2048
option      SHMALL=4096
option      NMBCLUSTERS=32768
option      MAXFILES=8192
```

Table D-3 and Figure D-3 summarize the OpenBSD results. The choices for Open-BSD are similar to those for FreeBSD. Unfortunately, however, *coss* doesn't run on OpenBSD, which lacks the aio_read( ) and aio_write( ) functions.

Table D-3. OpenBSD benchmarking results

Storage scheme	Filesystem	Mount options	Throughput	Response time	Hit ratio
diskd(1)	UFS	async, noatime, softupdate	91.1	1.45	56.3
diskd(2)	UFS		63.7	1.44	56.2
ufs(1)	UFS	softupdate	27.6	1.51	56.3
ufs(2)	UFS	noatime	25.1	1.52	56.3
ufs(3)	UFS		22.7	1.52	56.1
ufs(4)	UFS	async	22.1	1.51	56.6

In general, the OpenBSD results are slightly worse than FreeBSD. This isn't too surprising, given that the OpenBSD project emphasizes security and perhaps spends less time on filesystem performance.

One odd result is that using the async option (alone) caused a slight decrease in performance for the *ufs* storage scheme.

NetBSD

These results come from NetBSD Version 1.6.1 (released April 21, 2003). Table D-4 and Figure D-4 summarize the NetBSD results. NetBSD actually performs almost the same as OpenBSD. The best configuration yields about 90 transactions per second.

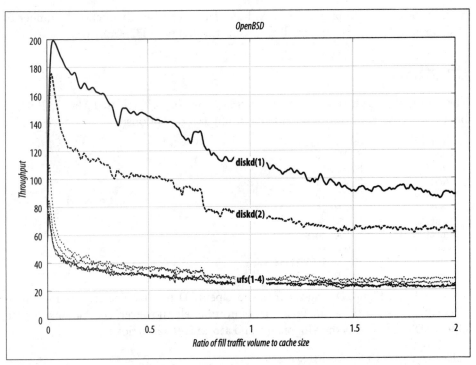

Figure D-3. OpenBSD filesystem benchmarking traces

Unfortunately, NetBSD doesn't support *coss* or *aufs*. I built a custom kernel with these options:

```
options        NMBCLUSTERS=32768
options        MAXFILES=8192
options        MSGSSZ=64
options        MSGSEG=512
options        MSGMNB=8192
options        MSGMNI=40
options        MSGTQL=2048
```

Table D-4. NetBSD benchmarking results

Storage scheme	Filesystem	Mount options	Throughput	Response time	Hit ratio
diskd(1)	UFS	softupdate,noatime,async	90.3	1.49	57.2
diskd(2)	UFS	softupdate	73.5	1.51	55.8
diskd(3)	UFS		60.1	1.48	55.9
ufs(1)	UFS	softupdate,noatime,async	34.9	1.51	56.2
ufs(2)	UFS	softupdate	31.7	1.52	55.5
ufs(3)	UFS		23.6	1.53	55.4

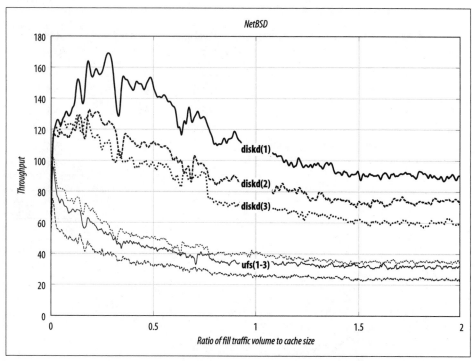

Figure D-4. NetBSD filesystem benchmarking traces

Solaris

These results come from Solaris Version 8 for Intel (released February 2002). Solaris 9 was available when I started these tests, but Sun no longer makes it freely available. I tweaked the kernel by adding these lines to */etc/system*:

```
set rlim_fd_max = 8192
set msgsys:msginfo_msgmax=8192
set msgsys:msginfo_msgmnb=8192
set msgsys:msginfo_msgmni=40
set msgsys:msginfo_msgssz=64
set msgsys:msginfo_msgtql=2048
set shmsys:shminfo_shmmax=2097152
set shmsys:shminfo_shmmni=32
set shmsys:shminfo_shmseg=16
```

Table D-5 and Figure D-5 summarize the Solaris results. This is the only other operating system, in addition to Linux, in which the *aufs* storage scheme works well. Interestingly, both *aufs* and *diskd* have about the same performance on Solaris, although the actual numbers are much lower than on Linux.

Table D-5. Solaris benchmarking results

Storage scheme	Filesystem	Mount options	Throughput	Response time	Hit ratio
diskd(1)	UFS	noatime	56.3	1.53	55.7
aufs(1)	UFS	noatime	53.6	1.49	56.6
diskd(2)	UFS		37.9	1.53	55.5
aufs(2)	UFS		37.4	1.49	56.4
coss			32.4	1.47	54.6
ufs(1)	UFS	noatime	24.0	1.53	55.6
ufs(2)	UFS		19.0	1.50	56.3

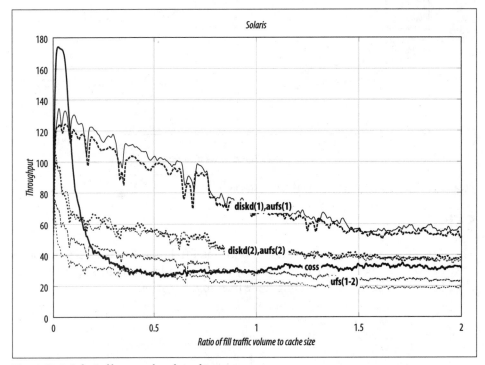

Figure D-5. Solaris filesystem benchmarking traces

Solaris also supports *coss*, but at nowhere near the rates for Linux and FreeBSD. For some unknown reason, *coss* on Solaris is limited to 32 transactions per second.

Number of Disk Spindles

In this section, I compare Squid's performance for different number of disk drives (spindles). These tests are from the Linux system with the *aufs* storage scheme and *ext2fs* filesystems.

Table D-6 and Figure D-6 summarize the results. The test with no disk drives has the best throughput, but the worst response time and hit ratio. Note that Squid does serve a few cache hits from memory, so the hit ratio isn't zero.

Table D-6. Comparison of 0–3 disk spindles on Linux with aufs

#Disks	Throughput	Response time	Hit ratio
0	332.1	2.99	0.4
3	109.6	1.44	56.2
2	85.3	1.49	53.9
1	66.0	1.50	53.5

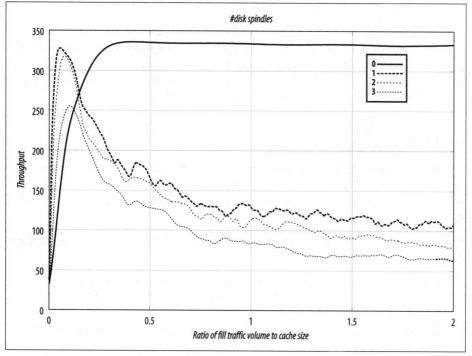

Figure D-6. Benchmarking results for 0, 1, 2, and 3 disk drives on Linux with aufs

The primary purpose of these tests is to show that Squid's performance doesn't increase in proportion to the number of disk drives. Excluding other factors, you may be able to get better performance from three systems with one disk drive each, rather than a single system with three drives.

APPENDIX E

Squid on Windows

Squid has been designed to run on Unix, but you can also get it to run on Microsoft Windows. Perhaps the easiest way is to use Red Hat's Cygwin emulation layer. It gives a Windows box everything it needs to run a variety of Unix applications. Another option is to use SquidNT. This is a version of the source code that has been modified to compile under a native Windows C compiler.

Cygwin

Cygwin is a Unix emulation package for Microsoft Windows. It provides an environment that allows you to build and run software primarily designed for Unix. You can also download and install a number of precompiled binary packages, including Squid.

Cygwin runs on Windows 95, 98, ME, NT, 2000, and XP. The Cygwin FAQ, however, makes this disclaimer:

> Keep in mind that Cygwin can only do as much as the underlying OS supports. Because of this, Cygwin will behave differently, and exhibit different limitations, on the various versions of Windows.

When writing this appendix, I installed Cygwin Version 1.3.21 on Windows 2000.

Installing Cygwin

The first step is to install Cygwin on your Windows system. Visit the *http://www. cygwin.com/* site and click on the *Install Cygwin* link. After running Cygwin Setup, you'll have the base environment with a number of standard Unix tools. You might want to spend a little time playing with it to see how it works. Once you're comfortable with the Cygwin environment, decide if you'd like to use the precompiled package or compile Squid from its source.

The Squid Package

The Cygwin project provides a precompiled Squid binary. To download and install it, run the Cygwin Setup program again. When you see the *Select Packages* window, find the *Web* group and select *squid* for installation. Continue with the setup procedure as before.

When *Setup* completes, you should find the Squid binary at */usr/bin/squid* and the configuration file at */etc/squid.conf*.

Compiling Squid

You can also compile the Squid source code under Cygwin. This might be necessary if you want to run a more recent version than the precompiled binary available from the Cygwin site. To compile on Cygwin, you need to install at least the following packages:

- *Archive/sharutils*
- *Devel/make*
- *Devel/gcc*
- *Interpreters/Perl*

After installing those tools, you should be able to configure and compile Squid as described in Chapter 3.

Configuring and Running

Since Cygwin is essentially a Unix environment, you can run Squid as described throughout this book. Some special features may or may not work. For example, you won't be able to build certain authentication helpers without additional libraries and header files. Here are a few things to watch out for:

- The *cache_effective_user* directive is set to *nobody* by default. When you run Squid under Cygwin, you may get an error that the *nobody* doesn't exist. You can either create that user or set *cache_effective_user* to a username that does exist.
- Cygwin doesn't have a */etc/resolv.conf* by default, and Squid won't pick up your DNS server settings from the Windows registry. You can either create a fake */etc/resolv.conf* or list your name server addresses in *squid.conf* with a *dns_nameserver* directive.

SquidNT

Guido Serassio is maintaining a project called SquidNT. It is branch of Squid's development tree that contains changes necessary for a native port of Squid to Windows NT, 2000, XP, and 2003. In other words, you can compile and run this version of

Squid on Windows without any Unix emulation libraries. The code is known to compile with Microsoft's Visual C++ 6.0 compiler and under the MSYS+MinGW environment. Guido also provides some precompiled SquidNT binaries. You can find his work and more information on SquidNT by visiting *http://www.serassio.it/ SquidNT.htm*.

Configuring Squid Clients

This appendix contains information on setting up various browsers and user-agents to use Squid. Although it is more extensively covered in my O'Reilly book *Web Caching*, I'll include some brief instructions here.

I have instructions for the following HTTP user-agents: Internet Explorer v6, Konqueror v3, Lynx v2.8, Netscape v7 a.k.a. Mozilla v5, Opera v7, libwww-perl v5, Python's urllib/urllib2, and Wget v1.8. If you think this is all a huge hassle, consider using HTTP interception, as described in Chapter 9.

Manually

Web browsers and other HTTP-based user-agents have methods for explicitly setting a proxy address. For large organizations, this is a real hassle. You may simply have too many desktops to visit one at a time. Additionally, this approach isn't as flexible as the others. For example, you can't temporarily stop the flow of requests to the proxy or easily bypass the cache for certain troublesome sites.

Browsers usually give you the option to send HTTPS URLs to a proxy. Squid can handle HTTPS requests, although it can't cache the responses. Squid simply tunnels the encrypted traffic. Thus, you should configure the browser to proxy HTTPS requests only if your firewall prevents direct connections to secure sites.

Netscape/Mozilla

To manually configure proxies with Netscape and Mozilla, follow this sequence of menus:

- *Edit*
- *Preferences*
- *Advanced*
- *Proxies*

- *Manual proxy configuration*
- Fill in the *HTTP Proxy* address and *Port* fields. Enter the same values for *FTP Proxy* if you like.

Explorer

To manually configure proxies in Internet Explorer, select the following sequence of menus:

- *View* from the main window menu
- *Internet Options*
- *Connections* tab
- *LAN Settings*
- Enable *Use a proxy server* and enter its address in the *Address* and *Port* fields

The *Advanced* button opens a new window in which you can enter different proxy addresses for different protocols (HTTP, FTP, etc.).

Konqueror

You can manually configure proxies in Konqueror by clicking on the following sequence of menus:

- *Settings*
- *Configure Konqueror*
- *Proxies & Cache*
- *Use Proxy*
- Fill in the address for *HTTP Proxy*, and *Port*. Use the same values for other protocols if you like.

Opera

Here's how to find the proxy configuration screen in Opera browsers:

- *File*
- *Preferences*
- *Network*
- *Proxy Servers*
- Enter an IP address (or hostname) and port number for HTTP, FTP, and other protocols as necessary.

Lynx

The Lynx browser uses a configuration file, typically */usr/local/etc/lynx.cfg*. There you'll find a number of settings for proxies. For example:

```
http_proxy:http://proxy.example.com:3128/
https_proxy:http://proxy.example.com:3128/
ftp_proxy:http://proxy.example.com:3128/
```

Lynx also accepts proxy configuration via environment variables, as described in the next section.

Environment Variables

Some browsers and other user-agents look for proxy settings in environment variables. Note that the variable names are lowercase, unlike most environment variable names:

```
csh% setenv http_proxy http://proxy.example.com:3128/
csh% setenv ftp_proxy http://proxy.example.com:3128/

sh$ http_proxy=http://proxy.example.com:3128/
sh$ ftp_proxy=http://proxy.example.com:3128/
export http_proxy ftp_proxy
```

I've convinced myself that the following products and packages check for these environment variables:

- Opera
- Lynx
- Wget
- Python's urllib and urllib2
- libwww-perl

Proxy Auto-Configuration

Proxy Auto-Configuration is a technique that allows more control over the way user-agents select a proxy. The configuration file is simply a text file containing a JavaScript function. Browsers download the configuration file when they start up and then evaluate the function before each request. The function's return value determines where the request is sent.

Proxy Auto-Configuration is attractive because it gives the network administrator more control. For example, you can temporarily disable your caching service, implement load balancing, or migrate the service to new systems. Additionally, the function can return a list of proxy addresses, which the browser tries in sequence. If the first is unavailable, it tries the second, and so on.

The following browsers support Proxy Auto-Configuration:

- Internet Explorer
- Opera
- Netscape
- Konqueror
- Mozilla

All these browsers have a place in which you can type in the Proxy Auto-Configuration URL. You'll find it in the same place as the manual proxy settings, earlier described in the section "Manually." Configuring hundreds or thousands of workstations is a real hassle, which is why a handful of companies came up with WPAD, described in the next section.

Writing a Proxy Auto-Configuration function is relatively straightforward. The function, named FindProxyForURL, takes two arguments and returns a list of proxy addresses, separated by semicolons. The word DIRECT instructs the browser to forward the request directly to the origin server, rather than to a proxy. Here is a simple example:

```
function FindProxyForURL(url, host) {
    if (isPlainHostName(host))
        return "DIRECT";
    if (!isResolvable(host))
        return "DIRECT";
    if (url.substring(0, 5) == "http:")
        return "PROXY 172.16.5.1:3128; DIRECT";
    if (url.substring(0, 4) == "ftp:")
        return "PROXY 172.16.5.1:3128; DIRECT";
    return "DIRECT";
}
```

The first if statement makes the browser connect directly to the origin server if the user types a single-component hostname, such as *www*. This is generally a good idea because the browser's interpretation of the hostname might be different from the proxy's. The second if statement ensures that the hostname exists in the DNS. If not, the user sees an error message from the browser itself, rather than from Squid. The next two if statements return a proxy address, followed by DIRECT for HTTP and FTP URLs. If the proxy doesn't respond, the browser attempts to make a direct connection to the origin server.

 If you have a firewall in place, the browser probably won't be able to make a direct connection.

After writing the function, save it somewhere in your web server's data directory. Next, you need to configure the server to return a specific content type for the file.

The convention is to give the file a *.pac* extension, such as *proxy.pac*. Then, ensure that the HTTP server returns the content type application/x-ns-proxy-autoconfig. With Apache, you can add this line to your server config file:

```
AddType application/x-ns-proxy-autoconfig .pac
```

Refer to Section 4.3 of *Web Caching* (O'Reilly), for more information on Proxy Auto-Configuration files, including more complicated FindProxyForURL ideas and examples.

WPAD

The Web Proxy Auto Discovery (WPAD) protocol is a technique for user-agents to find a nearby caching proxy automatically. The idea is relatively simple. The protocol provides a number of methods for generating a URL that refers to a Proxy Auto-Configuration file. Those methods include DHCP, DNS lookups, and SLP (the Service Location Protocol).

DHCP is the first method the user-agent should try. It sends a query for "option 252" to a local DHCP server. The response is a string: the URL. Here's how to configure ISC's DHCP server for WPAD:

```
option wpad code 252 = text;
option wpad "http://172.16.1.1/proxy.pac";
```

The second method is SLP. However, its implementation is optional. I do not know if any user-agents actually support WPAD via SLP.

DNS is the last resort. The protocol specification outlines a number of DNS techniques a user-agent might use to find a *wpad.dat* URL. The most straightforward technique is to perform an address lookup for the hostname *wpad* in the local domain. For example, if the system's hostname is *orion.example.com*, the agent requests the IP address of *wpad.example.com*. If the lookup is successful, the agent makes a TCP connect to that address on port 80 and requests */wpad.dat*.

To make this work in Apache, you need to set the content type for the *wpad.dat* file like this:

```
AddType application/x-ns-proxy-autoconfig .dat
```

This may have negative side effects if your server has other files that end with *.dat*. One trick some people use is to redirect requests for *wpad.dat* to *proxy.pac*, with commands like this in *httpd.conf*:

```
Redirect /wpad.dat http://wpad.example.com/proxy.pac
```

Note that you probably won't be able to set up a separate virtual host for the *wpad* name in your domain. This is because some user-agents set the Host header to the IP address, rather than the hostname. The following is an example.

```
GET /wpad.dat HTTP/1.1
Accept: */*
User-Agent: Mozilla/4.0 (compatible; MSIE 6.0; Win32)
Host: 206.168.0.13
```

WPAD is enabled by default in Microsoft Internet Explorer. Konqueror also supports WPAD but disables it by default. You can enable WPAD in Konqueror by visiting the proxy configuration page (described in the "Konqueror" section) and selecting *Auto Configure Proxy*. Although the current stable versions of Netscape (v7. 02) and Mozilla (v5.0) don't implement WPAD, future versions will.

Summary

Table F-1 summarizes the various proxy configuration options for the user-agents mentioned in this appendix.

Table F-1. Proxy configuration techniques for popular user-agents

User agent	Manual	Environment	PAC	WPAD
Explorer	Yes	No	Yes	Yes
Konqueror	Yes	No	Yes	Yes
libwww-perl	N/A	Yes	No	No
Lynx	Yes	Yes	No	No
Netscape/Mozilla	Yes	No	Yes	No
Opera	Yes	Yes	Yes	No
Wget	N/A	Yes	No	No

Index

We'd like to hear your suggestions for improving our indexes. Send email to *index@oreilly.com*.

debugging (*continued*)
 replicating problems and, 326–328
 reporting bugs, 329
 segmentation violations and, 323–326
 stack traces and, 323–326
 swap directory error, 315
 system speed, 318
debug_options directive, 347
 cache.log, 213
delay, cache manager page, 283
delay pools
 configuration, 402
 monitoring, 406
 overview, 401
 subnetting scheme and, 406
delay_access ACL, 80
delay_access directive, 386, 403
delay_class directive, 386, 402
delay_initial_bucket_level directive,
  387, 403
delay_parameters directive, 386, 403
delay_pools directive, 385, 402
deny_info directive, 374
DEVEL releases, 9
developers, devel.squid-cache.org site, 12
devices, interception caching and, 130–141
diffs, applying, 32
Digest authentication, 194
 API, 203
 auth_param directive, parameters
  supported, 201
digestauthenticator, cache manager
  page, 250
digest_bits_per_entry directive, 393
digest_generation directive, 393
digest_rebuild_chunk_percentage
  directive, 394
digest_rebuild_period directive, 393
digest_rewrite_period directive, 394
digest_stats, cache manager page, 270
digest_swapout_chunk_size directive, 394
direct options, 178
directories
 cache directories, initialization, 46
 disk cache, object allocation, 100
directory argument, cache_dir directive, 94
directory number field, store.log, 229
disk cache
 cache_dir directive, 94
 cache_replacement_policy directive, 101
 cache_swap_high directive, 99

cache_swap_low directive, 99
 directories, object allocation, 100
 I/O bottleneck, 108
 object removal, 102–104
 object size, 99
 refresh_pattern directive, 104
 replacement policy, 101
 usage, 99
disk space, process size and, 96
disk spindles, benchmarks and, 416
diskd, cache manager page, 245
diskd storage scheme, 115–119
diskd_program directive, 352
dns, cache manager page, 247
DNS name lookup tests failed message,
  debugging and, 316
dns_children directive, 350
dns_defnames directive, 351
dns_nameservers directive, 351
dns_retransmit_interval directive, 350
dns_testnames directive, 373
dns_timeout directive, 351
domain names, ACLs, 57
dst ACL type, 61
dst_as ACL type, 70
dstdomain ACL type, 62
dstdom_regex ACL type, 72

E

emulate_httpd_log directive, 341
 access.log and, 224
environment variables, proxy manual
  configuration, 423
environments, chroot, 50
ephemeral ports, 17
err_html_text directive, 374
error checking, squid.conf file, 45
error messages, surrogate mode and, 313
error_directory directive, 382
ESI (Edge Side Includes), 4
/etc/inittab scheme, 50
/etc/rc.local script, 49
events page, cache manger pages, 244
expires field, store.log, 230
Explorer, manual configuration, 422
ext2fs, 93
extension_methods directive, 395
external ACLs, 74
 authentication helpers and, 207
 writing, 208
external_acl, cache manager page, 250

Q

query_icmp directive, 379
quick_abort_max directive, 360
quick_abort_min directive, 360
quick_abort_pct directive, 361

R

-R option, command-line, 45
range requests
    range_offset_limit directive, 362
range_offset_limit directive, 362
rc.d scheme, 49
read-only option, cache_dir directive, 98
read_timeout directive, 363
Ready to serve requests message, 47
realm parameter, auth_param directive, 196
redirect_children directive, 189, 190, 353
redirector, cache manager page, 250
redirector pool, 189
redirector_access ACL, 79
redirector_access directive, 191, 353
redirector_bypass directive, 191, 354
redirectors
    access controls and, 185
    AdZapper, 193
    buffered I/O, 187
    configuration for, 190
    definition, 185
    filters and, 185
    interface, 186
    Jesred, 192
    samples, 187
    squidGuard, 192
    Squirm, 192
redirect_program directive, 190, 353
redirect_rewrites_host_header
    directive, 191, 353
referer field, referer.log, 232
referer.log, 231
referer_log directive, 346
referer.log file, 211
refresh, cache manager page, 280
refresh_pattern directive, 360
refresh_pattern directive, disk cache, 104
regular expressions, ACLs type, 59
releases of Squid, 9
reload_into_ims directive, 380
reloads, surrogate mode and, 312

removing objects
    entire cache directories, 104
    groups of, 103
    individually, 102
replacement policy, disk cache, 101
replicating problems, debugging
    and, 326–328
reply_body_max_size ACL, 80
reply_body_max_size directive, 368
rep_mime_type ACL type, 74
reporting bugs, 329
req_mime_type ACL type, 74
request method field, access.log, 217
request_body_max_size directive, 360
request_entities directive, 396
request_header_max_size directive, 359
requests
    denying, access controls and, 89
    different proxy, 182
    single proxy, 182
request_timeout directive, 363
Request-URI
    FQDN, 186
    HTTP redirect messages, 187
    ident_lookup_access directive, 186
    whitespace, 187
resources for support, 5
response time field, access.log, 216
responses, median time, 238
restricting usage, access controls and, 86
result code, access.log, 218
result/status codes field, access.log, 216
root, starting as, 37
rotating log files, 53, 235
routers
    application-layer, 153
    content routers, 153
RTT (round-trip time), netdb and, 163
rules
    access controls
        checks, 84
        matching, 81
        syntax, 80
    ACLs, 78
running processes, reconfiguring, 52

S

-s option, command-line, 44
samples, redirectors, 187
SASL (Simple Authentication and Security
    Layer), authentication and, 199
scaling, ICP, 165

scheme argument, cache_dir directive, 94
security
    log files, 236
    surrogate mode and, 302
segmentation violations,
        debugging, 323–326
server acceleration, 302
    content negotiation, 311
    overview, 303
    (see also surrogate mode)
server_list, cache manager page, 286
server_persistent_connections directive, 395
servers
    FTP servers, 2
    Gopher, 2
    HTTP, 2
    multicast ICP, 170
    origin servers, 2
server-side of Squid, 1
sever acceleration, access controls, 310
shells, file-descriptor limits, 15
shutdown, 51
shutdown, cache manager page, 254
shutdown_lifetime directive, 365
sibling caches, 153
    false hits, 154
size argument
    cache_dir directive, 95
sleep_after_fork directive, 398
slow speed, debugging and, 318
SMB (authentication helper)
    Basic authentication, 199
    NTLM authentication, 205
SNMP
    monitoring and, 290
    snmpget and, 292
    snmpwalk and, 292
SNMP MIB, 237
snmp_access ACL, 79
snmp_access directive, 383
snmp_community ACL type, 71
snmpget, 292
snmp_incoming_address directive, 383
snmp_outgoing_address directive, 384
snmp_port directive, 383
snmpwalk, 292
soft updates, filesystem tuning and, 110
Solaris
    file descriptors and, 17
    filesystem benchmarks, 415

source code
    CVS and, 11
    patches, applying, 32
    precompiled binaries, 9, 11
    shared libraries and, 10
    Squid ports, 9
    unpacking, 14
speed, debugging and, 318
Squeezer, 227
Squid
    as daemon process, 47
        squid_start script, 48
    history of, 3
squid -k shutdown command, 51
Squid MIB, 292–301
Squid ports, 9
Squid RPMs, 11
squidaio_counts, cache manager page, 244
squid-announce mailing list, 7
squid-cache Web site, 5
squidclient utility, Cache Manager and, 240
squid.conf
    access controls, 39
    cache_mgr directive, 42
    case sensitivity, 36
    directives, 35, 331–398
    error checking, 45
    http_port directive, 38
    syntax, 35
    visible_hostname directive, 40
squid-dev mailing list, 7
squidGuard redirector, 192
SquidNT, 419
squid.pid file, shutdown and, 51
Squid-RRD, cache manager and, 290
squid_start script, Squid as daemon
        process, 48
squid-users mailing list, 5, 6
Squirm redirector, 192
src ACL type, 60
src_as ACL type, 70
srcdomain ACL type, 63
srcdom_regex ACL type, 72
SSL connections
    https_port directive, 331
    surrogate mode, 304
ssl_unclean_shutdown directive, 332
STABLE releases, 9
stack traces
    debugging, 323–326
status code field, store.log, 230
stderr, terminal window and, 46

V

-V option, command-line, 45
-v option, command-line, 44
vary_ignore_expire directive, 397
versions of Squid, 9
via_headers, cache manager page, 252
visible_hostname directive, 40, 369
vm_objects, cache manager page, 264

W

wais_relay_host directive, 359
wais_relay_port directive, 359
WCCP (Web Cache Coordination Protocol)
        interception caching, 138
    configuration, 147
    FreeBSD, 144
    Linux systems, 142
    NetBSD, 146
    OpenBSD, 145
wccp_incoming_address directive, 385
wccp_outgoing_address directive, 385
wccp_router directive, 384
wccp_version directive, 385

web caching, 2
Web Polygraph, workload file
    filesystem benchmarks, 408
Webalyzer, 227
whitespace, Request-URI, 187
winbind authentication helper
    Basic authentication, 200
    NTLM authentication, 205
Windows, Cygwin, 418
workload files, Polygraph, 408
WPAD (Web Proxy Auto Discovery) proxy
        configuration, 425

X

-X option, command-line, 45

Y

-Y option, command-line, 45
YP authentication helper (Basic
        authentication), 200

Z

-z option, command-line, 44

About the Author

Duane Wessels has been active in the field of web caching since 1994 when he worked on the Harvest project. Later he joined the National Laboratory for Applied Network Research to work on IRCache and Squid. His first book, *Web Caching*, was published by O'Reilly & Associates in 2001. He is currently co-owner of The Measurement Factory, Inc., a company that specializes in evaluating the performance, compliance, and security of HTTP intermediaries.

Colophon

Our look is the result of reader comments, our own experimentation, and feedback from distribution channels. Distinctive covers complement our distinctive approach to technical topics, breathing personality and life into potentially dry subjects.

The animal on the cover of *Squid: The Definitive Guide* is a giant squid (*Architeuthis dux*). Of the class *Cephalopoda*, which means "head foot," the giant squid holds much fascination for humans, part of which has to do with the fact that it has never been observed alive in its natural habitat. Scientists have only been able to study specimens that have been caught or found washed up on beaches. This invertebrate can grow to 60 feet in length and weigh as much as a ton. It's a deep-sea dweller (660–2,300 feet) that is found throughout the world's oceans.

A giant squid consists of seven parts. Its head houses a complex brain. Its eyes are the largest in the animal kingdom—up to 10 inches in diameter. (Most deep-sea animals have very large eyes so they can gather the small amounts of light available in the depths of the ocean.) Its fins are relatively small and help it to balance and maneuver as it swims. Its main body is called a mantle: it's a muscular sac that contains most of the organ systems. Its eight arms are studded with two rows of suckers; it also has two much longer feeding tentacles, the ends of which also have suckers and are called clubs. Finally, its funnel is a multipurpose tube used to breathe, squirt ink, lay eggs, expel waste, and propel itself.

To eat, a giant squid captures its prey with its two long feeding tentacles. Holding the intended dinner with its shorter arms, its sharp horny beak cuts the food up, and a file-like radula sends it down the throat and esophagus; the food then passes directly through the brain to the stomach. Scientists believe giant squid may be solitary hunters because no more than one has ever been caught in the same fishing net.

Mary Anne Weeks Mayo was the production editor and copyeditor for *Squid: The Definitive Guide*. Sada Preisch proofread the book, and Marlowe Shaeffer and Claire Cloutier provided quality control. Jamie Peppard and Mary Agner provided production assistance. Johnna Dinse wrote the index.

Ellie Volckhausen designed the cover of this book, based on a series design by Edie Freedman. The cover image is a 19th-century engraving from the Dover Pictorial Archive. Emma Colby produced the cover layout with QuarkXPress 4.1 using Adobe's ITC Garamond font.

Melanie Wang designed the interior layout, based on a series design by David Futato. This book was converted by Joe Wizda to FrameMaker 5.5.6 with a format conversion tool created by Erik Ray, Jason McIntosh, Neil Walls, and Mike Sierra that uses Perl and XML technologies. The text font is Linotype Birka; the heading font is Adobe Myriad Condensed; and the code font is LucasFont's TheSans Mono Condensed. The illustrations that appear in the book were produced by Robert Romano and Jessamyn Read using Macromedia FreeHand 9 and Adobe Photoshop 6. The tip and warning icons were drawn by Christopher Bing. This colophon was compiled by Mary Anne Weeks Mayo.